HD 6955 RHO

Critical Representations of Work and Organization in Popular Culture

This book challenges traditional organizational theory by appreciatively examining how work and organizations have been conceptualized and critiqued in mass mediated popular culture. Through a series of essays, Rhodes and Westwood examine popular culture as a compelling and critical arena in which the complex and contradictory relations that people have with the organizations in which they work are played out. By articulating the knowledge in popular culture with that in theory, they provide new avenues for understanding work organizations as the dominant institutions in contemporary society.

Rhodes and Westwood provide a critical review of how organizations are represented in various examples of contemporary popular culture, from David Mamet's *Glengarry Glen Ross* to Ridley Scott's *Blade Runner* to the songs of Bruce Springsteen. This book demonstrates how popular culture can be read as an embodiment of knowledge about organizations – often more compelling than those common to theory – and explores the critical potential of such knowledge and the way in which popular culture can reflect on the spirit of resistance, carnivalization and rebellion.

This book will be of great interest to students and researchers engaged with organization and management studies, cultural theory and the sociology of organizations.

Carl Rhodes is Professor of Organization Studies at the University of Technology, Sydney. **Robert Westwood** is Reader at the University of Queensland Business School. Their book *Humour, Work and Organization* (2007) is also published by Routledge.

Routledge advances in management and business studies

Critical Representations of Work and Organization in Popular Culture

Carl Rhodes and Robert Westwood

Routledge
Taylor & Francis Group

LONDON AND NEW YORK

First published 2008
by Routledge
2 Park Square, Milton Park, Abingdon, Oxon OX14 4RN

Simultaneously published in the USA and Canada
by Routledge
270 Madison Ave, New York, NY 10016

Routledge is an imprint of the Taylor & Francis Group, an informa business

Typeset in Times by Wearset Ltd, Boldon, Tyne and Wear
Printed and bound in Great Britain by TJI Digital, Padstow, Cornwall

British Library Cataloguing in Publication Data
A catalogue record for this book is available from the British Library

Library of Congress Cataloging in Publication Data
A catalog record for this book has been requested

ISBN10: 0-415-35989-9 (hbk)
ISBN10: 0-203-00787-5 (ebk)

ISBN13: 978-0-415-35989-4 (hbk)
ISBN13: 978-0-203-00787-7 (ebk)

Contents

Acknowledgements

Some of the ideas and text that are included in this book were given outings in other formats, both published and unpublished. Parts of Chapters 1 and 3 were written as a paper presented at the 2005 Standing Conference on Organizational Symbolism (SCOS) as: Rhodes, C. and Westwood, R. (2005) 'Organizations, Organization Studies and the Mimetic Excess of Popular Culture', *The Standing Conference on Organizational Symbolism XXIII*, Royal Institute of Technology, Stockholm, 8–10 July 2005. This annual conference has provided ample support for our work both in terms of providing a venue for its presentation and reception and for its general encouragement and legitimation of the development of new ideas in management thinking. Indeed, Chapter 7 of this book was presented in 2003 in an earlier format as: Rhodes, C. and Westwood, R. (2003) 'Does McDonald's Really Suck? Comparing Perspectives from Sociology and TV Animation', *The Standing Conference on Organizational Symbolism XXI*, University of Cambridge, United Kingdom, 9–12 July 2003. A different version of the discussion of *South Park* in that chapter also appears in the SCOS journal as: Rhodes, C. (2002) 'Coffee and the Business of Pleasure: The Case of Harbucks vs. Mr. Tweek', *Culture and Organization*, 8(4): 293–306. A version of the material that now makes up Chapter 6 was presented at the 2nd Art of Management and Organization Conference in Paris in September 2004 and we wish to acknowledge the contribution of Allanah Johnston of the University of Queensland Business School to that paper. Finally, an version of Chapter 8 was previously published as: Rhodes, C. (2004) 'Utopia in Popular Management Writing and the Music of Bruce Springsteen: Do You Believe in the Promised Land?' *Consumption, Markets and Culture*, 7(1): 1–20.

1 Introduction

Organizations and popular culture

A plausible story...

Imagine for a moment a person, maybe your neighbour, maybe yourself ...
after having finished the house work, sitting down in her living room one
Sunday afternoon she switches on the television. She is greeted by the
familiar show *The Simpsons* and laughs out loud as the evil industrialist Mr.
Burns hatches a plot to eliminate health insurance as an employment benefit
in the nuclear power plant he owns. When the episode ends she picks up the
newspaper to see what else is on TV that afternoon and pauses at the syndi-
cated comics section. She smiles wryly at the strip about the arch white
collar loser Dilbert when she reads that "Leadership isn't only about selfish
actions. It's also about empty, meaningless expressions". Just then her kids
come storming into the room, grab the remote and switch to the cartoon
channel. They laugh uproariously as Wiley Coyote hatches an elaborate
plan to catch the Roadrunner, having just been delivered a new set of
purpose built gadgets from the customer-focused Acme Corporation.
Seeking a retreat from the cacophony, she goes into her bedroom, lies back
and switches on the radio. It is tuned to a classic rock station which is
playing Roy Orbison bemoaning his fate of "Workin' for the Man": she
hums along to the familiar tune. This is followed quickly by Bruce Springsteen singing about death in the eyes of factory workers. A little bored with
such oldies, and looking for a more hip contemporary station, she soon finds
herself tapping her feet to Planet Funk's hit "Who Said" and singing along
"I've never been to the USA; I'm a slave for the minimum wage; Detroit,
New York and LA; But I'm stuck in the UK".

Later that evening she visits the video shop to look for a DVD and can't
decide what to borrow. She pauses, considering Wesley Snipes and Sean
Connery in *Rising Sun* – a story about cultural and strategic intrigue in a
Japanese company operating in the U.S.A. Thinking of a more family oriented film, she looks at *Hook* in which a workaholic manager, and largely
absent father, rediscovers himself and his relationship with his children when
forced to confront his earlier life as Peter Pan. Still undecided, she finds the
original *Star Wars* movie replete with its moralistic tales of good against evil.

Still in the science fiction section, she eventually settles on *Judge Dredd*, in the hope it might deliver a sense of judgment, redemption ... and action.

Back home, she falls asleep on the sofa watching the movie. Waking at 5 am with a crick in her neck and a tired burning pain in her eyes, she reluctantly gets ready to go to the office – an entirely different place ... or is it?

Considering popular culture

Our work on this book began with a quite simple observation: many of the forms of popular culture that we were both familiar with and enjoyed were inherently and explicitly critical of work and its organization. As academics whose interests, broadly defined, revolve around a critical analysis of the practices and culture of contemporary organizations, this was most interesting. What we also observed was that many of the themes that were present in critically oriented management and organization studies were closely paralleled in popular culture. Of course this critique is not prevalent in all of popular culture. But this is another parallel – for the most part management and organization theory too lacks critique, instead settling for a role as a functional handmaiden for enhancing organizational effectiveness, efficiency and so forth. As has long been the case, social science finds its identity as a 'servant of power' (Baritz, 1960).

Despite this initial observation, we also knew that there was a long history of skepticism towards the popular amongst academics and intellectual elites (Rhodes, 2004). This is a view where "the popular is often suspect. It can't be intelligent and it is linked to vulgarity, tastelessness, gaudiness and even to a certain laziness [... by ...] those who think they do not belong to the populus" (ten Bos, 2000: xiii). In contrast to this, our starting point is that popular culture, neither as an essential totality nor as a social specificity, cannot be relegated *toute courte* as intellectually vacuous or critically meaningless. Quite the contrary, it is within popular culture that we can locate some of the most innovative, insightful and penetrating critical commentaries on work and organizations. It is examples of such commentaries that we are most interested in in this book. The plausible story introduced above highlights not only that position, but also signals some other key issues. First, that our daily lives are saturated by this culture and that representations of work and organizations are ubiquitously present in it. Second, that many of these representations are inherently questioning and critical in their portrayal of organizations, work and our lives within them. Third, that popular culture has been the basis on which to practise organization theory for a small but significant number of theorists, particularly in more recent times – indeed, the examples used in this story were chosen, in part, because each has been the subject of study or discussion within the academic discipline of management and organization studies.[1]

Those examples notwithstanding, and despite the ubiquity of representations of work and organization in popular culture, it is most common for organization and management researchers to eschew (or at least ignore) such representations as a legitimate source of material or knowledge from which to conceptualize work and/or organizational phenomena or as a resource with which to approach theorizing practice. Representational forms such as those associated with popular culture are not commonly taken seriously in terms of their knowledge potential – echoing a form of reasoning that can be traced back to Plato (1955), it appears that the contemporary imitative arts have no place in the republic driven by science and philosophy. Those people who approach popular culture with scholarly intent are often targets of deep scepticism and suspicion – a fact that is not only suggestive of the belief that popular culture is debased, but also reflects "the persistent disbelief that academic theories and methodologies can shed new light on phenomena whose meanings seem so transparently obvious" (Harrington and Bielby, 2005: 2). As Novitz (1992: 21) pointed out some time ago, this is a paradoxical attitude:

> the popular arts are seldom seen as the bearers of our cultural heritage or our national heritage. If anything, most are denigrated as valueless and crass, but they continue all the while to be sought out as objects worthy of our attention. The high arts, by contrast, earn lavish praise but are seldom the object of popular attention.

The academic distrust of popular culture was given intellectual coinage in the Frankfurt School, especially by Theodore Adorno and Max Horkheimer (1944; Adorno, 1941). Their argument, in summary, was that the cultural industries were merely a device for duping the masses and were part of the domination perpetuated by consumer capitalism. While such a totalizing perspective is largely eschewed by contemporary scholars, it still defines the contours of much contemporary debate over whether popular culture is an authentic expression of 'the people' or a ruse for the interests of the powerful (Harrington and Bielby, 2005). Indeed, work of the Frankfurt school "set the terms of debate and analysis for the subsequent study of popular culture" (Strinati, 2005: 46).

To this day, the ethos that regards popular culture as inauthentic or even manipulative lives on; despite various attempts, often in the name of postmodernism, to collapse the high/low culture distinction. That there is 'no respect' for the popular is suggestive of an intellectual history that has constructed a powerful division between the 'educated' and the 'ordinary' – the latter to be treated by intellectuals with disrespect, paternalism, authority and/or elitism (Ross, 1989). For many, it remains current for popular culture to be viewed as a medium that panders to and exploits the 'low' tastes of the general public, even to the extent that we might be 'amusing ourselves to death' (Postman, 1987). Such views combine cultural cynicism with retrograde historicism and mythical nostalgia so as to promote the idea that in contemporary society "collective and personal identities are being eroded, that modern culture is a trash culture, that art is under threat and that the enlarged role of the mass media allows them to exercise a powerful ideological influence over their audiences" (Strinati, 2005: 222). Even more pessimistically, some see the distinctions between high and low culture as perpetuating particular hierarchies in society. Thus, it is argued that the "distinction between fine and popular art loses credibility in Postmodernism because they are seen more as fostering polit- ical illusions than worthy ambitions" (Krukowski, 1992: 200). By such accounts, it would seem that we are embroiled in a cultural pessimism that locates the present in a narrative of decline, a fall from a truer state, suggesting a psychological disposition that regards the world as being in intellectual downfall (Bennett, 2001).

For most of those who study management and organizations, popular culture does not even seem worthy of scholarly attention. Despite a minority who have made occasional use of, or reference to, 'low culture' and mass culture representations as a part of organizational theory and research (see Chapter 3), the majority appear to consider that if one wants to study work and organi- zations then she/he should enter into the offices and the factories, the board- rooms and the lunch rooms; the places where organizations seem to 'exist' in their material forms and where real work is directly experienced. The proclivi- ties and ethos of the positivist orientation that continues to (at times subtly) pervade organization studies' orthodoxy conspire to perpetuate a realist ontol- ogy in which only materially 'real' phenomena of work and organization are admitted as legitimate and viable objects of study and theorizing. Representa- tions distributed by the media, and especially those constructed in and through popular culture, are considered less than real – at best marginal, possibly illegiti- mate and inadmissible and at worst damaging.

Such an ontology (with its accompanying epistemology) has increasingly been challenged, as has the ordering of representations into rigid categories such as the real and objective versus the imaginative and the subjective. This is a position that has, for example, long been rejected within the field of cultural studies as demonstrated some time ago by Fiske (1987: 5) who argued that what passes for reality in any culture is the product of that culture's codes. From such a perspective, 'reality' is always already encoded, it is never 'raw'. Further, work and organizations have such cultural centrality and primacy that it is arbi- trary, artificial and limited to confine and define them within the materialist bounds of the factory and the office or within the material practices of office hours, time clocks and factory whistles.

As our introductory story suggested, organizations also exist as experienced representations – cultural narratives and images constructed, in part, in an effort to make meaning and sense of the institutions and activities that dominate people's lives. It is in the various genres of popular culture in particular that such representations can be found contemporarily – in written narratives, paint- ings and graphics, cartoons, television, cinema and popular music. It is to the latter three that we turn in this book in order to both understand and construct some relationships between popular culture and work organizations. Our overall aim in this book is to provide a set of theoretically *and* culturally informed essays that exemplify such relationships.

It is not our aim to generalize culture by presuming to offer the last word on the subject and so to totalize the meaning of culture, nor do we claim to pin down the meanings of culture for its various audiences. Rather, we explore how popular culture can be productively regarded as a manifestation of knowledge about organizations that has important implications for scholarly research. Our approach engages actively with particular instantiations of culture as a set of meaningful and meaning generating texts. We read popular culture as an embodiment of knowledge about organizations that can be more compelling than that common to theory and that can provide avenues for advancing the study of organizations. More particularly, this book focuses on how popular culture often manifests in a popular critique of organization and that such manifestations are important, as examining the narratives of popular culture is critical to understanding cultural discourse more generally (cf. Czarniawska and Rhodes, 2006).

Rejecting a priori hierarchical distinctions not only between high and low culture, but also between popular culture and academic discourse, this book seeks to demonstrate how popular culture can be fruitfully engaged with for examples of the popular interrogation, understanding and critique of work and organization. We are encouraged in this position by the small but significant minority (represented by those referenced in relation to our opening story, as well as others) who have already productively explored the possibilities of popular culture representations in studying organizations. We are further encouraged by the recent assertion that one of the founders of contemporary organization theory, Max Weber, might be best understood as less a classical management theorist and rather more a student of culture, practising what today we would call 'cultural studies' (Clegg, 2005). Even William Whyte (1957) in his classic *The Organization Man* bolstered his thesis by analysing the 'organization man in fiction' – a means for him to gauge popular belief as it appeared in novels and films. There is a provenance to our discipline that has until recently been neither recognized nor realized.

This heritage provides a worthy rationale for the aims of this book and for considering why popular culture has been, and might further be, of value to the formal study of organizations. As noted, on an orthodox surface reading, discussing things like cartoons or song lyrics seems redundant and unnecessary in that it focuses on that which is 'outside' organizations, irrelevantly extra-organizational. The question is then, why not remain focused on the goings on in 'real' organizations instead of risking such 'whackademic' pursuits? One response might be that there is value because popular culture provides some form of *reflection* of culture more generally – as implied by Weber and Whyte. For us, however, such positions are not entirely satisfactory because popular culture is only being considered in terms of the relative accuracy or inaccuracy of its representations without considering the possible productivities of such representational practice. It is precisely such productivities that the chapters in this book seek to interrogate. These are possibilities available because popular culture representations of work and organization are different to, or even excessive of, those present in both managerial and theoretically oriented accounts. It is in that extra, excessive space that new knowledge about work and organizations is constructed and creative ways of (re)theorizing organization emerge. The claim here is that organizing is "a cultural matter and that engagement with other cultural texts might enable a more diverse collection of ways of organizing organization" (Parker *et al.*, 1999: 588).

In approaching popular culture, we do not make any neophiliac claims to radical newness, but rather we seek to draw on and further develop ideas that are already in circulation. The idea that popular culture can be a valid source of knowledge about culture and society was suggested 20 years ago by Marcus and Fischer (1986) who positioned the study of popular culture at the heart of a 'repatriated anthropology'. Much of contemporary cultural studies also does not treat popular culture merely as a set of representations but as a productive site of meaning enmeshed in knowledge/power circuits – significant for subjectivity and subject positions as any other text (e.g. Collins, 1995). Following such inspiration, this book is based on the conviction (and a desire to demonstrate) that popular culture is an embodiment of meaningful knowledge about organizations and that it can provide avenues for exceeding the orthodox study of organizations.

Popular culture provides a valuable set of representations of work and organization. These representations, however, need not be considered or read blandly in terms of their capacity to accurately (or inaccurately) copy or reflect what goes on in organizations – instead, they can be construed as containing within themselves creative value and intelligent reflections. In popular culture's difference to (or even lack of respect for) theory, it opens up a space for the creative questioning and critique of the organizational realm – both theoretical and pragmatic – in the popular spirit of resistance, carnivalization, parody, rebellion and subversion.

The limits of popular culture

Given that the focus of this book is on popular culture, we feel that it is incumbent upon us to clarify how we are using the term. Since first being identified by Johann Gottfried Herder in the eighteenth century (see Burke, 1978), the term 'popular culture' has been subject to substantial definitional contestation. That definitional diversity notwithstanding, the term casts a wide net in that it can refer to anything from Levi jeans, to Mills and Boon novels, to the habits of skateboarders in Nebraska, to the goings on in holiday camps in Blackpool. Attesting to such variety, Storey (1998) discusses six different ways that popular culture can be defined. It is that part of culture that:

1   is appreciated by many people,
2   is opposed to high or elite culture,
3   is massified and commercialized,
4   emanates from 'the people',

5   is a site of contestation over meaning between subordinate and dominant cultural groups and
6   is resulting from the interpenetration of commerce and culture.

Street (1997) notes that perhaps the most dominant definition of popular culture sees it in terms of its production, distribution and consumption such that it is "a form of entertainment that is mass produced or is made available to large numbers of people" (Street, 1997: 7). This, like Storey's, is in part a relational definition that perpetuates the distinction between popular culture and the more exclusive high culture. As Street goes on to discuss, however, such a definition fails to give substance to popular culture and does not account for its actual content. Yet another approach defines popular culture in terms of styles and genres – hence we know that rock is a form of popular culture but opera is a form of high culture (although even such distinctions are contested now, see Collins, 1995). This issue of definition is, as Street points out, a political one because "each definition, by its nature, entails selecting particular cultural forms from amongst other, and making evaluations of their worth" (Street, 1997: 8).

Notwithstanding the significant differences between these definitions, Storey (1998: 17) points out that "whatever else popular culture might be, it is definitely a culture that only emerged following industrialization and urbanization". This commonality is important to us because it immediately positions popular culture in relation to market and consumer capitalism, and hence to the principal way that work is organized and popular culture produced in the modern era, through industrialism and post-industrialism. Such a relationship has led to considerable research, especially in the fields of cultural studies and critical theory, into how organizations are the producers of culture. This is manifested in the long-standing debate over whether "commodified cultural practices feed back into the ongoing production and maintenance of the hegemony of capitalist social relations" (Gunster, 2000: 41). For some, this has resulted in a tendency towards 'unreflexive grand theorizing' (Rowe, 1995: 21) of the impact of capitalism that suggests that the production of mass culture is purely economic and its effects unilateral and exploitative. As Frith argues:

> Academic approaches to popular culture still derive from the mass cultural critiques of the 1930s and 1940s, and particularly from the Marxist critique of contemporary popular culture in terms of the production and circulation of commodities [... this argues that ...] in creating markets for their goods, cultural entrepreneurs developed manipulative sales methods that ensnared consumers into self-delusion, in the continual pursuit of false (and easily satisfied, easily dissatisfied) desire.
>
> (Frith, 1996: 13)

However, the complex institutions, relationships, practices and intersections of mass culture are not reducible to an overarching economic regime and its ideologies (ibid.). The products of mass culture are not merely products of such regimes and they are not containable within them. Similarly, the meanings of cultural products, processes and practices cannot be contained and fixed by producers or by other dominant elements in society. Popular culture and its meanings can be appropriated and creatively turned by its consumers and altered and differentially made use of by subcultural groups. The products of mass culture themselves can be read, constructed and reconstructed variously as meaningful representations with resistive and interrogative potentialities vis-à-vis the producers and the dominant system. They are not just artefacts available for critique by theorists adopting an external and privileged position relative to popular culture and the masses. Thus, in approaching our subject, we do not seek to construct a totalizing, abstract definition of popular culture, but rather to focus on some particular ways that it can be engaged with. Such an engagement, for example, can connect with products of mass culture as a form of resistance and critique – they can offer defiance as a weapon to deny power such that "actions of political resistance are commonly played out within popular culture" (Street, 1997: 13). This does not mean that all mass culture is necessarily a form of 'serious' debate or of political resistance, but rather that there are examples in mass culture that can be considered as such – and it is these that we are most interested in.

Popular culture and critique

In terms of the critical potential of popular culture, early last century Gramsci (2001) quite explicitly recognized that, in a plural society, alternative cultures can be a source of resistance, even revolution, once brought outside of the influence of the bourgeoisie. For Gramsci:

> popular fiction, such as adventure stories, can generate beauty and educate readers through presenting an alternative reality to that of a dehumanizing capitalist rationality and the increasingly industrialized, disciplined world of mechanized labour. Thus popular songs [for example] express a positive commitment to a social world different from that of "official society".
>
> (Swingewood, 1998: 19)

The point here is not to deny that popular culture is a form of commodity, but rather that its commodity status does not fully saturate its possible meanings and uses. As Swingewood (1998: 50) explains: "The argument that art has become a commodity does not necessarily suggest that it is experienced and interpreted as a commodity, or that commodified art-forms necessarily translate into commodified modes of reception."

Swingewood uses the example of rock music, and particularly its more radical and avant garde forms, to illustrate how forms of popular culture are resistant to incorporation into the dominant culture. Indeed, in many respects, such music is conceived, constructed and performed within marginalized (and often intendedly so) subcultural groups in agnostic and oppositional positions to the dominant culture. The same is true of other musical genres such as rap, hip hop, punk, even jazz. He suggests that the form and language of such music is such that it militates against appeal to a wider, mass audience. More simply put, *if your grandma likes it, it ain't rock an' roll!* Even when rock or rap are appropriated by the mainstream, as they are, they can still be reappropriated and meanings and uses constructed that escape the clutches of the orthodoxy and the dominant culture. Further, the very act of appropriation creates a tension and acts as a motivation for differentiation as members of subcultural groups creatively find new modes of popular expression that is positioned again in opposition to a conception of the mainstream. All this argues forcefully against those theories of popular culture that see it monolithically and unilaterally as something imposed on the docile masses as part of a dupery that manipulates their desires and seduces them into a dominant hegemony, or that position (and denigrate) the people as merely passive consumers. As Swingewood (1998: 50) further argues: "To analyse popular music as 'confirming' and reinforcing a 'psychological debasement', which violates human dignity and reduces aesthetic distance, is to ignore the living involvement, the imaginative grasp and creative use of popular music within distinct communities" (see also Cohen, 1991; Finnegan, 1989).

In terms of what we are trying to achieve with this book, popular culture is a productive space, one in which meanings and practices emerge that are other than those intended by the dominant culture. Moreover, these meanings are often oppositional, resistant and critical with respect to the dominant culture. We argue more specifically that there is significant value for (organization) theory in seeking to engage with those aspects of popular culture that are mass mediated and that have large audiences, but which also contain within them critical examinations of the relationship between organization, work and human life. We invoke the term critical here in that we are interested in those texts (broadly construed) which overtly question the way that work is organized in contemporary capitalism – a questioning that is related directly to an unease with the dominance of managerialism, capitalism and positivism both in the academy and in society more generally (Fournier and Grey, 2000). This is not to say that we limit our attention to various exercises in negative 'fault finding' (cf. Williams, 1976), or finger pointing, but rather that we are concerned with the various problematics of work and organization as they appear in culture. As Parker (2002a) has clearly stated, "many (though not all) contemporary books and films contain implicit or explicit representations of management and organizations that reflect a fair degree of ambivalence and often hostility" (135). Looked at this way, the relationships between popular culture and the critical study of organizations are both palpable and ripe for continued exploration.

What you might find in this book

Having introduced the background and aims of this book, it is important to reinforce that with this book we are neither attempting nor claiming a totalizing or encyclopaedic review of how organizations are represented in popular culture. Avoiding the theoretical hubris and practical impossibility of such a venture, we have chosen instead to use this book to present a series of essays each of which examines a particular area or example of popular culture and discusses it in terms of how it relates to knowledge about work and organizations. Each of these essays are by and large 'stand-alone' pieces in that while they are connected together by the overarching aims and themes of this book, they do not proceed as steps in a grand argument. Our intention is that each chapter develops its own argument in relation to its chosen subject matter as contextualized within the project as a whole.

The examples on which we draw are taken from across the range of contemporary western popular culture as distributed through the mass media – with a particular emphasis on the late twentieth century. We have tried to incorporate a mixture of recent as well as more 'classic' and well-known illustrations. The selections are ours – we made them in part because they are those parts of popular culture that we are familiar with, that we participate in or that we appreciate. We also chose what to include because we felt that it was relevant to the issues we wished to discuss. While we hope that readers will be able to relate to this book based on their own cultural experience, we recognize too that this might not be the case – not all of us watch the same films, listen to the same music or tune in to the same television programmes. To limit this, we have, by and large, written about popular culture that is 'mainstream' in the sense that it is widely available and broadly consumed – we hope that you find things in this book that connect in some way with your own cultural experiences, even if those connections are different to ours.

Following this introduction, this book starts, in Chapter 2, by problematizing the very distinction between popular culture and management knowledge. Acknowledging the cultural cache in sustaining this distinction, we also note the recent explosion of mass-mediated representations of management in the popular media – especially through the provinces of the 'management guru'. We argue that this burgeoning phenomenon means that management has entered the popular domain and *is* a form of popular culture. By examining popular management representations and the academic responses to them, we suggest that while scholarly approaches commonly position themselves as distinctive and elitist, solid boundaries between the popular and the academic are increasingly hard to sustain. The point is that the academic study of management is already deeply and problematically related to popular culture, in terms of both the creation of its identity in relation to an inferiorized popular 'other' and the interpenetration of ideas between the two.

Despite the relations between the study of management and organizations and popular culture discussed in Chapter 2, the distinctions between the two are culturally salient. This is the case especially in academic culture and especially again when it comes to those areas of culture not explicitly making claims to contain representations of management knowledge – we are thinking here of television, cinema, popular music and the like. In Chapter 3, we concern ourselves with how these two might be productively connected in a manner that avoids the elitism that so often prevails when management academics consider the popular. This begins with a review of those academic studies of management and organizations that have explicitly studied organizations in popular culture in a critical, constructive and affirmative way. The chapter also sets out our position on why we see value in the academic study of management and organizations in popular culture, as well as establishing a methodological position on how we might do so. The perspective we develop is one that suggests that there are many important and critical representations of work and organizations in popular culture – representations that exceed those available to theory. Taking inspiration from Laclau (1977), Laclau and Mouffe (2001) and Hall (1996), we argue that there is value in articulating this popular knowledge with theoretical knowledge. By attending to the 'critique *in* culture' rather than the 'critique *of* culture', we take the position that academically sanctioned knowledge can benefit from taking seriously the many examples of popular culture that focus critical attention on contemporary work and organizations.

Following the first three chapters, the remainder of this book consists of a series of essays each of which examines a different example of popular culture in terms its critical relationship to work, management and/or organizations. Following on from the position outlined in Chapter 3, these chapters provide different manifestations of how popular culture can be articulated with management and organization theory. This begins, in Chapter 4, with a discussion of masculinity, identity, violence and language in organizational contexts and in relation to the capitalist ethos. We surface these issues by discussing the 1992 film version of David Mamet's *Glengarry Glen Ross*. We argue that Mamet not only offers a considered critique of contemporary capitalism in terms of its dehumanization, criminality and corrosion of values, but also of the way that capitalism and its institutions reproduce patriarchal and phallocentric social structures. Moreover, he goes further, relating that to the reproduction of particular forms of masculinity and limited ways of 'performing masculinity' that men become entrapped in, and through the performance of which they reproduce and perpetuate the masculine capitalist ethos and the structures of patriarchy in society. This is a critique that provides insight commonly lost in mainstream academic analysis within management and organization studies and an area of analysis neglected until recently. We conclude that Mamet's work is an exemplary and vanguard critical practice that contains significant conceptual resources for those academics interested in researching gender and masculinity in organizations.

Drawing on another example from the cinema, Chapter 5 turns to a classic science fiction film: Ridley Scott's *Blade Runner* (1982). Locating this film within the genre of science fiction, we examine its critical salience in relation to the exploratory potential of science fiction and its ability to critically interrogate contemporary organizational behaviour. We argue that this critique is made possible through a 'cognitive estrangement' (Suvin, 1979) that represents a world different to our own such that we can consider our own reality more critically.

Having charted the relations between organizational critique and science fiction in general, the chapter turns to *Blade Runner* in terms of its commentary on how the ethos of late capitalism emerges from the relationship between technology, subjectivity and commerce. This ethos reflects how technology has come to be central in what it means to be a person in the world, and the implications of this for the very notion of humanity. We argue that the film provides a critical representation of the way that morality might be understood in an era where corporate power increasingly encroaches on all aspects of life and identity.

In Chapter 6, we shift our attention from the cinema to television. Here we give a discussion of British situation comedies and how they have represented gender, class and difference at work. By reviewing these television comedies, from the 1950s to the present day, we interrogate the way that they explore the politics of difference in workplaces, and in particular how they relate gender difference to class and power differences. In making a comparative analysis over time, the chapter also looks at how changes in television comedy in Britain are related to the dynamics of gender politics in society more generally. The analysis suggests that while television comedy is often accused of characterizing women in a limited and/or negative ways, there is actually significant variation and nuance – variation that includes subtle yet insightful commentary of gender politics that critically questions the stereotypes they so often draw on.

In Chapter 7, we switch channels from British situation comedies to American television animation. The chapter discusses the way that the phenomena of fast-food restaurants in general, and of McDonald's in particular, have been represented both in academic work and in popular culture. The chapter draws an explicit comparison between the critique of McDonald's and McDonaldization as it can be found first in the sociological work of Ritzer (1996, 1998, 2004) and second in animated television programmes such as *Beavis and Butthead* (1993–1997), *The Simpsons* (1990–) and *South Park* (1997–). We review Ritzer's theorization of McDonaldization as a deterministic process where a homogenized culture associated with fast-food restaurants is becoming globally dominant. By comparing this to what we find in the cartoons, we argue that while the sociological critique has merit in highlighting problematic aspects of contemporary culture, it does so in a way that is elitist and overdetermined in its consideration of the effects of that culture. We argue that within popular culture itself, there lies the resources and representations for different yet equally cogent and nuanced forms of critique that are engaged and reflexive in their approach. This attests to the idea that popular culture can be a site for a kind of inside-out, reflexive, auto-critique – the type that in our examples not only deeply problematize McDonaldization in relation to the labour process, consumer society and cultural invasion, but also more fully locates itself within the complexities and ironies of its cultural context.

Having worked through some examples from television and the cinema, the remaining three chapters focus on popular music. This begins with Chapter 8 which interrogates and contrasts representations of work and Utopia in two examples of popular culture. Building on the discussion in Chapter 2, the examples referred to are a sample of contemporary popular management books and a sample of work-related themes in the popular music of Bruce Springsteen. In comparing the two, the chapter examines how they both use utopian representations as a key element of their claims, yet do so in markedly different ways. We argue that Springsteen uses a 'voice from within' to explore the ambiguities and paradoxes that emerge from the gap between real experience and utopian desire. Conversely, we show how the popular management books tend to speak from a 'voice from above' that actively suppress ambiguity and ignore power in order to reproduce the dominant ethos of contemporary capitalism. We use this to argue that while popular management literature provides uncritical support for its imaginary Utopia, Springsteen provides a compelling critique of the promises of economic freedom through capitalism – promises which management writers are so often complicit in (re)producing.

Chapter 9 turns its attention to the musical phenomena of punk rock, with specific reference to the archetypal 1970s British band *The Sex Pistols*. While *The Sex Pistols* have been discussed extensively in the academic literature, we focus specifically on the relationship the band had with their various record companies and what this might mean for how we understand resistance and authenticity in capitalist work relations. By considering the culturally located actions of *The Sex Pistols* in relation to Foucauldian-inspired resistance theory, we both question and rethink the way that popular music discourse is deeply implicated with notions of authenticity – most particularly through the culturally inauthentic practice of 'selling out' to commercialism. We argue that *The Sex Pistols'* subversive practices in relation to the music industry point to the possibility of forms of authentic subjectivity that are forged in relation to the cultural sedimentation of capitalism, but are creatively excessive of them.

In the final chapter, Chapter 10, we look at the musical technique of sampling which, while clearly associated with contemporary rap and hip-hop musicians, has a long and diverse history. Sampling is a practice which intersects with work practice and technology and can be seen as a form of tinkering in which samplers make appropriations of heterogeneous materials that are at hand to produce new compositions. Considering such musical practice as a form of bricolage (in terms of both tinkering and the appropriation of technological malfunctions), the chapter seeks to open up a new space for exploration in organization studies. This is a space that offers the prospect of enhanced understanding of the nature of work practice and the intersection of work and technology. Sampling challenges conventional notions of originality and authenticity but is also an example of other appropriative and tinkering practices that do likewise. We argue that such practices are forms of bricolage and that they are more prevalent and widespread in organizations than is commonly acknowledged. The consideration of notions of tinkering and bricolage opens up a space for the examination of the value of the unintended uses of technology and practice and how this constitutes resistance to the ordered regimes of organizational sanctioned technological deployment. This provokes, we argue, a challenge to and potential subversion of the ordered, intended, rational structures and processes that are often presumed to be essential for effective organizational functioning.

We started this introductory chapter with a plausible story about the cultural prevalence of representations of work of an organization. As we have tried to outline, this book is about taking such representations seriously, and in a sense as equals in the critical study of management and organizations to more formally academic modes of knowledge and representation. We do this informed by an ethos that there are positive and productive relations to be drawn between those representations of work and organizations found in popular culture and those found in theory. Our project is a critical one, but also an affirmative one – it aims to draw together the critical knowledge that can be found in theory with that which can be found in popular culture such that that knowledge might be enhanced. We do this in part to suggest that the two have much in common, but also to suggest that being critical as an academic need not mean being disparaging about culture. Old elitist positions present within the academy might be both common and attractive to those who wish to bolster their own egos at its expense, but as we hope to show they are neither necessary nor necessarily desirable. If the study of management and organizations is to be a critical project, then popular culture is not the enemy.

2 Management as popular culture

A VCR, a rented video, a tub of popcorn and a copy of *Movies for Leaders: Management Lessons from Four All-Time Great Films* ... management training doesn't get any better than this!

This quotation is taken from the homepage for the website *Management Goes to the Movies* (*MGTM*) (2006), which, in their own words "uses popular films to teach Management 101". The site currently has ten management topics listed with corresponding films for each (with several others noted as in the pipeline). The topic with the largest number of corresponding films is 'Leadership', to learn about which you are instructed to watch *The Bridge on the River Kwai*, *The Wizard of Oz*, *Hoosiers* and/or *Moby Dick*. With regards the latter, clearly, modern business leaders have much to learn from Captain Ahab's obsessive, vengeful pursuit and killing of the white whale – the symbol of what lies outside human dominion. Somewhat more prosaically, to learn about 'corporate traders and raiders' – note, not to learn about greed or the unacceptable face of capitalism – one is advised to view *Wall Street*. Less obviously, and almost quixotically, to learn about 'Leveraging Resources', one is offered insights from *Zulu*, whilst lessons from either *Bugsy* or *Fitzcarraldo* are offered to develop an understanding of 'Vision'. The intertextuality of the former provides irony given that the film is an adaptation of a book by Dean Jennings (1967) about the real-life Benjamin Siegelbaum – the extremely violent, sociopathic mobster who was a multiple murderer, rapist, fraudster, extortionist, gambler, bootlegger and womanizer (possibly bigamist). In relation to the latter, the mad vision of Brian Sweeney Fitzgerald (*Fitzcarraldo*) is perhaps matched by, and is as salutary a lesson as, director Werner Herzog's own egomaniacal vision. It is interesting to note that online at *MGTM* you can also earn a 'Hollywood MBA'.[1]

An interesting representational twist emerges from the *MGTM* list. The film chosen for the topic 'The Role of the Firm' is *Roger and Me*, written/directed by Michael Moore and released in 1989. It is a documentary that portrays the impact on the US town of Flint in the state of Michigan of a series of General Motors' (GM) plant closures that resulted in laying off 30,000–40,000 employees in the area. It also documents Moore's attempts to interview Roger

Smith, the then CEO of GM. The film is, then, a critique of the downsizing strategies of large corporations, especially when little consideration seems to be
given to the consequences for the towns and communities so dependent upon
them. It is also a critique of the exploitative off-shore outsourcing of jobs to
developing countries – as plants were being closed in Michigan, new ones were
being opened in Mexico. At the time, the film was the most successful documentary in US history.[2] The notes from *MGTM* (2006) refer to the film as an
example of 'guerilla journalism' and to Moore as a 'muckraker', whilst Smith is
described as 'embattled'. Whilst offering it as a useful vehicle for an exploration
of "public-relations management, crisis management and the responsibilities of
firms to their shareholders, employees and communities", *MGTM* dismisses the
film as 'just a rant' that "sheds maximum heat but little light on issues of corporate responsibility". Perhaps indicative of the orientation of those running
MGTM, it asks rhetorically if the situation GM faced was "primarily a 'corporate responsibility' problem or a 'public relations' problem? Even without changing its approach to the layoffs, could GM have minimized the PR damage?"

   MGTM provides an example of a complex intersection of spheres of action,
knowledge and modes of representation. There is, in the first instance, an action
from the realm of practice, presumably based upon some knowledge of how to
run a large corporation. This action is then subject to representation in popular
culture as a feature documentary. That representation is then taken up, represented on a website and made use of in the form of popularist pedagogy for
the training of managers. They are supposedly then to put the lessons learnt into
their own management/business practice. There are still other modes of
representation associated with this circuit that run off from it in rhizomatic
fashion – reviews and critiques of the film in the press and other media, news
coverage of the events themselves, but also of the film as news, websites
devoted to the film with other 'links', and so on in a cornucopia of popular
media representations. Interestingly, penciled in as a future offering for an
assessment of the 'Role of the Firm' are *The Godfather Parts I and II.*

   We used the phrase 'in the first instance' above, but this is a misnomer; there
is no starting point to these circuits. We do not know what events, texts,
representations or what 'knowledge' might have impelled Smith to initiate the
actions and strategies that he did. Those actions might have been impelled by a
particular discourse about business management – one constituted by particular
academic theories perhaps, or by popular representations of business practice, or
by some pedagogical material he might have been exposed to, or by some
mélange of these various modes of representation of management 'knowledge'.[3]

   MGTM is an exemplar of the varied and somewhat problematic representational space that management knowledge has come to occupy in recent times.
Within its own confines, it constructs a space in which academic management
representations, popularist management pedagogic representations and popular
cultural representations of management are brought into cohabitation. In this
chapter we want to explore such representational spaces, suggest that they have
expanded significantly in recent decades and propose that the lines of demarca-

tion between the various modes of representation are becoming increasingly blurred. Management knowledge is by now in a representational space that runs from scholarly academic texts (in journals say) to popular management texts (particularly those emanating from what some refer to as the management guru or management fashion industry) and on to representations in the full gamut of popular media (literature, movies, television and cartoons). The distinctions between these various modes, and hence between the knowledge status of what they represent, are increasingly indistinct.

The cultural elevation of management and its expanded representational space

The cultural significance – in tandem with the organizational, occupational and economic significance – of 'management' has grown enormously since the industrial revolution, but particularly since its professionalization and certification as initiated in the USA from around 1881.[4] It is worth noting that formal management education was established coterminous with the emergence of the management/business consulting industry. Arthur D. Little started his consulting company in 1886, Frederick Taylor was functioning as a consultant around 1890 and the Emerson Company was founded in 1889, almost ten years before the incarnation of the Harvard Business School. As the Harvard Business School states: the School "is *nearly* as old as the concept of management education itself" (Harvard Business School, 2006, italics added). A practitioner focus remained a strong feature of early management education with relatively little attention to scholarship and research. Even by the late 1950s, a number of reports slammed US business schools for being more akin to vocational colleges, with low academic credibility. Since then, management and business studies has endeavoured to prove its academic credentials, mainly through striving for scientific status by adopting the methods of the physical sciences and a functionalist paradigm. More recently, the pendulum has turned and business schools have been accused by notables within the field of being too enamoured of quantitative academic research, detached from business realities and/or lacking relevance to practitioners (Bennis and O'Toole, 2005; Gosling and Mintzberg, 2003, 2006; Pfeffer and Fong, 2002).

Following the expansion of management as a practice and academic discipline has been a massive expansion of the representational space for management 'knowledge' in recent decades. Where once such representations were confined to academic journals and specialized trade and practice magazines, they have now exploded across all available and emergent media, including those with popular access and appeal: teaching-related texts, practitioner-related texts, summaries and synopses for practitioners, guru texts, business leader biographies and autobiographies, print and online management magazines, blogs and other internet-mediated products, business journalism, films and documentaries, audio tapes, CDs, videos and DVDs and so on. Certainly, Mazza (1998) argues that management and business 'knowledge' has increasingly been disseminated through channels other than academic ones and that the popular media, newspapers and magazines in particular, have been significant in diffusing and legitimating certain forms of management 'knowledge'. Sturdy (2004) also describes the diffusion channels for management as extending beyond academic outlets to encompass consulting companies, newspapers and magazines, professional associations and management gurus. That management has increasingly been the subject of such varied media representation is hardly a surprise given its enhanced social, economic and cultural salience.

With respect to management 'knowledge' representation, a form of circularity has developed in which management ideas (and managers) are popularized through a range of media, thereby raising their visibility, and indeed constituting or reconstituting the very notion of management and the manager, such ideas are enacted in practice and may attract further media attention, resulting in additional representations being constructed, which reconstitute management/the manager – and so on. Guru theory, for example, is actually constitutive of the notion of 'management' and what it is to be a manager (du Gay, 1996; Watson, 1994). It creates representations of 'manager' that enter popular discourse and inform modes of practice, modes of being and subject positions that become aspirational for practicing managers (Clark and Salaman, 1998). Guru 'narratives' work on management values, skills, roles and identities; they "define senior manager's identities, and legitimize manager's status claims. They tell managers they are important, why they matter, why their skills are critical [... they are essentially about ...] redefining and reconstituting the subjectivities of managers" (Clark and Salaman, 1998: 153). They typically represent the senior manager as heroic, central and critical to the success of the organization – if not the whole economy. It is typical for guru theorists to individualize and personalize their message – so although some focus on techniques or practices, more often what is at issue is the manager and his/her personality, talent, competences or other personal attributes. Narratives of organizational success are anchored to tales of heroism, courage, integrity, vision, charisma, emotional intelligence and the like. Furthermore, the narrative is often cemented by making such characteristics resonate with the prevailing values within the wider community. In the USA as such, this might include individualism, risk taking, optimism, simplicity, the valourization of leadership and the value of a dream or vision – a resonance with the American Dream (Guest, 1990, cited in Clark and Salaman, 1998; see also Chapter 8).

These newly constituted narratives of management/the manager become objects of desire and are taken up by practicing managers. Indeed, Furusten (1999) has argued that the representations of management/the manager in popular/guru-based management texts create an accessible, legitimized and desirable image and subject position such that isomorphic pressures are created, compelling the kind of homogenization of management that we are witnessing on a global scale. Furthermore, practitioners will invoke such narratives to justify who they are, how they behave and the actions they initiate (Zorn *et al.*, 2000): they provide a kind of rhetoric of motive. The texts and their representations come to provide the resources for identity formation and for the justification and legitimation of practice. They coalesce into a discourse within which managers locate a viable subject position. As such they cannot be dismissed as superficial epiphenomena, as mere rhetoric devoid of substance – in the occasions of their use, they are 'world making' (Chia, 2003).

A number of commentators see this as a deliberate, manufactured process – one initiated and kept in motion by a management 'fashion-setting industry' (Abrahamson, 1991, 1996; Spell, 2001). Leaving that aside for the moment, what is at issue is this popular constitution of the manager as a notable, not to say heroic, figure of high cultural significance. Clark and Salaman (1998: 157) argue that the representations of management gurus have built a "conception of the nature and importance of the manager in a way that would have been inconceivable 20 years ago where managers and management were, if anything, regarded negatively".[5] Certainly, if the representation of managers in British sitcoms is anything to go by that would certainly be the case (see Chapter 6). Going further, Micklethwait and Wooldridge (1997: 5) have been moved to suggest that management popularizers, such as Peter Drucker, have supplanted the poet as the 'unacknowledged legislators of mankind' through "reshaping our institutions, refashioning our language and, above all, reorganizing people's lives".

That latter phrase is significant since Hancock and Tyler (2004) argue that management discourse has entered thoroughly into our everyday, non-work lives. Lifestyle magazines, they argue, have been especially influential in popularizing and re-presenting management 'knowledge', especially through applying management ideas to the management of self. They argue, following Habermas, that management discourse has come to 'colonize' the lifeworld and is part of the dissolution of the boundaries between work and non-work life spheres. Involved is a penetration of the 'performance imperative', of "both the performative reflexivity and quantification that characterizes contemporary managerial texts", into all life spheres, and lifestyle magazines particularly deploy that to urge that lives are things to be 'managed' (Hancock and Tyler, 2004: 632–3). Citing Grey (1999) and Parker (2002a), they argue that management has increasingly become a "universal framework for negotiating the myriad human experiences and interactions" (Hancock and Tyler, 2004: 621). It has to be noted, however, that the separation of life spheres was very much a project of modernity (Godelier, 1980; Kumar, 1984) and that a fresh implosion has emerged within postmodernity. Popular management 'knowledge' is, as noted, often directed expressly at the individual manager as a 'discourse of mastery' (Garsten and Grey, 1997) through which the manager is urged to enhance self-mastery and performance. Senge (1990), particularly his principle of 'personal mastery', and, again, Tom Peters are cited as instrumental in promoting this discourse and imperative. It is Peters who advocates "the importance of reconceptualising the self as an entrepreneurial project or what he terms 'ME, INC'" (Hancock and Tyler, 2004: 630) and who promotes the imperative that we make ourselves into a brand (Peters, 1999).

Modes of representation of management in popular culture

'Management' has entered popular culture through a marked elevation of its cultural significance, its central location as a key role and subject position in organizational, economic and other domains, and by its colonization of the lifeworld. Its location in popular culture is also marked by the massive proliferation of modes and forms of representation. Mazza (1998), for example, argues that the success of popular management books from the early 1980s on has irrevocably linked management knowledge with popular culture, implying that such texts *are* forms of popular culture. The early 1980s are significant since they witnessed the publication of such enormously popular management texts as Peters and Waterman's (1982) *In Search of Excellence*, Deal and Kennedy's (1982) *Corporate Cultures*, Johnson and Blanchard's (198) *One Minute Manager*, Handy's (1983, 1985) *Understanding Organisations* and *The Gods of Management* and Ouchi's (1981) *Theory Z*. It could be argued (the role of Peter Drucker notwithstanding) that this period initiated the true entrance of management 'knowledge' into the popular culture sphere and the emergence of the so-called guru industry. Certainly, the popular appeal is undeniable: *In Search of Excellence*, for example, has sold more than five million copies globally – 122,000 copies within two months of being published – it also recently topped the list of the most influential business books of the last two decades (cited in Pagel and Westerfelhaus, 2005). Stephen Covey's *Seven Habits* has sold ten million copies.

The industry has grown significantly since the early 1980s. For instance, by 1991, 1,421 popular management books were sold, but a decade later that had risen to over 5,000, generating sales in excess of US$938 million (Pagel and Westerfelhaus, 2005). The market grew strongly through the 1990s but also diversified and broadened such that the notion of what constitutes a business book has greatly extended and the proportion of academics writing such books declined (Jackson, 2001a). Indeed, Huczynski (1993) has offered a threefold classification of management gurus: (1) 'academic gurus' (e.g. Rosabeth Moss Kanter, John Kotter and Kenneth Blanchard); (2) 'consultant gurus' (e.g. Tom Peters, Edward de Bono, Robert Waterman) and (3) 'hero managers' (e.g. John Harvey-Jones, Lee Iacocca, Jack Welch), but the boundaries, especially between (1) and (2), are indistinct. Some see the guru industry as involved in the creation of celebrities (Clark and Greatbatch, 2004; Khurana, 2002) and thus involved in more than just the production of one or two texts; the lecture/seminar circuit, guest appearances, videos/DVDs, websites and other media spin-offs are part of the package. Again, in line with commercial popular culture, some have referred to the creation of a 'brand' (Clark and Greatbatch, 2004), an idea Collins, D (2003) takes further suggesting that popular management 'knowledge' should be analysed by drawing on contemporary thinking on brands and branding, particularly in terms of identity formation and other social construction processes. Referencing this notion of branding, one of the editors in the industry interviewed by Clark and Greatbatch (2004: 408–9) said "The author is all-important. What we want is to build a brand so that the author has instant recognition" and another that:

> When you publish these books you have to work on the assumption that most people who buy it won't read it. It needs to be seductive for reasons other than content. The package is the total package, the book and the person [...]. Packaging the author is as important as packaging the book [...]. What you are selling is an attachment to a particular person and their brand or ideas.

Under pressure to maximize returns by keeping the guru in the market and diversifying product offerings, it is reported that fabrication occurs in which material for core texts is actually made-up (Clark and Greatbatch, 2004).[6] Furthermore, material is often not actually written by the guru himself/herself; the production process often involves extensive editorializing and even the use of ghost writers (Clark and Greatbatch, 2004; see also Crainer, 1998a).

The market for popular management books is clearly very significant and is exemplified by the proverbial 'airport' book. The texts are marketed through such popular channels, are widely known and secure very good sales, as noted. Their diffusion to practitioners is very apparent. A panel assessed the most influential business books for *Forbes* magazine; the top five included: Peters and Waterman's *In Search of Excellence*, Collins and Porras' *Built to Last: Successful Habits of Visionary Companies*, Bryan Burrough's *Barbarians at the Gate*, Hammer and Champy's *Reengineering the Corporation* and Michael Porter's *Competitive Advantage* (see Table 2.1). A ranking by readers included two of

Table 2.1 Forbes – the most influential business books

Title	Author(s)	Publisher	Year
In Search of Excellence: Lessons from America's Best-Run Companies	Thomas Peters, Robert H. Waterman	Harper and Row	1982
Built to Last: Successful Habits of Visionary Companies	James C. Collins, Jerry I. Porras	HarperCollins	1994
Reengineering the Corporation: A Manifesto for Business Revolution	Michael Hammer, James A. Champy	HarperCollins	1993
Barbarians at the Gate: The Fall of R.J.R. Nabisco	Bryan Burrough, John Helyar	HarperCollins	1990
Competitive Advantage: Creating and Sustaining Superior Performance	Michael E. Porter	Free Press	1998

Source: Ackerman, *Forbes Magazine*, 2002.

those (*In Search of Excellence* and *Built to Last*) but also had Stephen Covey's *Seven Habits*, James Collins' *Good to Great* and Geoffrey Moore's *Crossing the Chasm*. HarperCollins listed its all-time best-selling management books in 2000, and the list also included *Barbarians at the Gate, Built to Last, The Effective Executive* and *In Search of Excellence* – but also Tichy and Cohen's *The Leadership Engine: How Winning Companies Build Leaders at Every Level* and Scott Adams' *The Dilbert Principle*. The latter warrants a small divertisement.

The presence of Adams' (1996) *The Dilbert Principle* in the list is significant in that it represents another mode of popular culture representation for management knowledge, but also because it signifies some pertinent representational contortions and intertextual perambulations. Adams' work represents the comic bathos of organizational life and is particularly critically satirical about managerialist practices and pretensions and their effects on the 'average' worker (see Czarniawska and Rhodes, 2006). It is enormously popular, extensively diffused and widely read. The cartoon strip appears in 2,500 newspapers across 65 countries worldwide and has over 150 million readers. It has its own spin-off businesses with associated books, a television animation series, computer games and assorted merchandise. *The Dilbert Principle* was also rated by the *Washington Post* as "the management book of the century" and by a *Wall Street Journal* writer as "the best management book I have ever read" (cited in Kessler, 2001). More importantly, it has also impelled a traversal of the boundary between the popular and the academic. It has been the subject of academic commentary (including from Drucker) and has been the subject of academic enquiry, including a number of PhD theses (e.g. Carter, 2000; Davis, 2000). For example, Solomon (1997) offers a scholarly critique of Dilbert suggesting that despite its apparent satire, it fails to be subversive, offers no critical acuity, is ultimately supportive of power asymmetries and is disrespectful of the average working person. Others invoke Dilbert as a signifier for pervasive organizational cynicism regarding management policy and action (Feldman, 2000) or used it as a motif with which to interrogate other aspects of organizational and work life (Brown, 1996, 1997; Dyrud, 1998; Johnson and Indvik, 1999). In other words, *Dilbert* is read as offering a valid critique of certain aspects of contemporary management and organization practice. That a cartoon should be considered by some commentators to be the repository of valid and critical knowledge about management and organization, sufficient for it to be deemed a pre-eminent source of such knowledge by the popular press and worthy of the highest level of enquiry by academia, is very notable. Indeed, it problematizes the nature and status of management knowledge and provides a location for a significant blurring of the boundaries between various modes of representation of management knowledge.

Adams' work is indisputably in the domain of popular culture, but there is little ground for resisting locating the best-selling management books discussed above as also belonging to that domain. However, the issue we want to address is not whether such texts are part of popular culture but rather to ask the question, Where does the popular end and something else begin? More specifically, our prime concern in the rest of this chapter is with the question of whether a distinction can be sustained between such 'popular' modes of management 'knowledge' representation and academic modes of representation. It is a question we shall return to shortly. However, the potential blurring of that distinction is not confined to a potential conflation between guru management (including cartoon manifestations) and academic representations.

First, the 'fashion-setting industry' includes not only the gurus themselves, but large organizations with media, consulting, education and even development interests, and it is these organizations that control the marketing, diffusion and distribution of management 'knowledge' with mass appeal (Clark and Salaman, 1998; Sturdy, 2004). The networks and flow of people through these organizations are significant – they are far from discrete domains – and popular management ideas and representations are co-constructed in the mix (Spell, 2001). Second, the popular representation of management knowledge is appearing in all manner of media, not just those emanating from management gurus. There are, for example, academic texts that draw on representations of management and organizations as already constructed in popular culture – in literature or film for example – as a pedagogic device through which to explore aspects of management 'knowledge'. The *Management Goes to the Movies* site is a clear example, but movies have been progressively used in management training (Champoux, 1999; Dubnick, 2000; Clemens and Wolff, 1999; Jurkiewicz and Giacalone, 2000). The use of literature in management pedagogy is perhaps even more prevalent. Examples are numerous, including such texts as: Czarniawska and Guillet de Monthoux's (1994) *Good Novels, Better Management*, Puffer's (1991) *Managerial Insights from Literature*, Brawer's (2000) *Fictions of Business: Insights on Management from Great Literature*, Clemens and Mayer's (1999) *The Classic Touch: Lessons in Leadership from Homer to Hemingway* and Whitney and Packer's (2000) *Power Plays: Shakespeare's Lessons in Leadership and Management*. Works relating management/business to other cultural forms such as poetry or music are rarer but do exist (see Vaill, 1981; Powell and Veiga, 1986, repectively, for examples).

The above presupposes, naturally, that there are representations already present in art and popular culture that deal with management/business issues as a key point of focus that can be so drawn upon for pedagogy. Again, the examples are legion across a range of media, some of which are discussed in this book: David Mamet's play *Glenngarry Glen Ross* and others in his 'business trilogy' as discussed in Chapter 4; Ridley Scott's film *Blade Runner* in Chapter 5; various television situation comedies such as *Dinner Ladies* in Chapter 6; satirical television cartoons such as *The Simpsons* in Chapter 7 and in the music of Bruce Springsteen in Chapter 8. Of note is a small but also growing genre of management/business novels. Some, such as Goldratt's (1984 and 1997, respectively) *The Goal* and *The Critical Chain*, Roberts' (2001) *The Invisible Heart: An Economic Romance*, Jevons' (1998) *Deadly Indifference: A Henry Spearman Mystery*, Loebbecke's (1999) *The Auditor: An Instructional Novella* or de Marco's (1997) *The Deadline: A Novel About Project Management*, are expressly written to make a point about management practice and are basically pedagogical. Others, such as Coupland's (1996 and 2006, respectively) *Microserfs* and *JPod* or Kemske's (1996 and 1993, respectively) *Human Resources: A Business Novel* and *The Virtual Boss*, are less managerialist and more literary. Still others are spoofs or parody, such as Kehlog Albran's (1974) *The Profit*!

What is notable is that academics are invoking some of these alternative modes of representation in ways that, ipso facto, raise questions about the status of management 'knowledge' in its various representational forms. Some are using popular culture modes and suggesting that they constitute valid forms of management 'knowledge', sometimes disparaging or downplaying more ortho-dox academic modes of representation in the process. For example, in recent issues of the *Harvard Business Review* (HBR),[7] it has been suggested that liter-ature contains important 'knowledge' about management that is as valid and useful, if not more so, than academic modes. For example, in the May 2005 issue, Bennis and O'Toole (2005) argued that the focus on quantitative analysis in management research had skewed the delivery of management education, leading it away from relevance and application. They then argue that students can learn more about issues such as leadership and decision making from liter-ature than they can from academic textbooks. More recently, Badaracco (2006a) suggested that "You could learn as much about leadership from that [Shake-speare's Julius Caeser] play as you would from reading any business book or academic journal." Indeed, Badaracco (2006b) has published a book exploring management, especially leadership, through literature and has courses and exec-utive programmes at Harvard Business School doing exactly that. Here we have a senior academic from one of the USA's most prestigious business schools informing us that the management 'knowledge' to be found in literature is more valuable than that derived from academic journals and based on empirical research. He is careful to make clear that he is focusing on 'serious literature' as he calls it, seeking perhaps to sustain a high culture–low culture distinction, but it is perhaps a moot point whether Conrad or Auchincloss is part of popular culture or not. That notwithstanding, we would argue that Badaracco's own *Questions of Character* is part of a popular management knowledge industry and more clearly a part of popular culture.

Of further note are the particular interpretations that Badaracco offers of the texts he elects to examine. One of those happens, fortuitously, to be Arthur Miller's *Death of a Salesman*. Badaracco suggests a different reading to the standard one which typically sees Willy Loman as suffering through his pursuit of a chimerical American Dream and the play being a critique of contemporary capitalism (see Chapter 4). His reading internalizes, individualizes and depoliti-cizes *Death of a Salesman*. It suggests that Loman's dreams are inappropriate: 'naively optimistic', 'gossamer' not anchored to reality and more delusion than dream. This turning of matters of political economy into ones of individualized psychology is not untypical in US business academic discourse.

The examples above, particularly perhaps the latter one, demonstrate that the boundaries between the different forms of representation of management 'knowledge' are becoming increasingly blurred. It is a blurring that occurs across what has become a broad continuum of forms of representation ranging from those emanating from the arts (literature for example) that focus on management/business issues because they are such a key aspect of the contemporary cultural landscape to empirically grounded academic representations. We argue that management 'knowledge' has increasingly been represented in forms and through processes that justify its inclusion in the location of popular culture and that the blurring of the boundary between representations in the academic mode and those in the popular culture mode is of particular interest. Further, whilst arguing that the boundaries between all these modes of representation are becoming blurred, we want to give particular attention to those associated with the *management guru industry* since that is perhaps most acute in any contestation over the nature and status of 'management knowledge'.

Tom Peters live at…: consuming gurus

The guru industry is that which produces 'texts' and products aimed at a wide and popular market and includes popularizations of management thinking. It includes texts produced by gurus and experts that are targeted beyond the academic market and includes such products as biographies and autobiographies of business leaders and other non-textual media (e.g. videos, DVDs) typically associated with core texts. As noted, the guru industry really took off in the early to mid-1980s following a spate of highly successful and popular texts published at that time. It has grown into a significant industry, and the impact of popularized management ideas has been enormous – of such significance that Huczynski (1993), with suitable hyperbole, suggests that guru theory is one of a group of six core management ideas to emerge over the last century.

There is a growing subgenre in organization and management studies which analyses and discusses guru theory. It tends to be critical, but there are exceptions. Much of the focus has been on explaining the uptake and popularity of guru management ideas by practitioners. Such explanations have been varied: one commentator identifies eight different theoretical perspectives related to the adoption of (management guru) ideas and discusses their rationales and relative merits (Sturdy, 2004). A summary table from Sturdy is reproduced here (Table 2.2).[8]

It is not our intention to precise these perspectives but rather to comment on some of them as they bear on the interests of this chapter.

Sturdy's psychodynamic perspective is of interest. It corresponds to the psychological explanations discussed by others (Abrahamson, 1996; Clark and Salaman, 1998). It argues that guru ideas resonate with practitioners because they apparently offer a way of coping with underlying anxieties and desires they experience by providing a sense of understanding, order and control. Clark and Salaman (1998) suggest that the texts often display rhetorical devices that play to this, for example, by suggesting that the organization and/or its managers

Table 2.2 An assessment of theoretical perspectives on the adoption of ideas and practices

Perspective	Reason	Strength	Weakness
Rational	Effective for organization	Prescriptive	Idealistic
Psychodynamic	Anxiety/identity	Emotion focus	Essentialism
Dramaturgical	Rhetoric	Integrative	Mono-directional
Political	Interests/effects	Critical	Functionalist
Cultural	Fits values	Contextual	Apolitical
Institutional	Imposed/legitimation	Comparative/integrative	Deterministic
Multi-dimensional	Various	Inclusive	Non-integrative
Contingency	It depends	Flexibility	'Relativist'

Source: Sturdy, 2004: 168

confront a threat, thereby inducing anxiety, but then proffering a solution, a way to reduce the threat and restore order. Sometimes the discourse here engages in a kind of 'othering' of the manager – we will return to this later. Managers are depicted as so anxious and uncertain that they will gladly embrace any solution seductively offered. They are portrayed as psychologically weak, damaged and somewhat infantilized. Sometimes a mimetic process is implied whereby managers adopt ideas because others have. This can be seen as a simple desire to be in vogue but can also be seen as reflecting a more complex dynamic in which the very notions of management and manager are constructed within the interchanges between managers, gurus and others and that practicing managers naturally seek to embody those constructions. Furthermore, management is a language game and if it is constituted and framed by influential others, including gurus, then it is expedient that managers seek to participate in that language game.

The cultural perspective points to the cultural embeddedness of ideas and practices and that adoption is a function of the extent of resonance of ideas with the cultural values and practices prevailing within a particular context at a particular point in time. For example, many of the guru management ideas promulgated in the early 1980s were embedded in a language and context that pointed to the threat from Japanese business but which offered a solution through an appeal to American values and practices. The resonance of popular management ideas with wider cultural values has already been commented upon, but additionally, texts will often trade in myths and symbols resonant within the culture, leading some to see management gurus as primarily myth makers, symbol manipulators and storytellers (Clark and Salaman, 1998). This is claimed as if there were an alternative, objective, unmediated, non-rhetorical way of representing management ideas. Indeed, it is argued that gurus revert to these rhetorical manipulations as "rationality surrogates" invoked in the absence of an "objective and functionalist knowledge base" (Clark and Salaman, 1998: 148).

The notion of the purely rhetorical and symbolic content of management gurus' representations is further reflected in Sturdy's invocation of the dramaturgical perspective. Indeed, labelling guru representations as merely rhetorical and examining their rhetorical devices has been a common strand of commentary and criticism in the literature (e.g. Clark and Greatbatch, 2004; Grint and Case, 1998; Roberts, 2005). Kieser (1997), for example, focuses on the rhetorical in popular management books and explicates the devices which help make them popular and marketable, including the importance of narrative and story, especially if a heroic motif can be incorporated (Hegele and Kieser, 2001). The value of stories is also noted by Sturdy (2004), and he suggests that management 'knowledge' is a matter of constructing 'credible stories' (citing Alvesson, 1993), especially if they relate to known real managers/executives (Clark and Greatbatch, 2004). For Sturdy though, it is more than rhetoric, it is about marshalling all the dramatistic elements so as to produce a persuasive performance, especially since guru texts are often accompaniments or additions to the live performances on the lecture/seminar circuit. Again, we would raise the question as to whether such rhetorical and dramaturgical practices are confined to guru management or whether they are, in fact, also inherent to any discursive construction including those within management academia (see Rhodes and Pitsis, 2007).

Pursuing the notions of rhetoric further, a number of writers have provided more detailed analysis of the form and content of guru representations, noting some distinctive features, including a range of specific rhetorical and stylistic devices (Furusten, 1999; Jackson, 1996; Pagel and Westerfelhaus, 2005). For instance, Kieser (1997) identifies ten characteristics of top-selling management books which include staying focused on one crucial factor, linking to wider values, deploying known managers as examples, simplistic yet ambiguous language, linked to empirical research (but vaguely), and accessible style. Echoing the latter point, it is argued that stylistically the texts are "immediate, practical, concrete, superficial and easily read and assimilated", features that reflect the nature of managerial work (Clark and Salaman, 1998: 142). Clark and Greatbatch (2004: 412) similarly argue that guru texts need to be simply and clearly written requiring that "the main elements of the ideas be reduced and simplified into pithy lists, acronyms, concepts, mnemonics, metaphors, and stories that are immediately graspable, understood, and assimilated". These features are also an echo of consultant-speak with its simple, direct language employing few flourishes and relying a lot on bullet points (Bloomfield and Vurdubakis, 1994). It is a style that research suggests is actually preferred by managers (Pagel and Westerfelhaus, 2005). Practitioners described academic texts to them as being too detailed, complex, indirect, abstract, too lengthy and not convertible into action. Indeed, the length of a text was the single most significant factor in a purchase/read decision.

Popular representations contra academic representations of management

Popular culture's empty spectacle

Critics of the guru management representations often point to their stylistic and dramaturgical features in order to disparage guru theory, implying that it lacks substance and presents only a superficial, merely rhetorical, set of representations (Abrahamson, 1996; Hegele and Kieser, 2001; Kieser, 1997; Lewis *et al.*, 2006; Roberts, 2005). In doing so, they cast doubt on the value of the representations and the 'knowledge' they presume to encompass. Called into question too are the practices that derived guru theory which are deemed to be deficient, lacking efficacy, exhibiting high failure rates and doing more harm than good (Abrahamson, 1991; Clark and Salaman, 1998; Hilmer and Donaldson, 1996). For example, Roberts (2005) argues that the rhetorical and persuasive tactics present in popular management texts produce 'knowledge-lite' outcomes and that if management knowledge is left to the dictate of the market, there will be an erosion of a "substantial knowledge base" (Roberts, 2005: 56). The knowledge status of guru representations is thus challenged. Even when guru management representations are constructed via such 'heroic' and deeply experienced practitioners as Jack Welch, they are still seen as superficial, deliberately simple and vague (Kieser, 1997). There is also then an implied disavowal of the knowledge of the practitioner. Others also see popular representations as some form of distortion, deformation or impoverishment of 'proper' management 'knowledge' which is presumed to be derived only from academic sources and dismissively refer to 'fads' and 'fashions' (Abrahamson, 1991; Hilmer and Donaldon, 1996; Jackson, 1996).

These critiques seek to establish a clear differentiation between popular and academic representations of management 'knowledge'. They also, of course, imply the obverse; that academic management 'knowledge' is 'proper', adequate, facilitative of effective practice and free of the dismal exigencies of fashion. Further, it is presumed that there is 'true' management 'knowledge' and that academics have privileged access to it and that their representations are the only valid ones. As Collins (2000: 28) puts it, it is a view that "suggest[s] that management's gurus live in a false or deluded world, while critical scholars of management enjoy unique access to a world which provides true and objective information regarding the nature and performance of organizations". He continues, arguing that the totalizing world view of the guru is critiqued but replaced by the totalizing world view of the academic, but that neither seems to resonate properly with the world as experienced by the practitioner.

Even among those who resist dismissing guru management out of hand as empty and vacuous, there is still often an implicit assumption that the mode of knowledge representation it trades in is somehow flawed. Clark and Greatbatch (2004), for example, argue that popularizing management texts are part of the age of the spectacle and that they make their popular appeal on the basis of the manipulation of image and presentation rather than content and are thus "fundamentally an aesthetic form" (Kieser, 1997). Kieser intends by that notion the alignment of guru management with other forms of fashion and thus making it available to analysis via aesthetics. Popular management ideas are an aesthetic form and they function at the level of appearance. This critical strand invokes the work of Best, Kellner, Baudrillard and of course DeBord to reinforce the view that there is an increased ambiguity in separating image, simulation, spectacle and hyper-reality from the real. The management fashion industry is then portrayed as a purveyor of spectacle, of pseudo-knowledge and synthetic products (Clark and Greatbatch, 2004: 398–9). Its products are seen to serve an aesthetic function rather than any utility for practitioners. The problem, of course, is that this can lead to a reversion to a realist ontology and an assumption that there is a reality behind the spectacle that can be accessed and represented. Additionally, for some the interpretation seems to be that the spectacle, the simulacrum, is inferior to the supposed original and further that the original can be accessed and represented but only by the privileged keepers of knowledge; in this case, the management academic. Whilst this might not be what the likes of Baudrillard intend, it does seem to be apparent in the critics of guru theory.

All this again echoes debate in cultural studies where there has long been a move away from the idea that texts represent reality in any untrammelled manner or that representations can lock reality or specific meanings about reality into texts so that they become carriers and delivers of that knowledge. A move away also from the idea that authors or critics are the proper keepers of knowledge with privileged access to it. This identification of popular management representation with the age of the spectacle or with other moments in postmodernism is one line of critical reflection, but it should not be allowed to instil a closure on the meanings of such representations. Those arguments notwithstanding, whilst it might legitimately be argued that there is an aestheticization of management, this does not preclude it having other discursive positions, nor other modes of engagement with practice. Furthermore, there appears to be an implicit assumption that orthodox academic representations are devoid of aesthetics and that their authority and impact is not dependent on aesthetics; something denied by certain contemporary theorists (e.g. Czarniawska, 1999; Richardson, 1994; Rhodes, 2000, 2001b; Van Maanen, 1995) and confounded by those academics who deliberately incorporate aesthetic, poetic and popular stylistic forms into their work (e.g. Kostera, 1997, Rhodes, 2000; Westwood, 2004).

Proper and improper management knowledge

Clark and Greatbatch (2004) do, in fact, acknowledge that popular management theory is not mere appearance – that it is consequential for practitioners. It is argued that management gurus provide mutually understood ways of talking about, defining and thereby knowing management issues in organizations (Clark and Salaman, 1998) – something we shall return to shortly. However, it is still nonetheless claimed that their authority rests on the ability to convey the *impression* of authoritative knowledge. We still want to ask how this is different from any other act of representation, any discursive knowledge claim – including those mounted by academics? Academic management knowledge is a representation and is constructed and discursively arranged like any other with its own particular genres, metaphors and other tropological qualities, even though claimed by neo-positivists to be objectively and neutrally derived and based on 'hard facts'. Its reception, interpretation, acceptance and legitimacy rests as much on these features as on content – as with any other mode of representation.

The authority of academic representations also rests on the ability to convey the impression of authoritative knowledge and such an impression is equally a tropological accomplishment. It is of course aided in this by its location within specific discourses and associated institutions, which already, in certain socio-cultural conditions, bolster such authoritative knowledge claims. It is important to note that the representation still needs to be constructed in such a manner that it achieves that discursive and institutional location – otherwise alternative, less authoritative readings might emerge. We are reminded of Burrell's (1993) account of his attempt to have a video accepted as a viable academic representation. However, this is a dynamic process and very much depends on the audience at issue in a particular act of consumption–production. For management practitioners, there are clearly barriers to the reception of academic management representations. There has been a clear failure to find resonance, and practitioners do not necessarily read academic texts as definitively authoritative. Indeed, if the research and commentary discussed in this chapter are an indication, they are more likely to find greater resonance and authority in guru representations. Indeed, Collins (2001: 27) maintains that guru theory is a "persuasive and substantial representation of an organizational reality" and academics should take it seriously (see also Collins, 2000; du Gay, 1996; Grint, 1997). That guru representations have been more influential with practitioners has been a cause for comment and even lament among management scholars (Pagel and Wester-felhaus, 2005).

There is a discernible tendency then, even among critical scholars, to set up a bifurcation of rhetorical, superficial and improper guru knowledge opposed to a real, valid and proper academic management knowledge. We suggest that this is not a sustainable distinction. Not least because current theorization, at both a general level (Angus and Langsdorf, 1993; Brown, 1992) and an organizational level (Czarniawska, 1995; Gowler and Legge, 1983; Linstead, 2001; Watson, 1996), sees all representations as rhetorical and rhetoric as not merely a surface artifice of language but as implicated in the constitution of meaning and 'reality' and the determination of action in relation to it. As we have noted above, there is no reason to exclude academic representations from aesthetics or to assume that their interpretation and authority is not dependent upon its tropological qualities – while such distinctions remain culturally sedimented, there is no reason for them not to be troubled. Collins (2001) and others would argue for the importance of taking guru theory seriously precisely because it constitutes managerial reality and plays a part in the determination of organizational practice. It is not simply that rhetoric and aesthetics are constitutive of organizational reality, they are constitutive of knowledge too.

The argument that presumes to instantiate a sharp differentiation between popular and academic representations of management by suggesting that the former is superficial artifice and the latter delivers 'proper' knowledge also welcomes a naïve realism back in by suggesting that there is a real, objective truth about management and organization that can be unearthed by academic practice and that this can be done free of the artifice of rhetoric and metaphor. It is orthodox organization studies that pursues a positivist, objectivist epistemology which holds that knowledge can be constructed and represented in a neutral language detached from the subjectivity of the researcher, theory and the epistemological processes that 'uncover' the knowledge of a pre-existent objective reality. Such an epistemology privileges the academic researcher and his/her knowledge claims. Such views of realism, objectivity and truth in the social sciences and humanities have been under attack going as far back as Myrdal (1958) and Cicourel (1964) amongst others and neither constructivist nor postmodern epistemologies admit to such positions within organization studies (e.g. Chia, 1996; Clegg and Hardy, 1999; Hassard and Parker, 1993).

The othering of managers

In the critiques of popular texts outlined above, there is a form of 'othering' of the practicing manager. The practicing manager, as is often the case in management and organization studies, is absent in these representations and silenced in the rarified and distant pontifications of the academic. Sometimes the 'othering' rests on very negative essentialisms: Huczynski (1993), for example, suggests that guru texts have an appeal to managers and are a substitute for academic representations because of their limited intellectual capacities, short attention spans and inability to process complex material. Although managers themselves have expressed preferences for short and simplified material (Pagel and Westerfelhous, 2005), Huczynski's criticism is blind to the mundane realities of managerial life and the enormous pressures on time and information processing. A rejection of an academic representational style by practitioners is not a cause for inferences about their intellectual capacity. As one of Pagel and Westerflehous's (2005: 440) management interviewees said about one of the management texts he/she had read:

> Yea, I started, but I didn't finish. It is a horrible book. Great ideas, but a terrible, terrible writer. There is no life to it. It is just like a professor writing. It is more of a textbook than it is something to read. It is like reading an engineering textbook.

Commenting on the various explanations for the market success of guru representations, Clark and Salaman (1998: 146) suggest that typically:

gurus are defined as the dominant, initiating partners, exploiting the naivete, vulnerability of their client managers, selling them glib promises, fads, empty slogans; confusing them through their rhetoric, dazzling them with their performances. Managers, on the other hand, are conceived largely as passive, docile consumers of gurus' ideas and recommendations, inherently vulnerable to gurus' blandishments, anxiously searching for reassurance and support, looking desperately for new ideas.

They also, in this regard, cite Thomas (1993) who goes on to say that managers' needs are depicted as being like those of "a petulant infant, insecure, desperately seeking predictability and order, easily bored and distracted, fixated on instant gratification and filled with yearnings for dependence and authority figures".

The manager, then, is depicted as a helpless dupe who is a passive and seduced consumer of the wares marketed by the management fashion industry – as 'marks' in a managerial 'shell game' (Collins, D. 2003: 189) or as victims of the 'witchdoctors' of popular management (Micklethwait and Wooldridge, 1996). It is a view which essentializes and 'others' managers in unwarranted ways. It also offers a very restricted and theoretically outmoded view of diffusion and consumption processes (Sturdy, 2004).

The production and consumption of management in popular texts

The notion that consumption is a unilateral and unidirectional process in which the customer is the passive recipient of the manipulations of the market and that the meaning of consumptive items is ineluctably encoded within them at production has long been contested within cultural studies and culture theory. Fiske (1987, 1989), for example, has long since rejected conceptions of the production–consumption process that positions the consumer as passive cultural dupe. He points to the operation of a 'cultural economy' (running in parallel with a financial economy) within which meanings, pleasures and identities are constructed in an *active* process of consumption/production. As Fiske (1987: 313) says, "the power of audiences as producers in the cultural economy is considerable".

Within the discussion of guru management and its impact, there is, then, a reprise of old arguments in cultural studies about the impact of the cultural industry on the consumer wherein writers like Willis (1990) and Fiske (1989) argue that consumption is a productive process and that the meaning of a consumptive item is not encoded at production, but constructed in usage, versus those who argue that such a view of the sovereign consumer deflects from the structural conditions that the culture industries and the mechanisms of late capitalism exploit to dupe the consumer into consumption patterns that suit their interests (e.g. Golding and Murdock, 1991; McGuigan, 1992). D. Collins (2003), for example, takes issue with du Gay (1996) whose analysis appears to construct an asymmetrical relationship in which the practitioner is a victim to the management fashion industry, preferring to side with Clark and Salaman

(1998) in conceiving of the guru–practitioner relationship as characterized by higher levels of interaction, dynamism and mutuality. Clark and Salaman (1998) suggest the situation is not one of gurus, or the guru industry, imposing meanings upon a passive consumer, rather there is interaction and negotiation in which "gurus' success lies in reflecting and modifying managers' meanings" (Clark and Salaman, 1998: 151) and incorporating their understandings and values into the representations they construct. Indeed, it is maintained that gurus are likely to be re-presenting or re-packaging ideas and practices that already exist in some form (Grint, 1994; Huczynski, 1993; Micklethwait and Wooldridge, 1997; Roberts, 2005; Spell, 2001). The recycling associated with quality control circles and MBO are two examples. This has led some to refer to the life cycle of management ideas, and for some this is less like a typical product life cycle and more like the processes to be found in the fashion or entertainment business.

The extra complexity here is that practicing managers may experience pressure from such life cycles through feeling impelled to appear as modern and up to date and to be aware of the latest 'management ideas'. There are certain mimetic qualities then in the uptake and utilization of popular management ideas as practitioners compete to be perceived as at the vanguard (for an international dimension to this, see Westwood and Kirkbride, 2000). It is in the interests of the management fashion industry to foment this dynamic. It is important to note that management and organization studies is itself a 'discipline' that has consistently and repeatedly picked up ideas, concepts and theories from other domains and applied them to its own – the notion of corporate culture being a prime example (Bartunek and Spreitzer, 2006). It is also worth noting that some ideas and concepts appear to whither away and die – for example in organizational studies, anomie and alienation have seemingly passed on.

Such patterns and processes of production and consumption are as likely to be applicable to academic texts, but, as far as we are aware, there has been scant attention on such processes in relation to academic products. The whole diffusion and consumption of academic texts and other 'products' has not been explicated, but although it might have a particular patina, there is no reason to suppose that academic outputs are immune from such processes. This remains an omission in the literature and might legitimately be undertaken as part of the reflexive turn in organization studies (Alvesson and Skoldberg, 2000).

Like any consumption process, practitioners will appropriate what is offered by gurus, invest them with meanings that fit their purposes and use them to account for and legitimize their actions in situated ways. Collins (2000, 2004), for example, points to a complex consumptive process in which practitioners take vague and ambiguous representations and invest them with meaning in the context of practical situated action. He sees this, loosely following Latour, as a process of translation. The meanings of the representations launched by management gurus are not enduringly inscribed at the point of production; the practitioner participates actively in processes of consumption/translation. The relationship between guru and practitioner is dynamic and dialogical (Collins, D.

2003) and the construction of management 'knowledge' emerges in a dynamic interaction between the practitioner and the guru or other members of the management fashion industry such as consultants. Practitioners are tactical in their appropriation and use of guru ideas within their own spheres of action (Benders and van Veen, 2001). Of most significance, though, is the notion that guru representations actually constitute what management is and what it is to be a manager. Guru representations provide the resources for the co-construction, by practitioners, of managerial and organizational realities that are consequential and cannot be dismissed as delusional fads obscuring more objective realities to which academics claim privileged access. As Collins (2001) argues, guru representations are troublesome not because they obscure some supposed other objective reality, but because they offer a 'totalizing' account of management and organization that leave little space for the many varied interpretations and representations available. One might, however, say the same of academic representations, particularly from within particular paradigmatic positions. Indeed, as Collins (2001) argues, the whole notion of a management 'fad' tends to assume a homogenous field of management and organization studies which responds uniformly to ideas circulating within the discourse: a notion that is clearly untenable.

One might say that guru management representations help managers to co-construct subject positions for themselves within the shifting terrain of management and organizational discourse. The representations provide a rhetoric of motive, the resources for the legitimation and justification of who they are and what they do. It would be fallacious to suggest that there is a distinct boundary between these processes and the processes of management 'knowledge' production within the academic sphere. The constructed bifurcation which delineates academic from popular representations is at best misleading, in part, because it ignores the equal reliance of academic representations on the rhetorics of persuasion, stylistics, narrative and other tropological devices. Misleading, too, in privileging academic representations as if they have exclusive and objective access to the reality of managerial work and organizational life. Such privileging is especially at odds with the demonstrable inability of academic representations to resonate with the practitioner and with the fact that guru texts cannot be dismissed as superficial and inconsequential when they clearly have an impact on practitioners and help to constitute the world in which they function and the identities they assume. As Wilkinson *et al.* (1998 from Collins, 2001: 31) maintain,

> The problem with this dualistic form of analysis, however, is that the so-called fads of the guru industry have been used by consultants and others to engineer real changes in our working lives and in the conduct of our hospitals, our schools and in the apparatus of our governmental structures.

The poverty of academic management representations

Clark and Salaman (1998: 147) argue that management guru representations cannot have recourse to "formal, authoritative, theoretical professional knowledge to underpin their work", and then add, "because there is no such knowledge". Others have also pointed, albeit less radically, to the limitations of management knowledge – noting, for example, its deeply decontextualized and ahistorical nature (Collins, D. 2000, 2003). Micklethwait and Wooldridge (1997) argue that the poor quality of management knowledge in part rests on the relative immaturity of its scholarship. It is noteworthy that some bastions of management/organization studies orthodoxy come to similar conclusions but respond in a radically different way. Pfeffer, in particular, has analysed the poverty of the field, suggesting it lacks maturity (Pfeffer, 1982, 1993, 1997) and famously made a plea for the field to rally around an agreed paradigm (unsurprisingly, he advocates an orthodox, structural functionalist, neo-positivistic paradigm) and carefully police itself through institutional mechanisms to ensure that the paradigm is adhered to and the field not polluted or diluted by alien paradigms. Latterly, Pfeffer (with Sutton) has continued his attack arguing that management practice is undermined by seeking management knowledge in the wrong places – in flawed best practice, in mere experience, in emulation or in the blandishments of a raft of self-proclaimed management experts. The answer, they argue, is to emulate contemporary medical practice and pursue evidence-based management wherein actions and decisions are based on evidence – on 'hard' facts derived from proper research (Pfeffer and Sutton, 2006a, 2006b, 2006c, 2006d). They make claims for a realist ontology and objectivist epistemology, asserting that the 'facts' of good management and business are uncoverable through positivistic research and that the truth so revealed should be the basis for action.

What is interesting here is the acknowledgement from management academic orthodoxy that their representations fail to resonate and have an impact on practitioners, but that does not cause a reflexive examination of the processes of representation, diffusion and consumption and accompanying stylistics, but a retreat to a realist ontology and objectivist epistemology. That they should invoke the 'sacred' discourse of medicine is, of course, an astute rhetorical move since medicine is a discourse with the highest levels of legitimacy in terms of applied knowledge available today. It is also notable that there is no reflection on the fact that the authoritativeness of their own proclamations is facilitated by their work being embedded in the valourized institutional and discursive frame of the USA's elite university system. There is no apparent reflexive awareness of the politics of signification as evidenced by Pfeffer's overtly political moves to control the discourse, control meanings and police boundaries. It is also of high significance that Pfeffer and Sutton's work has begun to bear the imprimatur of the very 'fashion-setting business' they seek to disavow – replete with high exposure, strong marketing, mediation and dissemination through popular media and standard rhetorical devices such as pithy typologies or steps: Six

Flawed Management Beliefs, Five Principles of Evidence Based Management and so on. Like Tom Peters, they also have their own website to promote and popularize their ideas,[9] as well as (one imagines) fatten their wallets. That their work is abound with rhetorical and tropological practices might be anathema to their notions of objective knowledge, but it is inescapable. Almost paradoxically, Pfeffer and the representations he constructs and promulgates, whilst auto-positioned as within academic orthodoxy and promoting all that the orthodoxy holds sacred in terms of its ontological, epistemological and methodological commitments, actually end up as a good exemplar of the blurring of the boundaries between the academic and the popular.

In the search for the surety and order of a totalizing discourse, others have made similar pleas for paradigm closure and for a disciplining of the field, often on the basis of an assessment of its parlous state, and particularly through pointing to the immaturity of its theoretical development and its inability to resonate with the practitioner. Thus, Donaldson (1996, 2001, 2003) has repeatedly maintained that objective organizational truths can be uncovered through positivism and contingency theory and the field should hold no truck with other perspectives. McKinley (2003; McKinley *et al.*, 1999; McKinley and Mone, 1998) has also expressed dismay at the lack of development and relevance in the field and argued for greater construct consensus through imposing a construct dictionary that would pin down requisite construct meanings and which those participating in the newly policed field would be required to adhere to.

Trajectories of representation

There might be agreement that academic management knowledge fails to talk to practitioners, that it fails to resonate, but clearly not all would agree with the solutions offered by Pfeffer, Donaldson, McKinley and others. It might, in any case, be argued that it is this disjuncture between the academic domain and its knowledge production and dissemination regimes and the domain of the practitioner that has created a space within which alternative modes of management knowledge representation – such as guru theory – could emerge. The situation, however, is complex with dense interconnections and interplay between practitioners, gurus/consultants and academics such that neither they nor their texts can be separated by any clear boundaries – temporal, physical or discursive. It is critical, as we have noted, to recognize that the ideas and practices that management gurus promulgate *are* impactful and are taken up and acted upon by practitioners. Additionally though, it also needs to be recognized that such acts of practice are then often themselves the site for academic research scrutiny. Such scrutiny might lead to the production and dissemination of management knowledge representations – perhaps confined to academic outlets (perhaps not). Such ideas might be picked up by management gurus or consultants, repackaged and disseminated through other media and again taken up by practitioners. This is one possible trajectory for the circulation of management ideas. Indeed, some have argued that it is management gurus and not academics that actually define and constitute management and business practice and, given the trajectory described above, set the research agenda (Gerlach, 1996).

The trajectory of management ideas – from guru, to practitioner, to academic – is imperfectly described, since the starting point for any particular idea is undecidable and there are a number of possible trajectories. However, there is support for the notion that the trajectory, at least on some occasions, is that guru representations precede those of academics or, put differently, that management ideas appear within popular culture before they are taken up in the academy. Spell (2001: 359), for example, shows empirically that ideas often appear in the popular press before they appear in academic publications (see also Mazza, 1998). A more specific example is that of corporate culture which analysis shows received significant representation in the popular press before receiving academic attention (Barley *et al.*, 1988). Spell also quotes Galbraith (1980) as saying that he knew of no new management techniques or forms of organization that were initiated by management academic theorists. Is it, then, that management research simply reports on what popular management ideas have promoted with practitioners? Are academic representations parasitic upon popular culture representations?

Spell's (2001) analysis certainly suggests that management ideas do appear in the popular media before the academic literature, thus profoundly questioning the assumption of the typical trajectory being that management ideas are developed in academia and diffused through to the practitioner, mediated by gurus and popularizers or not. Research by Bartunek and Spreitzer (2006) also notes how management ideas often appear in other disciplines and then are diffused into management; they specifically trace the emergence of 'empowerment' from other disciplines such as religious studies. It is likely that the trajectories are actually multiple and multi-directional (Sturdy, 2004). One trajectory that might be salutary to consider is the auto-circulaton of management ideas among academics: ideas simply re-circulate between academics with no substantive diffusion out to practitioners or others. In this sense, management academics are cannibalistic, devouring their own progeny. This might be a more primary trajectory than we would perhaps care to admit. It might be more accurate to say, given management and organization studies' polysemous and contested nature (see Westwood and Clegg, 2003), that management ideas tend to circulate, be consumed and truth claims upheld within the paradigmatic communities of which the field is composed and not even travel very well across paradigms let alone across the multiple spaces occupied by practitioners.

Politics of representation

This chapter has sought to problematize the distinctions that are commonly drawn between different modes of representation of management 'knowledge'. It has done so by considering the nature of such representations emanating from the popular and academic domains and more specifically focused on the so-called management guru modes. Such distinctions have been upheld, often by constructing a bifurcation which privileges academic representations whilst downplaying or disparaging popular representations as superficial and 'knowledge-lite' (Roberts, 2005). It is argued that the boundaries between these different modes of representation are increasingly blurred and that there is a fundamental interpenetration of popular culture with academic modes of representation. This is not merely a matter of the material carriers of representations, nor of stylistics; the boundaries are sustained on assumptions of ontological and epistemological differences between the different modes with a reversion to realist ontology and objectivist epistemology often surfacing to sustain a separation. Hence, a demonstration of the blurring of boundaries actually represents a problematization of the status of management 'knowledge' and of the ontologies and epistemologies that might be invoked to sustain one form or another.

There is a politics of representation here. As usual, the discourse of management turns out to be a contested terrain through which power and its effects endlessly circle. As we have seen, even among the more critical, poststructuralist management scholars, there is a tendency to denigrate popular management knowledge and to mask the power effect in which an alternative form of knowledge, one produced by the academic community, is privileged. The management fashion business is, of course, involved in the same project of having their preferred representations constructed, disseminated and consumed. As Collins (2001: 31) puts it, these areas of contestation are "at root a fight for the monopoly rights to organization [management] studies, and the right to lecture others about their own lives and experiences". Ironically, whilst management academics have mounted a sustained attack on popular management theory asserting their privileged access to proper knowledge about management and organization, the management fashion industry has not really felt it necessary to respond – other than to continue to produce and disseminate their form of management knowledge. As we have seen, and self-admittedly, academic management has failed to have its representations resonate with the practitioner, whilst guru theory continues to be widely consumed. The high culture of academic management knowledge is clearly losing out to the low culture of guru theory! Perhaps this is not surprising when academic discourse continues to 'other' the manager, engage in a monologue that condemns them to silence and treats them as passive dupes. Popular culture, if nothing else, has resonance with its audiences and offers a space of active engagement and productive consumption. The academic domain of management knowledge has remained unreflexive about the nature of the production–consumption process in relation to its own practice and outcomes. It continues to be willfully blind to its own status as producer of popular culture and largely silent about the stylistic and rhetorical practices it ineluctably engages in.

3 Articulating organization studies and popular culture

Over the past 20 or so years, the concept of 'culture' has become central to both the theory and the practice of management – in particular, through the notions of 'corporate culture' and 'organizational culture' (see Linstead and Grafton-Small, 1992). It is on account of this that the stories, myths, symbols and values that circulate in organizations have long been seen to be central to how organizations function and to the possible meanings of work (e.g. Boje, 2001; Boyce, 1996; Deal and Kennedy, 1982; Frost *et al.*, 1991; Gabriel, 2000; Phillips, 1995; Pondy *et al.*, 1983). Whereas organizational culture and symbolism have become core constructs in mainstream organization studies, less attention has been placed explicitly on popular culture, even though, as we argued in the last chapter, the two are implicitly connected. This is not to say, however, that over the years there have not been important contributions from people who have sought to incorporate popular culture into their theorizing about work and organization – for some, such a practice offers a creative opportunity through which to better understand the culture of work. Indeed, it is the further pursuit of such opportunities that informs the ethos of this whole book.

Our concern in this chapter is with both offering a brief review of some of the different ways that people working in organization studies have incorporated the study of popular culture into their work and with addressing the question of the relationship between cultural representations and organizational realities. In Chapter 2, we saw how the distinction between management as theory and management as popular culture is hard to sustain given all of the evidence that suggests that they are deeply interpenetrating. What we also saw, however, was that despite this, these distinctions continue to be upheld by those who seek to privilege the types of knowledge produced in the academy. In this chapter, we continue to work against such an elitist position. Specifically, we do so to outline a particular methodological position from which popular culture might be productively connected to the critical study of management and organizations.

Drawing on Taussig (1993), we argue that while popular culture representations of organizations are in a sense mimetic of actual organizations, this mimesis is also characterized by an excess of meaning and that it is this excess that constitutes the possibilities for the knowledge value and potential of popular culture. To further develop this argument, we also turn to the theory of articulation (Laclau and Mouffe, 1985; Hall, 1996) as a way of exploring how the excess of popular culture can be used to generate new connections and expressions of the meaning of work and organization. As a means through which to open up the remainder of this book, we conclude the chapter with a discussion of the implications of our arguments for the study of popular culture within organizational studies.

Reading popular culture, writing organizations studies

Popular culture offers the organizational researcher a number of possibilities. It can sometimes provide access to arenas of life that academics (and others) might otherwise not think about or may have trouble entering and experiencing. More importantly though, popular culture often opens up a critical space with respect to issues, behaviour, structures and/or practices that much of organization studies neglects, marginalizes or misses out altogether. Further, the types of observations and critiques located in popular culture are capable of creating new spaces for the theorization of work and organizations for organizational studies, either afresh or in juxtaposition to or fruitful interpenetration with existing theoretical formulations. A small but significant number of writers in the field have pursued such opportunities. Contributions have included examinations of the organizational world of science fiction (Parker *et al.*, 1999; Smith *et al.*, 2001), the common emplotment of popular culture narratives and management practice (Czarniawska and Rhodes, 2006), the representation of organizations in the cinema and literature (Hassard and Holiday, 1998; Foreman and Thatchenkery, 1996), the treatment of work in popular music (Rehn and Skold, 2005; Rhodes, 2004, 2007), the relationship between organization theory and detective stories (Czarniawska, 1999) and the carnivalization of organizations in animated cartoons (Rhodes, 2001a, 2002).

More specific examples of uses of popular culture texts have included using Hitchcock's *Vertigo* to explore the tragic sublime and its relation to the debilitating pursuit of organizational idealizations (Höpfl, 2002), comic strip character Dilbert as a management iconoclast (Kessler, 2001), the history of the efficiency expert in popular culture (Lee, 2002), science fiction as a way of disrupting the development of management theory (Grice and Humphries, 1997), the dynamics of identity and stigmatization among *Star Trek* fans (Cusack *et al.*, 2003), examining cross-cultural issues in foreign-located companies via the film the *Rising Sun* (Foreman and Thatchenkery, 1996), consideration of masculinity and public management in the British television programme *The Bill* (O'Sullivan and Sheridan, 2005), the exploration of envy in workplace via Richard Russo's novel *Straight Man* (Patient *et al.*, 2003) and the way that Ronald McDonald can be considered a transformational leader (Boje and Rhodes, 2005, 2006). These illustrative examples point to a broad array of issues and topics.

In general terms, Phillips (1995) suggests fruitful alignments between narrative fiction and a range of organizationally relevant issues:

Narrative fiction can illuminate issues such as racism and sexism (Spike Lee, *Do the Right Thing*), the experience of job loss (Arthur Miller, *Death of a Salesman*), and the frustration of white collar work (David Mamet, *Glengarry, Glen Ross*). It can also provide baby-boomer managers and academics with access to the otherwise inaccessible culture of the twenty-something generation.

    (Dougles Coupland, *Shampoo Planet*, and he might have added Coupland's
Microserfs)

Elsewhere, Clegg (1992: 32) has discussed how organizations have been sensitively and innovatively critiqued in popular culture, particularly in films such as Chaplin's *Modern Times* (1936), Lang's *Metropolis* (1927), and Gilliams' *Brazil* (1985), and that this has been of scholarly value. Other scholars have turned to popular culture as a way of inspiring or embellishing academic arguments – Clegg and Hardy (1996) cite the James Brown classic song 'It's a man's, man's, man's world' to discuss organization and representation; Linstead (2003) turns to Bob Dylan's 'Love Minus Zero/No Limit' to explore silence and organization. Popular culture can even be used to find models which those doing academic work might use to guide their own practice (Rhodes *et al.*, 2005).

The examples pointed above are more or less direct engagements with aspects of popular culture to stimulate or engender theorizing about organizations and work. There is also a further deployment of popular culture that has grown in recent years and that is as a pedagogic device. For example, in their best-selling text book *Organizational Behavior: An Introductory Text*, Buchanan and Huczynski (2003) supplement each chapter with a précis of various movies and television programmes that are useful in illustrating the various formal theories that they discuss. They have more recently commented in detail on the use of *Twelve Angry Men* (1957) and *Thirteen Days* (2000) for such purposes (Buchanan and Huczynski, 2004). Such pedagogical uses of popular culture are indeed well established – for example Comer and Cooper (1998) advocate the use of Michael Crichton's *Disclosure* (1994) as a means of teaching people about sexual harassment in the workplace (although Brewis, 1998, has pointed to the dangers of the film in terms of sexual politics). Elsewhere, Hobbs (1998) has sought to use television as a way of integrating media literacy into management education, Champoux (2001) has explored at length the uses of film sources to examine organizational behaviour topics and Puffer (2004) has done the same for fiction and international management. Other texts that have argued for the use of fictional and popular culture representations for pedagogic purposes include Brawer (2000), Higgins (1999) and Czarniawska and de Monthoux (1994) – although this latter goes further than advocating pedagogy to suggest that the study of literature can overcome some of the drawbacks of organizational theory such as the difficulties of handling multiple levels of analysis.

For some in organization and management studies, including many of those cited above, one of the most common reasons cited for a turn to popular culture is that it provides compelling and realistic accounts of organizational life that seem to have congruence with what actually goes on in organizations; in other words, it seems to resonate with people's everyday experience of work and organizations in a way that more traditional academic accounts cannot. Indeed, it has even been pointed out that the bifurcation between scientific and non-scientific writing as genres of realism is one that was very much artificially constructed through various waves of 'scientization' from the advent of the social sciences in the nineteenth century up until the late 1970s (Czarniawska, 1999). Greenwood (2000: 156), for example, in her promotion of the Dr Seuss story *The Lomax* as a means of highlighting issues of business ethics, argues that popular literature "offers an opportunity to present the organization in all its truly complex and contradictory forms, since in literature more room exists for doubt, uncertainty and paradox".

Orthodox organization and management theory tends to 'clean up' its texts and to smooth out inconsistency, paradox, doubt and uncertainty (Pullen and Rhodes, 2008). It would seem that popular texts enable a better and more dynamic appreciation of the lived experience and affectivity of organizational life. Hassard and Holliday (1998: 1) also point to the uninspirational nature of much management theory when they claim that "popular culture offers more dramatic, more intense and more dynamic representations of organizations that management texts". Accepting that (some) popular culture provides for better (and different) representations suggests that they might also lead to a broader and deeper understanding of the social realities of work and organizations. Thus, fiction can be regarded as a "valuable means through which by which organizations and working life might be understood and informed" (Rhodes and Brown, 2005) so as to provide "legitimate alternative ways of understanding organizations" (Parker *et al.*, 1999: 585).

For other researchers and theorists, the texts of popular culture warrant attention since they are seen as providing a form of data suitable for scrutiny and analysis. DeVault (1990: 887), for example, suggests that "many sociologists of literature and some literary critics, recognizing that cultural works are produced in social context, have argued that novels can be taken as sociological data and used as indicators of prevailing attitudes and social relations". Such an approach enables, for example, studies that examine how particular conceptions of work and workers are embedded in culture – for example the culturally pervasive figure of the organizational 'efficiency expert' as one which is "laughed at but never admired" (Lee, 2002: 881). Such a perspective, however, also suggests that there is some form of homology between cultural texts and social reality such that the study of those texts might provide useful and otherwise unavailable materials through which to understand the social. This is not to suggest that cultural texts offer factual accounts or deliver a factual chain of events, but rather that they can "weave a pattern of truth in a way quite parallel to the theories of organizational analysis" (Phillips, 1995: 634) and that they can provide "a valuable complement to traditional ethnographies and to more quantitative approaches to organization" (ibid.: 639). This value may well be because "the work of an artist expresses inexplicitly what is dealt with more directly in the work of prose expositors" (Foreman and Thatchenkery, 1996: 48).

The brief overview discussed above demonstrates that there has been a small but steady stream of work by scholars involved in the study of organizations that engages with, and locates productivity in, popular culture. It also illustrates why they have done so. Various claims have been made as to the benefit of incorporating popular culture into organizational studies. These claims extend beyond the mere notion of popular cultural texts offering an alternative and exoticized representation of various aspects of work and organization. It has also been argued that popular culture resonates more fully with certain facets of work life than is traditionally offered by organization and management studies texts. It is worth noting here the work of Frost and colleagues whose hugely successful *Reports from the Firing Line* (Frost *et al.*, 1997) and *Managerial and Organizational Realities* (Frost *et al.*, 2004) force us to recognize that work and organizational realities are often not properly captured in orthodox texts of organization studies and of the value of presenting accounts of organizational life by those who actually live them. More importantly perhaps is that popular culture can contain an assessment and a critique of work and organization that is sometimes absent in organization studies and that an engagement with popular culture offers an alternate space for conceptual exploration and theoretical development.

Excessive popular culture

In the previous section, we suggested that to date the use of popular culture in organizational research has been concerned, inter alia, with popular culture as compelling representations of work, popular culture as a reflection of society and popular culture as a form of data to be subjected to analysis. Now we wish to explore more directly and problematize the status of popular culture as a form of *representation* by considering its excessive potential. At the outset, we note it is no longer contentious (other than in steadfast and insular bastions of positivistic orthodoxy) to assert that the relationship between text and meaning is highly problematic. In attesting to the possibilities of connecting popular culture with organization theory, we are thus cautious about assuming that mass-mediated culture offers a simple homological representation of culture more generally – as if to say that because, for example, a movie, television programme or song is popular, its content is a direct, accurate and/or proper representation or reflection of the goings on in society. Indeed, it would be naïve to suggest that just because *we* can find interesting or even critical examples of the representation of work in popular culture, that the meanings we so locate are somehow identical (or even commensurable) to either the intention of their producers or other audiences who may make quite different readings.

Take, for example, popular music. Quite clearly, for many people the lyrical content of the music is relatively unimportant, and to the extent that lyrics are acknowledged or remembered, sometimes certain phrases or lines are taken out of context. For example, the British conservative party, who, at the height of Thatcherism, were found singing John Lennon's 'Imagine' at the end of their annual conference. It is safe to say that this was not Lennon's intention. As Frith surmises, there is no reason to believe that the meaning of songs as intended by the author, or as interpreted by an analyst, is the same as it is for other listeners; nor is their reason to believe that the content will necessarily form or reflect listeners' beliefs. One might note the appropriation of the songs of ABBA and Kylie Minogue by the gay community or of Gerry Marsden's *Ferry Cross the Mersey* by the fans of Liverpool Football Club. The same holds for other forms of popular culture.

This complex and ambiguous relationship between the meanings of popular culture and the lives of its audiences/consumers is an important consideration in the study of culture. As Negus has pointed out, "[t]he sounds, words and images that have been distributed via the media and music industries can be used in different ways and provide possibilities for a variety of conformist or oppositional selves" (Negus, 1996: 2; see also Chambers, 1985). Such a realization has been acknowledged in "active audience theory" (Negus, 1996: 35), which explores how, in the act of consumption, music audiences are active creators of meaning rather than simply being capitulated by the corporate mechanisms through which it is produced. This is a point broadly consonant with Barthes' (1977) suggested "death of the author" (which also heralds the birth of the reader) such that the active process of consumption is always productive of meaning beyond authorial intentions. Within such theoretical approaches, the construction of meaning from culture has been considered in terms of, for example, youthful rebellion (Hall and Whannell, 1964), oppositional subcultures (Hebidge, 1979), community and identification (Lewis, 1992) and resistance to everyday life (Chambers, 1985). For Frith (1996), for example, popular music has the potential to be a form of social critique that can have a positive influence on people's real lives.

> Music certainly puts us in our place, but it can also suggest that our social circumstances are not immutable (and that other people – performers, fans – share our dissatisfaction). Music is not itself revolutionary or reactionary. It is a source of strong feelings which, because they are also socially coded, can come up against common sense. It may be that, in the need, I want to value most highly that music, popular and serious, which has some sort of disruptive effect, but my argument is that music only does this through its impact on individuals, and that this impact is obdurately social.
>
> (Frith, 1996: 277)

On this perspective, culture is at once involved in the creation of meaning as well as in the representation of life. It is also involved in the construction and maintenance of identities and subjectivities. There is a further dynamic wherein the meanings constructed in relation to popular culture become autonomized and re-enter the social realm and may feed into subsequent popular culture constructions. One of us lived and worked in Hong Kong during late 1980s and early 1990s. The film *Wall Street* had come out in 1987. It was intriguing to note the local employees of Salomon Brothers, CitiCorp, Goldman Sachs and others don braces (male suspenders) and slick back their hair in a mimesis of Gordon Gekko – a character who was portrayed negatively in the film itself. What we suggest is that it is out of this complex, dynamic process that emerges the possibilities and value of popular culture to the study of organizations. To explain and theorize this possibility, we turn to Taussig's (1993) discussion of mimesis and "mimetic excess".

As a starting point, despite the problematics of representation noted above, it cannot be avoided that popular cultural representational practices engender an element of 'copying' – and this would be as true of representations of work and organization as any other. We make sense, for example, of the behaviour of the executives of the Omni Consumer Products (OCP) corporation in the *Robocop* films, because they resonate with understandings we hold of actual corporations. The vision of a "commercial world in which executives manipulate their bodies to climb the career ladder, observe the dress codes, the washroom status hierarchy and talk a corporate newspeak to conceal the basic amorality and immorality of what they are doing" (Parker, 2002a: 148) makes sense because it somehow resonates with an understanding of what goes on in actual corporations. Mimesis is at play, but it is not just representational copying. As Bhabha (1994) and others have noted, a mimesis is not an exact copy, there is movement and difference involved. The mimetic is always other than the original and in this sense is in excess of the original. Thus, a popular culture presentation of, say, a bureaucratic organization (as in the film *Brazil* for example) may be mimetic of real bureaucracies but is more than a copy; it is something other than the original, something excessive to it. Further, as Taussig (1993: 23) notes, the commoditized world of popular culture involves opening up "new possibilities for exploring reality and providing means for changing culture and society along with those possibilities". These possibilities emerge because the mimetic faculty, the faculty to "copy, imitate, make models, explore difference" (xviii) is not passive. Instead:

> To ponder mimesis is to become sooner or later caught, like the police and the modern State with their fingerprinting devices, in sticky webs of copy *and* contact, image *and* bodily involvement of the perceiver in the image, a complexity we too easily elide as non mysterious, with our facile use of terms such as identification, representation, expression, and so forth – terms which simultaneously depend upon and erase all that is powerful and obscure in the network of associations conjured up by the notion of the mimetic.
>
> (Taussig, 1993: 21)

What this implies is that the mimetic faculty is both the ability to copy and the "capacity to Other" (19), while it also implies that a mimetic process is an act of engagement, an almost tactile engagement, with the original and with the copy *and* with the process by which we construct and see them together – their relationship. A mimesis is not merely the production of a copy, the construction of a mimetic object; it is a process, a productive process and one of oscillation, of a dynamic interplay between original and copy. Mimesis and alterity are not un-entangleable, they are intimate and interconnected. This is a fecund and productive interplay, a space of creativity and possibility. So,

> pulling you this way and that, mimesis plays this trick of dancing between the very same and the very different. An impossible but necessary, indeed an everyday affair, mimesis registers both sameness and difference, of being alike, and of being Other
>
> (Taussig, 1993: 129)

These are the in-between spaces, the hybridities that Bhabha (1994) sees as productive and mobile in (national) cross-cultural affairs. Interestingly, Bhabha also sees these spaces as sites of resistance as an antidote to the view that the dominant culture is monolithic and that the power effects in the relationship between the colonizer and the colonized are unidirectional and unilateral. There are echoes here in the mimesis in the cross-cultural affairs involving popular culture. It is precisely here, in these spaces, that the possibilities for interesting and alternate modes of analysis, critique and theorizing are opened up.

It is through mimesis that the copy assumes the characteristics and power of the original while at the same time being excessive of it. In terms of the case when organizations are represented in popular culture, this suggests that a doubling is at play here too. Organizations depicted in popular culture are representations of organizations, yet they are different to them, as indeed they are different to themselves. It is this "mimetic excess" (Taussig, 1993) – the power to both double and become other – that imbues cultural representations with some sense of 'magic'. The possibility of mimetic excess is that of "an excess creating reflexive awareness as to the mimetic faculty [...] the magical power of the signifier to act as if it were indeed real, to live in a different way with the understanding that artifice is natural" (Taussig, 1993: 255). This is precisely the power of popular culture and of art, to allow a suspension of belief, to recognize a mimetic process but to respond to the mimesis as if it is real, whilst at the same time not responding necessarily in the same way as one would to the real. Gazing upon, say, Andy Warhol's soup cans conveys this sense of mimetic doubling, but also difference, distance and alterity. The soup cans are a copy, and we respond to the paintings as a real object, but the response is not the same as looking at a Campbell's soup can on the supermarket shelf – much less than the ostensive purpose of eating the contents. It needs to be noted that the Campbell's soup can is itself just an image. It should also be acknowledged that once seeing Warhol's version, the 'original' is rarely perceived and read in the same way.

The representation of organizations in popular culture is too a mimesis, but it is also a difference. In terms of organizational theory, this begs the recognition that the representations of organization in theory, in academic scholarship are also representations and also mimetic – representations of something that they are not. In this sense, popular culture representations might be considered just as 'accurate' as any other representation – but of course, accuracy is not the main issue. The difference is that with fictional popular culture, the suspension of disbelief is closer to the surface, and that is so one might say, 'accidentally' since the suspension of belief in academic representations is less on account of knowledge-power relations that have come to privilege that mode of representation over others and the mimetic (and hence creative) qualities are backgrounded. Ironically, however, the retention of the sustained reflexive awareness of mimesis and alterity in considering popular cultural representations is exactly where additional value resides. It is the inclusion of the dynamics of the mimetic process that enriches the space and offers fresh possibilities for thinking and theorizing. Part of this productivity resides in the realization that mimetic excess suggests that an 'actual' organization, as it is understood through representational means, requires just the same suspension of disbelief. In other words, the whole relationship between original and copy is thrown into disarray and we are compelled to question and reconsider the status of the supposed 'original', the supposed 'actual'. As Taussig puts it, "Mimetic excess provides access to understanding the unbearable truths of make believe as foundation of an all-too-seriously serious reality, manipulated but also manipulatable ... [to] engage the image with the reality thus imagized" (255). This is particularly acute when we have not just a popular cultural representation presumably mimetic of, say, a presumed real (or normal) organization, but when we also bring into the mix the social science representations of supposedly 'real' organizations, representations which are themselves presented as accounts of the real and as real things in themselves. We have, then, (at least) a triumvirate of representations circulating in complex relationships of mimesis, alterity, movement, difference and power. The distinctions between the original and copy, between the real and the representation of the real are problematized through the reflexivity of mimetic excess, and this is where lies the creative possibility to connect with culture as a means of understanding actual and possible organizations. This mimetic excess, this reflexive awareness of the power of representation and the arbitrariness of the real, is an "invitation to begin the critical project of analysis and cultural reconstruction ... a preamble to investigation" (Taussig, 1993: xvi). What this might mean is that organization can become regarded as *subjunctive* – as contingent, conceived and possible rather than being fixed in representational prisons or conceptual straightjackets.

Connecting with popular culture

Having suggested that the cultural representation of organizations is a form of mimetic excess whereby the representation copies but also exceeds the actual, and in so doing also problematizes the reality of that actual, we now move on more directly to discuss what this might mean for the study of popular culture and organizations. The first consideration is the implications for identity formation and for strategies of resistance. As noted previously, Negus has pointed to the use of popular culture to construct various identities and sometimes these are identities constructed in opposition and resistance to the status quo and to dominant cultures and systems. There is indeed empirical backing to such assertions (e.g. Hebidge, 1979). Typically in such cases, people use popular culture as a resource, taking different aspects of culture and connecting them together to provide a new means of cultural expression and resistance. It is in this way, for example, that the resistant subculture of Rastafarianism was created through the articulation of different elements such as biblical scripture, Jamaican folk music, contemporary rock music and modern media to create both a new language and the new political identity of the Rasta (Hall, 1996). The punk movement in the United Kingdom in the late 1970s and early 1980s similarly and deliberately engaged in a bricolage of cultural elements that in combination were a parody of the dominant culture, a resistive distancing from the status quo and an assault on bourgeois orthodoxy.

The means by which popular cultural artefacts, such as music and clothes fashion, contribute to such reformulations is through what Hall (1996, 1994, drawing on Laclau, 1977 and Laclau and Mouffe, 1985) refers to as *articulation*. Articulation is defined as "any practice establishing a relation among elements such that their identity is modified as a result of the articulatory practice" (Laclau and Mouffe, 2001: 105) – it involves articulation in the sense of establishing both new connections and new expressions (Hall, 1996). The articulatory practices are not necessarily ordered, sequential or guided by any systematic or predefined logic; they may be somewhat arbitrary, fortuitous or accidental in nature. Applying this to discourse, the implication is that rather than being connected by "inherently logical relations", discourses are "bound together simply by connotative or evocative links which custom and opinion have established between them" (Laclau, 1977: 7). For Hall (1996: 143), this means that in cultural formations, "[i]t is not the individual elements of a discourse that have political or ideological connotations, it is the ways those elements are organized together in a new discursive formation". Thus, for example, the cultural elements brought together in a garish bricolage by punks – types of clothes, readymades and dislocated everyday objects, music, attitudes and expressions – individually are rather inert, but when brought together constituted a distinctive creed of nihilism and a political message of anarchy. It is through the creation of such discursive formations that the excess of mimesis can be seen to be at play. The articulation of elements copies them, but renders them different to that which is copied – it is excess that enables articulation. The safety pin is an almost iconic example in the case of punk. Its social codings in the orthodox realm are mundane and utilitarian, but when pushed scarily through the nose of a punk those codings are challenged and the hegemonic values of utility, and one might add of beauty and adornment, are deconstructed and reframed. In the same move, the codes of consumer culture are challenged and the value of goods decomposed and repositioned. Some years ago, one of us witnessed a punk female using a metal kettle as a handbag – shades of a dadaesque affront to the bourgeoisie and critique of consumer culture are all there in one elegant gesture!

The point of invoking articulation and mimesis is not to suggest that occasionally they are activated as exotic and somewhat aberrant practices, rather it is precisely to appreciate that the fixity of meaning is always arbitrary and political and can be both disputed and disrupted. The unity of a discourse is only ever an articulation of elements that might always be subject to different and excessive re-articulations. Any notion of unity is constructed out of particular linkages – articulation is "the production of identity on top of difference, of unities out of fragments, of structures across practice" (Grossberg, 1992: 54). With a specific focus on culture, the point is that cultural transformation occurs through new articulations where new political identities can be formed through a "reorganization of the elements of a cultural practice, elements which do not in themselves have any necessary political connotations" (Hall, 1996: 143). These new identities always being excessive of the discursive materials out of which they are formed. Similarly, we can surmise that different organizational and workplace identities are realizable in relation to excessive articulations of organizational culture.

Power effects are not far away in these arguments. Certain discursive arrangements, constituted by specific articulations, come to inscribe a particular place in the order of things. They presume to appropriate forms of knowledge and to have that discursive arrangement accepted as a proper and viable location of that knowledge. Like all discourses, there is a power effect which attempts closure such that the knowledge claims of that particular discourse are promulgated as the real and true and alternatives are cast out as false, deviant or mad. Particular discourses within and about culture attempt articulations which present particular knowledge and values as the only viable ones for a group of people and thus to exercise a hegemonic effect. However, this is always a partial exercise and the intended closure of meaning, knowledge and values are always capable of deformation and reformation – is always defeasible. Not least because closure is an illusion of temporal fixity that occurs in a moment that always passes – there is always difference and differment, there is always possibility of new and different articulations. Not least too, because of the need to always repeat and re-say, and in the reproduction to fail to reproduce the original. In other words, there is always an excess such that mimicry is never a copy and always a difference, an Other. Hence, despite the articulation of elements into hegemonic discourses that seek to eliminate the possibility of mimetic excess, society (or organizations) are not "sutured or self-defined totalit[ies]" (Laclau and Mouffe, 2001: 111). The sutures can come undone, the totalities can be shown to be merely temporary conglomerations of elements that can split asunder and reform into new articulations.

This 'theory of articulation' interpolates a productivity in that it recognizes the multiple elements that constitute culture and how any cultural form is a somewhat arbitrary and tenuous set of articulations. It explains how such constitutions might come to appear natural/hegemonic, but also how they can be decomposed, deconstructed or dissolved and 'new' seeming articulations embodied (Middleton, 1990). The concept of articulation has been used to argue that the study of popular culture should not simply involve assuming the linear and exact communication of messages from producers to consumers as if the ongoing trace of meaning lacks any excess or mutation. Such approaches suggest that the formal study of popular culture should entail examining processes of 'articulation' in which particular forms of culture "have to seek out, be sought by and connect with particular audiences" (Negus, 1996: 134).

Adding to the discussions above, and in a sense defining our core methodological interest, a point we make is that articulation is not only a way of thinking and theorizing the practices of others, but also a manner by which theory can engage with different people and perspectives – an engagement which performs 'articulation at work' (Slack, 1996) rather than an observation of articulation. By this, we wish to register that the researcher or scholar might position himself/herself as a practitioner of articulation through his/her work – rather than assuming that he/she should just be in the business of unreflexively representing the articulations of others (indeed, in relation to our earlier discussion, such attempts are futile anyway on account of their unavoidable excess).

In relation to the possibility of theorizing, care needs to be taken about the assumed position of the critic or theorist. Theory commonly enacts a powerful delineation of types of persons that makes a clear and wide demarcation between the audiences of popular culture and the critics or analysts who write about it. In such a demarcation, the critic is neither a producer nor considered to be an audience member (or even worse a fan). Instead, the critic resides in a privileged third space which is presumed to allow him or her to comment on the relationship between the culture and the audience. Here theory is constructed and positioned as a 'theory *of* culture'. Conversely, what we suggest is the possibility of a theorizing that places the theorizer in relation to popular culture rather than outside of it. The theorist is not immune to the reflexivity of mimetic excess. While we recognize that popular culture might be (but is not necessarily) a source of inspiration for the reformation (even revolution) of everyday life, we do not want to restrict the role of 'theory' (or more accurately theorizing) about popular culture to an examination of the impact on *other* (non-theorizing) people. Thus, we insist that researchers too are within culture not apart from it and that they too participate in, receive and respond to popular culture. There is no critical position external to this other than one falsely erected on the pedestal of hubris. We suggest that researchers (i.e. ourselves) need to be reflexive about this engagement and to include an assessment, analysis or at least an acknowledgement of the impact on them and then write about this impact as it occurs in an overlapping space between social science and popular culture. This means writing about culture without locating oneself outside of it. This means that, as academic writers, we place ourselves squarely within the category of audience member rather than assuming the position of external commentator, critic or interpreter. Of course, our location in academia means that our possible readings of popular culture might be different to others – but it is such differences that form the basis of a creative mimetic excess. The result, we might hope, can be a mimetic excess that critiques organization and changes the conceptions and theories we hold of them – such critique and challenge occurs when mimetic excess reveals the arbitrariness of any notion of organization. In this sense, we say that the value of connecting organizational theory with popular culture is not based on commenting on the 'effects' of popular culture on society or on particular people but rather to forge productive connections between theory and culture such that both might be exceeded. It is such an engagement that we see as being of value because it articulates different organizational and cultural theories with popular culture and its explicit statements in order to develop an innovative way of understanding the culture of contemporary work.

Such articulations are valuable because popular culture provides insightful elucidations of the cultural meanings of work in contemporary society, but whilst these are often consonant with the critical study of management and organization, they remain largely unexploited. This is perhaps so because management and organization studies that pursues (either explicitly or implicitly) a copied scientism has long been suspicious of the popular. This parallels a more general elitist academic position that sees popular culture as "without seriousness and aesthetic quality, not art, not knowledge, a mess down there that has to be regulated, cleaned up, if possible removed" (Docker, 1994: 128; see also Crainer, 1998b). As ten Bos points out, popularity, per se, is considered vulgar, tasteless and gaudy by "those who think they do not belong to the *populus*" (ten Bos, 2000: xiii, italics in original).

Appreciating this means taking seriously the many examples of popular culture that focus critical attention on contemporary work and organizations. The value of appreciating such examples is not to assess their truth value, or compare their accuracy with some other mode of representation, or to perform a 'critique *of* culture', rather it is to engage with the 'critique *in* culture' – that is the critique embodied within popular culture itself – as a valuable source of knowledge for understanding organizations and organizational life that is *positively* excessive of it.

Concluding the beginning

As we have explained, the approach to studying popular culture that we elucidate eschews the commonly held critical view that implies that 'good' criticism involves "moral/superiority/understanding over the mass spectator together with the illusion of clarity and unambiguity" (Brereton, 2001: 49). We argue that the researcher engages reflexively and positively as a participant in and consumer of popular culture and uses that position to enhance a productive critical and theoretical practice. We also have argued that although not true for all popular culture, in many cases the representations of work and organization often offer critical insight. The argument we articulate is not intended to suggest that Britney Spears is theoretically on a par with, say, Jürgen Habermas, but it does mean that some aspects of popular culture can be engaged with for the value of the observations, commentaries, critiques and ideas. Because it is popular, it is not, a priori, trash. Indeed, whilst mass culture is not necessarily a form of "'serious' debate or of political resistance [...] there are examples in mass culture that can be considered as such" (Rhodes, 2004: 3). Thus, in attesting to the value of popular culture, our attention has been drawn to issues of representation that question what it *means* to write about something in the first place and the status of supposedly different modes of representation (see Rhodes, 2001b).

In terms of an analytic, the excessive articulation between theory and culture that we are arguing for is intended to open up new spaces in which to create texts that are *about* theory *and* culture. It can be said that this *about* is a way of writing a new text that in some way relates to, but is not the same as, its subject – articulation in writing can thus be explicit and reflexive in creating difference and excess. In Van Kerk's terms, this is a position where "instead of using a purely stand-back-and-objectively-look-at-this-work approach, the critic writes a narrative that may not actually reflect on the work but that reflects beside it" (van Herk in McCance, 2002: 4). The writing space is one that is both outside of something and in something. It means writing about culture in a way that is concerned with it, engaged with it and connected to it, and it does not mean assuming that 'describing' culture is tantamount to being the same as culture, mapping it or representing it. Thus, a text *about* popular culture and organization might be considered as a theorization that connects with popular culture in particular ways, rather than being a way of representing or mapping it – and further that it is the excess of cultural representations that enables this (Rhodes and Brown, 2005).

Focusing on the articulation of work and life in popular culture is also a matter of appreciating the aesthetic representation of work. Dealing with popular music in particular, Frith has argued that "we are drawn, haphazardly, into affective and emotional alliances with the performers and with the performers' other fans [...]. Pop songs are open to appropriation for personal use in a way that other popular cultural forms [...] are not" (Frith, 2004: 37). In this example, it is music's lyrical, rhythmic and affective ability to generate emotionality and effect that makes it a promising means through which to understand the possible realities of the lived experience of work. Here, the aesthetics of pop music's expressiveness is a means of developing, understandings of the possible cultural meanings of work that would scarcely be available in other forms of representation.[1] Thus, while Frith (1996, 2004) argues that an aesthetics of popular music suggests a focus on how songs produce social values, what we have been arguing, using the theoretical resources of mimetic excess and articulation, is that there is also the possibility for researchers and theorists to connect with popular culture as a means of producing a discussion of social values without recourse to functionalist or representational readings of the relationship between culture and the 'people' or the organization. Here, culture is considered not as a form of data that can be analysed in terms of relation with society, but is taken as an aesthetic form of knowledge that is different to, but connectable with, more formally accepted forms of knowledge. If culture provides a way of making sense of the world through experience and collusion, surely this sense-making activity may be extended to include, and be of value to, scholars and theorists. It is such value that we seek in this book.

4 Men, non-men and masculinity in *Glengarry Glen Ross*

The retardations of the masculine in contemporary capitalistic organizations

This chapter opens a space within which the interrelated themes of masculinity, identity, violence and language in organizations and in relation to the capitalist ethos[1] can be explored. Whilst these are clearly significant issues for organizations and organizational understanding, it needs to be acknowledged that "The major traditions of organisational analysis have not been characterized by a significant and explicit concern with gender, sexuality, and violence" (Hearn, 1994). The space is opened by an examination of the treatment of these issues in *Glengarry Glen Ross* (hereafter abbreviated to *GGR*), the film based on David Mamet's Pulitzer prize-winning drama. Whilst the analysis will be based primarily on the film version, use will also be made of the published play.[2] Since the themes are tackled by Mamet in some of his other works, the space is widened by locating the analysis in this broader oeuvre. Furthermore, given similarities of content and even theme, *GGR* can scarcely be critically considered without some reference to Arthur Miller's (1958, 1961) classic *Death of a Salesman* (*DoS*) even though there is a gap of more than 30 years between the two. *DoS* premiered in 1949 and was itself made into a film – in fact, there have been three film versions.[3] The space so opened provides an opportunity to juxtapose the critical treatment of these issues by Mamet, and other popular culture depictions, with their representation and theorization in management and organization studies.

We argue that Mamet offers a complex and trenchant critique of the ethos of contemporary capitalism and its effects on those who labour within it. It is a multifaceted critique, one that exposes inter alia the myth of the American Dream, the damaging and dehumanizing effects of hierarchy and competition, the venal and criminogenic nature of work and the corrosion of values, character and community within business organizations operating under that ethos. Mamet goes further though, arguing that the patriarchal and phallocentric dominance present in our social structures is reproduced in and recursively reconstituted by the mechanisms and institutions of capitalism and business. The capitalist ethos is infused with and underpinned by the discourses of patriarchal and masculine power and this extends into the more micro-domain of organizations within the system. Mamet, however, chooses not to explore the implications of this for the gendering of work and organization and the disadvantage of women or other marginalized groups, rather he focuses on the implications for men – for notions of masculinity and identity that confront men functioning under this ethos. From his perspective, contemporary organizations are ineluctably reproducing not only a masculine ethos but a particular and severely restricted one. Business organizations provide a context and a culture that reproduces a stunted version of masculinity in the mundane language and practises, permits and legitimizes it and in turn reproduces the masculine ethos and hence the systems of patriarchy and dominance that constitute the wider capitalist system. Men find themselves locked into an iron cage of patriarchy that impels them to perform gender in ways not only limiting to self and identity, but which, for most of them, for most of the time, is stultifying, limiting and violent. It constructs a restrictive regime that inhibits their capacity to explore alternative masculinities, alternative selves and that erodes their values, sense of self-worth and relationships.

We suggest that Mamet offers a critique that is rare in its nuanced complexity, penetration and insight when compared with what can be found in mainstream academic analysis within management and organization studies at that time. Indeed, we go further, arguing that in dealing with the isomorphism between masculinity and the capitalist ethos, in exploring the corrosions of self, value and community under that ethos and in revealing the consequences of a restricted masculinity in organizations, Mamet was at the vanguard of critical analysis. We barely see attention to the gendered nature of organizations and the selective production of identities in organizational analysis until the late 1980s in management and organization studies. In his work, Mamet has not only drawn attention to some vital areas of critique and analysis, he has also provided an exemplary critical practice and significant conceptual resources for those within management and organization studies to take the analysis further.

Plot and themes in *GGR*

The film/play actually has a relatively simple plot line and structure. It focuses exclusively the interactions of men in a real estate agency and locations adjacent to it. The protagonists are four real estate salesmen[4] and their immediate manager. The salesmen are tasked with pursuing leads provided by the office in order to sell parcels of a distant property development or land release – the *GGR* of the title. This is highly competitive and their earnings are commission based. The company adds to the pressure by making it into a competition between the men. The pressure is heightened when the manager from the office visits with new leads and tells them that failure in that month's competition will result in dismissal. This creates consternation amongst the salesmen and there is much discussion, including talk about breaking into the office to steal the new leads. The next day, it is apparent that there has indeed been a break-in. As things unravel, it is the character called Levene who is in the end incriminated.

The film opens with salesman Levene and Moss in adjacent telephone booths. Levene is talking to his daughter and trying to reassure her about something. Moss is making a pitch to a potential customer. Some themes and motifs emerge immediately. First, the film immediately exposes the lies and deceit involved in the sales pitch. Moss's patter, and that of all the salesmen, clearly is full of lies and untruths. In this business, and by extension in any capitalist business, the imperative is to sell: if you sell, you win, and winning and beating the competition is an overarching imperative that displaces everything else – including values, morality and the truth. After his sales call, Moss complains bitterly about the leads the salesmen have been given and, introducing another motif, deploys considerable verbal aggression and profanity. The introduction to Levene contains the seeds of more subtle themes in the drama. Levene is talking to his daughter, one of the two absent/present women in the play. It is the only moment in the drama where the language is not aggressive and violent, indeed, the only moment that in any way signifies real human feeling and tenderness. There is a forlornness and desperation about Levene. The pressure of selling quickly pulls him away though impels him back into the masculine world of competition with its violent argot. The moment gestures to the idea that only the presence of women allows some relief, some alternative, to the violent, aggressive and competitive world of men's business.

From this point on, a relatively simple plot unfolds: the narrative is clearly not the vehicle for Mamet but rather a space for the themes to emerge and for a focus on the language deployed. The four salesmen are trying to sell distant, dubious and possibly non-existent developments to customers. The 'leads' the company provides are supposedly contacts to potential buyers, but there is perpetual discussion and criticism of them by the salesmen and it is apparent that they are often little more than addresses and not genuine prospects. As Moss says irately: "Bunch of bullshit trying to make a living on these bullshit leads .... They don't give you the leads, they don't give you the support, they don't give you dick."

After each of the salesmen has been introduced in various short scenes, a sales conference takes place in the office. Blake, a younger, brasher manager visiting from the head office, berates the staff and explains the new 'policy directive' from Mitch and Murray – the owners/senior partners of the business. The office runs a competition every month based on who sells the most property. Blake informs the group that they are

> adding a little something to this month's sales contest. As you all know, first prize is a Cadillac Eldorado[5], anyone want to see second prize ... second prize (he holds them up) a set of steak knives ... third prize is you're fired. Do we get the picture ... you laughing now?

This provides the dramatic set-up for what unfolds. The competitive stakes have been suddenly raised and intensified. Blake is a quintessential manifestation of the masculine-capitalist ethos and he rams home the prime imperative: making the sale is all that matters and winners are rewarded and losers punished.

The added pressure fuels the salesmen's desperation and immediately we are shown the impact of the prime imperative in the corrosion of values, ethics and character. In a pathetic mix of obsequiousness and aggression, Levene tries to persuade Williamson to give him the new leads, eventually resorting to bribery by offering Williamson a share of the commission plus cash for the leads. Williamson feigns interest but in the end does not give up any of the leads. Elsewhere, Moss is privately talking to Aaronow and suggesting that someone should break in and steal the leads and sell them to a competitor. It becomes apparent that Moss is serious and that he is trying to cajole, even blackmail Aaronow into doing the break-in. At this stage, we are left uncertain as to what is agreed. Meanwhile, Ricky Roma is in the restaurant making an opportunistic, complex and subtle pitch to another incidental customer – James Lingk. There is virtuosity in Roma's performance, but ultimately it reveals that the prime imperative feeds inauthentic behaviour, inauthentic relationships and even inauthentic philosophy. His quasi-philosophical pitch is a seduction; it seduces Lingk by offering him inclusion into the world of independent action in the pursuit of individual desires; the world of 'real men'.

The second act begins back in the office the next morning, and it is immediately apparent that someone has in fact broken in. Detective Baylen has arrived to investigate. Roma comes in and frantically tries to ascertain if the contract he got Lingk to sign the night before has been filed or stolen since it would ensure his prime spot in the competition and the Cadillac. Williamson tells him, it has been filed. A buoyant Levene enters claiming to have made a significant sale to customers, the Nyborgs, and performs the macho, assertive, successful salesman. Moss exits fuming from the adjacent office where he has been interrogated by Baylen, argues with Roma and leaves. Shortly after, Lingk arrives, after discussing the deal with his wife, he has returned to cancel it. Roma invokes Levene to join him in a bit of trickery to try and put Lingk off. Roma feigns an urgent need to be out of the office whilst seeking to placate him by saying that the cheque has not yet been cashed, leaving time to discuss it later. He is about to get away with the hoax when Williamson emerges and thinking that Lingk is concerned about his contract assures him that it has been filed and the cheque cashed. Lingk leaves. Roma explodes at Williamson for blowing his deal and Levene joins in the verbal assault. Roma goes into the back office to be interrogated by Baylen. During his tirade, Levene reveals that he knew Williamson was lying to Lingk about the contract being filed, knowledge only the burglar would possess. When confronted, Levene confesses, but then tries to bribe Williamson again. In a final ignominy, Williamson reveals that the Nyborg deal will not fly; the Nyborg's are known unreliable customers. Williamson goes to inform Baylen about Levene. Roma comes out and offers to go into partnership with Levene sharing commission, but later, as Roma talks to Williamson, we realize this to be yet another scam to ensure Roma's victory in the competition.

The simplicity of the plot belies the complexity of the actual focus. At one level, Mamet is critiquing contemporary US-centred capitalism and its effects on people and their relationships. Like Miller in *DoS*, it is in part a critique of the American Dream, an attempt as Mamet (1988: 96) says to "tear down [...] some of the myths about this country". But, in focusing on a microcosm of this, on the homosocial world of these salesmen, he demonstrates the corrosive effects of the masculine-capitalist ethos on men's values, behaviour and character. Ostensibly, what is portrayed is the intense competition between salesmen as they vie for the best leads and closed deal. However, the competition spills over so that almost every interchange between the men is a verbal contest of one-upmanship and braggadocio. The men are locked into brutal and dysfunctional masculine behaviours, reinforced by a management style and set of expectations that creates a climate devoid of ethical standards. There is an obvious text here about the demeaning nature of work in contemporary organizations, but there is also a significant subtext concerned with masculinity and identity. The drama deals, then, with a range of issues – the corrosion of character, the immorality of business, the collapse of community, the violence of language, the violence of men, but particularly the limitations of a particular mode of masculinity. This chapter explores the representation of those themes in this film/play and links them to their theorization (or not) in management and organization studies.

Castigating the capitalist-masculine ethos

We begin with perhaps the most straightforward aspect of Mamet's critique in which, as with Miller in *DoS*, he exposes the corrupting impact of the capitalist ethos. Again, as with Miller, the critique is extensive since it deals not with the localized politics of business, work and organization, but with the decay of the American Dream and the erosion of values in society as a whole. As we shall see, however, this provides the platform for a more nuanced critique of the corrosive effect of this on community, ethics, relationships and character.

Clearly present in *GGR*, and in other areas of Mamet's work – particularly in the so-called 'business trilogy'[6] – is a powerful exposure of the corrosive effects of contemporary US capitalism and critique of the ideology of rabid individualism and its concomitants in destructive competition, greed and selfishness. Indeed, like *DoS*, it can be read as a dissection of the myth of the American Dream as men pursue false hopes in a system ultimately based on brutalizing and destructive competition. Furthermore, participation in the structures of capitalistic competition defines their masculinity and identity, thus as the myth of the American Dream unravels the limitations and corrosiveness of the masculine identities and subject positions they have felt compelled to adopt are exposed. Part of the unravelling and of the corrosion of contemporary capitalism is the bastardization of values and the displacement of ethical judgement and reasoning through the injunctions of economic success and economic rationalism. Success, of individuals as well as systems, is measured only in terms of economic gain. Furthermore, success in these terms is valourized: hence, competition, winning and economic gain have positive valence, indeed are virtues.

As Silverstein (1995: 115) suggests, Mamet documents the

> disappearance of criteria for grounding value judgements by reminding us of what happens when we pervert the meaning of "good", wrenching it from

its place as the vital centre of an ethical vocabulary and transforming it into a synonym for "success".

Silverstein cites Lyotard's (1993: 18–19) similar assessment of the capitalism's crisis of legitimacy wherein "success is the only criterion of judgement [our culture] will accept. Yet it is incapable of saying [...] why it [success] is good, just, true, since success is self-proclaiming". Such critiques echo Bauman's (1993, 1995) assessment of postmodern ethics and the trouble locating a moral compass in the displacements of rampant capitalist consumerism and the 'humiliation' of being excluded from capitalism's games. In *GGR*, this stunted ethic is exemplified in the act of selling – everything is about selling. To sell is to win, to beat the competition and to beat the competition is to attain material and economic gain. The salesmen are impelled to see securing a sale as the prime directive and to consider any means legitimate to that end.

This imperative is most starkly laid bare in a scene that encapsulates the drama's key themes and sets up the unfolding narrative. Quite early on, Blake, arriving from head office, berates the staff and delivers the ghastly ultimatum of the terminal competition, thereby crystallizing the imperatives embodied in competing–selling–winning. At one level, the scene signifies the stark and simple logic and ethic Mamet sees at the heart of contemporary capitalism. Blake assumes a hectoring tone and, with the aid of camera positioning, a lecturing posture. Before outlining the new hyper-competitive regime, he spots Levene pouring himself a coffee off to the side. Blake bellows at him, "PUT THAT COFFEE DOWN ... coffee is for closers only." 'Closers' being those able to take leads, make a sale and close a deal. A little later, when Moss asks his name, he explodes: "Fuck you. That's my name. You know why mister ... 'cos you drove a Hyundai to get here tonight, I drove an $80,000 BMW, that's my name." His whole speech is a series of demeaning put-downs accompanied by self-aggrandizement and braggadocio. The put-downs include a vicious emasculating tone. He turns to Levene: "Your name is 'you're wanting', and you can't play in the man's game. You can't close them? *(as a rhetorical question)*, then go home and tell your wife your troubles." Then to the rest "'cos only one thing counts in this life, get them to sign on the line which is dotted ... you hear me you fucking faggots".

Mamet has said that *GGR* is a play about a society based on business, a "society with only one bottom line: How much money you make" (quoted in Gussow, 1984: C19) – Blake is the dramatic embodiment of that, an iconic representation of contemporary capitalism and the ethos of business upon which it rests. He is young, sharp-suited, aggressive, thrusty – a model of testosterone-driven masculinity of a particular hue. He even has the swept back and gelled hair reminiscent of Gordon Gekko in *Wall Street*. He embodies an ethos in which the business imperative of material success is the *only* imperative and the only value. Those unable to obey these imperatives and be successful are losers ... worse, they are emasculated, are non-men; indeed, it is implied, they are without identity.

In a comment that is almost an echo of a line he might have given Blake, Mamet (in Lahr, 1983) says, "American capitalism comes down to one thing [...]. The operative axiom is 'Hurrah for me and fuck you.'" It is an axiom Mamet critically explores in different ways in the business trilogy. For example, he says of *American Buffalo (AB)* that it deals with:

> The predatory aspect of American life. The whole Horatio Alger myth in America is false. It's a play about honour among thieves and the myths this country runs on .... Calvin Coolidge once said "The business of America is business." The ethics of the business community is that you can be as predatory as you want within a structured environment.
>
> (quoted in Carroll, 1987: 32)

Elsewhere, he tells us that *AB* is about a corrupted American business ethic, one that justifies all manner of betrayals and ethical compromises (Gottlieb, 1978). It is, he asserts, a system that legitimizes unethical behaviour, engenders impoverished values and encourages criminality (Roudané, 1986). Part of American mythology, signified by the 'frontiersman' (Prasad, 1997), is the cult of the individual and the enshrined freedom of the individual; values deformed under the regime of contemporary capitalism it is suggested. As *Teach*, the protagonist of *AB*, says:

> You know what is free enterprise? The freedom ... Of the Individual ... To Embark on Any Fucking Course that he sees fit [...] In order to secure his honest chance to make a profit [...] The country's founded on this.
>
> (Mamet, 1977: 72–3, emphasis in original)

In many respects, *GGR* is bleaker than the earlier *AB* since in the latter there are at least intimations that the main characters might sustain a meaningful relationship, whereas in *GGR* the competitive imperative pollutes *every* relationship. Mamet sees the ethical decay as pervasive, suggesting that "there's really no difference between the lumpenproletariat and stockbrokers and corporate lawyers who are the lackeys of business [...]. Part of the American myth is that a difference exists, that at a certain point viciousness becomes laudable" (quoted in Gottlieb, 1978: Section 2, p. 1). He makes it clear, like Miller in *DoS*, that it is the collapse of the American Dream that causes the anguish and moral decay. Mamet (quoted in Leahey, 1982) makes the following blunt observation: "the people it [the American Dream] has sustained – white males – are going nuts". It is the alienated, dehumanized and desperate condition of the characters that provides the dramaturgical impetus for the play, rather than any narrative (see Savran, 1992).

We can, of course, find a swathe of critiques of the capitalistic enterprise and business ethos in the literature. It is, however, less common to anchor those critiques so intimately, as Mamet does, to the corrosions of community and character,[7] and even less common to relate them to the deformations of identity and confinements of stunted masculinity. In *GGR* and other plays, he reveals the penetration of the caustic effects of the capitalistic ethos – particularly its rampant individualism and machismo-driven competitiveness – into the values systems, relationships and souls of members of the culture. It is a penetration so trenchant and pervasive as to have "commodified and objectified the private sphere of interpersonal relationships to the point where it becomes impossible to locate any affective dimension uncontaminated by the inexorable logic of capital" (Silverstein, 1995: 112). Thus, in *GGR*, there is no person, no relationship and virtually no action left untouched by this logic.

There is a danger, of course, of overstating these impacts and of making everyone a passive victim and dupe incapable of resistance. In *AB*, Mamet does leave a glimmer of hope that men can find the grounds for a meaningful relationship, but in *GGR* there are no meaningful relationships, they are all polluted by the motives of selfish material advancement and winning at all costs. Indeed, it is worse than that since the residual values of character, camaraderie, family and community are all *used* and exploited to manipulate others in pursuit of self-interest. Bigsby (1985a: 262, 290) argues that such positive values are never apparent in the characters' actions, only in their language which thereby represents "the vocabulary of a world which has slipped away". Thus, for example, Roma uses the language of camaraderie to apparently support Levene, but only so as to secure a portion of Levene's sales, or Moss uses the rhetoric of community to dupe Aaronow into breaking into the office. Indeed, the penetration of the capitalist ethos and its corrosive business culture is so all-encompassing that Mamet doubts the efficacy of mounting a critique directly into the political/economic sphere since that sphere is also so penetrated as to nullify any such intervention. This explains his choice of the arts and popular culture to pitch his critique – hoping to access the collective conscious, indeed the dreams, of people in the culture through dramaturgy (see Mamet, 1986; Savran, 1988).

Mamet is ambitious in his critique for, as Demastes (1988: 87) points out, whilst *GGR* details the corrosive effect of the ethos in the workplace and upon the salesmen, there is "a much broader topic that Mamet is addressing – the decaying of America as a result of this ethic, not just in business, but throughout". The effects of this decay penetrate the structures, values and relationships of society and community. The uniqueness of Mamet's critique is to offer the kind of multi-level analysis rare in management and organization studies at the time.[8] He charts how the corrosive capitalist ethos not only penetrates and erodes societal-level values and structures, but does the same to the individual and his (in this case) identity, ethics and relationships. He explores the mutually constitutive relations between patriarchy, masculinity and the capitalist ethos at the societal level with gender politics and identity issues at the micro-level. The masculine-capitalist ethos creates the conditions for and constitutes particular masculine identities which are performed in the workplace, performances and enactments which are in turn reproductive of the masculine-capitalist ethos. Mamet's analysis suggests that men functioning within this circuit become entrapped in a recursive masculinist code that is inhibiting and debilitating. As Vorlicky (1995: 31) makes clear:

> The ethics of Mamet's business world, and its intended metaphoric and actual associations to American patriarchy, are directly linked to the culture's masculine ethos. As dramatized by Mamet, this gendered ethos appears unethical: it promotes corruption, exploitation, prejudice, and violence

It is this dramatization of such a complex set of relationships that represents Mamet's unique critique.

Mamet's male tribes

Mamet has pursued the issue of masculinity in a number of plays – indeed, it has been suggested that he has a "fascination with the male tribe" (Friedman, 1985: 40) – and a degree of controversy has ensued from that. That is hardly surprising; Mamet has courted controversy since the production of his first play *Sexual Perversity in Chicago* in 1973. The controversy then centred on the profanity of the language; something that continues. It is very much in evidence in *GGR* but functions to reflect both the violence and the restricted codes of masculine language. Controversy around his treatment of gender issues reached a nadir with the staging of *Oleanna* (Mamet, 1992), which deals with the repercussions of an accusation of sexual harassment against a male university professor by a female student. Mamet's treatment of those issues led some to accuse him of misogyny (Showalter, 1992); it certainly seemed to evoke misogynistic responses from some audiences (Silverstein, 1995). Others, however, see this as a misreading of the play (Badenhausen, 1998), preferring to interpret it as a satire on political correctness. Commenting on the accusation of misogyny, Mamet (1989a: 32) himself famously said, "We feel, based on constant evidence, that women are better, stronger, more truthful, than men. You can call this sexism, or reverse sexism, or whatever you wish, but it is my experience." The issue of misogyny notwithstanding, we elect to focus here on a reading of Mamet as constructing a critique of masculinities as limited and stunted, and exploring the implication for matters of identity, and for social and organizational dynamics.

Mamet's work has frequently explored male characters in depth, for example in *AB, The Lakeboat, The Duck Variations, Edmond, Speed-the-Plow* and, of course, *GGR*. As in *GGR*, the drama is often set in intensely male, indeed, male-dominated, even homosocial, domains. All the interactions in *GGR* are between men, the four salesmen and Williamson their office manager, with women totally physically absent. There is, however, an off-stage female presence of significance with two females invoked as absent/present others – absent since not physically present, present since they are implicate and necessary to the treatment of masculinity in the visible domain. One is the apparently sick and hospitalized daughter of Levene, the other the wife of Lingk, a duped and weak customer. We will have more to say about this female presence later.

As noted, in *GGR* and other plays in the business trilogy, Mamet explores the imbrication of the ethos of capitalism and masculinity. It is an imbrication, which suggests that the capitalist business values/practices of extreme individualism, aggressive competition and selfish materialism are isomorphic with a certain masculine code, one that equates with Connell's (2005) 'hegemonic masculinity'. The link is so strong that men define themselves and are defined by their jobs and by their success in the competitive games of business. We are not, of course, suggesting that there is only one type of masculinity, nor engaging in any essentialism here. That masculinity is a social construction and that there are a range of masculinities within most cultural groups has been made very clear (Beynon, 2002; Connell, 2005; Lorber and Farrell, 1991). We are suggesting that there is a way of 'doing masculinity' that has a particular contour and which resonates with, indeed is produced by and reflexively reproduces, the values and ethos of the capitalist enterprise. There is a strong stream in management and organization studies which has since considered the construction of gender in the workplace (e.g. Alvesson and Billing, 1992; Cleveland *et al.*, 2000; Game and Pringle, 1983; Gherardi and Poggio, 2001; Knights and Kerfoot, 2004; Mills and Tancred, 1992). However, there has been a 'silence' around masculinities in management and organizations (Collinson and Hearn, 1996) that has only recently been broken (Kilduff, 2001).

There have more recently been significant reflections on masculinity and organization and management (e.g. Chalmers, 2001; Cheng, 1996; Collinson and Hearn, 1996, 2005; Hearn, 1994; Roper, 1994) but still only a limited number exploring the complexities, situatedness and nuances of performing masculinity (Alvesson, 1998; Barrett, 1996; Catano, 2001; Collinson and Hearn, 1994; Dasgupta, 2000; Dellinger, 2004; Lupton, 2000; Mills, 1998; Mumby, 1998; Prokos and Padavic, 2002; Smith and Winchester, 1998). These latter demonstrate how various modes of masculinity are an accomplishment resulting from the situated social interactional and identity work of men in different organizational contexts. There is, as Connell (2005) and others (e.g. Barrett, 1996) have suggested, a hegemonic form of masculinity prevalent in society that produces and reproduces society's patriarchal structures, but there are other forms that are possible and are enacted. Research has examined, for example, the masculine identity work of men in atypical male organizations and occupations, and female-dominated work contexts (Alvesson, 1998; Dellinger, 2004; Henson and Rogers, 2001; Lupton, 2000; Simpson, 2004; Williams, 1995). Nonetheless, the literature in management and organization studies infrequently explores the dynamics of masculinity with the acuity and complexity displayed by Mamet, and few have traced, as he does, the relationships between the ethos of capitalism and the construction of a form of masculinity. There is some limited research that does show how under the ethos of work, business and capitalism, men are often positioned to construct a particular identity and perform a particular type of masculinity (Connell, 2005; Craib, 1988; Hodgson,

2003; Roper, 1994). As with Mamet, it is argued that these constructions and performances of management and work behaviour produce and reproduce the capitalist ethos and the power structures inherent therein and within society's patriarchal formations (e.g. Collinson, 2003; Hopton, 1999; Kerfoot and Knights, 1998). It needs to be noted that Mamet's dramaturgical critique pre-dates this work in management and organization studies by a considerable margin.

Within *GGR*, it is the person adhering most to the hegemonic masculine/capitalist ethos that comes to occupy positions of power, but this is a shifting hierarchy – a pecking/pecker order – of power/masculinity (Vorlicky, 1995). It is Blake, a caricature of the masculine-capitalist ethos, who is positioned as the most powerful person in the hierarchy in *GGR*. The pecking order then descends down through the office manager Williamson, to Roma the top salesman, to the angry and bitter Moss, the failing and aging Levene, with the weak Aaronow at the bottom; the latter two both in danger of shading into the category of not-men. For, as Vorlicky (1995: 30) suggests, within the dominant white male culture in the USA, a person has "no identity outside his culturally coded power of domination". Beyond Blake, there are the absent Mitch and Murry who as business owners or 'bosses' signify masculine-capitalist power. As we will see though, the play is structured so as to make apparent that significant power – albeit of a different form – actually remains absent, invisible and external to the action among the men.

The organizational environment in *GGR* represents a male-only, homosocial environment typical of many organizational contexts. Mamet constructs it thus because he wants to explore the dynamics, relationships and identity issues in precisely such contexts. He is, at the same time, seeing this as a microcosm, a homology, of the wider hegemonic masculine culture that constitutes and is constituted within the contemporary capitalist ethos. It manifests a form of masculine culture founded upon myths of masculinity embedded in, for example, the American Dream, but it is a dream shown to be deformed under the motivations and mechanisms of capitalism. Almost syllogistically, if masculinity is constituted by capitalism, and capitalism is a deformed project, then this form of masculinity is deformed. *GGR* dissects and lays bare these deformations. But, it is men who reproduce the structures and values of capitalism through their continued (re)enactment of the 'American masculine ethos'. An alternative, feminist account might argue the reverse – that capitalism is constituted by a particular mode of masculinity, a masculine mode that is stunted and deformed, hence capitalism is itself a deformed, limited and limiting mode of social organization.

GGR is not, then, just an indictment of capitalism and the falseness of the American Dream, but also "a reproach to a particular discourse of masculinity that capitalism fosters" (Greenbaum, 1999: 43). The capitalist ethos and the delusions of the American Dream traps the men into a stunted, destructive and unfulfilling mode of performing masculinity – one corrosive of self, character and community. The equating of masculinity and masculine identity with modes of work and work-related success has been explored in the academic literature but mostly only recently and still in a limited way (Brittan, 1989; Collinson and Hearn, 1994, 1996; Haywood and Mac an Ghaill, 2003; Hearn and Morgan, 1990; Parkin and Maddock, 1995; Roper, 1994; Tolson, 1977). *GGR* reveals a particular male subject position and specific masculinity; a dominant mode constructed and performed in many other homosocial work environments as documented, for example, by Barrett (1996) in relation to the Navy. Indeed, Hopton (1999) argues that the hegemonic masculinity traditionally constructed within the military is now being reproduced within the domain of managerialism. Hearn (1992) argues that throughout the twentieth century, paid work has provided men with a sense of identity as well as power and status – reiterated starkly in *GGR* by Levene who simply states the blunt homologue, 'A man's his job'. Pertinently, Collinson (2003) relates this to Miller's *DoS* and notes the collapse of identity of those who, like Willy Loman, fail at work in the phallocentric world of capitalism and for whom the American Dream remains a chimera. Grey (1994) similarly shows how the pursuit of a successful career supports particular masculine identity claims, but often also brings demands and challenges that cannot be met, thus ultimately undermining a sense of identity. There has, then, been growing recognition in academic discourse of the centrality of work to the male identity. As Sinclair (2000: 85) says in summary, "This research leaves little doubt that for many men and for most managers, work accomplishes masculinity. In organisational life, the two identities of manager and man have fitted hand in glove." However, this makes sense only if we hold to an essentialized view of masculinity, to only one, albeit pervasive and perhaps hegemonic, mode of performing masculinity.

The non-male Other

We signalled how Blake is a signifier of this dominant mode of masculinity; how he represents the machismo and the aggressively competitive and selfish ethos of contemporary capitalism. In that emblematic scene in which, as noted, he berates the salesmen and establishes the cut-throat ground rules for the sales competition, he provides the drama's set-up. After establishing these ground rules, he turns and, with his back to the men, opens his executive briefcase and removes something from it. He turns and reveals a pair of oversized brass balls that he dangles strategically in front of his crotch. The message is clear, you need balls, big ones, to play in his game and to compete under his rules. He not only berates the men's performance, but maligns their manhood. If they cannot sell, cannot close the leads, not only are they 'shit', not only are they 'weak', they are not men: "you can't play in the man's game, you can't *close* them? ... then go home and tell your wife your troubles ... you faggots...?"

To close deals, to succeed in business, is to affirm one's masculinity; to fail is to become less than men. Blake's last phrase in the above tirade – suggesting that failed salesmen are 'faggots' – is significant. This is a common motif in Mamet, especially in *GGR*, wherein hegemonic 'masculinity' is constructed in relation to some Other, some 'not-man'. Typically and traditionally, that Other is the female, is woman, but it can also be the homosexual, or the emasculated, effeminate male. For example, confronting Williamson, Levene, after asserting that 'a man's his job', then says "you're fucked at yours ... You don't have the balls." The most scathing and violent comments in the film are constructed in this manner, directed at those who fail, who are not deemed able to compete and succeed in the male world. To be so judged typically leads to the further attribution that the person is less than a man.

In the *Company of Men* (Mamet, 1989a), Mamet discusses how a homosocial environment constructs its own rules with its own language games and subject positions. In *GGR*'s world, the rules are the cut-throat rules of business competition with the pre-eminent one being 'always be closing'. The language game is 'selling' – everyone is either selling or engaged in manipulative talk that manoeuvres towards a sale. The available subject positions are the restricted ones of a male salesman, constructed within the limited language of selling and a location within the discourse of phallocentric American business, the enfolded space of masculinity-within-capitalism. It is a testosterone-fuelled world that works a violent inclusion–exclusion practice whereby the male and the masculine is defined by participation in the competitive game of manipulative selling, but also by being counter-pointed in relation to the Other – a less than 'male' Other, a homosexual or the ultimate Other, a woman. It is a world both misogynistic and homophobic. As Vorlicky (1995: 52) notes, the two survivors in *GGR* – Williamson and Roma – survive because they know how to play within the masculine ethos, "to exploit other men in order not to become one of the 'other' (non-)men". Part of the competitive game is not only to ensure the maintenance of one's own masculine identity, but also to challenge others' masculinity, through constructing positions of otherness, thereby further affirming one's own masculinity. This resonates with the work of Kerfoot and Knights (1993, 1998) who have examined such processes of differentiation and identification by which men seek to construct their masculine identities.

People unable to achieve accreditation as bona fide members of the dominant masculine world are castigated as non-men. In *Speed-the-Plow* (Mamet, 1988: 70), when Fox finds out he has been duped by Bobby Gould, he vents his sexist invective "... you fool – you fuckin' sissy film ... you squat to pee. You old woman ...". For Moss in *GGR*, the power hierarchies of companies like his also emasculate employees. He bemoans the diminuitions the bosses inflict on the salesmen "Look, look, look, look, when they build your business, then you can't fucking turn around, enslave them, treat them like children, fuck them up the ass ..." (36). The bosses are accused of treating the salesmen as less than men, signified on this occasion by the conflation of slave, child and homosexual. A similar conflation occurs in what is perhaps the most violent attack in *GGR* when Roma berates Williamson and assaults his masculinity in a stream of invective:

ROMA: You stupid fucking cunt. You idiot. Whoever told you you could work
     with men? .... I don't care ... whose dick you're sucking on. You're going

out …. What you're hired for is to help us – does that seem clear to you? To help us. Not to fuck us up … to help men who are going out there to try to earn a living. You fairy …. You fucking child

(96–7)

The analysis Mamet offers shows how modern organizations and the masculine-capitalist ethos work to reproduce a restrictive hegemonic version of masculinity; in doing so, those not included within those constructions are positioned as 'Other', as non-men. Within that world, customers too are positioned as passive recipients of masculine-capitalist power and so as also less than men: Levene, for example, refers to them as 'cocksuckers'.

The restricted codes of masculinity

The masculine-capitalist ethos corrodes not only identity and character, but also language. The men in *GGR* are constantly seeking to reproduce their masculine identities through processes of differentiation and identification, particularly as noted, through differentiation from non-men and women. Furthermore, they inscribe and are inscribed by a restricted language that recirculates the codes of masculine power and dominance within the language game of capitalist business competition. It is a language that reproduces hegemonic masculine codes and the limits and possibilities they contain, including roles, relationships, identities and subject positions. It is argued that:

> Mamet's male characters are locked into culturally coded roles as speaker and listener, that is, the men activate a socially sanctioned, predetermined relationship to one another simply because they are discussing, in a non-personal manner, a topic determined in accord with the masculine ethos.
>
> (Vorlicky, 1995: 28)

They are locked into a discourse that constructs the permissible and legitimate modes of talking, behaving and being for 'men-like-them', for 'proper' men. They are, in other words, locked into a specific mode of performing masculinity; men "trapped in their worlds, and their words are trapped in their culture" (Demastes, 1988: 91). Mamet makes it clear that it is a restricted language, but also the only one available to them through which they seek to affirm their sense of identity, including a collective identity itself derived from the common, restricted codes[9] the language engenders. It is a stunted language constructing stunted empty relationships and stunted masculine identities.

The salesmen have a particular way of using language, centred almost exclusively on selling (broadly construed) and the capacity to sell "is central to the characters' identities and relationships to each other" (Worster, 1994: 375). Language is misappropriated by the characters in *GGR* and "this unethical [use of] language is committed to the business of deliberate obscuring of the truth; it encourages illusion, not the actual, as it fosters frustrated isolation rather than meaningful connections among those who speak it" (Vorlicky, 1995: 31). The men in *GGR* use language like a weapon to abuse and to bludgeon, but also to manipulate, to seduce. The prime exponent of the latter is Roma, particularly as exemplified in his sophisticated sales pitch to Lingk, using an ersatz-philosophical disquisition to engage Lingk, then appealing to the myth of the independent man that Lingk has lost before segueing into his sales pitch. The language is manipulative in both style and content and geared towards moving the 'mark' towards a sale. The same motive and dynamic persists in talk amongst the salesmen themselves: Levene trying to induce Williamson to give him the leads, Roma trying to flatter Levene into sharing his leads, Moss seeking to seduce Aaronow into breaking into the office. Almost the whole linguistic space available to these men is taken up with this language of selling and seduction in one form or another.

The linguistic code available to them is at times so restricted as to appear as a disabling inarticulateness, particularly in contexts when the language and codes of business and selling are not available to them. Thus, when their language is not constructed to sell and seduce, they typically revert to an even more restrictive code, a language of violence, using it to bludgeon, bully and control others. Indeed, much of Mamet's dramaturgy rests on and explores language as violence (Bigsby, 1985a; Malking, 1992). It is a language with a limited lexicon characterized by cliché and expletive. Almost every sentence contains one swear word or another. All the exchanges between the main male characters are characterized by this brutal language. It is, of course, part of performing this particular mode of situated masculinity. It does so not merely by the invocation of masculine aggression, but also through the restrictions of the code, which leave little space for the expression of such sentiments as tenderness, compassion, caring or even inclusion. As in *AB*, Mamet reveals how the restricted codes available to men mean that they have very limited access to a language that builds and sustains relationships, engages with feelings or fosters intimacy. As Bigsby (1985a: 123) plainly puts it, Mamet's men "no longer have access to words that will articulate their feelings". In the masculine world of *GGR*, doing business requires the suppression of a personal self and because of this the men "favour familiar and predictable, socially engendered roles that feed off cultural clichés and stereotypes of maleness" and "revere a social dialogue that perpetuates the game of business, of male mythology, of power" (Vorlicky, 1995: 34–5). Indeed, it is argued that their "thraldom to the imperatives of 'business' at any cost has stunted them and prevents them from knowing either themselves or others" (Carroll, 1987: 50).

This incapacity to reveal a personal side or engage in any intimacy is again dramatized in *GGR* by female absence. In this case, that absence is represented by Levene's daughter who we only see him talk to/about on the telephone. There are indications that she has a significant health problem, but it is both indicative of and an indictment of the masculine ethos that Levene is unable to discuss this with anyone at work. The personal is displaced, existing in some other location away from work and not allowed to intrude into that arena. The personal and the intimate are weaknesses and have no place in the masculine-capitalist world of 'men'. Levene must suffer his personal trials in silence. Besides, within the circuits of the masculine-capitalist ethos, the solution to personal problems, as with all problems, is to be successful.

Even the most articulate person in the drama, Roma, distorts and debases his language facility since all his language is, in the end, the language of selling. In the early encounter with Lingk in bar, Roma conjures an articulate, almost quasi-philosophical exegesis that intimately draws Lingk in:

> I say this is how we must act. I do those things which seem correct to me today. I trust myself. And if security concerns me, I do that which today I think will make me secure. And every day I do that, when that day arrives that I need a reserve, [a] odds are that I have it, and [b] the true reserve that I have is the strength that I have of acting each day without fear .... According to the dictates of my mind.

The language circles around notions of masculine engagement, decision, action and power. Roma intimates to Lingk that he can (re)gain control of this life, his destiny and indeed his manhood, and solve his powerlessness by re-engaging in the masculine world of business, by exercising his right to action through the vitalizing transactions of commerce. This is especially so, perhaps, when the transaction specifically deals with land and invokes American myths of land and ownership. It is men's right and nature, Roma suggests, to act: this is the essence of male power and privilege, to assert the freedom to act. Roma's appeal to Lingk is this promise of freedom, the freedom to act, to decide, on his own, as a *man*. The apparent camaraderie and inclusiveness proffered by Roma is, of course, a sham, it is only ever part of his manipulative selling technique, his attempt to seduce Lingk and make a sale. Once again, "What masquerades as intimacy is in fact the betrayal of intimacy, confidence, trust, the shared experience implied by language" (Bigbsby, 1985: 119). As the play unfolds, there is an extra gendered dynamic since Roma is appealing to a man whose power to act is subject to the will of another – his wife, a woman.

We see the same dissembling in Roma's professions of the camaraderie of the salesman to Levene: a charade Levene colludes in. Roma almost ritualistically invokes the language of the frontier "Your partner ... a man who's your partner, depends on you ... you have to go with him ... or you're a shit, you're shit, you can't exist alone." This imagined bonding is real in one sense, that by all sticking to the restricted codes of masculine-capitalism, the salesmen reproduce that very world. It is a world they seemingly cannot escape from. The men cannot break out of their restricted language and its codes, cannot genuinely self-disclose, cannot conjure intimacy and cannot imagine an alternative way of being.

The corrosion of character and community

The caustic and limiting masculine-capitalist ethos depicted in *GGR* entails a restrictive language game and deformations of values and ethics that constitute a criminogenic environment and ultimately lead to a corrosion of character. It is argued that "In Mamet's world of men, thieves and salesmen are one in the same. They are all perpetrators of the corrupted American frontier ethic of exploitation in the name of economic gain" (Vorlicky, 1995: 53). At the heart of the language game is a fiction. The men trade in a fiction, telling lies in order to sell pieces of land that are not what they say they are. But, the film suggests, this fictive and unethical game is not merely at the centre of these men's behaviour in *GGR*, it is at the centre of the practice of selling in general, and ultimately at the heart of the masculine-capitalist regime. It is underpinned by the dictum 'always be closing' and a competitive mindset encouraging the pursuit of results at any price, where ends always justify means if the ends are success and material advancement ... get the leads, make the sale, always be closing. Closing is success, is the proper action of a 'man', success is winning the game, winning the game is getting the Cadillac, the Cadillac symbolizes masculine success.

Commenting on *DoS*, Collinson (2003: 561) notes the effect of this ethics of success on identity: "It illustrates how the disciplinary ideology of 'achieved selves', which insists that salespeople 'are only as good as their last sale', can have a corrosive impact on employees' sense of identity and well-being." For Willy Loman,[10] the pressure to sell meant an estrangement from family and friends, the dissolution of his sense of identity, an erosion of sanity and, ultimately, his suicide. For the men in *GGR*, it entails a brutal and brutalizing competition in which selling and winning overrides everything else: friendship, genuine human engagement, integrity, values and ethics. It provides the context for a criminogenic ethos and a logic and justification for theft. Other values and ethical considerations are displaced by the same logic. As Mamet himself has said:

> The play concerns how business corrupts, how the hierarchical business system tends to corrupt. It becomes legitimate for those in power in the business world to act unethically. The effect on the little guy is that he turns to crime.
>
> (quoted in Roudané, 1986)

But more important for Mamet's critique is that whilst this corrosive and criminogenic effect is of concern, of far greater significance is that lies and untruth become the norm, the taken-for-granted, the 'way things are'. The salesmen lie to their customers, they lie to each other, but most importantly they lie to themselves; they are "caught in a matrix of self-perpetuating deceptions" (Geis, 1992: 62). They pursue these into humiliation, isolation, crime and self-destruction; a clear echo of Willy Loman and his pathological adherence to the myth of the American Dream – unto his own death.

The theme of community has been prevalent in the Mamet oeuvre. This theme as Silverstein (1995: 109) suggests, is one "of the need for a community in which recognition of our commonality becomes the basis for establishing universal values that transcend the limits of strategic, instrumental action", limits inherent to the logic of capitalism and business. Mamet (1986) considers the values of community and connection as universal and holds that they are corroded by the machinations of contemporary capitalism and only retrievable through the "magic force of words capable of assuring the truth in oneself or in others" (6–7). He has said in an interview that we need to rediscover community since it provides the only proper site of "ethical interchange" (Savran, 1988: 134). For Mamet, the erosion of community is deeply connected with the erosion of ethics and of character. Community has been eroded and can only be rediscovered through rebuilding proper relationships developed through proper and meaningful communication. He draws a distinction between groups, such as the group of salesmen in *GGR*, and communities. Groups are not accountable, and as he says in *Writing in Restaurants* (Mamet, 1986: 108), "We cannot *talk* to them." In a mode not dissimilar to Habermas, Mamet suggests that the mutual understanding and ethical reinforcement instantiated in serial acts of talking within a community have been eroded by a sterile and instrumental manipulation of language in and among disconnected speakers. Thus, the 'group' of dysphasic and anomic individuals joined only by the necessities of capitalistic employment within the frame of the real estate office exist in conditions that are destructive of both communication and community. The relationships and interactions between the salesmen in *GGR* are devoid of real and meaningful communication and interchange and fail to generate a community. As Bigbsby (1985a: 119) reminds us, there is no real intimacy, sharing, inclusion or trust in the relationships between these men. There is no connection in their talk. The talk of business leaves no space for meaningful connection. Talk is instrumental – or it is nothing. Everyone in *GGR* – the customers, the salesmen themselves, even the audience – exist to be 'sold' – that is the game par excellance, and in this stunted world, the only game (Zeifman, 1992). Any talk appearing to be about establishing, building or maintaining a relationship is in fact shown to be merely instrumental, serving the self-interest of the speaker and an element in the competitive game of selling–winning.

In a number of key exchanges, the ersatz nature of the relationships between the men is revealed: for example, in Moss's talk with Aaronow. The conversation begins with Moss seeking to establish a mutuality, an alignment of the salesmen against the unfair and exploitative behaviour of the bosses. However, as it becomes obvious that the initially hypothetical idea of breaking into the office is actually a real suggestion, it also becomes obvious that Moss is really trying to seduce Aaronow into doing the break-in. Then there is the exchange between Roma and Lingk. Actually, it is more of a monologue as Roma engages Lingk in what at first appears to be a casual barroom conversation. Roma engages in a pseudo-philosophical discursus that has a surface sophistication and degree of self-disclosure that attracts Lingk's attention by its very atypicality as barroom chat between two men. It gestures to a serious conversation between two intelligent but worldly men. Lingk is seduced and drawn into the relationship, only then does Roma turn, mantis-like, to reveal his real intentions and begin his sales pitch.

It is clear that making a sale was all that Roma was interested in and this sophisticated engagement with the mark is just an instrument to that end. Genuine interaction and human exchange is violated in pursuit of economic gain. There is another revealing exchange between Roma and, this time, Levene, towards the end of the film. It occurs after the break-in and after Williamson has inadvertently ruined Roma's negotiations with Lingk. Roma suggests they form a partnership and share leads so that together they can compete and win. He talks of the old school salesmanship and camaraderie they both represent. Roma says, "We are the members of a dying breed. That's ... that's ... that's why we have to stick together." Interestingly, he also says, "I've wanted to talk to you for some time. For a long time, actually ... I never said a thing. I should have, don't know why I didn't." It is almost as if he is using the inarticulateness of these men to carve out a difference, a difference that will seduce Levene and draw him into a relationship. But, even this 'talk' of partnership is shown to be motivated by a purely selfish strategy – to secure a share of his sales. As soon as Levene is led off by the detective after being exposed by Williamson, Roma turns to Williamson and immediately betrays the 'partnership':

ROMA: when the leads come in ... listen to me: when the leads come in I want my top two off the list. For me. My usual two. Anything you give Levene .. .. I GET HIS ACTION. My stuff is mine, whatever he gets for himself, I'm talking half.

Escape routes: alternate masculinities

In the masculine-capitalist ethos of *GGR*, weakness and failure is associated with a lack or absence of masculinity. The irony is that almost all the men featured display one form of weakness or another. But Mamet is subtle here. Within the ethos, power is presumed to reside in a particular mode of masculinity, one founded upon aggression, competition and winning. Those unable to play are positioned as weak and weakness is equated with a loss of male identity, the non-male domain and the feminine. Mamet embeds this in the full complexity of gender politics. The absence of women in *GGR* further dramatically signifies that "the values the male characters traditionally associated with the 'feminine', compassion, tenderness, empathy, spirituality, are seen as threatening to their business ethos; in the business world such values are characterized as weakness" (Zeifman, 1992: 124–5) and as a threat (Bigbsby, 1985b). By absenting women, Mamet is able to focus on the dominant masculine values of "machismo, toughness, strength, cunning which have become appropriated and apotheosised by American business, alchemised into the fool's gold of power, greed, and competition" (Zeifman, 1992: 125). However, this equation of power with a particular mode of the masculine within the masculine-capitalist ethos is not only shown to be destructive, corrosive and dysfunctional, it is also undercut by two subtle turns in the drama. These turns involve Aaronow (who, positioned as perhaps the weakest of the salesmen, has his masculinity placed at risk) and an absent woman, Lingk's wife.

There is nuance surrounding Aaronow's role. At one level, he is positioned as a weak male within the dominant masculinist world of the sales office, one of those Others, those less than men, in relation to which the dominant masculine subject position is constructed. He is certainly portrayed as a failure in the sales competition, but also as a rather brow-beaten, bemused, non-assertive, some-what melancholic person. However, he is the only person to display a modicum of an ethics that transcends the 'sell at any cost', 'always be closing' world Mamet recreates. Despite Moss's best seductive techniques, he fails to persuade Aaronow to break into the office. He is not, in fact, the only person to resist such seductions, the other is Lingk's wife. This synchronic association might suggest that Aaronow is once again being positioned as less than male, as Other. But another reading is that Mamet is positioning him more positively as representing an alternative form of masculinity, one able to escape the destructive dialectical relationship between the masculine and capitalist ethos, and the amoral, corrosive world engendered therein. On this reading, there is an ironic critique in that power, presumed to reside within the masculine-capitalist ethos, is actually shown to exist in those who resist, in those who say 'no'. It is Aaronow's 'no' to Moss and Lingk's wife's 'no' to Roma that provide the two alternatives to the dominant ethos, ethical alternatives and exit routes to the circuits of power and patriarchy in the masculine-capitalist ethos.

In Roma's convoluted sales pitch to Lingk, he seeks to detach him from his absent wife, to seduce him by suggesting that a man, a real man, has his own things, his own desires, decisions and own power. The marital relationship and the values of women are a threat to that male order.

ROMA: I want to tell you something. Your life is your own. You have a contract with your wife. You have certain things you do jointly, you have a bond there ... and there are other things. Those things are yours. You needn't feel ashamed, you needn't feel that you're being untrue ... or that she would abandon you if she knew. This is your life.

Lingk is invited to re-enter the world of men by taking the independent action that is its strongest mark by making a decision to buy the piece of land. Desperate for the 'company of men', Lingk is so seduced. However, away from the clutches of Roma, his wife compels him to return to retrieve the contract. The drama is heightened when unethical actions elsewhere in the capitalist domain create the conditions by which the full extent of Roma's deceitfulness surfaces. However, of more significance is the fact that it is the absent wife who is able to resist the power of the male domain. Power, then, is made to reside in the absent wife's capacity to derail the contract and subvert Roma's hermetic world of men, commerce and power. As Vorlicky (1995: 50) points out, Lingk's admission to Roma that "I don't have the power" is an "astounding admission for a (white) male character to make". The intrusion of the Other, of the feminine, together with Aaronow's resistance and ethical location represent alternatives to the dominant masculine mode. Vitally, it is Aaronow's ethical resistance that shifts the course of action down a particular path; one that signals the break-up of that masculine world. That break-up is also signalled by Lingk who, when forced by his wife to rescind the deal, is devastated and, Judas-like, begs forgiveness for letting the male world down: "Oh, Christ ... Oh Christ. I know I've let you down. I'm sorry. For ... Forgive ... for ... I don't know anymore. [Pause.] Forgive me."

Mamet's critique of the limits and degradations of the masculine-capitalist ethos is trenchant, one rarely located in the academic literature, certainly at that time. As Novick (1984: 89) asks, "Has any professed feminist ever given us so unsparing a picture of the masculine ethos at its most barren, destructive, anguished, futile?" The critique devastatingly exposes the hermeticism of the homosocial world that is *GGR*; a stultifying environment within which the only way of being masculine and validated as a 'proper' male – and hence 'proper' person – is breached by the ambiguity represented by Aaronow and penetrated and subverted by the absence that is woman. These 'openings' may be mere cracks in the wall enclosing the hegemonic masculine world of business and capitalism in *GGR*, but they are cracks exposing the limits of that world and the possibilities of alternatives.

Nonetheless, most of Mamet's male tribe remain locked in their impoverished locations seemingly resisting the "discovery of new identities that would release them from a stance which is antagonist to the female without as well as to the feminine within them" (McDonagh, 1992: 205). They appear unable to engage with alternate ways of doing masculinity. The dominant, hegemonic masculine ethos that is constantly being reproduced in capitalist workplaces, continues to enfold them and obliterate horizons of possible other selves they could become. They are ensnared by the ineluctable logic that maintains that to fail in selling and business is to fail to be male. But the reverse logic is also operable: to become other than orthodoxly masculine is to fail to equip oneself properly to compete in business and the game of selling. The very notion of their (masculine) identity is embroiled in this calculus. It is also deeply implicated in society's patriarchal roles and expectations, including their domestic roles and identities. As Mamet (1989a: 90) notes: "the competition of business [...] is most times prosecuted for the benefit of oneself [i.e., the male] as breadwinner, as provider, as paterfamilias, as vestigial and outmoded as you may feel those roles to be". This is despite other masculinities or other possibilities of performing maleness being available, especially in the post-1960s era when gender politics and gender roles had received substantial scrutiny and a degree of experimentation and liberation had widened the options.

More recent research on masculinities, whilst recognizing the persistence of a hegemonic form of masculinity, has clearly shown the multiplicity of masculinities available. Indeed, one of Connell's (2005) major contributions is the articulation of these alternatives providing, for example, a "powerful analysis of masculinities on the fringe of, or outside, traditionally work-defined maleness: among young unemployed men, feminist-influenced environmentalist men, and men in conventional jobs who are homosexual" (Sinclair, 2000: 86). It is not that these possibilities are just on the fringe or outside the traditional space; the very notion of gender and masculinity has been reconfigured, leading to the deconstruction of the hegemonic hold of traditional masculinity.

The theoretical turn reveals the socially constructed nature of gender and of masculinity (and femininity), leading to the conception of multiple gendered discourses and multiple gendered subject positions that individuals can locate and be located in. Indeed, post-structuralist theory, particularly feminist post-structuralist theory, has analysed the fragmentary, plural, fluid and dynamic nature of identity and identity formation in organizational contexts (Henriques *et al.*, 1984; Kondo, 1990; Martin, 2001; Nkomo and Cox, 1996). The formerly presumed coherence of traditional gender locations has been undone by the notion that people occupy simultaneously multiple subject positions, identities and their associated relationships. Identities are characterized by ambiguity, tensions and contradictions, not coherence and stability. Furthermore, identities and identity-formation processes are implicated in and formed by power relations and through which they are under threat (Kondo, 1990). Identity thus becomes both an interactional accomplishment and a contested terrain in which power effects seeking to locate identity positions in particular ways are resisted and deconstructed (Kondo, 1990).

More specifically and in relation to the concerns of Mamet, it has become clear that men may legitimately perform masculinity in a variety of forms. Even within organizational contexts and the masculine-capitalist ethos, opportunities exist for the construction of alternative masculine identities (Martin, 2001). However, it still needs to be acknowledged that these are contingent modes of identity, dependent on particular discursive locations and specific conditions of their enactment and legitimacy. It has been noted that although there may, *in principle*, be a range of masculinities available to be performed, in specific contexts some have more legitimacy and privilege, whilst others may be stigmatized or marginalized (Hearn and Morgan, 1990). The idea of identity formation as a playground in which actors are at liberty to assume and cast off an identity at will is a chimera that neglects the centrality of power relations in identity formation and fails to attend to the discursive and institutional frames that provide the conditions for the production and reproduction, and the privileging and legitimation, of particular modes of masculinity.

Mamet in many respects significantly prefigures these theoretical developments and provides in *GGR* and elsewhere a trenchant critique of hegemonic masculinity and its embeddedness in and imbrication with the ethos of business and capitalism. Significantly though, he also reveals how, given that such modes of masculinity are enmeshed within the power regimes of the dominant patriarchal capitalist formation, they are robust and not easy to challenge. This is especially so for men heavily socialized into those regimes and forms of masculinity and who remain locked into a socio-economic world and a language game that reinforces and reproduces them. It is one thing to argue theoretically for the social constructedness of gender identity and posit alternative masculinities, it is quite another for that to translate in practice into the ready availability of a repertoire of masculinities that men, such those in *GGR*, are at liberty to call upon. As Mamet demonstrates, such men are locked into a complex web of forces that reproduce restricted forms of masculinity. They might well be socially constructed, but they are constructed within power relations and associated knowledge-power discourses, the effect of which cannot be dismissed out of hand or overturned without struggle and consequences.

There is a need for further conceptualization and research on the processes of gender construction, gendered identity work and gender performance in organizational settings. Such analysis needs to explore the dynamics of gender/identity work and the contingent and contextual conditions surrounding particular forms of such work in particular contexts. It requires an analysis and deconstruction of the discursive regimes that sustain limited gender/identity options and offers the emancipation of genuine choices and options with respect to gender formation and gender performance in a range of organizational contexts. It is precisely this mode of critique, rare in the academic literature, that Mamet offers. Looked at more broadly, *GGR* and other elements of Mamet's work stand as exemplars of how the (popular) culture domain contains the resources through which to mount a critique not only of the organizational domain, but also the wider socio-political domain. Popular culture, by working with and through the discourses that not only resonate with people's experiences, but also are constitutive of social world in which we function and the meaning frames we co-construct, is part of a transformative process in which change is wrought in those discourses and frames of meaning. Popular culture as text and discourse helps to expose the aporia – the inconsistencies, arbitrariness and contradictions – in the dominant formation and in so doing open up spaces for change and transformation. In this case, *GGR* stands as a popular cultural intervention that does precisely that with respect to the dominant masculine-capitalist ethos and the hegemonic modes of masculinity it depends upon.

5 Commerce is our goal

Corporate power and the novum in *Blade Runner*

In a crucial scene in Ridley Scott's 1982 film *Blade Runner*, the business magnate and technological genius Dr Eldon Tyrell asserts: "Commerce is our goal here at Tyrell. 'More human than human' is our motto." With this sloganeering, he is referring to Rachael, the most sophisticated android (or 'replicant' in the film's terms) that his organization, The Tyrell Corporation, has produced. The Tyrell Corporation specializes in manufacturing replicants who are virtually indistinguishable from 'real' humans – the advanced models such as Rachael are even given false memories from childhood on so that they are not cognitively aware of their own status as being not 'real' humans. Eldon Tyrell, as the mastermind behind the production of the replicants, exercises his technological innovation and commercial power from high above an imagined 2019 Los Angeles. As the city decays and the earth's ecosystem is in ruins, replicants are built to perform the role of technological slave labour in the 'off-world' colonies to which humans escape from their own dying planet. Despite all of this devastation, Tyrell seems to be animated by only two things – doing business and realizing the potential of technology.

As a film, *Blade Runner* exudes a 'postmodern structure of feeling' contextualized in mass-media culture, information technology and globalized capital and characterized by the fragmentation of identity, the disassembling of reality and the loss of faith in humanity (Milner, 2004). In *Blade Runner*, we see a most bitterly ironic juxtaposition – an irony located between the fetishization and valourization of a technically advanced commercial system and the dystopic vision of a world whose 'progress' has long since outlived its value. The very meaning of humanity lies in the balance.

Some 25 years after its initial release in 1982, *Blade Runner* still holds a key place in the history of science fiction cinema – together with *Alien* (1979), it is said to have "ushered in the postmodern era in SF[1] film" (Booker, 2006: 15). Such a periodization can be understood in terms of the four stages of science fiction identified by McCracken (1998: 103):

(1) Pre nineteenth century: travel and fantasy literature, tales of other lands; (2) nineteenth century: reactions to the industrial revolution; (3) late nineteenth century to mid twentieth century: the "modernist" visions of the

Scientific Enlightenment; (4) late twentieth century: the "postmodern" visions of a post-industrial, often post-holocaust age, including feminist futures and cyberpunk.

McCracken suggests that the latter of these periods emerged from a growing dissatisfaction with scientific enlightenment "fed by fears of nuclear war and an increasing awareness of the role of technology in the destruction of the environment" (108). This is now a world "in which the modernist dream of solving social problems through technology no longer holds" (112). Postmodern science fiction has been a fertile ground for examining the implications of "the 'globalization of the world's economy, the growth in population movements, [...] the speed and quantity of information exchanges" (109) and so forth. The relevance to studying work and organizations is palpable.

While science fiction has been studied most extensively as a form of literature, its existence as a cinematic genre is increasingly regarded as important. As Milner (2004) argues, while science fiction's history is one that can be traced back to literature (e.g. Mary Shelley's *Frankenstein*) and to the 'pulp' newsstand magazines of between-the-wars United States, it has a very particular relationship to the cinema. Science fiction is not only one of the earliest cinematic genres (dating back to 1902), but the technology of the cinema enables the ideas of science fiction to be displayed in a spectacular visual form. In contemporary times, science fiction is established as one of the most popular cinematic genres. As Roberts (2006) states, if we examine the list of the all-time top 15 movies as measured by total global sales, all of them bar one (1997s *Titanic*) is science fiction or fantasy, with four of the top five being science fiction [*Star Wars* (1977), *ET: The Extra-Terrestrial* (1982), *Star Wars: The Empire Strikes Back* (1980) and *Star Wars: Return of the Jedi* (1983)]. By now, thanks to the cinema, science fiction is "part and parcel of the modern lived environment" (Higgins, 2001: 2).

The development of science fiction, in recent times, is very much linked to the cinema. Roberts (2006) argues that in the period between 1960 and 2000, there were two main changes in science fiction. The first was that it became a "genre dominated by 'visual media' and especially by 'visual spectacularism', a special sub-genre of cinema that is predicated primarily on special effects, the creation of visually impressive alternate worlds, [and] the realization of events and beings liable to amaze" (264). The second, and related, development is a move away from science fiction as a 'literature of ideas' and a move towards an 'imagistic aesthetic' that combines literary imagery with the powerful visual imagery of popular culture. In particular, the adding of visual special effects to science fiction narratives has become core to the meaning and value of the form. For Roberts, the turn to 'visual science fiction', especially in the form of the Hollywood blockbuster, has led to the creation of many 'masterpieces' that both extend science fiction's aesthetic dimensions and give it a much deeper and more extensive cultural penetration. Roberts argues that the increasing dominance of Hollywood in science fiction was marked with 1977s *Star Wars*, and since then has, as its most important films, *Alien* (1979), *Blade Runner* (1982) and *The Matrix* (1999) – all of which are marked both by the creation of alternate worlds and immense visual power.

In this chapter, we are concerned with how work and organizations are represented in the cinematic spectacle of the science fiction genre, with a particular focus on how these films present a critical perspective on the development of humanity. In exploring this we examine how this form of popular culture can be valued as a form of critique (Suvin, 1979). This specific interest emerges from the way that science fiction cinema, of the postmodern dystopic variety, might also have something to say about the present – the present state of humanity in relation to corporatization. The impetus here, and its relation to this book as a whole, lies in the way that:

> Science fiction sheds light on theory by providing an ideal-typical setting through which theory can be represented, clarified and developed. Conversely, it gives insight into the empirical world, while partly suspending the epistemological conundrum of the double hermeneutic that afflicts every empirical study in the social sciences.
>
> (Kavanagh *et al.*, 2005: 157)

To explore organizational dystopia in science fiction cinema, we turn our attention specifically to the 1982 science fiction film *Blade Runner* introduced earlier – a film that is "widely regarded as one of the most influential science fiction movies of the 1980s" (Srinivas, 1999: 617) and as "the most visually influential SF film of all time" (Booker, 2006: 15). *Blade Runner* is also one of the most academically discussed and critically influential science fiction films of the contemporary era (Booker, 2006; see UC Berkely, 2006), especially by those academic critics "who have found science fiction film (and science fiction in general) to be among the paradigmatic expressions of postmodernism" (Booker, 2006: 15). Through this example, we examine science fiction as interesting in that, by nature of its genre, it enables visual and discursive explorations that go beyond the representational confines of more realistic or naturalistic forms of film and text.

Given that corporate organizations are frequently represented in science fiction (in *Blade Runner*, The Tyrell Corporation), we argue that the exploratory potential of science fiction is its ability to critically interrogate contemporary organizational behaviour. Science fiction's dominant concerns have included a range of topics including globalization, worker exploitation, the corporatization of society, the role of technology in society and the effect of business behaviour on the environment. In this chapter, as well as discussing the relations between organizational critique and science fiction in general, we examine *Blade Runner* in particular to see how it critiques the idea of a particular corporate ethos that emerges from how the film constructs the relationships between technology, subjectivity and commerce and what this means for humanity. This is an ethos expressed in terms of how corporately produced technology and attempts at panoptic corporate control have come to be central in what it means to be a person in the world, yet one where corporations lack any reflexive responsibility for these effects, drowning them out in the discourse of commercial achievement and technological progress. If it is the case that science fiction "has supplied narratives of modernity which attempt to map the shifting cultural boundaries brought around by rapid social change" (McCracken, 1998: 102), then changes to work and organization are central to science fiction's critical potential.

Science fiction and/as critique

Science fiction is often classified, even by those who write it or write about it affirmatively, as 'pulp' (McCracken, 1998; Sterling in Parker *et al.*, 1999, Higgins, 2001; Milner, 2004). Historically, science fiction has been considered amongst the lowest of the low genres: "lower than literature, lower than film, perhaps even lower than television" (Milner, 2004: 260). This is a conception that follows the view that:

> it is easy to see science fiction as trash [...]. Space ships, ray guns, aliens, cyborgs and mysterious journeys to unknown worlds means that it is classified together with fantasy [...]. And, as for the movies, they are usually a mix of high style and violent action.
>
> (Parker *et al.*, 1999: 579)

The irony of science fiction is that despite its low genre status, it is widely heralded for its critical potential. Freedman (2000) argues that science fiction should be privileged as a genre for critical theory – an important connection being that both insist on "historical mutability, material reducibility, and, at least implicitly, utopian possibility" (32). The connection between science fiction and critical practice has been explored at length in academic discourse including critical theory (e.g. Freedman, 2000), utopian studies (e.g. Jameson, 2005), literary criticism (e.g. Suvin, 1979), feminism (Lefanu, 1988), eco-feminism (e.g. Jenkins, 1997), cultural studies (e.g. Milner, 2004), social and cultural theory (e.g. Kuhn, 1990), queer theory (Science Fiction Studies, 1999b), sociology (e.g. Stableford, 1987) and anthropology (e.g. Battaglia, 2001). The academic interest in science fiction is so entrenched that since 1973 there has been an academic journal, *Science Fiction Studies*, dedicated to the topic, and the corpus of critical writing on the subject is extensive and expanding (see, Science Fiction Studies, 1999a).

The academic fascination with science fiction has not gone unaccounted for amongst those who study management and organizations. This is, however, a relatively new development, given that until very recently "management and organization studies [... had not ...] fully appreciated the rich resource that science fiction would appear to offer" (Higgins, 2001: 3). The development of this interest, however, was very much enabled and accounted for with the publication of two key edited collections by a group of British academics. The first was the special issue of the journal *Organization* in 1999 entitled 'Organization

Studies as Science Fiction' and edited by Martin Parker, Matthew Higgins, Geoff Lightfoot and Warren Smith. The second was the 2001 book *Science Fiction and Organizations* by the same editors (Smith *et al.*, 2001). This work, as well as emerging from the editors' mutual interest in and fascination with science fiction, is more formally premised on the idea that science fiction, like a science of organization, uses creativity to explore the meaning of lived reality such that bringing the two into proximity might create a space for the creation of 'new knowledge' (Parker *et al.*, 1999). The value of creating such proximity, they argue, is that those things which are produced in each's name can be understood as artefacts of contemporary culture. Moreover, using science fiction in the study of organizations is productive in that "engagement with other cultural texts might enable a more diverse collection of ways of organizing organization" (588). What they were hoping for was the forging of connections between science fiction and organization in order to make manifest their concern for creating "legitimate alternate ways of understanding organization" (585).

Of central importance to the academic study of science fiction is the idea that "within and throughout SF we can find things to say about contemporary society" (Higgins, 2001: 2) and that these 'things' might both complement and add to how this society is understood in more formal and theoretical representations. In terms of the study of management and organizations, a key interest has been in the way that science fiction has explored the creation and use of technology by organizations and the meaning of this for humanity. Phillips and Zyglidopoulos (1999) suggest that science fiction has an important place in the study of organizations not only because of the allusions of both to science, but first because "science fiction is, in many cases, explicitly about work organizations" and second because "science fiction has an abiding interest in the development of new technologies [... which have ...] important ramifications for organizing and the organizational effects of the technologies" (606–7). This is not surprising given that, as Haley (2001) elucidates, the development of the science fiction genre has not only been "intimately connected with the technological progress of the 20th century" but also that science fiction "has sought to make perceptive comments about emerging technology and cultural tendencies" (Haley, 2001: 31) – in particular, human-centred technologies (Corbett, 1995). Science fiction can thus be understood not just as a form of entertainment, but also as a form of critical commentary in its own right (well before the academic critic appropriates it). Common to this critique is a technophobic impulse: "sf films have long fostered dystopia images of the machine as a sinister agency that propagates itself and threatens to strip humanity of its soul; its human-centredness" (Corbett, 1995: 215). This is a theme that can be traced back to Fritz Lang's genre defining 1927 silent movie *Metropolis* – a film whose dystopic depictions of technology has influenced generations of science fiction film makers to this day. *Metropolis* "works out in an almost archetypal way the [science fiction] genre's simultaneous fascination with and fear of the technological, and it anchors this contradictory attitude in the centerpiece of special effect – the creation of robot in our human image" (Telotte, 1995: 16).

Dystopia

Of course, the critical potential of science fiction is not always sophisticated: "SF has a long tradition of moralizing about a monstrous version of scientific rationalization that corrupts and destroys fragile humans" (Parker *et al.*, 1999: 581). Nevertheless, the potential for critical connections are always possible – one of the key areas through which this is enabled is in how science fiction has represented images of utopia and dystopia (cf. Suvin, 1979). Central to the science fiction genre and to many of its narratives are the issues of "utopian and dystopian [...] alternatives and the opportunities and dangers of scientific experimentation" (McCracken, 1998: 103). In terms of the critical study of science fiction, it is such themes that were central to the groundbreaking studies by Raymond Williams and Darko Suvin in the 1970s (Milner, 2004). It is also in relation to these themes that organization is connected to science fiction.

Parker *et al.* (1999) argue that the most pervasive connection between organization and science fiction is also related to the description of utopia and warnings of dystopia. They suggest that for managers and management academics speculating on the possibilities of a utopian organized future – what they refer critically as a "pro-capitalist fantastic fiction within the management context" (582) – is very much set in relief by the dystopian pre-occupations of twentieth-century science fiction. It is, in fact, the case that the "vast majority of sf films produced for general public release offer a dark and dystopian view of our technological future" (Corbett, 1995: 216). This has meant that science fiction has "foregrounded fiction as a method of throwing a sharply critical light on the present" for example by developing storylines around "warring corporations, universal commodification and a disenfranchised underclass" (Parker *et al.*, 1999: 382).

As part of its projection of dystopian futures, Parker *et al.* (1999: 382) note also that science fiction has a long history in the "demonizing of cold bureaucrats". But, representing imagined dystopias is not just a game for the depressed and inactive to fuel their own despair and cynicism, it can also "provide us with the opportunity for creatively exploring imaginative ways of dealing with 'real' problems by vacillating between [...] the utopian (or dystopian) and the real" (Kavanagh *et al.*, 2005: 158). Dystopia is then not necessarily the domain of the doom-saying hopeless cynic, it can also be understood in relation to what Moylan (2001) refers to as 'critical dystopia' – "a negative cousin of the Utopia proper, for it is in the light of some positive conception of human social possibilities that its effects are generated from Utopian ideals its politically enabling stance derives" (Jameson, 2005: 198).

In general terms, we can surmise, with Srinivas (1999: 610), that:

> Dystopian themes in SF mark an awareness of the economic, political and ecological perils of modernity. By describing a bleak future, dystopias generate inevitable comparisons with worlds real to the reader [...]. The success of dystopias depends on their familiarity. The more real and intriguing the fictional world, the greater its impact on the reader [or viewer].

Such dystopias can be both "critiques of the contemporary world as well as reflections on the possibility of action" (ibid.) as they vacillate between the contrast between dystopia and reality and dystopia and utopia. It may be the case that science fiction dystopia is one where "future social organization is represented as a living hell with totalitarian technology holding humankind in its thrall" (Corbett, 1998: 250), but the question to be asked is what this says about the world we experience now.

Sciences fiction, cognitive estrangement and the novum

The interest in the critical potential of science fiction has burgeoned since the 1970s. As introduced earlier, crucial in this development has been the massive influence of the writing on Darko Suvin (1979, 1988). As Milner (2004: 259) surmises, "[c]ritical theory has transformed science fiction studies from a 'fan' enthusiasm into a scholarly subdiscipline in the years since 1979, when Darko Suvin first published his *Metamorphoses of Science Fiction*". It was in this work that Suvin introduced two central and related analytical concepts to the study of science fiction – these were 'cognitive estrangement' and the 'novum'. Seeking a structural definition of the genre, Suvin (1979: 8–9) argues that science fiction is "a literary genre whose necessary and sufficient conditions are the presence and interaction of estrangement and cognition, and whose main formal device is an imaginative framework alternative to the author's empirical environment". For Suvin, a hallmark of science fiction is this 'cognitive estrangement'. It is cognitive in that it presents an image of a different world as understandable in the terms of contemporary reality, and "it sees the norms of any age, including empathetically its own, as unique [and] changeable" (Suvin, 1979: 7). It is estranged in that it presents itself in a "strange newness, a *novum*" (ibid.: 4). This novum being a deviation "from the author's and implied reader's norm of reality" (ibid.: 64). Taken together, cognitive estrangement means that the genre is:

> both nonrealistic – that is, it presents readers with settings and situations that are alien to them, from which they are estranged – as well as understandable; in other words, the estrangement can be explained, for the most part, in logical or rational terms. The element that introduces this sense of estrangement Suvin terms the "novum" or new thing.
>
> (Harris-Fain, 2005: 5)

The point then, for Suvin (1979: 18), is that science fiction is an endeavour that can illuminate human relations "by creating a radically different formal framework – a different space/time location or central figures for the fable, unverifiable by common sense". It is this potential for 'illumination' that renders science fiction critical. When done well, Suvin (1979: 36) argues, science fiction "demands from the author and reader, teacher and critic, not merely specialized, quantified positivistic knowledge (*scientia*) but a social imagination whose quality of wisdom (*sapientia*) testifies to the maturity of his [*sic*] critical and creative thought". While such a call to 'demands' draws on the assumption that science fiction can be defined formally and structurally rather than culturally, what the idea of cognitive estrangement still leaves us with is the potential for the *fiction* in science fiction to provide a critical reading of the contemporary world. Science fiction's difference from today makes today all the more clear.

By its most general definition, science fiction is a cultural discourse of a world that it somehow differentiated from the actual world which the reader or viewer inhabits and understands as 'real' (Roberts, 2006). This differentiation is key to science fiction's critical potential in that it fuels the ability of its viewers to engage in Suvin's (1979) notion of 'cognitive estrangement' – while the narratives are set elsewhere (for example in time and/or space), this actually provides a distance such that the present can be interrogated more critically. The idea is that the "new reality overtly or tacitly presupposes the existence of the author's empirical reality, since it can be gauged and understood only as the empirical reality modified in such-and-such ways" (Suvin, 1979: 71). While this might be true of much fiction, it is exaggerated in science fiction to the extent that it becomes a defining feature of the genre. This is a particularity of science fiction in that the genre rests on the device of creating an "imaginative framework alternative to the author's [and reader/viewer's] empirical environment" (Suvin, 1979: 1) such that it creates an interaction between estrangement from one's own world, as well as an awareness of the relation between the fictional and the empirical. This is the "imagination that informs science fiction, that takes from and revises history, puts it out there, in a (de)familiarized but cognitively plausible and contextually recognizable 'future'" (Grewell, 2001: 27). Thus, a characteristic of the best science fiction is that it pertains "more to our own world that to its fictional world of the future" (Booker, 2006: 184).

It is on such grounds as those explored above that it has been argued that while "[s]cience fiction is perhaps one of the most innovative of popular forms [it] is also one of the most critical. The representation of new worlds involves a process of reflection and comparison with society as it is now" (McCracken, 1998: 123). What enables this, in Suvin's (1979) terms, is that at the core of science fiction is the 'novum' – "the fictional device, artifact or premise that focuses the difference between the world the reader inhabits and the fictional world of the SF text" (Roberts, 2006: 1). The novum helps create cognitive estrangement because it "balances radical alterity and familiar sameness" and enables the conditions of our own world in a different, even revolutionary way (ibid.).

It is the sense of estrangement provided par excellence by science fiction that can enable us to think differently. As Kavanagh *et al.* (2005: 157) outline: "[s]cience fiction shares with all imaginative fictions the potential to think ourselves away from the contexts of action and the mundane realities in which we are constrained to think and act" – it is just that this is amplified in science fiction on account of the radical difference of its setting from our own world. This is directly pertinent to thinking about organizations because science fiction facilitates "a critical imaginary [that] can enable us to envision a variety of organizational alternatives with which we can assess out own practices and the theories that constitute them" (ibid.: 158). And, in its dystopic forms, science fiction can also permit an assessment of what not to do or what to stop doing – lest the dystopic imaginary be realized in the future or be horrifyingly recognized in the present. The cognitive estrangement of science fiction points directly to the possibility of creating critical accounts or work and organizations, for example in relation to "the rise and supersession of technical-industrial modes of production, distribution, consumption and disposal" (Broderick in Roberts, 2006: 1). That science fiction films, from *Metropolis* to *Blade Runner*, "are critiques of an organizational society is obvious, but they are also quite detailed interrogations of what organizations do – and how these practices might be resisted" (Parker *et al.*, 1999: 582). What science fiction enables is for the frame through which such matters are understood in the discourse of the cultural present to be rendered different through a plurality of speculative possibilities that might enable us to see the limits of current thinking or even free us from the restrictions of that discourse (Roberts, 2006).

The key issue that emerges from this consideration is that of temporality – science fiction is a genre whose novum is most often related to its temporal location, usually in the future. But as we have suggested, this does not fully remove science fiction from the empirical world. The future projections of science fiction are both "eerily alien and securely familiar" so as to generate "a dialogue with existing social conditions" (Higgins, 2001: 1). Indeed, it is the skill of the science fiction writer or film maker to work the tension between the familiar and the unfamiliar so as to construct the positions of intelligibility within which the audience can locate itself and possibly be reflexively aware of that location. A key part of this that is particular to science fiction, as McCracken (1998: 102) suggests, is that "[at] the root of all science fiction lies the fantasy of alien encounter. The meeting of self with other" so as to "offer new possibilities of being and the exploration of new alternative realities". Moreover, these possibilities are very much rooted in a critical concern with issues of the present and the changes being encountered within it. Not the least of these are changes associated with business, corporate behaviour and the organization of work.

Blade Runner

As a film adaptation of Philip Dick's (1968) novel *Do Androids Dream of Electric Sheep?* 1982's *Blade Runner* was directed by Ridley Scott, famous earlier for directing 1979's *Alien*. Although it did not have the box office success of science fiction blockbusters such as the *Star Wars* films, the *Alien* films or the *Matrix* films, *Blade Runner* "is considered a classic of SF cinema not only by critics but by a large fan base". This is a reputation enhanced by its origins in Dick's novels (with Dick being a "talismanic figure for many SF fans") (Roberts, 2006: 284). *Blade Runner* had two major releases – the original film from 1982 and the 'Director's Cut' version from 1992 – the latter of which "restored the film's original darker vision" (Srinivas, 1999: 617, 622).[2] As an example of science fiction, *Blade Runner* is very much a cinematic event; it is exquisite in its appearance and "revels in a density of visual affect" (Roberts, 2006: 285). The film is of interest to us here not just because of its popularity and genre-defining qualities, but also, as we introduced at the beginning of the chapter, because one of the chief 'characters' is an organization – The Tyrell Corporation. The film not only offers "a serious exploration of numerous political and social issues, making it one of the most politically engaged of all SF films" (Booker, 2006: 178), but more particularly, it explores "the relationship between high-tech corporate capitalism on the one hand, and individual modes and styles of personal behaviour on the other" (Byers, 1987: 326).

Prior to the appearance of any of the actors, the film starts by placing corporate power at the centre of the narrative. The rolling introduction tells us that:

> Early in the 21st century, THE TYRELL CORPORATION advanced robot evolution into the NEXUS phase – a being virtually identical to a human – known as a *Replicant*.
>
> The NEXUS 6 *Replicants* were superior in strength and agility, and at least equal in intelligence, to the genetic engineers who created them.
>
> *Replicants* we used Off-world as slave labor, in the hazardous exploration and colonization of other planets.
>
> After a bloody mutiny by a NEXUS 6 combat team in an Off-world colony, Replicants were declared illegal on earth – under penalty of death.
>
> Special police squads – BLADE RUNNER UNITS – had orders to shoot to kill, upon detection, any trespassing replicant.
>
> This was not called execution.
>
> It was called retirement.

It is clear from the very start that it is an organization – The Tyrell Corporation – that is central to the plot. But Tyrell is not *Blade Runner*'s novum – its behaviour is all too familiar. It is the urban future setting with its new technology and the existence of the replicants that provide the film with its 'new thing'. In *Blade Runner*:

> the architecture of the dystopian cityscape functions as a synecdoche for the wider catastrophe that has overcome [… its …] populations. […]. The city *is* the dystopian novum, the shape of the prior catastrophe encoded deep within its social and architectural forms
>
> (Milner, 2004: 267)

Tyrell resembles in so many ways the actual late twentieth-century mega corporation – but one estranged through its location in this dystopian near-future world.

The film is set in Los Angeles in November 2019. Bursts of flame shoot through the sky, as hover cars pass over the city at high speed looking down on a city of lights that looks ironically like a clear starlit sky. But no stars can be seen above, just a haze of pollution. Looming high in this cityscape is the building of the Tyrell Corporation – glistening and gleaming spectacularly over the filthy and dangerous streets below. From the beginning, *Blade Runner*'s narrative and spectacle are very much enabled by its cinematography, special effects, design and attendant visual imagery – indeed, "the *look* of the film has proved so enduring" in providing visual imagery that enhances the plot (Roberts, 2006: 284). It is this imagery that announces the 'post-catastrophic dystopia' in which the film is set – "a city soaked with acid rain and choking on pollution, where the most healthy humans have already moved 'off-world'" (Milner, 2004: 268).

Loud and clear through the streets can be heard advertisements announcing that "a new life awaits you in the Off-world colonies. The chance to begin again in a golden land of opportunity and adventure." This marketing announcement repeats again and again all over the city, interspersed with advertisements for replicants 'made especially for your needs'. Huge neon signs advertise Coca-Cola, TDK and PanAm – a suggestion of corporate longevity that links to the viewers' known empirical world. The critical motif is set: "commerce is everybody's goal here in Los Angeles [and] this is what has brought the city to its present impasse" (Milner, 2004: 268) – an impasse where life on earth is barely tenable.

It is in this environment that we find Rick Deckard – a former Blade Runner. Deckard gets called up to return to his former profession for a special task. The task is to track down and 'retire' (i.e. kill) four replicants who stole a space shuttle off-world, killed its crew and passengers and returned to earth. He does not want to do it. And we know that the Blade Runner's work of 'retiring' replicants, as a euphemism, positions the replicants directly in a deadly new form of 'career development'. They retire when they are no longer fit for purpose – and to retire is to die. When asked to perform these retirements by his boss, Police Captain Bryant, Deckard responds "I was quit when I came in here. I'm twice as quit now." Bryant agrees but sees the implications differently: "you're not cop now, you're little people". Feeling powerless in the face of authority, Deckard sees that he has no choice. He gets to work. He has not yet learned how to resist.

The escaped replicants made themselves known on earth when they tried to break into the Tyrell Corporation. Deckard asks Bryant, "What do they want out of the Tyrell Corporation?" a question that impels the film's narrative. There are four replicants Deckard has to locate and retire: Roy Batty and Leon who are both combat models, Zhora who has been trained for an off-world murder squad and Pris who is a 'basic pleasure model' for use by military personnel in the outer colonies. Each of them is a NEXUS 6 replicant – designed to be exactly like humans in all ways, except their emotions. We are told, however, that the designers suspect that after a few years of being 'alive', they might have developed their own emotional responses. Concerned that the development of emotions would make them uncontrollable, the designers built a planned redundancy into the replicants – a four-year lifespan. This lifespan is critical to the film's narrative since it is knowledge of this that has led to the replicants' fear of death and wish to extend their lives. Their return to earth, their return to their corporate maker, is a quest to reverse the death sentence which was built into their creation. And this death is approaching fast – especially for Batty.

Meanwhile, Deckard is asked by Bryant to go to the Tyrell Corporation to test the 'Voight–Kampff machine' on a new replicant. This is a machine that Blade Runners use to determine whether a subject is a human or a replicant by measuring their physical emotional responses (heart rate, breathing, capillary dilation, pupil fluctuation and 'blush response') to questions designed to provoke such responses. Evoking a fear of the inability to determine humanity, when Deckard asks "and if the machine doesn't work", Bryant looks away with worry in his face. The crux of the plot of the film is thus set out: the possibility of the inability of the central character, Deckard, to distinguish between the 'real' and the 'artificial' (Roberts, 2006), the human and the machine. The film "projects a world in which technologies of image and memory production render human experience and memory ultimately indistinguishable from the experience of, and the memories created for, the replicants" (McNamara, 1997: 423).

Deckard meets with Dr Eldon Tyrell – the founder and head of the Tyrell Corporation who has a strange resemblance to Nazi scientist Josef Mengele (Kerman, 1991: 2). His office is at the top of the corporation's building. So high an elevation that the sun can be seen shining in the background – a sight no longer possible on the streets below, enveloped as they are in a blanket of pollution. Deckard then meets Rachael – the most advanced form of replicant, and the one he has been sent there to test. The advance is that unlike the others, she does not know she is a replicant – again, the distance between human and non-human is slowly being disintegrated by big business's technology. She has been programmed with memories, with a past – in this case, those of Tyrell's own niece. The corporate rationale is that this enables it, as Tyrell puts it, "to control them better" because they are better able to handle emotional responses – the organizational production of the 'appropriate individual' (Alvesson and Willmott, 2002) is taken to its logical extreme. In keeping with Tyrell's motto of 'more human that human', Rachael is the most advanced experiment. Deckard performs the Voight–Kampff test on her. Tyrell looks on with a wry grin. It takes him more than 100 questions to determine that she is a replicant – the norm is 20–30.

Deckard proceeds in hunting down the team of escaped replicants. First Zhora, then Leon, then Pris. But before Deckard gets to Batty, Batty has found a way to meet and confront Eldon Tyrell – the man he believes to be the only person who knows how to extend his life. "It's not an easy thing to meet your maker." Batty says to Tyrell as he approaches him. Batty is clear, his problem is death – he wants more life, more than his allotted four years, the end of which is loomingly close. But, Tyrell knows that this is impossible – the end is built into the replicants' cells. Batty realizes his quest is futile. Tyrell refers to him as the prodigal son and looks at him admiringly. Batty holds Tyrrell's neck and kisses him on the lips and then kills him by pushing his thumbs into his eyes. Batty "commits the Oedipal crime [... and ...] thus seals his (lack of) destiny, denying him absolute resolution and salvation" (Bruno, 1987: 71).

Deckard is still pursuing Batty. Of the two of them, only Deckard has a gun, but Batty is an intelligent and formidable opponent who turns the tables on Deckard. Deckard tries to escape and loses his gun. But Batty is dying – "not yet" he says to himself and pushes a building nail through his hand to bring himself back from apparent loss of consciousness. Deckard clambers out of the window onto a ledge high above the city in an attempt to escape. He climbs on to the roof, but as Batty approaches he tries to leap to the roof of the next building, an attempt that fails and he ends up hanging precariously from a beam. Batty catches up to him and says "quite an experience to live in fear isn't it? That's what it is to be a slave". Just as Deckard is losing grip and about to plummet to a certain death, Batty grabs his wrist and pulls him up to safety. But by now it is Batty's time to die, and he knows it. He hangs his head and is then motionless. Deckard's job is done – the enforced retirement was not necessary.

The film ends with Deckard going back to his apartment. Rachael is there, asleep. "I love you" she says to him – their relationship having developed through the course of the film. "Do you trust me?" he replies. "I trust you." This echoes back to an earlier scene in the film where Rachael was also in Deckard's apartment. She is concerned that he thinks she is a replicant. She shows him photographs of her childhood. But Deckard also has photographs, which, among other things suggest to the viewers that he might be a replicant too. Rachael asks him "you know that Voight–Kampff test of yours. Did you ever take that test yourself?" He does not answer. It is with this knowledge that at the end of the film the two of them enter the elevator outside his apartment and descend to street level. What lies ahead of them is left unclear. We know though that he disobeyed his order to retire her and together they were leaving for somewhere else.

A better humanity?

As an iconic film of the late twentieth century, *Blade Runner* embodies an extreme distrust in the trajectory of capitalism – a distrust epitomized by the life of fear of the replicants, who are far more easy to sympathize with than the film's human characters. This is what Jones (1998) has referred to as *Blade Runner capitalism* – one where increasingly powerful transnational corporations, fuelled by a rampant desire for capital accumulation and institutional rationalization, contribute to the proliferation of a global consumer society where everything is capable of being produced and consumed – even humanity. But Jones' *Blade Runner capitalism* also has built in an alter ego "outside of the institutional structure of the formally regulated and taxed economy" – a "grunge economy" (292). Jones' point is that the existence of this 'other' form of life, outside of corporate power, is where there lie possibilities for indigenous culture not beholden to the commodification and homogenization so central to advanced capitalism. But this relation is not just one of economy, but also one of humanity.

Under the purview of the Tyrell Corporation and in the middle of its off-world markets, humanity is not just bought and sold – it is manufactured. But what is required in their corporatized society is not fully human – or perhaps, rather, it is more than human – more in the sense that it has the intelligence and strength of a human being, but is more easy to control, at least in principle. If it is the case that the organization's desire is an 'exemplary worker' – "an idealised worker who is automated, compliant and mechanical" (ten Bos and Rhodes, 2003: 403) – then why not manufacture them? After all, real humanity is far too recalcitrant to live up to such imposed ego-ideals. The problem that The Tyrell Corporation finds, however, is that the replicants too lack such an impossible exemplarity – as with the problematic humans, free will still raises its head. And it is free will itself that the film suggests is most antithetical to organizational ideals – ideals that harbour the desire for the worker to be human without humanity. But even when taken to their most extreme measures, it seems that the megalomaniacal desires of complete organizational control through the expulsion of free will cannot be realized. There is something positive to be found in *Blade Runner*'s dystopia – the idea that, ultimately, even the most monolithic and powerful corporations cannot fully control people. The four replicants knew this all along; Deckard learned it as the film progressed.

Despite setbacks, Tyrell is very much a modern corporation in that it continues to believe in perfectibility. Whereas the attempt to control humanity in the NEXUS 6 is through the 4-year lifespan, the apparent failure of this is to be rectified in the new model as prototyped by Rachael. The fix is the addition of fake memories of an idyllic bourgeois childhood. This all demonstrates how the "replicants' capacity for human feeling resists their raison d'etre for their producers, their use value for powerful agents of capital production" (Battaglia, 2001: 511). Ironically, while emotional control is part of the design of the replicant as a 'perfect worker', it is also what is demanded of Deckard as a Blade Runner. In order to do his job, he constantly denies himself an emotional reaction to it and its consequences. Moreover, his character development comes from him coming to terms with this. While Tyrell seeks to create replicants as 'more human than human', it seems that Deckard starts off as being 'more replicant than replicant' – at least in his emotional sophistication. And as the film progresses, he moves towards a fuller humanity through dealings with the replicants (but then perhaps he too is a replicant). In an ironic reversal of the Tyrell motto, we might say that the human is less than human.

Estranged as we are in *Blade Runner*'s futuristic novum, what comes home to roost in the present is the extent to which corporate power increasingly pervades all aspects of life. And this is a life made easy by the existence of quasi-human slave replicants to displace the human need for physically demanding work as well as to fulfil sexual desire. Here slavery and prostitution are the newest professions. It is clear that capitalism is a central theme of the film and this is one of its links back to our own world – especially in its portrayal of Tyrell, who:

> while participating in the long SF film tradition of the mad scientist [...] is far less interested in advancing scientific knowledge that he is in turning a

tidy profit [...] all of the scientific achievements of Tyrell and his minions [...] are harnessed strictly in the interests of business

(Booker, 2006: 184)

The corporate power that *Blade Runner* portrays is of a particular type – one that produces humanity, but also exceeds it. When Batty murders Tyrell, there are "no perturbations in the circuits of power, because power circulates through sophisticated management systems that are so internationalized, so technical that they are beyond the control of any one person or cartel" (McNamara, 1997: 431). The present and the future do not seem so different after all.

But *Blade Runner*'s dystopia is not entirely pessimistic. Rather than display-ing a distrust in technology (cf. Corbett, 1995), *Blade Runner* connects with our own times and world in its demonstration of a distrust in humanity – particularly as manifest in corporations. This is not so much about dehumanization by science and technology (cf. Byers, 1987) – a common theme in SF – but rather about the failure of humanity in the legacy of its modern form; a failure of humanity to recognize itself, a failure to distinguish itself from its own techno-logical mirror and a failure to have the emotional power to resist domination. Like in many science fiction films, *Blade Runner*'s Tyrell Corporation is "popu-lated by utilitarian capitalists, power hungry careerists or selfish research scien-tists. In a sense there is no humanity here, merely economic imperative and the language of strategy, accounting and marketing" (Parker, 1998b: 81). But it is the possibility of some humanity outside of corporate relations that the film promises.

In *Blade Runner*, "the will to dystopia is [...] overwhelmingly the effect of corporate power and its extension into policing, but not [...] that of the totalitar-ian state per se" (Milner, 2004: 269). This is not a fear of politics but a fear of business – an activity that has made politics weak and passé. And it is this busi-ness that gains its power through its manipulation of (and manufacture of) human interiority: "*Blade Runner* shows us not only the product becoming the consumer, but also the effect of such a move on individual freedom. Marketing methods generate new consumer needs" (Srinivas, 1999: 619).

Restoring humanity

As Jameson (2005) has commented, *Blade Runner*

signals the passage from the classic or exotic alien to the representation of the alien other as the same, namely the android, whose differentiation from the earlier robot secures a necessarily humanoid form. This may be said to be the moment of [...] reflexivity in the genre, in which our attention and preoccupation as readers [viewer] turn inward, and mediate on the "android cogito", which is to say on the gap or flaw in the self as such.

(141)

It is this reflexivity that is central to *Blade Runner*'s critical potential in relation to the present – it is the opening up of the possibility of a life not entirely circumscribed by Tyrell-style capitalism. This potential is realized most specifically in Deckard – the only character who really develops in the film's narrative. At the beginning of the film, he is portrayed very much as a pawn in a game in which he lacks a sense of agency. When asked to return to his duties as a Blade Runner, he does so not out of desire, but because he feels that he has no choice if he is to retain the privileged life that he leads. At this point in the film, it is only the replicants who seem capable of agency, even through Deckard dismisses them as being machines. The replicants are portrayed as the "oppressed and exploited in capitalist society" such that the film evokes "feelings of resentment and anger against a repressive status quo", with the replicants as being those that resist (albeit futilely) (Fitting, 1987: 340).

Through the film, Deckard's sense of agency increases – perhaps because of his relationship with the replicant Rachael, and perhaps also because of the possibility that he himself is a replicant. The replicant here is the alter ego of a failed humanity that is more human than human indeed. Deckard's character development comes to a climax in his fight with Batty – who despite being a replicant actually saves him from a certain death in "a Christ-like gesture of compassion" (Lev, 1998: 33) just before he dies himself. This suggests the possibility that the replicant has a superior sense of morality than the human, they are "more than human" (Lev, 1998: 33) – a matter that cuts the morality of corporations at its heart. Deckard's decision, as the film ends, is to escape – having abandoned his sense of helplessness, he finds that his only way to resist the corporation is to live outside its domain, always in fear that he might be hunted down by its protectors. Agency, for Deckard, means striving for a location outside of an all-demanding, all-encompassing corporate power. The plot thus develops, through the Deckard character, as a crisis of (capitalist) ideology that is resolved when Deckard "comes to recognize the lack of reasonable justification for what he does" (McNamara, 1997: 437).

The ending of the film offers a final nuanced critique of contemporary organized society that is more sophisticated than just being a nostalgic yearning for a romanticized vision of pre-industrialized, pre-postmodern society. The film can be seen as "a critique not only of multinational capitalism but also of regressive critiques of postmodernism that long for the certainty of some natural order or a past that is imagined to be simpler and more comprehensible" (McNamara, 1997: 443). Instead, what *Blade Runner* proposes is "the commencement of our task to re-imagine the conditions of our subjectivity in the complex, often contradictory space of postmodern culture" (McNamara, 1997: 443). And, as part of this, it also invites us to re-imagine the possibilities of our relations to and involvement with organizations, and what this means for our relationships with ourselves.

In the novum of a 2019 science fiction dystopia, *Blade Runner* exposes a vision of today's hard corporate realities. Realities where corporations seek to control not just business, but the very notion of what it might mean to be human.

Gazing on this future world, we might be brought back to our own so as to see a little differently – a little more clearly even. "I am not in the business" Rachael says in one scene, "I *am* the business." The encroachment of business on all aspects of life such that the two are indistinguishable is palpable. But as the film also shows, the pursuit of a different life is always a possibility. A dangerous possibility, but a possibility for humanity nonetheless.

6   From '*The Rag Trade*' to '*Ab Fab*'

Representations of work, gender and
the politics of difference in British
sitcoms

British television situation comedies (hereafter 'sitcoms') have productively
mined the inter-related themes of work, work relations and work behaviour since
the advent of television. They were present in some of the earliest sitcoms such
as the *Army Game* (1957–1961), the *Dustbinmen* (1968–1970), *Bootsie and
Snudge* (1961–1963, 1974) and *The Rag Trade* (1961–1963), and have continued down to the present with comedies such as *The Office* (2001–2003),
Absolute Power (2002–2005) and the *Green Wing* (2004–2007). A subtext
running through much of these popular cultural representations has been that of
gender and gender relations, particular as they intersect with hierarchy and
power relations. Ineluctably, given the deeply embedded class structures and
sentiments within British society, class and class relationships also often intersect with gender relations. In other words, British sitcoms provide a space for
the exploration of the politics of difference within the workplace.

The sitcom as television genre has been the subject of significant analysis (e.g.
Bowes, 1990; Dalton and Linder, 2005; Hamamoto, 1989; Marc, 1997; Mintz,
1985a and b; Morreale, 2002). The analysis of gender in sitcoms specifically is
more limited (Apter, 1982; Douglas and Olson, 1995; Fouts and Burggraf, 1999;
Lee, 1995; Olson and Douglas, 1997; Spangler, 2003) as is work (Brabazon,
2005). There are even fewer studies of the representation of men and masculinity
in sitcoms (e.g. Good *et al.*, 2002; McEachern, 1999). There is, however, a body
of literature exploring the representation of gender and the dynamics of gender
relations in other television genres (e.g. Clark, 1990; Elasmer *et al.*, 1999).
Looking at the issue from a different direction, there is a relatively small amount
of work on gender differences with respect to comedy and humour in general
(Finney, 1994; Gallivan, 1999; Gray, 1994; Hengen, 1998; Kotthoff, 2000, 2006;
Lampert and Ervin-Tripp, 1998; Rowe, K. 1995; Sochen, 1991). Much of this has
taken the form of presumed differences in humour perception and appreciation
(e.g. Henkin and Fish, 1986; Herzog, 1999; Mundorf *et al.*, 1988), but other
gender issues, focusing on how comedy is enacted, communicated and received or
with how gender is reproduced in comedy, have also received some attention
(Crawford, 1989; Kotthoff, 2000).

A relationship between depictions of women in the media and the prevalence
of gendered attitudes in society has commonly been argued (Durkin, 1985;

Morgan, 1987; Signorielli, 1989). Whilst this view has been challenged for being too simplistic and lacking nuance, it is supported by research exploring the specific and often gendered, not to say stereotypical, manner in which women are portrayed in the mass media in general and in television in particular (Carilli and Campbell, 2005; Elasmer *et al.*, 1999; Gunter, 1995; Lotz, 2006; Meyers, 1999; Spangler, 2003). However, the analysis of the representation of women in television has moved away from relatively unsophisticated depictions proclaiming bias and negative stereotypes. There has been increased recognition of more positive, reversed or even liberatory depictions of women in television in general (Clark, 1990; D'Acci, 1994; Heinecken, 2003; Helford, 2000; Lotz, 2006) and in situation comedy in particular (Apter, 1982; Holbert *et al.*, 2003; Lee, 1995; Mayerle, 1991).

In this chapter, then, we examine the representations of gender and gender relations in the workplace in British sitcoms. We explore the production and reproduction of gender and gender relations in and through this mode of popular culture. At the same time, this chapter pursues the intersection of class and gender and the representation and reproduction of class structures and relations in work-related sitcoms. By looking at depictions of class and gender relations and their inter-relationships in sitcoms, an analysis of changes in such representations is provided. The analysis also seeks, albeit in a somewhat limited way, to relate the representations in popular culture to the dynamics of gender politics and gender discourse manifest in the wider society. Pressing that analysis, we seek to question whether sitcoms have the capacity to transgress particular ideological stereotypes and assumptions and to open up and transform wider discourses. For instance, can gender and/or class relations be challenged by sitcoms and/or do sitcoms have the potential to initiate a questioning and possible change to the social/cultural status quo? We argue here, as we have elsewhere (Westwood and Rhodes, 2007), that comedy has a particular potential for critique through parody, breaking frames and transgression.[1]

Sitcoms: genre, formula and content

Situation comedy has been a staple of television since its commercial inception and has exhibited a remarkably stable semiotic history (Hartley, 2001: 65). As Marc (1997) notes, the sitcom's narrative structure can be directly traced back to prior forms on radio from which the genre is derived. For example, in the United Kingdom, a television version of *Hancock's Half Hour* (1956–1961) emerged directly from the radio show equivalent. The core narrative structure to the sitcom is represented as: familiar status quo – problem – resolution and lesson learned – familiar status quo. However, it would be misleading to oversimplify or homogenize the genre; although the genre is in many respects formulaic, alternative forms and narrative structures are discernible. *The Fall and Rise of Reginald Perrin* (1976–1979) being one example of a British sitcom that deviates from that typical structure.

Hartley (2001) categorizes sitcoms as being either family or workplace based, but in both the British and US family-centred forms have dominated. However, as Hartley notes, the notion of family has broadened and latterly includes forms that are far from the nuclear 'norm' (e.g. the three generations of women in *Absolutely Fabulous* (1992–2005). Note that this is an illustration of the ways in which sitcoms parallel changes in the wider society. Families may also be represented metaphorically; indeed, the workplace has often been represented as a pseudo-family of co-workers, a kind of proxy for the traditional family (Hartley, 2001) – the British sitcom *dinnerladies*[2] might be considered an example. However, others (e.g. Gray, 1994; Feuer, 2001) argue that workplaces are more typically portrayed as the last bastion of the 'male domain', providing a space within which male characters can operate beyond the shackles of domesticity. Whilst this may be true of some sitcoms, it is certainly not true of all and glosses the nuances present in them.

Variations in characters, location/context and ensemble structures notwithstanding, sitcoms have mostly relied on a simple framework, and innovation has been limited. Nonetheless, they have proven extremely robust and popular; the genre has exhibited great longevity spanning the entire history of television. Sitcoms are a vehicle for reflecting/commenting on social, cultural and economic changes. For instance, we can laugh as we watch two women from the 'baby boomer', 'me' generation struggle with a variety of more contemporary beliefs and ideologies in *Absolutely Fabulous,* or enjoy the satire, in the *Brittas Empire* (1991–1997), of an incompetent and bombastic manager enunciating the argot and fads of modern management to no great effect. Sitcoms can draw attention to sensitive, challenging and even confronting issues and the way people react to them and provide the basis for audience identification, but it is comedy – and so it is not lecturing and hectoring.

Class and class structure constitute a distinctive and relatively unique subtext within British comedy. Indeed, British sitcoms have pervasively acted as a vehicle for the exploration of class relations, often providing farcical representations of this feature of British social relations. Such material was present from the outset in the earliest radio comedies such as *ITMA* 1939–1949.[3] The characterizations tended to be strongly based on class stereotypes, for example, Colonel Humphrey Chinstrap the upper class dipsomaniac, Mrs Tickle the office tea lady and Tommy Handley – the show's writer and lead actor – playing the Minister of Aggravation and Mysteries at the Office of Twerps. In terms of gender, the names say everything – The Minister's secretary was 'Dotty' and in a vicious commentary on body image and gender, Hattie Jacques played the characters 'Ellie Phant' and 'Sophie Tuckshop'![4] In one of the very earliest televised sitcoms, *Emney Enterprises* (1954–1957), Fred Emney played a cartoonish, stereotypical upper class man who wore a monocle and was in a state of virtually permanent inebriation. The hierarchical structures of British class relations have been represented repeatedly in sitcoms from the 1950s to the 1980s in programmes such as *The Army Game* (1957–1961), through *The Rag Trade* (1961–1963), *'Til Death Us Do Part* (1965–1975), *Dad's Army* (1968–1977) and *Brass* (1983–1984). The epitome of the comedic representation of class structure – although not a sitcom – was in *The Frost Report* (1966–1967) where

John Cleese, Ronnie Barker and Ronnie Corbett performed sketches in which they represented members of the three classes arranged according to size, from the tall Cleese presenting the upper class to the diminutive Corbett as the working class person. The semiotics of size is telling.

It is not incidental that the decline of the British aristocracy has been traced to the disasters and disenchantments of the First World War with further amplification and acceleration following the Second World War (Cannadine, 1990). The decline became very apparent in the post-Second World War period and provided the conditions within which the aristocracy and upper classes became figures of fun and derision; they rarely get a sympathetic representation in British sitcoms. A series of comedies appeared in the 1970s that dealt with the new realities of a declined and repositioned aristocracy, dealing, in different ways with the socio-economic displacement of aristocrats or upper class people who found themselves in circumstances well below the station in life they might have enjoyed half a century before. Economic expediencies had forced them into new domains, those populated by the lower classes. These included the sitcoms *The Last of the Baskets* (1971–1972), *A Class by Himself* (1972), *His Lordship Entertains* (1972) and *To the Manor Born* (1979–1981).

It is perhaps unsurprising given the complexities of the British class system that the way the issue is represented in sitcoms is itself complex and nuanced. The working class is, for example, sometimes fondly depicted, but at other times they are held up for ridicule. This ambiguity is apparent in one of Britain's most successful sitcoms *'Til Death Us Do Part* (1966–1975), which is overtly working class and addresses class issues in society. The writer, Johnny Speight – himself from that class – was keen to represent the working class on television, not to romanticize it but to reveal its own bigotries and irrationalities. Much of the humour (and biting commentary) of the series rests on the irony of the fact that the main character, Alf Garnett, although deeply working class, is a monstrous, bombastic, bullying, racist, Tory, monarchist who is disdainful of his own class and its values. The conflict with his son-in-law, Mike, who held almost diametrically opposed views, was the interactional location for much of the comedy. Garnett is a grotesque and was intended as such. Speight is a socialist satirist who intended that Garnett and his views look foolish, ignorant and outmoded – he was not, however, read that way by everyone. In terms of gender, Alf's daughter Rita was backgrounded and mainly an adjunct and support to her husband Mike's views, whereas Alf's wife Else was portrayed as a rather stupid woman who was abused by her husband who most often referred to her as 'a silly moo'. In terms of work, Alf upheld the work ethic and was fastidious in his starched collars. Mike was ideologically opposed to work and was critical of the capitalist ethos and its demands.

It is arguable that class structures are less overtly part of British sitcoms from the 1990s onwards, but as Cannadine (1999) argues, the British continue to understand and describe their social world through the lens of class, and social relationships are still finely graded and mediated through class awareness. This is a challenge to the political rhetoric begun with British Prime Minister Margaret

Thatcher in the 1980s and sustained by Tony Blair that the United Kingdom is becoming a classless society. On this reading, class is still present in sitcoms, but is more nuanced and less discernible in crude social stereotypes and social positions as it is in the subtle semiotic codes to which the British are so finely attuned – codes of speech and language, dress, taste etc. In this way, it is easy for a British person to read that Basil Fawlty is not upper (barely middle) class – despite the aspiration, the tweeds and the appropriated accent. Equally, it is easily read that Edina Monsoon (Eddy from *Ab Fab*) is not upper class despite the wealth, speech inflections and designer wear. The difference is that by the end of the 1990s, Edina does not care that she is not classified as upper class, and is not aspiring to be so.

In an analysis of class and gender representations in American sitcoms across four decades up to 1990, Butsch (1992) reported that the majority were based on middle class families, with working class families less represented. Conversely, in Britain, the working class family was more apparent in the early sitcoms of the 1950s, 1960s and early 1970s; for example, in such programmes as *On the Buses* (1969–1973), *Queenies' Castle* (1970–1972) and *'Til Death Us Do Part* (1965–1975). From the mid-1970s onwards, the middle classes featured more prominently (Wagg, 1998); for example *The Good Life* (1975–1978) and *Butterflies* (1978–1983). This is not to say that working class themes and locations disappeared after this time, but there was a distinct emergence of interest in the middle class. Although family sitcoms predominate in the United Kingdom and the USA, in the United Kingdom, there has been a wide array of comedies with work and organizational settings apparent throughout, from *Emneys Empire* (1954–1957) to *Absolute Power* (2003–2005).

Gender has been a recurrent theme running through British sitcoms, at times directly tackled (e.g. *The Lovers*, 1970–1971; *Coupling*, 2000–2004) or with foregrounded (e.g. *The Likely Lads*, 1964–1966/1973–1974; *Butterflies*, 1978–1983). More generally though, gender is an implicit or nascent issue in most sitcoms. As noted, the problematics of gender representations in the popular media have been tackled by a number of authors (Dow, 1996; Signorielli, 1989; Tuchman, 1978). Such work traces how such representations reveal the articulation between gender structures and relationships with wider societal structures and power relations. It has been argued that such media representations mirror the prevailing gendered attitudes in society in a clear manner (Durkin, 1985; Morgan, 1987). However, whether popular culture merely reflects the attitudes and significations prevailing in society or is actually constitutive of them is more debatable. The rather passive, mirroring role of popular culture has been challenged and a more dynamic relationship to social and cultural formations and processes articulated. Some would argue, for example, that prime-time television has such cultural presence as to play a constitutive role in wider social formations and processes (Holbert *et al.*, 2003). It has also been argued that television programmes provide a forum where issues of gender and equity are discussed and a challenge and contestation mounted (Dow, 1996; Tuchman, 1978). Once again, as we have shown in this book, popular culture cannot be positioned as a mere reflection of matters occurring in society, rather it is in dynamic relationship, at least offering the ground for a critique of social practice, but also folding back into the social and institutional to be constitutive of them.

Representations of class and gender in British sitcoms: chronological patterns in social context

In this section, we review and analyse the representations of gender, class and their intersections in a series of workplace sitcoms over a period of time from the 1950s to early 2000s. We focus primarily on five sitcoms – *The Rag Trade/On the Buses*, *Hi-de-Hi*, *dinnerladies* and *Absolutely Fabulous*. Our purpose is to use these exemplars to open a broader discussion of the trends and developments in television comedy and society at large.

The Rag Trade: *female power and eccentricity*

One of the earliest sitcoms to deal with the working class in a specifically work context is *The Rag Trade* (1961–1963), which was set in a London-based garment business – Fenner Fashions. At the time, this was an innovative setting for a sitcom and the direct focus on a factory and working class issues was unusual. Written by two writers who were to become major players in British sitcom, Wolfe and Chesney,[5] the series was also unusual in that the lead roles were mainly occupied by females. Furthermore, the roles were fulsome, well-rounded and for the most part not sexualized. It might be argued that the programme and its gender structure were an exception[6] however, it is apparent that conditions were such that a sitcom in this form and with this structure and thematic content was not only possible, but, given its popularity and longevity, highly resonant to society.

This early example rather goes against some analyses, which have characterized British sitcoms as relying upon the absence or relative erasure of women. Gray (1994), for example, argues that there are a number of comedies, beginning with the seminal *Hancock's Half Hour*, that work because they offer a counterpoint to the 'norm' of heterosexual relationships and ultimately marriage and familial domesticity, which the character transgresses from a mixture of personal choice and his own inadequacy. Gray perceives a form which relies on the idea of a lone male eccentric struggling against an establishment he will never escape, but which benevolently contains his eccentricity (other sitcoms which might be read in this way include *The Fall and Rise of Reginald Perrin* (1976–1979) and *Shelley* (1979–1992). In gender terms, women are merely part of the establishment, their absence freeing men from the confines of the family 'norm' and permitting their individuality/eccentricity. On this view, women are important in sitcoms only as a backdrop, whereby their "absence is existentially liberating" and a reminder of the 'norms' which help the viewer identify the comic incongruity. As such, they are comedically crucial, but are denied the possibility of being the source of the comedy (Gray, 1994). This is certainly not true of *The Rag Trade* or indeed of many other sitcoms since then where the comedy *is* centred on and created by the women. It is not exclusively female, but men are not the centre of the comedy and, indeed, in many respects the chief male, Fenner, is the straightman to the women. What is particularly acute here is that Lily (a key female character) – or more properly 'Lilian Lavinia Lulu Sawn' – is a genuine *female* eccentric.

It is further suggested that far from being the site of an alternative family, the workplace is a location that 'nourishes' the type of masculine selfish individuality and eccentricity noted above since there are no women around to 'spoil things' with 'common sense'. Here, the workplace plays a special role in the pursuit of male freedom. Gray (1994) contends that sitcoms such as *Steptoe and Son* (1962–1974), *Porridge* (1973–1977), *Dad's Army* (1968–1977) and *Yes, Minister* (1980–1984) allow the male 'character' all his comic glory by situating him in an all-male setting. It is acknowledged that are some exceptions in terms of the presence of women on screen and 'behind the scenes'; for example, Gray (1994) allows that *Fawlty Towers* (1975, 1979) is one of the few sitcoms in which female characters are permitted to act as well as react. Basil Fawlty's eccentricity is not liberated by Sybil's absence, but by her presence, and her eccentricity is equally liberated by her hatred for him.

There clearly are sitcoms that are total male arenas, and there is some sense in an analysis which suggests that it is the erasure of women that provides a playground for male individuality. It also makes sense to suggest that females have repeatedly been positioned as the sensible, able and 'normal' adjunct to the 'funny' (in both senses – humourous and eccentric) male. However, equally clearly, this is not the only gender structure in British sitcoms, and quite possibly not even the dominant one. As *The Rag Trade* and other sitcoms demonstrate, even from an early period, television sitcoms were produced that created spaces for strong female characters and for humour to centre on and emanate from them. They are not erased, they are very much present – and funny.

It is notable, for example, that some time after *The Rag Trade* one of its actors, Sheila Hancock, was given the lead in a sitcom entitled *Better Than a Man* (1970) in which she played the managing director of a steel company. It depicts her as expressly fighting and overcoming male sexist attitudes and behaviours. The show never made it past the pilot, but the fact that it could be constructed and aired is indicative of a real counterpoint to the notion that British sitcoms were merely a vehicle for male ego and fantasy. Indeed, we would argue that Gray is incorrect in identifying *Fawlty Towers* as an exception to the rule of female reactivity. Is it really the case that Yootha Joyce's Mildred is merely an empty vessel to George's plenitude in *Man about the House* (1973–1976) and *George and Mildred* (1976–1979) – that she is not also a centre of the humour and an active creator of comedy? Is Wendy Craig's Ria Parkinson in *Butterflies* (1978–1983) a mere comedic adjunct? Most certainly not. Indeed, all of Carla Lane's comedies[7] feature women in strong or leading roles in which they are the active generators of comedy. It is important to note that one of those, *The Liver Birds*, was first aired in 1969 and portrayed young independent women pursuing jobs, careers and sexual satisfactions. There is clearly a more central and non-occluded role for women in British sitcoms than Gray's rather gloomy picture portrays, and *The Rag Trade* was an early and innovative example of this.

The Rag Trade was not dominated by one individual but was an ensemble piece. The main characters[8] were Harold Fenner (Peter Jones) the owner-manager of the business, Paddy (Miriam Karlin) the female shop steward, Carole (Sheila Hancock) and 'Little Lil' (Esma Cannon) two shop floor workers and Reg (Reg Varney) the foreman. The show exploited the divisions between management and workers to derive its comedy, but the conflicts were short-lived and readily resolved, and the relationship between the sides was never bitter with many moments of mutual support. It was certainly not offering a radical socialist critique of sweatshop labour and the brutalities of oppressive capitalist management. Fenner was in fact positioned as a somewhat fumbling, harassed and asinine manager, and certainly not as someone able to dominate the strong character represented by Paddy. Reg as the foreman was also often a dupe to the machinations of the women, and was located in that proverbially debilitating and unenviable role foremen are habitually seen to occupy between workers and management. Whilst Lily was portrayed as a rather scatty, fidgety woman, it was not an insubstantial role, and the character was more eccentric than merely silly. Although the series did create strong female roles that cannot be read as reproducing stereotypical depictions of the female, Barbara Windsor did, nonetheless, play her typical busty-blonde character, but not until the last series. We would argue that *The Rag Trade*, particularly in view of its historical location, signifies the subtleties of gender relations as portrayed in British television sitcoms, subtleties that make gross summary analyses dangerous and misleading. It is also reflective of the changes and subtleties in gender relations in society in general. The role of women in the workplace was altered significantly during World War II as large numbers of women were pulled into the labour force to help the war effort – something that *The Rag Trade* gestures to.

On The Buses: *male infantilism and the authenticity of class location*

Wolfe and Chesney went on to write a very different comedy that, whilst it also dealt with working class people in a low-level work context, had little in common with the *The Rag Trade* in terms of innovation and avoidance of stereotype. *On the Buses* (1969–1973) became one of Britain's longest running and popular sitcoms. It focused on the escapades of bus driver Stan (Reg Varney) and his conductor partner Jack (Bob Grant) and their repeated run-ins with the Bus Inspector 'Blakey' (Stephen Lewis). Stan is the focus, and the comedy alternates between his workplace trials and tribulations and his domestic relationships with his mother, his sister Olive and her husband Arthur. The style here is simpler, almost cartoonish – the characters stereotypical and the jokes based heavily on entendre or slapstick.

Blakey is the archetypal, rule-following supervisor – anal in his slavish pursuit of rules, symbolized by the ever-present clipboard and pen. He is rigid in persona and in stature – retentive, officious, repressed, miserable and rather pathetic. He represents a long line of supervisors/middle managers who are invariably unsympathetically portrayed as bureaucratic, incompetent or both, and usually as dupes to a quicker witted, lower-level employee. In work-based comedies, supervisors/middle managers are almost uniformly presented in this way, especially if they belong to the middle classes or, worse, are working class aspirants to the middle/managerial class – whereas characters that are authentically working class or upper class are often treated in more varied, nuanced and even sympathetic ways. Bloody Delilah, the 'Corporation Cleansing Department's' inspector in *The Dustbinmen* (1968–1970), is a similar character – officious, and loathed and derided by the workers. Middle class or aspirant middle class middle managers include Captain Mainwaring in *Dad's Army* and Captain Peacock from *Are You Being Served?* – as to some extent are Basil Fawlty and latterly Gareth Keenan (*The Office*).

At one level, the characterization suggests a cultural antipathy to authority figures, interference from bureaucrats and minor officials, pomposity and officiousness and an overly rigid adherence to rules and regulation. However, there is also a deeper issue concerning the middle and aspiring middle classes. Clearly working class and clearly aristocratic figures are in known and fixed locations, with the textures of history and tradition behind them. The lower-middle classes and those middle class aspirants are a disturbance to that order. Perhaps sitcoms, especially the earlier ones in the 1960s and 1970s reflect disquiet about that disturbance. It is certainly the case that British popular culture, including sitcoms, has been often critical and disparaging about those who shift or aspire to shift their class position. Those who aspire to the middle classes and try to adopt the accoutrements of that class in an inauthentic way were particularly derided and often the focus for scathing humour in British sitcoms.

In *On the Buses*, Stan remains avowedly, unashamedly working class, and shows no inclinations for upwards mobility. Indeed, in Episode 5 of Series 1, he gets promoted to inspector, but it is short-lived and he returns happily to his role as driver and his mates. In this sense, there is something of a celebration of working class culture that has been pervasive in popular culture representations – not just in comedies but in 'soaps' such as *Coronation Street* and *East Enders*. However, in *On the Buses*, as with other sitcoms, the portrayal is not entirely saccharine and one-dimensional. Although Stan as the main character is usually able, with the help of Jack, to outwit Blakey, he is not portrayed as either of two stock male characters in British sitcoms. He is neither the worldly wise, confidently dismissive and crafty 'jack-the-lad' (a role assumed by Jack in *On the Buses;* also characterized by Ted Bovis in *Hi-de-Hi*, Sid James in *Citizen James* and Del in *Only Fools and Horses*), nor as the amiable 'bludger' or free-rider (as characterized by *The Artful Dodger*, Terry in *The Likely Lads* and *Shelley*). Rather, Stan appears to be perpetually on edge and fraught; he is harassed by Blakey, niggled at by Arthur and dominated by his mother. He is in many respects a pathetic figure characterized by pathos rather than masculine braggadocio. Although he mostly avoids being totally put upon by Blakey and management, he never overcomes them either. Socially and sexually, he is often thwarted by and/or comes second best to Jack.

In terms of gender relations, the programme has been frequently criticized for its misogyny and sexploitation, for reputedly having groups of mini-skirted girls gratuitously present for Stan and Jack to leer at. Whilst this does occur, it is more prevalent in the later series and in the film offshoot. In the original series, there are no such female representations until the fifth episode. Interpreting the treatment of gender issues in the series in this simplistic manner is to miss some more interesting and ambiguous gender politics. Stan's relationship with his mother is telling; especially given that he is clearly into his thirties, employed, yet still living with her. She is the dominant figure whom Stan is always trying to please, invariably giving in to her requests and interests. Indicative of her dominance and Stan's subservience is the episode 'The Darts Match' (Episode 7, Series 1). Stan and Jack have been challenged to a darts match by two female 'clippies'. During the game, Stan flirts with one of them, Iris, and she invites him back to her place. Stan is childishly excited, but he is supposed to take his mum home. She is manipulative and he caves in, informing Iris that he can't go. To further accentuate Stan's status as perpetual loser, Jack invites Iris to join the darts team and drops Stan, it is then Jack who goes off to Iris's house. As an adjacent issue, it is also worth noting that in this episode, although the two 'clip-pies' might be considered to be cast as 'dolly birds' and are the subject of ogling and jokes from Jack and Stan, they manipulate the men and win the darts match. They also make fun of the men, including comments on their capacities as sexual partners. It is the men, and Stan in particular, who are made to look foolish and pathetic.

In another instance (the episode 'Family Flu', Series 2), both Stan's mother and sister are in bed with the 'flu'. They both have broomsticks, which they hit on the bedroom floor to get Stan's attention. He is rushing around in a very harassed state trying to meet their needs. His mother frequently says to him 'Be a good boy Stan' or some equivalent, and there is a childlike quality to Stan – certainly boyish at home, childish in the pranks at work and immature in his attempted relationships with the opposite sex. He rather pathetically tries to play 'jack-the-lad' at work, competing with the more authentically laddish Jack; but at home, he is a 'mummy's boy', childish in his need to please her and deeply dependent on her. He is infantilized and indeed emasculated in his relationships. His emasculation is exemplified in the episode 'Late Again' (Series 2, Episode 5), when he discovers that Jack has stolen 'his' girlfriend and slept with her. Indeed, Jack frequently pre-empts or frustrates Stan's erotic aspirations by 'getting the girl'.

The characterization of male figures in British sitcoms as childish, childlike or even infantilized is quite common. Certainly, the working class male is fre-quently pictured as inept and foolish, but sometimes this goes further with the male portrayed as either emasculated and/or infantilized by a stronger and more capable wife or partner. One can think of Terry Scott's infantilized figure in *Happy Ever After* (1974–1978) and *Terry and June* (1979–1987), and similarly

George Roper in *George and Mildred* and *Man About the House*. Frank Spencer in *Some Mothers Do 'Ave 'Em* (1973–1978) is perhaps the quintessential 'baby-man'. In another prominent example, Basil Fawlty, (in *Fawlty Towers*, 1975, 1979), is emasculated by his wife, the monstrous Sybil. He also exhibits child-like qualities, with his tantrums and tears when his schemes are frustrated, and his frantic and absurd attempts to cover up his blunders. There are elements too in *The Likely Lads* (1964–1966/1973–1977) and more deliberately latterly in *Men Behaving Badly* (1992–1998), although here the regression is to the prank-ishness of pre-pubescent teens rather than the more childlike Frank Spencer. It has been suggested that the re-emergence of 'laddishness' in popular cultural representations such as *Men Behaving Badly* and in contemporary magazines such as *FHM* and *Loaded*[9] was something of a male backlash against feminism (Kenny and Stevenson, 2000).

In an interesting related analysis of class and gender representations in American sitcoms, Butsch (1992) found that most sitcoms were based on a middle class family, with frequently successful, reasonable, 'super-parents'. While there are variations and exceptions, across nearly five decades of television, the middle class 'standard' has been remarkably robust. However, when a working class context was used, the father was usually presented as inept, irresponsible, stupid or lacking in maturity, while the wife is portrayed as competent, able and in control of things; similar to the middle class male in terms of maturity and sensitivity. In this sense, the working class man effectively has his gender status inverted – he is feminized, and disparagingly so. This inversion, Butsch argues, buttresses the social order by confirming the status order of class; middle classes are 'refined', reasonable, able and ordered, while the working classes are surrounded by chaos and disorder. In British sitcoms, it is not just *working class* men who are infantilized and feminized. Terry Scott's characters are more lower-middle class than working class and the same is true of Basil Fawlty.

There is another gender issue in *On The Buses* that deserves comment. It concerns the relationship between Stan's sister Olive and her husband Arthur. They both live at home with Stan and his mum. Arthur is a booking clerk for British Rail and Olive often is not working, although in Episode 3, Series 1, she does get a job as a clippie for one episode. The relationship between Arthur and Olive is distant, to say the least. He seems to be barely able to stand her company and often belittles her. Olive is depicted as frumpy and unattractive. She is, however, clearly possessed of a healthy sexual appetite and periodically tries to get Arthur interested. Arthur, though, is not at all interested and is always finding ways of avoiding any sexual or intimate contact. This is an ongoing subtheme in the comedy and crops up in most episodes.

This type of dysphasic and conflictual relationship between partners is common and is a version of the classic 'battle of the sexes' subgenre. However, in *On The Buses*, the sexual focus for the humour together with a reversal of the stereotypes through the portrayal of the female as sexually active, almost voracious, and the male as sexually muted and avoiding makes for a more distinctive form, but again, one not uncommon in British sitcoms. At one level, Olive is a female harridan and nagging wife and hence an example of a common female characterization in sitcoms. Indeed, Porter (1998) suggests that there are only a limited number of female characterizations in British sitcoms such as the "tarty, giggly blonde" (exemplified by Barbara Windsor in a swathe of roles), "plump matriarchs" such as Hattie Jacques and female grotesques/harridans (examples here would be Yootha Joyce in *George and Mildred*, Sybil Fawlty in *Fawlty Towers*, Nora Batty *Last of the Summer Wine* and Anna Karen's 'Olive'). He argues that what unites this narrow spectrum of female types in the traditional modes of popular British comedy is the a priori definition of physicality and sexuality: the 'tart' or 'dumb blonde' by her over-determined sexuality and the 'tyrant' or 'spinster' by her asexuality. He then maintains that both extremes are represented as threats to men and male order in comic narratives. Once again, we consider this to be a simplification if not a distortion. For example, Olive is at one level a harridan, but she is not asexual, rather it is her insipid husband who is asexual. Olive is shown as lusty, but it is an unrequited lust because of her husband's disinterest.

Unrequited female lust (most often from middle-aged women) is apparent in a number of sitcom characters: Mildred in *Man About the House* and *George and Mildred* is almost a carbon copy of Olive's situation; Mrs Slocombe in *Are You Being Served* is a clearly sexualized character and frequently pursues Capt Peacock who ignores or shuns her; Gladys Pugh perpetually lusts after the wan Mr Fairbrother in *Hi-de-Hi* to no avail; and both Joan and Miss Erith in separate series have their desires for Reggie Perrin in *The Fall and Rise of Reginald Perrin* unreturned. It is tempting to invoke a misogynist discourse and say that the message is that the women are spurned because they are not attractive enough and so the humour is cruel in commenting on sexual desire and attractiveness. This is a possible reading in some situations, but it clearly will not do in all. There is clearly a commentary on male sexuality here as well; one that perhaps references an inherent male fear of female sexuality, especially when exhibited in an open and voracious fashion. Perhaps there are resonances with men's fears and doubts about sex and their own sexuality in general and about sexual performance in particular. It is apparent that the humour is not just directed at women but also at men and their sexual incapacities and fears. There are other counterpoints to Porter's restricted typology. For example, Nora Batty in the *Last of the Summer Wine* may be a grotesque and herself rather asexual, but she is, nonetheless, the object of the unrequited lust of 'Compo'. Furthermore, there are many female characters that are neither tart nor harridan – those in *The Rag Trade*, *dinnerladies*, *Ab Fab*, the *Vicar of Dibley*, *Butterflies* and almost all of Carla Lane's characters. Indeed, we can think of very few straight tarts and not many harridans that do not also have complexities of character – for example Sybil Fawlty.

In summary, *On the Buses* whilst simple in its comedy, contains nuances in terms of characterization and gender relations. True, there are the occasional 'dolly birds' in mini-skirts and Jack and Stan do engage in sexist behaviour, but often the joke is on them. Stan in particular is not successful with women; they manipulate him, spurn him and leave him for Jack. He is a 'mummy's boy, harassed, inept and mostly has his pleasures withheld or mediated by other obligations. There is considerable pathos in the role: in the frequent failure and the inability to enjoy himself. This is not the image of the rampant, oversexed, laddish, cad who makes women the object of his fun and humour. The comedy (and the twinge of tragedy) focuses on him and these failings. The celebration around Stan, if there is one, is that he keeps trying: and that he remains true to his class.

In terms of work relations, *On The Buses*, at one level, has a simple 'us-and-them' structure with the workers and management (in the character of their representative Blakey) perpetually sparring. Most of the time, this is rather insignificant and the commentary on class and workplace relations muted. The conflicts are really at a more localized and personal level. It is noticeable that no managers ever appear; they are only alluded to and remain forever absent. The conflictual structure of workplace relations were more apparent in the first episode, where there was a strike, but rather tailed off subsequently. So as with *The Rag Trade*, the class conflict was relatively mellow and tame and neither show represents much of a critique of industrial relations. If anything, for their time, both were comedies that were affirmations of working class culture and of remaining authentically attached to one's class.

Hi-de-Hi*: high jinx and high farce in a working class holiday camp*

The hit sitcom *Hi-de-Hi* provides an interesting case since it was aired in the 1980s (1980–1987) but set in the 1950s. The location is the working class holiday camp of Maplins (thinly disguised Butlins[10]). The comedy centres primarily on the relationships and activities of the holiday camp's staff responsible for entertaining the guests as well as the management of the camp in the figure of Mr Fairbrother (Simon Cadell). The programme has certain class themes and relationships running through it. This type of holiday camp was a mainstay for many working class people in the post-war austerity era, providing a holiday by the sea that they could afford. The accommodation was basic, but there was an attempt to entertain people with shows and an ever-present team of staff to get people involved in various activities (Ward, 1986) – at Maplins called 'Yellow-coats'. In addition to Fairbrother, there is an ensemble of characters, the main ones being Ted Bovis (Paul Shane) as the resident comic and Spike (Jeffrey Holland) his understudy, Gladys Pugh (Ruth Madoc) the senior Yellowcoat and would-be assistant to the manager, Peggy (Sue Pollard) a chambermaid and Yellowcoat aspirant, the Stuart-Hargreaves (Barry Howard and Diane Holland) as dance instructors, Mr Partridge (the Punch and Judy man), and Fred Quilly (Felix Bowness) who looked after the horses and donkeys. There were some young female and male Yellowcoats in more minor parts – the latter in oddly short mini-skirts for the period they were playing.[11]

The humour resides in the intersection of these various characters and their relations with the 'guests'; class issues are pervasive throughout. One of the key intersections is between Bovis and Fairbrother. Fairbrother is a former

Cambridge academic archaeologist. He is not quite the stereotypical 'upper class twit', but he is rather weak and ineffectual as a manager. Whilst Fairbrother tends not to be pretentious, his class location is made a figure of fun. In Episode 2, his former Dean visits him at work and says pompously "Do I need a visa". Bovis later advises in reference to the Dean – "Never buy anything from a man with a poof voice." In the figure of Fairbrother, there is something of a spoof on English amateurism and on the fact that for a long time, management in the United Kingdom was not seen as a specialist profession and was undertaken by amateurs. There is also an implied critique on the class system that enabled those privileged enough to go to Oxford or Cambridge University to assume leadership positions, even where they had no real experience or competency. Bovis, on the other hand, is another of those unashamedly working class characters who has a lot of streetwise capability and usually outmanoeuvres Fairbrother. He is another 'wide-boy' or 'jack-the-lad' who is always looking for an angle, a way to 'turn a buck' and to avoid work if possible. In terms of class politics, here the working class clearly has it over the upper-middle class.

Fairbrother suffers from the working class from the other direction. His boss, and the owner of Maplins, Joe Maplin, is an uncultured, uncouth bully from the working class who has made good through the holiday camp business. His behaviour and business ethics are at odds with Fairbrother's more refined view of the world. In Episode 3 'A Matter of Conscience', the council wants to develop a hospital on the land adjacent to the camp. It is the land that Maplin wants to acquire and develop himself. He instructs Fairbrother to ensure that there are enough noises and smells when the council inspection team comes to look at the site to put them off. Bovis informs Fairbrother that Maplin has half the council in his pocket and says they should comply with Maplin. Fairbrother becomes morally haughty and says he will refuse. In a telling speech, Bovis says: "Joe Maplin pays my wages, when he says 'jump' I jump. I can't afford morals on my salary. If you get the sack you can go back to ... [being an archaeologist]". Fairbrother, who as noted earlier is the object of desire for Gladys Pughs, the Welsh senior Yellowcoat, receives a telegram from Maplin saying:

> No one leaves messages for me son. Get cracking and do what I've told you or your wife's solicitors will get wind of the goings on between you and a certain Welsh Yellowcoat who wiggles her rear at you.

Bullied and blackmailed by Maplin, Fairbrother caves in and does what he wants. Most of the Yellowcoats won't do it and go on strike, but with Bovis organizing things, the task is done. Later, Fairbrother sums up his actions: "I look upon today as the most shameful day of my life. I've sacrificed truth, friendship, and charity, just in order to save my wretched reputation".

The contrition does not hide the weakness and lack of ethical stature, but it is not only the upper class scholar who is lambasted in this episode, Maplin, the working class escapee is also portrayed as a blighted creature. It is interesting that both of these people have transgressed their class origins – Maplin ascending out of his working class roots through wealth, Fairbrother descending to join the *hoi polloi.*

There is a fairly common theme running through British sitcoms from the 1950s till the early 1990s that treats negatively such class transgressions, more particularly so when the aspirations are for upwards class mobility and the inauthenticities involved therein. It is a theme we have touched upon earlier. British sitcoms, then, seem to rest on humour that is derived from transgressions, common enough and indeed part of the comedic tradition (Westwood, 2004), but in this case the transgressions are of class location. It is clear that the comedy is critical of such transgressions and appears to offer support for some presumed authenticity of people adhering to their class roots and locations.

Whilst British humour has poked fun at the 'upper. class twit' and the working class fool and bigot, it appears to hold back its most bitter barbs for another species – the petit bourgeois social climber. It is here that the endless, fine semiotic gradations of the British class system and its residues come into play. Subtle cues in language use are enough to give real class location away. Indeed, the attempt to mask such cues is itself a cue. So as with Mrs Slocombe and Hancock, the aspirated 'haitchses' and occasional falling 'aitches' in their speech gives away their working class origins. Mrs Slocome's middle class pretensions are popped by such slippages and are the source of amusement at her expense. Old Mr Steptoe is forever undercutting his son Harold's pretensions to rise above his class. There is a certain pathos in the perpetual frustration of a man trapped in a social setting that he would rather not be in. The pathos is perhaps deliberate; there is the punishment of the permanent evasiveness of happiness and fulfilment awaiting those who seek to transgress their class. This can be read as a reaffirmation of the status quo ante, of the class structure *intacto.*

There is a similar enactment in *George and Mildred* and *Man about the House.* What is interesting there is that Mildred is the failed social aspirant, while George remains firmly attached to his working class roots. With George there as a permanent signifier of working class culture, ethos and background, Mildred's aspirations are doomed to failure. The same is somewhat true of Bob Ferris and his middle class aspirant girlfriend/wife Thelma in *The Likely Lads,* except in this case it is his best mate's doggedly down to earth working class attitudes and behaviour that anchors Bob and punctures many of his pretensions. The truly dreadful Hyacinth Bucket (*Keeping up Appearances,* 1990–1995) is perhaps the most recent exemplary incarnation of this characterization. There is an implicit critique in these sitcoms of the pretensions of class transgressions – of trying to appear as other than what you are. At the same time, there is a valourization of authenticity as defined by your class origins. In the end, socially and politically, it is a rather conservative, even reactionary critique.

Aligned with this critique of class transgression is a lambasting of social snobbery, also common in British sitcoms. In a subtle turn around this theme, the apparently genuinely upper class Sgt Wilson in *Dad's Army* often frustrates and exposes the snobbish and pompous middle class Captain Mainwaring. Basil Fawlty and Sybil are both snobs and are derided for their pretensions – although

Basil so much more so. In *Hi-de-Hi*, the dance instructor husband and wife team of Yvonne and Barry Stuart-Hargreaves are the social snobs. Again, the hyphen is an intricate part of class semiotics in Britain along with the so-called 'plummy' accent; both exhibited here. In this case, the whole pretension is undercut by the fact that the two are employed and live in a rather run-down, working class holiday camp. They refer to 'people of our class' and 'putting a brave face on it'. It is almost 'keeping a stiff upper lip' except that their trials and tribulations consist only of an affront to their own pretensions. In Episode 3, they try to hold a soiree in their 'chalet', replete with punch and canapé. Through a series of mishaps, the wrong 'guest list' gets circulated and the soiree is subverted into a 'boozy', working class 'knees-up'.

In a useful meta-commentary on the main manifestation of gender relations in the series, Yvonne comments on the apparent involvement of Fairbrother with Gladys Pugh:

> Someone of his breeding has no defence against a girl like that. If a man who hasn't had much experience of women comes up against such blatant, brazen sexuality you know as well as I do how he'll react.
>
> (Episode 3: The Pay Off)

The relationship between Gladys and Fairbrother is indeed central to the sitcom. Gladys is a working class girl 'from the [Welsh] valleys' who is obsessively in love and lust with the upper class Fairbrother. She is always smouldering around him, staring into his eyes and trying to entice him without being direct enough to ask. He seems aware and even to be stimulated by the attention, but does not seem able or perhaps willing to respond. One reading is that his class prevents him from embarking on an affair with someone of a lower class. It could also, though, be another commentary on male fear of female sexuality, especially when so obviously displayed. Gladys is another of those sexualized female characters who have their desires permanently thwarted – which is itself perhaps a commentary on women failing to find sexual fulfilment and on men's sexual inadequacies. It is also worth noting that neither is able to express their true feelings and desires – reflecting the emotional inarticulateness of British culture, perhaps compounded by class divides.

The other key female in the series is Peggy the chambermaid. She is good-natured but not very bright and often causes mayhem through her well-intentioned but not thought out actions. The sum of her ambitions is to become a Yellowcoat. She is dumb and blonde, but not the dumb-blonde of the cliché. There have been more recent manifestations of the 'gormless woman' latterly, notably Bubble in *Ab Fab* and Anita in *dinnerladies*. In all cases, these are rather sympathetically drawn and likeable fools and in the context of their sitcoms, not positioned to signify female gormlesness or stupidity in any general sense.

Hi-de-Hi replays some fairly typical class themes, but some of the more interesting nuances are again around issues of transgression and authenticity. In the end, the treatment of class conveys, indirectly, a rather conservative message. Adherence to one's class is valourized, whilst those who move out, seek to move out, or pretend to move out of their class locations are derided and through the derision, criticized.

In terms of the representations of gender, we again do not have simple or stereotypical representations. Granted there are two–three young women in mini-skirts, but they are rather insignificant. The other women in the series do have strong roles and are as much a part of the comedy as the men. Men do occupy the positions of authority and power, but the show is located in the 1950s when such gendering of organizations was the norm. Much of the humour is around intersections of roles and gender relations, but often cut across by class: Fairbrother, the rather inept upper class manager and the quietly lustful working class Gladys; Bovis the somewhat bovine, streetwise chancer and the upper class manager; the grumpy, booze-sozzled Punch and Judy man, and the sober and sensitive animal handler; the pretentious, snobbish Yvonne and her rather obedient and limp husband. The gendered nature of organizations has been attended too significantly in the management and organizational literature, but analysis still often fails to the complexities of gender with other identity issues and processes such as class or ethnicity. The sexuality inherent to organizations, so clearly a part of organizational life in this and other sitcoms, has also been neglected in the literature (Brewis and Linstead, 2000).

dinnerladies: *sex and pathos, with chips please*

In some respects, *dinnerladies* recalls *The Rag Trade* in that it is one of a small number of directly workplace-located sitcoms with a predominantly female cast. Broadcast at the end of the 1990s (1998–2000), *dinnerladies* is set in a workplace's canteen and focuses on the (mostly) female staff and their relationships and interactions. It was conceived of, written by and stars Victoria Wood as Bren, a supervisor of the canteen. The other women are mostly canteen staff and include: Dolly Belfield (Thelma Barlow) and Jean (Anne Reid), two middle-aged women who often engage in their own verbal jousting; Twinkle, (Maxine Peake) a young single woman who seems to lead an active social life, and appears perpetually tired and disengaged at work, she is, however, always there, has a sharp witty tongue and is kind-hearted; Anita (Shobna Gulati), a young Asian woman who is not well endowed intellectually and is vacantly pleasant. In addition, there is Phillipa Moorcroft (Celia Imrie) who is a stereotypical 'soft' HR manager, into 'issues', but who has a series of odd, often rampantly sexual, liaisons with men that never seem to work out. Finally, there is Julie Walters as Bren's rather surreal, eccentric, tramp-like, but somehow educated and well-connected mother. There are men, most notably Tony (Andrew Dunn) who is the canteen manager and plays something of a disjointed love interest for Bren. There is also Stan Meadowcraft (Duncan Preston) who plays a rather retentive and pedantic, but caring and gentle maintenance worker.

Although this is a working class environment, there are no real discussions of class issues or any class conflict. The only manager ever seen is the HR manager Phillipa, and she and what she represents are made fun of – albeit in a gentle way. There is a lampooning of modern management and its practices and systems. Stan, for example, claiming to not remember her name, refers to Phillipa as 'Human Resources' as if it were a name. Indeed, the whole comedic style is gentle and non-abrasive, but with a tinge of pathos. Almost all the characters are affectionately drawn. It could be read as a celebration of working class values and perhaps of 'feminine' values of mutuality, care and support, and this is something new in British sitcoms.

What is of significance is that *dinnerladies* is reminiscent of *The Rag Trade* in that it is a work-centred comedy in which the women make the humour and are at the centre of it. Tony, the main male character, is mostly a straight guy. Even in terms of gender relations, there is no clichéd battle of the sexes. Tony and Bren have an on–off (mostly off and unconsummated) relationship, but there is great affection and respect between them and it is a non-exploitative relationship. They have proper conversations, and Tony is able to open up to Bren emotionally in a way untypical of common masculine representations.

There is an edge of pathos centred on Bren's inability to find happiness. Part of this is due to her mother, the wildly eccentric Petula Gardeno. She arrives at the canteen periodically, usually when she needs help and money from Bren. For all appearances, she is a female tramp; dirty and unkept. However, she suggests an exotic lifestyle since she talks in so-matter-of-fact manner about her relations with the rich and famous, major celebrities from film, television and music. The tales are fantastic and can't possibly be true, but she delivers them with the aplomb of authenticity. This relationship is fraught for Bren and is the chief source of the pathos. For example, in 'Holidays' (Episode 3, Series 2), Bren has saved up enough money for a holiday with others from the canteen, including Tony. She brings the cash to work intending to do some holiday shopping and buy her ticket. Then Petula arrives in a more disheveled state than normal, looking singed in places. She has an elaborate tale about a fire in her caravan and that she needs a certain amount of money to sort things out – an amount very approximate to the sum Bren has. At first Bren is determined not to give in and she is urged not to do so by Tony and the others, but in the end she does and hands over all her money to her mum. Yet again, Bren is not able to get the pleasure and happiness she wants. This is a subtext in the series and indeed in a number of other sitcoms from Hancock, through Stan in *On the Buses* to Reggie Perrin and others. There is pathos and melancholy at the heart of much British humour, a decided inability for people to find fulfilment and happiness – and it might be tempting to suggest that this matches the national psyche – but perhaps, less grandly, it is just the nature of comedy.

Despite this pathos, the show bristles with one-liners and good gags, and everyone has a full comedic character with great lines, even the more incidental characters like Norman who delivers the bread. He is a large, languorous and melancholic man with severe hypochondria. One day, he arrives late and when Stan asks what happened, he responds in a slow and deliberate drawl "Oh, I couldn't get motivated. You get very bored of trays in my job." A little later, as he places a tray of goods on the counter, he says in the same monotone manner:

NORMAN: "I sneezed in these soft rolls, do you still want 'um?"
BREN: "How close?"
NORMAN: "About four feet ... but it were a biggun."

The relations between the men and the women in the canteen are mostly affectionate and supportive. We have already commented on the central relationship between Bren and Tony. The other main male character, Stan, whilst he is in many respects an officious pedant, fond of rules and regulations, he is still a positively drawn character liked by all the others. He displays warmth and sensitivity at times, and his officiousness is mainly confined to his work responsibilities, in which he takes great pride. He occasionally makes what could be seen as sexist comments, but again, this is confined to his immediate task area and in other areas he is polite and respectful. For example, in dealing with Christmas light decorations that he and Bren are trying to fix, he declares "I say this with the greatest love and respect, you're not a man and you don't know what you're talking about." In the context of mutuality the sitcom generates, this can pass, indeed, the women are happy to give Stan dominance over his domain – it is limited power and does not extend to power over them.

There is some interesting treatment of female sexuality in *dinnerladies* that is reflective of the time in which it is produced. Sex is a frequent topic of conversation – in an open, unembarrassed way. The conversations are risqué and full of double-entendres – more like a stereotypical 'lads' conversation than one between mostly middle-aged women. As noted, Phillipa has some rather complex relationships with men and she reveals herself to be a very sexualized person who talks openly about her sexual desires and activities. In Episode 4 of Series 2, for example, she decides to end a relationship with 'Michael' because 'its no fun'. She has, however, spotted a new man she has designs on and when he comes into the work area, she gleefully says to Bren: "Don't you think he is knicker-wettingly, groin-grindingly fab?" In the next episode, when she has begun a relationship with this new man, she tells Bren delightedly that they are having 'lots of sex' and is anticipating Christmas with him and more sex and says, "I've never had sex at Christmas before. Sex and no sprouts ... I'm so excited." This frank discussion of sex between women is rare in British sitcoms, indeed in most popular culture representations. The acknowledgement of sexuality in the workplace has also only latterly been made within organization studies despite its ubiquity.

In the same episode, Dolly comes to work with a big smile on her face. There is much talk about her new man, who is much younger. She maintains they have been having lots of sex – all over the house and several times a day. This frank discussion of female middle-aged sexuality is rare, but is perhaps also a reflection of the values and permissions of the times. The banter leads to various jokes about Jean's body. Bodies are another topic much discussed openly. There is a lack of embarrassment and often self-deprecation in these conversations, but there is little pandering to the media-mediated images of female sexuality or body image. As a plump nurse in one episode notes, "I don't eat biscuits – although I should do really, to keep my weight up."

dinnerladies is something of a rarity in that it produces great comedy without there being a conflictual edge or by having a target and at the expense of others. This is gentle, inclusive comedy – perhaps reflecting the female authorship. There are few instances of critique in class terms, although, overall, it could be argued that the programme is again a celebration of working class culture. There is some critique of management via the fun poked at Human Resources – so perhaps the target has narrowed. Gender relations are also mostly positive and supportive. There are some stereotypical residues, but they are embedded in the positivity and are not presented or handled as problematic. What is most telling about the show is the strength of the female parts and the humour they generate. In a sense, men have receded into the background. This is not women as a vehicle for or butt of men's humour, the women here generate their own humour. It is humour that circulates in a purely female domain and allows them to talk only about their interests, including their bodies and their sexuality. At the same time, it is not exclusionary in the way that male-dominated humour and sitcoms often are; there is a space for, accommodation of, and even an intersection of, male and female humour.

Ab Fab: *fabulously feminist?*

Written by comedian Jennifer Saunders (in production partnership with Dawn French), *Absolutely Fabulous* is a sitcom based around four female characters; Jennifer Saunders stars as the PR executive, Edina Monsoon, with Joanna Lumley as her best friend and sometime fashion editor Patsy Stone. Julia Sawahla is Edina's student daughter Saffron and June Whitfield plays Edina's batty mother. The show is set mainly in the 'designer' kitchen in Edina's large London house, equipped with the latest gadgets or in Edina's equally 'designer' office, although there are occasional trips to holiday destinations such as Marrakesh. First broadcast in 1992, the programme has gained a remarkably large following, not only in Britain but also internationally. In addition to critical acclaim, such as winning the 1993 British Film and Television Award for best comedy series, celebrity guest appearances by names such as Germaine Greer, Miranda Richardson and Elton John are testament to the kudos the show carries.

The show was conceptualized around the idea of a woman who refused to accept the need to behave 'appropriately', to grow up and move on from the hippie 1960s. The central character, Edina, is allegedly based around a very successful female PR executive. The PR work Edina does is part of the comedy of . the show, for what Edina does remains deliberately vague and apparently insubstantial. When there are substantive tasks, they mainly consist of developing ways of selling quite useless material objects (such as 'pop specs'). Mostly, she is making sure that she attends all the 'right' functions and is seen associating with the 'right' people. In this sense, the show can be seen as critique of the 1990s proliferation and vacuity of 'ideas' jobs such as those in the media, advertising and PR, filled with air kisses and hedonistic materialism. Edina is selfish, vacuous, narcissistic, but ultimately an anxious and empty reflection of the baby-boomer generation and the greed of the 'me-generation'. The PR industry is portrayed in *Ab Fab* as a shallow world where very little 'real work' is actually done and zero contribution made to society.[12] What other industry could employ a character like the weird and wacky assistant Bubble? What we may regard as actual work is quite peripheral to the real action in the show; what matters to both Edina and Patsy is their image, all the while drinking excessively and taking drugs. While Edina likes to regard herself as a modern 'career woman', Patsy makes no bones about her lack of career ambition. Indeed, one is never quite sure what Patsy actually does as a 'Fashion Editor'. Here work is represented as an afterthought, as at best a troublesome necessity, but not to be taken seriously and not to be allowed to interfere with more important things such as promoting self-image and enjoying oneself. This is a significant antidote to the rampant careerism, work intensification, 70-hour-week regimes of the 1990s and 2000s.

There are a number of reasons why *Ab Fab* has become so popular. One is the sheer hilarity of watching women behaving 'inappropriately', when they should be acting like 'responsible adults'. Common and orthodox values and expectations tell us that women in their forties should have 'proper' jobs and/or be 'good' mothers, who behave in a 'reasonable' manner, putting others' needs before their own. Edina and Patsy represent a rebellion against and transgression of these stereotypes and values, by acting selfishly, doing what they want when they want and making no attempt at being responsible or exhibiting reasonable behaviour. As a mother, Edina resists the contemporary blandishments to be a good mother and she is, in fact, a disastrous mother. Her daughter Saffron is a semi-traumatized, 'nerdy' person, who has had to become prematurely mature and assumes the reasonableness and maturity her mother avoids. There is, then, a role reversal, with the daughter being the mature person and looking after her immature and wayward mother.

As previously noted, the family is often central to sitcoms, but the family presented here is far from the nuclear norm. Edina is a single mother, Saffron's father is gay, Edina's mother is partially demented and the daughter assumes the role of 'mother'. The role and values reversal between Edina and Saffron is highly entertaining as we watch Edina's ineptitude at being a 'domesticated mother'. Interestingly, the fan culture that formed around *Ab Fab* would seem to indicate that many viewers identified with the 'bad mother' and therefore against the proper but dull daughter (Feuer, 2001). Kirkham and Skeggs (1998) argue that *Ab Fab* offers the viewer, and perhaps women particularly, the pleasures of transgressing feminine ideals of beauty, motherhood and proper behaviour. Both Edina and Patsy are what Rowe, K. (1995) terms 'unruly women', who are characterized by excess: excessive bodies (overweight or excessive clothing and hairstyles); excessive behaviours – drinking, smoking and drug taking; or simply exceeding the norms of femininity. *Ab Fab* is not the first television series to play on the theme of the 'unruly woman'. Rowe, K. (1995) first coined the term in reference to the US sitcom 'Roseanne', which made a comedy heroine of the unruly and irreverent mature woman. In some respects, Lucille Balls' character in *I Love Lucy* has also been considered somewhat in this vein (Gray, 1994) and demonstrates how far back but also disparate this form of female representation is. Lucy's role, however, is clearly more saccharine and less challenging to the status quo than Edina's.

Not only does *Ab Fab* present alternative ways of viewing women, but it also explores a number of social and economic contextual themes. According to Kirkham and Skeggs (1998), Edina and Patsy represent aspects of Thatcherism – emergent in the 1980s but seen by some as persisting into the 1990s and beyond – with their "bullish, selfish and hideously materialistic" behaviour (288). This dimension is, however, played against the remnants of their late 1960s/1970s laid-back and lazy lifestyle, represented, for example, by Buddhist chanting and the use of certain drugs synonymous with the 1960s and 1970s. The past and the neo-Thatcherite present are played off against each other to produce comedy and social comment while other points meld together in hilarious confusion.

The critique of the material values of Thatcherism, that some see as persisting under New Labour, is apparent in most episodes. A lack of collective values is arguably central to the Thatcherite project and its evangelical individualism, and this is accompanied by an economic rationalism in which business imperatives are paramount and the pursuit of profit a valourized instrumental goal. The emphasis on profits at all costs is taken to its limits in *Ab Fab* in the Romania baby episode, where Edina imports Romanian babies and works on the sales angles available as if they were simply another commodity. This lack of values, this corrosion of ethics, values and community is made explicit against the characterization of the daughter Saffron, who is used to represent a caring 1990s student, into ecology and social issues. "Mum", Saffron says in a moment of exasperation, "people don't get more interesting the more money you spend".

The current preoccupation with health and care of the body and self – the project of the self[13] – and its association with a healthy labour force has been associated with Thatcherism too. Whilst Edina is obsessed with her image and her body, this has not been converted into a genuine health and well-being drive except for occasional forays because of fashionable trends. Indeed, in general, the healthy body mantra is ridiculed and subverted by the excessive drinking and drug taking of Edina and Patsy. A further neo-Thatcherite and neo-colonial value exposed in the programme is the use of ethnic objects to signify distinctive taste and thus a lifestyle. The delight in 'Third World chic' and global commodification not only suggests that nothing is sacred from capitalism, but also that nothing is sacred from comedy. The following lines by Edina to Saffron illustrate this point:

> I got a load of those lip plates from dead Amazonian Indians. I thought they could be ashtrays. (To Saffron) Don't look at me like that, we can take the

lips off. Lots of kitchen pots and pans from Somalia. They don't need them, they've got no food to eat. But best news of all, you know all the villages that were deserted by the Kurds ... *I've* got the franchise.

There is a satire on the twin locations of the 'baby-boomer' generation, on the one hand carrying the baggage of the liberations of the 1960s forwards, but on the other, confronting the materialism of the 'project-me' ethos of 1990s Britain. Much of the humour resides in the tensions generated in that confluence. There is also a location with respect to feminism, which is to some extent also satirized. On the one hand, the show focuses on women and their independence, and the men are typically represented as weak, flawed or peripheral in some sense. The emphasis in the show on women as best friends, the flirtations with lesbianism, the way in which Edina and Patsy pursue their own goals, all seem to stem from feminist positions of independence and female worth. On the other hand, the vacuity and concern with image, including obsessions with body image, are antithetical to most feminist positions. Feminism, like other issues within *Ab Fab*, is handled through contradiction and contrast. It is a complexity that enables the obsession with fashion and image to be offered as both a source of identification for women and also a site for mockery and critique.

It could be argued that the programme offers certain viewers the satisfaction of looking down on vulgar hedonism, as Edina and Patsy open up for ridicule the vacuity and narcissism of the nouveau rich and the nouveau vogue. However, as Kirkham and Skeggs (1998) note, many viewers may not have access to this location of cultural critique and so not be in a position to make this reading. As Patsy and Edina playfully try to pass as knowing, consuming, global bourgeoisie and as successful, cultured women, they poke fun at those around them of similar ilk, but do sometimes laugh at themselves. But the comedy of all this depends on whether the audience is positioned to read their pretensions and passings as ironic. While *Ab Fab* can be understood as a critique of both greed and commodification of 1990s neo-Thatcherite politico-social values, and a celebration of unruly women, these critiques only work if the objects, identities and behaviours used in making the critique are still not seen as desirable by those not privileged enough to abandon them. The programme may, in fact, serve to reproduce the very desires and longings it mocks and works against. The parody also works in another way: *Ab Fab* is hyped by the very world it satirizes, as seen by the number of celebrities seeking to make guest appearances on the programme.

Changing dimensions of gender

This chapter has examined the intersection of class and gender in work-related settings, using British sitcoms as a site for the representation of such issues. It has done so by discussing a sample of work-related sitcoms that span more than five decades, and so, part of the aim was to look at shifts in representation of these issues in popular culture as well as, more speculatively, to see if that parallels or reflects changes in society at large. There have been shifts in the nature, style, narrative structure, characterization and themes of the sitcoms, and that is not surprising. There are also some commonalities that traverse the time period. Thus, the structure of class relations has shifted over time and that is reflected in the representation of the issues in the sitcoms, it is also true to say that class and class relations continue to inform the comedy and remain a preoccupation of this area of popular culture. Gender relations and politics have also shifted over time. The female-dominant comedies of *dinnerladies* and *Ab Fab* reflect the increased representation of women in popular culture and reflect increased presence and visibility in the public domain in society in general. However, it needs to be noted that *The Rag Trade* gave a similar focus to females and female humour back in the 1950s. What is different is the self-parody and irony as well as the foregrounding of certain themes such as female sexuality and the subversion of norms and expectations of proper behaviour.

It has been typically argued in the literature that representations of gender relations in British sitcoms have produced rather limited characterizations of women and that this has often taken sexist and misogynistic forms with a typical gender bias in the representation of gender relations. However, our analysis of a sample of British sitcoms across more than 50 years in fact reveals significant variation in gendered portrayals and a more nuanced treatment of gender politics than is typically supposed or than has been suggested. Indeed, the representation of these issues has often been more subtle and nuanced in British sitcoms than it has in other media, including the academic literature in management and organization studies. More recent sitcoms clearly show varied and nuanced representations of women and gender relations, but we have argued, and we hope have demonstrated, that earlier sitcoms also realized female characterizations that were not confined to simplistic categorizations such as asexual harridans or 'ditsy blondes', simply there to enhance the eccentricity of the male characters. As shown in such programmes as *The Rag Trade* and *dinnerladies*, sitcoms do produce female characters that go beyond the stereotypes, and can themselves be considered as eccentric. It is also the case that female characters have, across the time frame, been the centre of the humour, have influence, or even domination, over the male characters, and have been able to explore their own identities and sexualities within the genre. These characterizations are certainly not the one-dimensional charters we might have been led to believe they are. In this sense, popular culture representations of gender relations and politics, as manifest in sitcoms, offer a more nuanced and sophisticated treatment than is apparent in other domains and offer insights and dynamics of value and relevance to organization studies.

The representation of men and of masculinity has also exhibited complexity that defies simple categorizations and stereotypes. In terms of gender relations, although men have ostensibly been positioned in dominant positions and in hierarchical roles that seem suggestive of a reproduction of the structures of patriarchy, they are, on closer scrutiny, often represented in far more nuanced and, indeed, vulnerable ways than this. Managers, in particular, have been almost uniformly represented negatively, as inept, amateurish or in some other way flawed. In broader terms, men, whilst at one level appearing to be powerful and in control, are, in British sitcoms, often portrayed as weak and often very dependent on women. In some cases, this extends to a virtual infantilism and in others to an emasculation wherein their sexuality is threatened, muted or cuckolded, sometimes in the face of a more assertive and aggressive sexuality-exhibited female counterparts. Rather than macho figures with strength and power who exploit and dominate women, men are often represented as weak, dependent and rather pathetic.

In terms of class relations, however, our analysis shows that most often, extant class structures remain unchallenged in any radical sense, and essentially the comedy supports the status quo – if only by default. This is particularly noteworthy in the treatment of those characters who sought to transgress or transcend class origins. Such transgressions are usually derided and this, in a sense, serves to reinforce the value of existing class locations. At the same time, being authentic with respect to one's class is valourized, further reinforcing the status quo ante. In a workplace context, there may be some celebration of working class culture, and that has some cultural value and a counterpoint to dominance regimes in society, but there is not a trenchant critique of workplace relations based on class, nor much critique of capitalist exploitation. Any 'revolt' is more in the form of a localized attack on management and management ethos, practices and language, as to some extent in *dinnerladies.*

Therefore, while class ideology or politics is not directly challenged, gender relations are presented in a more complex and nuanced manner than has been suggested. There has always been what can be termed 'strong' female characters that are anything but 'wallpaper' to the action, or vehicles for male humour. Interestingly, male characters and masculinity are represented in sitcoms in more interesting and challenging ways than is typically acknowledged. This treatment of masculinity needs to be surfaced, discussed and the implications drawn for masculinities in organizational contexts where it remains understudied.

7 The reception of McDonald's in sociology and television animation

McDonald's restaurants are one of the twentieth century's most remarkable business and cultural phenomena – mammoth in size, global in reach, ubiquitous in presence and massive in popularity, McDonald's occupies a central place in the lives of many people across the world. This phenomenon has also generated considerable reaction in the sociological study of organizations and culture, most particularly in George Ritzer's (1996, 1998, 2004) critical evaluation and interpolation of the notion of McDonaldization.

For Ritzer, McDonaldization is "the process by which the principles of fast food restaurants are coming to dominate more and more sectors of American society as well as of the rest of the world" (Ritzer, 2004: 1) – these principles being efficiency, calculability, predictability and control though non-human technology. For critics like Ritzer, McDonald's and McDonaldization represent new forces for the homogenization of culture (Schlosser, 2001) – forces that are on a global scale and that are taking the place of the crusaders and politicians of the past (Belk, 1996). Ritzer's critique of the McDonald's rationalization process resonates with what others perceive to be pervasive disquiet at the prospect of an increasingly conformist and homogeneous world culture (Kellner, 1999: 188). In this respect, the McDonaldization thesis represents a continuation of the convergence debate that began in the 1960s (Harbison and Myers, 1959; Webber, 1969).

The debates surrounding McDonald's and McDonaldization present an important discussion of the role of organizations in society and their effects on culture. In this chapter, we turn to popular culture to argue that McDonald's is not as culturally monolithic as some proponents of McDonaldization thesis might suggest. Further, we contest the positioning of culture's recipients as dupes – largely uncritical and passive receptors of the intended workings of that cultural practice. To do so, we provide a discussion of various representations of McDonald's and related phenomena *within* popular culture – specifically within three animated television comedies from the 1990s: *Beavis and Butt-head*, *The Simpsons* and *South Park*. This seeks to show how popular culture contains a range of representations pertaining to McDonald's and related phenomena that demonstrate that within popular culture itself there exists different, yet equally compelling critical perspectives on McDonald's and related phenomena. Our argument is that the critique suggested by television animation cartoon shows that we will review are more reflexive and better anchored to current socio-economic and cultural realities and sensitivities. They eschew the sense of cultural elitism that elevates the critics of McDonaldization as being able to offer a privileged, unreflexive and extra-cultural perspective on culture. We thus explore some specific examples of how popular culture contains within itself the seeds of and resources for cogent critique of other cultural phenomena associated with business organizations: a kind of auto-critique.

McDonald's, McDonaldization and culture

Ritzer (1996, 1998, 2004) suggests that McDonald's has become more and more deeply ingrained into US and international culture. He uses the term *McDonaldization* to refer to how the production and consumption patterns associated with fast-food restaurants have become a model for many other production–consumption sectors, and increasingly so on a global basis (Ritzer, 2004: 1). He argues that the sectors so influenced include education, work, health care, travel and "virtually every other aspect of society" (2). For Ritzer, this process is deeply problematic as it "involves a wide range of irrationalities, especially dehumanization and homogenization" (vii). Thus, whilst the processes and practices involved are not restricted to McDonald's per se, McDonald's is seen as the most important manifestation of the globally pervasive neo-Weberian rationalization that Ritzer identifies. For Ritzer, McDonaldization is based on four principles:

- Efficiency: emphasis on "things like efficiency and profit maximization ... [and] little space for human values such as love or community" (Ritzer, 1998: 24)
- Calculability: The emphasis on "things that can be quantified" rather than on quality
- Predictability: Production of goods and services that are "the same from one time or place to another" (107)
- Control Through Non-Human Technology: Control of employees through technology rather than direct management, where such technologies "control employees, deskill jobs and ultimately replace people with machines" (108)

It is these principles and associated technologies, Ritzer claims, which entail that McDonaldization should be regarded as a 'threat' to "the entire cultural complex of many societies" (8). The hyperbole notwithstanding, the sentiment echoes the more general concern expressed by others that McDonald's problematically represents the homogenization of culture (Schlosser, 2001). Further, it suggests that "with Ronald McDonald leading the way, multinational consumer goods corporations are now breaking down international boundaries that have withstood the armies, missionaries, and crusaders of the past" (Belk, 1996: 25). Some even go as far as to say that "any truly global corporation exhibits most, if not all, of the tendencies of McDonaldization" (Peterson, 2006: 65). Such perspectives articulate "people's fears of increased conformity, loss of freedom and diversity, domination by external societal forces bound up with the evolution of modern societies" (Kellner, 1999: 194). Ritzer's analysis trades in the presumed zeitgeist of hapless dupes hopelessly locked into pointless patterns of production and consumption about which they fail to reflect and over which they have no control.

In his discussion, Ritzer rightly recognizes that McDonald's occupies a central place in American popular culture and acknowledges that "fast-food restaurants also play symbolic roles on television programs and in the movies" (Ritzer, 2004: 5). Elsewhere, he suggests that it would be valuable to critically explore McDonald's in terms of its relationship with, among other things, the media, culture, cultural imperialism and processes of resistance, and maintains that he would like to see "more scholarly attention devoted to resisting the process [of McDonaldization]" (Ritzer, 1999: 254). Despite this, Ritzer remains both pessimistic and nostalgic. He envisages McDonaldization as being like a deterministic Weberian iron cage that can become "an inhuman system that controls everyone, leaders included. With no people to appeal to, oppose, or overthrow in their efforts to escape, people may become even more hopelessly imprisoned" (Ritzer, 1996: 143). Thus for Ritzer, modern consumer capitalism is all enveloping; a space from which nothing can escape. He includes the cultural industries – of which the fast-food business is a component – within this capitalistic monolith. Ritzer appears to see that industry as an acute exemplar and to believe that "the culture industry is a seamless web in which all forms of resistance and all possibilities of change – being programmed by the system itself – are ultimately reified" (Zayani, 1997: 632). Even worse, it has even been suggested that McDonaldization has a "deleterious effect on culture" (Peterson, 2006: 85). It is this view in particular that we challenge in this chapter by showing that the 'culture industry' has *within itself* the resources for a very effective critique of certain aspects of consumer capitalism. That it comes from within does not devalue the critique – moreover, it might be argued that there is no other location available except for a falsely claimed externally neutral position in the academy. We thus acknowledge the possibility that "capitalism has not only a tendency to envelop the entirety of the social body, but also a proclivity to develop dysfunctionalities, create deficiencies, provoke deviations, and generate counter-processes that are more tendentious than Ritzer is willing to admit" (Zayani, 1997: 633).

There have been other forms of critique of the McDonaldization thesis and attempts to show how it might be resisted (see Smart, 1999), but it is our contention that there is additional merit in looking at how, within popular culture and within the machinations of consumer capitalism itself, representations of resistance, parody and alternatives have been constructed and to bring these into comparison with more sociologically orthodox critiques. We regard this as important as we fear that 'orthodox' sociological critiques of phenomena like

McDonald's – such as Ritzer's – echo earlier analyses of popular culture that paint a unremittingly "bleak cultural and political landscape" (James, 1998: 155). Thus, we would concur with James' summary of Ritzer's analysis as being "overly pessimistic and simplistic, falling too squarely in the camp of the old, elite, mass culture critics and failing to give adequate weight to the cultural aspects of McDonald's as a site for the active construction of meaning" (160).

Although it can be argued that Ronald McDonald, the Marlboro man and Mickey Mouse provide consumers with characters in a "sanitized version of reality, cleansed of strife, world problems, dirt, prejudice, exploitation or other problems of everyday life" (Belk, 1996: 23), these saccharine and idealized characters are not the only media characters that have global appeal. The same sanitized and wholesome characterization cannot be unproblematically associated with the likes of Bart Simpson, Krusty the Clown (from *The Simpsons*), Beavis, Butt-head (from MTV's *Beavis and Butt-head*) or the Stan, Cartman, Kyle and Kenny characters (from *South Park*). As we hope to demonstrate by discussing each of these examples of television animation, the totalization of culture can only be achieved with one eye closed, and that within popular and mass culture there exists an auto-critique to rival the critique of the most serious sociologist. This chapter is thus organized into three central parts as follows:

- An alternate consideration of the McDonaldized labour process, employment engagement and consumption patterns as represented in *Beavis and Butt-head*, with particular reference to the 'Burger World' restaurant.
- The critique of consumer capitalism found in *The Simpsons*, with particular reference to the 'cartoon a clef' (Rhodes, 2002) characterization of Krusty the Clown (Ronald McDonald?) and his hamburger restaurants 'Krusty Burger'.
- The nuanced critique of the cultural invasion process associated with the encroachment of multinational corporate cultures – with their accompanying consumer imperatives – into existing and localized cultural contexts, as represented in *South Park*, with a particular reference to the Starbucks coffee chain (Rhodes, 2002).

In selecting the animated cartoon as a locus of critique and counterpoint to sociological discussions of McDonald's, we are particularly making use of those forms of animation whose narratives draw on long-standing traditions of the 'carnivalesque' (Bakhtin, 1984a, 1984b). This cultural tradition is one where comedy and parody are used to oppose and destabilize official views of reality. Following Bakhtin, the carnival is a site which brings to life an inside-out view of the world through an excessive parody of non-carnival life through travesties, humiliations, profanity and the economic crowning and uncrowning of kings. Specifically, carnival is seen as a seepage and effluence out of the dominant and orthodox world. Emanating from within that world, the carnival escapes the bounds of reason and order and circulates as a parodying alterity – a disturbed and disturbing mirror to the mainstream, a transgressive celebration, a dark inversion.

Bakhtin and others who have followed him see the carnivalesque as a valid and powerful mode of social critique which offers "an ongoing challenge, to the narrowly conceived forms of reason of the 'public sphere', as well as to modernism desiring to legislate, in an equally imperial way, single standards for all culture" (Docker, 1994: 283–4). Contemporary animated film has been a significant site for such carnivalesque representations of 'official' culture (Rhodes, 2001a, 2002) that does not need to rely on the rationality, logic or consistency that might be expected from a more orthodox media (Lindvall and Melton, 1997). This enables a more playful, creative and sometimes more transgressive critique to be enacted. It is for these reasons that cartoons (both animated and still) can be seen to provide an important reflection on the society of our time and should not always be considered as the superficial and insubstantial media that is sometimes assumed (Kafner, 1997).

Beavis and Butt-head and the McDonaldized labour process

Beavis and Butt-head was a half-hour television cartoon that aired on MTV between 1993 and 1997 (although re-runs are still being played and new DVD releases have continued through to 2006). The show features two 13-year-old boys who spend time watching videos on MTV and engaging in various inane misadventures – usually involving "random destructiveness, defiance of school authority and [futile] attempts to score with chicks" (Morrow, 1999: 31). Beavis and Butt-head have been accused of many ills – from inciting children to light fires, to reflecting the worst characteristics of contemporary American youth. In the USA, they have featured prominently in congressional hearings on television violence (McConnell, 1994) and have been described by the US National Coalition on Television Violence as "Sesame Street for sociopaths" (cited in Bowman, 1993). Such 'moral panics' perhaps fail to recognize the irony with which the show treats its material – an irony directed at, for example the school system, political correctness, adults and, indeed, the stupidity of youths as represented by Beavis and Butt-head (Morrow, 1999). The show is not inviting viewers to agree with the moronic, inane and bigoted opinions that its characters profess, but rather to reflect on a society that creates and nourishes them. Of relevance to our discussion here is the fact that one such target for the show's critical irony is the iconic fast-food restaurant. Beavis and Butt-head work at a fast-food hamburger restaurant called *Burger World*. This restaurant is a very thinly disguised representation of McDonald's – not only are the décor, uniforms and product range similar, but the company's logo is a large W: looking suspiciously like an inverted form of McDonald's M-shaped golden arches.

Ritzer (1998) notes that one characteristic of fast-food restaurants is their reliance on low-paid, part-time, teenage employees who occupy what he calls 'McJobs'. These jobs are said to require little or no skill and to be both rationalized and de-humanizing. He thus proposes that people who work in such jobs are positioned "human robots" (60) who are expected to engage in routinized actions and scripted interactions as dictated by management. Beavis and Butt-head are ironic representations of the vast number of American youths who occupy such McJobs – and of youths so positioned in other cultures around the world. In one sense, Beavis and Butt-head are exactly the type of employees that Ritzer stereotypes. In contrast, however, as we shall see, they do not appear to be as over-determined as Ritzer (1998: 62) suggests when he proposes that workers simply "behave in accordance with the dictates of those [McDonaldized] structures". Beavis and Butt-head pay testament to the idea that the deterministic effects of work regimes and the expectations of specific behaviours and interactions are insufficient to evacuate the site of all possibility of alternative, counter or resisting behaviours. We acknowledge that the aspiration behind the design of such work regimes may be that the job occupant fully internalizes and believes in what is expected of them. However, this does not mean that there are any grounds for assuming that this is a necessary consequence or that there is no sense of agency or resistance on the part of workers.

Contrary to the implications of Ritzer's analysis,[1] as employees of Burger World, Beavis and Butt-head do not display the tendencies for self-regulation and obedience to internalized rules. For example, these two characters have something of a fascination with the deep-fryer in Burger World, and this is part of their widespread and ongoing infatuation with 'non-human technology'. In one episode (Burger World, Episode No. 17, first aired in 1993), they find an opportunity to subvert the intended functionality of this technology. They find it amusing to deep-fry a mouse and some insects and to serve them to a customer as a 'mouse burger and French flies'.

At another time, whilst Beavis and Butt-head apparently follow the dictates of the official procedures to change the oil in the fryer periodically, they undermine such formal expectations by procuring regular motor oil from a nearby gas station and use it to fill the deep-fryer. In the episode Citizens Arrest (Episode No. 168, first aired on February 28, 1997), the two stop an attempted robbery at Burger World. Filled with bravado, the boys proceed to try to arrest all of the customers they can find. There are innumerable other examples of them failing to adhere to the rules or subverting the regime such as: falling asleep on the job and dreaming of being rock stars (The Butt-head Experience, Episode No. 27, first aired on June 7, 1993); deliberately passing on an infection to Burger World customers by infecting the burgers (Tainted Meat, Episode No. 102, first aired on December 29, 1994); and repeatedly suggesting that 'customers suck'.

Clearly, these two employees have not been fully and effectively McDonaldized – and it is immaterial whether the failure to so indoctrinate them is due to wilful resistance or sheer stupidity. The interpretation of the McDonaldization process represented here is different to that promulgated by Ritzer. Where he seems to attribute ultimate and monolithic efficacy to the regimes of indoctrination and control that make employees into passive and helpless dupes, this interpretation from within popular culture is of a flawed and fallible process in which employees are agents of disobedience, subversion and parody.

The episode *Vaya Con Cornholio* (Episode No. 158, first aired on January 26, 1997) represents a different, but equally powerful critique of McDonaldization.[2]

In this episode, Beavis decides to 'chug' Burger World's new product 'Volt Cola'. The effects of the stimulants lead Beavis to pull his shirt over his head and become transformed into his alter ego Cornholio (who regularly features when Beavis has a caffeine or sugar 'spaz attack'). As Cornholio, Beavis becomes even more puerile and nonsensical than his normal self. In a bad Spanish accent, he repeats "I am Cornholio: I need T.P for my bunghole." Cornholio also appears in the acclaimed episode 'The Great Cornholio' (Episode No. 86, first aired on July 15, 1994). Here, he eats 27 chocolate bars and drinks six cans of root-beer and, when transformed into Cornholio, his already anti-social, anti-authoritarian behaviour is amplified. When asked to sit down by his teacher in class, he responds "Are you threatening me? I AM CORNHOLIO!" and then walks out of the classroom. He proceeds to the girls' bathroom and issues the demand "I am Cornholio!!! ... I need T.P. for my bunghole!! ... COME OUT WITH YOUR PANTS DOWN!!!" He is finally apprehended and taken to McVicker's, the school principal, office.

McVICKER: Uh ... look! I don't know what your problem is ... but I simply cannot have students wandering the hallways during class, interrupting other classes and giving prophesies of a great plague.

BEAVIS: Oh ... yeah. Sorry 'bout that

McVICKER: Wait! What was that? Did you just say you were sorry?

BEAVIS: Ummmmmmmmmm ... ummmmmmmmmm

McVICKER: You did! You just said you were sorry. Uh ... didn't you?

BEAVIS: Uhhhh ... yeah. Heh heh ...

McVICKER: You see! I knew it. You kids have never apologized to me once! Maybe this is a new day for you. Maybe punishment isn't the answer! I'm gonna let you go. Ya know ... I'm actually proud of you today. Take some candy with you ...

SECRETARY: Now, you're going right back to class, right Beavis?

BEAVIS: Yeah ... uhhhhh ... no. NO! I must get T.P. for my bunghole! I am the great Cornholio!!! Heh heh. ... Heh heh

SECRETARY: Do you need a hall pass?

BEAVIS: Are you threatening me? Heh heh ... yeah! I need no hall pass. I heed holio for my bunghole! I am the great Cornholio! I have no bunghole! BUNGHOLEEEEEOOOOOO! I need T.P. for my bunghole! We are without bungholes.

Representations such as this play back the negative image of youth that orthodox culture and society often construct. At one level, it portrays Beavis and, by extension, modern youth of his ilk as puerile – stupid even – rebellious, out of control and unable to operate in a socially normal and responsible manner. However, there are layers in the representation. On another reading, Beavis is an extreme carnivalized exaggeration of contemporary American youth – complete with the trademark carnival characteristics of exaggeration and comic reference to the 'lower body strata' (Bakhtin, 1984a). The critical turn offered in the episode is located in the fact that the extremes of behaviour exhibited by Beavis are brought about by him being seduced by the consumptive pleasures of McDonald's-type products with their drug-like qualities. It is the very bastions of contemporary consumer capitalism that are responsible for producing the personas and behaviours that the same orthodoxy bleats about and disparages as a cultural aberration. The show thus contains a reflexive critique of contemporary culture that mirrors back to the orthodoxy its own negative constructions of youth and teenage culture and can be used to interrogate social relationships and stereotypes (Fisher, 1997).

In asking why *Beavis and Butt-head* are so compelling, it has been suggested that "it may be that the part-fantasy, part-reality world that they inhabit is closer to the world we carry round in our heads, the images which guide our actions, than we care to admit" (Linstead, 2000: 63). This, of course, is not to promote Beavis or Butt-head as role models or as realistic representations. They are "crudely drawn cartoon adolescents ... [they] ... are neither intelligent nor glamorous nor attractive. To be blunt about it, they are a pair of scrawny, pencil-necked nerds" (Gardner, 1994: 60). But their very unattractiveness is part of the point. *Beavis and Butt-head* is a 'savage parody' of youth culture (McConnell, 1994) that challenges the view of McDonald's and McDonaldization as determining phenomena, producers of happy hamburgers, happy workers and happy customers. This offers a critique beyond the Ritzeresque which sees McDonaldization as an ineluctable process that brainwashes and pacifies the worker and consumer alike into mindless compliance. It shows youth engaged in McDonald's as knowingly disobedient and as subversive of the labour process regime and the consumption experience. It goes further still and offers a reflexive parody of a supposedly obnoxious youth culture that the society itself has produced. Beavis and Butt-head's behaviour contains an "implicit critique of the couch-potato mind-set ... severe in its condemnation of everything Beavis and Butt-head represent" (McConnell, 1994: 30). Where the critics of McDonaldization, such as Ritzer, appear both pessimistic and nostalgic, Beavis and Butt-head appear irrational and anarchic. They have the advantage of the jester in that because they are young, stupid and ugly, they are allowed to speak the truth because nobody cares what they say (Young, 1993).

The Simpsons, Krusty the Klown and consumer society

On air since 1990, *The Simpsons* is America's longest running television situation comedy. It airs in more than 60 countries and in 1999 was proclaimed by Time magazine as the best television show of the century. Its success, however, is not as a Saturday-morning cartoon watched exclusively by children – *The Simpsons* airs in a prime-time slot (8:00 p.m. in the United States) and, as such, draws in significant revenues from advertisers. Further, the merchandising machine that uses *The Simpsons* to sell a variety of products is also significant. This includes board games, trading cards, computer games, soft toys, electronic toys, replica figures, food, confectionary, apparel, clothing, books, comic books,

CDs and various novelty items. Looking at *The Simpsons* this way seems to confirm some of Ritzer's observations about the "fusion of consumption and entertainment" (Ritzer, 1998: 91). His argument is that contemporary society has witnessed the development of a new means of consumption which lead "consumers to consume in ways that are most advantageous and most profitable to manufacturers and sellers" (119) – particularly goods and services that consumers do not need or want. He thus suggests that there has been a shift in contemporary capitalism from the exploitation of workers to the exploitation of consumers. Taking what has become a common line of cultural critique, Ritzer agrees with Postman (1987) that we are "amusing ourselves to [cultural] death". *The Simpsons* seem to be wrapped up in this process of entertainment and consumption. Perhaps one might say that we are witnessing a *Simpsonization* of consumption?[3] This seems at odds, however, with *The Simpsons'* long pedigree of breaking the established 'rules', experimenting with subjects traditionally taboo for an animated series (Cohen, 1998) and satirizing the diverse social and political norms that define American culture (Korte, 1997; Marc, 1998) and in particular, work and organizations (Rhodes, 2001a; Rhodes and Pullen, 2007).

So, what does the text of *The Simpsons* have to say about this consumerism? To address this question, we focus specifically on a common sub-plot of the show – the business dealings of a character in *The Simpsons* known as *Krusty the Klown*. Krusty is a merchandizing madman. His core business consists of the Krusty Burger fast-food chain and the *Krusty the Klown* kids television show. He also has lines in Krusty brand vitamins (which give children rapid heart beats), Krusty Kalculators (which do not have a seven or an eight), Krusty brand pork products, a Krusty autobiography (notoriously lacking in veracity), a Krusty Kamp summer camp for kids, Krusty brand imitation gruel and Krusty's home pregnancy test (with the warning 'May cause birth defects'). He even has a series of Krusty legal forms – including a pre-made endorsement contract.[4] Further, Krusty is a smoker, a gambler, a drinker and a womanizer with mob connections. Of specific relevance to our discussion here, Krusty's fast-food outlet Krusty Burger is a direct parody of McDonald's.

Ritzer comments that:

> consumers always possess the capacity to refuse the new means of consumption, or to resist consuming […] however, these means are structured in a way that people are lured into them and, once in them, they find it extremely difficult not to consume
>
> (120)

In *The Simpsons*, a similar point is taken up, especially in terms of the relationship between consumption and children. For example, Bart Simpson, the ten-year-old underachiever who is one of the show's main characters, is a devoted fan of everything Krusty. He says himself that "He's my idol. I've based my whole life on his teachings" (cited in Richmond and Coffman, 1997: 28). The kids in *The Simpsons* are bombarded with Krusty culture from all directions –

they eat at his restaurant, they watch his television show, they buy his toys – all aspects of their cultural life is somehow Krusty related. Even baby Maggie sucks a dummy with Krusty's image on it. Such processes of identification are closely related to the sign systems that fast-food restaurants effect in an attempt to retain customer relationships through brand loyalty. Ritzer (1998) takes this further when he generalizes:

> As significant and highly visible sponsors, the fast food restaurants play a key role in the proliferation of signs by the media [...] in so doing, they contribute to the perception that everything is available for communication, signification, banalization, commercialization and consumption
>
> (125)

The issues of identification, sponsorship and the proliferation and entangle-ment of values are taken up in *The Simpsons'* episode 'Lisa's First Word' (Pro-duction Code 9F09, original air date December 17, 1992). Take the following scene where Krusty is filming a television commercial for his Olympic Krusty Burger in a flashback to 1984[5]:

KRUSTY: (on TV): Heyyy, kids! Summer's just around the corner, and Krusty Burger is the official meat-flavored sandwich of the 1984 Olympics!
(The scene switches to the studio where Krusty is filming the ad.)
CREW MEMBER: And, cut!
KRUSTY: Bleh! (He spits out the burger.) Oh, I almost swallowed some of the juice. (He takes a drink from his flask.) Uhhhh, I'll be tasting that for weeks.
ACCOUNTANT: Great spot, K. C.
KRUSTY: Put a sock in it, preppy. How much are these free burgers gonna cost me?
ACCOUNTANT: Not to worry, Mr. K. We've rigged the cards: they're all in events that Communists never lose.
KRUSTY: I like, I like.
WOMAN: This just came over the wires, Big K.
KRUSTY: [reads] Uh-huh. Soviet boycott. U.S. unopposed in most events. How does this affect our giveaway?
ACCOUNTANT: Let's see. [calculates] You personally stand to lose $44 million.

Krusty's failed attempt to align his meat-flavoured foods (which he himself will not eat) with a high-profile sporting event in order to market his restaur-ants to children is not a novel marketing ploy, but one that does acknowledge certain aspects of McDonaldized consumption. It also confirms Ritzer's point that "The new means of consumption are characterized, and to a very high degree, by simulacra [...] the entire distinction between the simulated and the real is lost" (Ritzer, 1998: 121). Of course in Krusty's case, however, in car-nivalesque style, the results are not as expected – after all, this is designed to be funny and the humour is engaging because it enables us to laugh at the crudeness of how such marketing works. One does not need to be trained in sociology to understand what is happening – one merely needs a sense of humour.

A key feature of the critique embedded in *The Simpsons* is its ironic and self-reflexive representation of the culture of which it is a part. As well as pointing to the effects of commercialized consumption, *The Simpsons* also alerts us to the nature of the reactionary backlash against such culture. An example of this can be found in the episode 'Krusty Gets Busted' (Production code 7G12, original air date 29 April 1990).[6] This episode sees Krusty framed for a robbery at the local convenience store – the Kwik-E-Mart. With his arrest broadcast on the television, the children of Springfield are devastated. As Bart stares sadly at the poster of Krusty on his bedroom wall, he pulls the string on his Krusty doll. It says: "You're my best friend ... Buy my cereal! Wuh-huh-huh-huh!" Meanwhile, Krusty is being referred to in the press as 'The Clown Prince of Corruption' and the town's people of Springfield are gathered together for a public burning of all Krusty-related merchandizing because they 'were inspired by an insane criminal genius'. Even souvenir stores are taking advantage of the situation by selling Krusty dolls with the marketing slogan of 'Buy 'em an' burn 'em!' Eventually, Krusty is found to be innocent. What we see from such examples is that *The Simpsons* provides a critique of commercialization and culture that is both located within that culture and that, through parody, is able to be critical of contemporary culture as well as to be critical of that critique. Further, *The Simpsons* does not exclude itself from this process – in talking to Krusty about the poor-quality nature of his merchandizing, Bart once remarked "... I'd never lend my name to an inferior product"[7] – a clearly ironic reference to the massive about of merchandizing that does in fact bear Bart's name.

A critique of commercialization can also be discerned in the episode 'The Last Temptation of Krust' (Production code 5F10, original air date August 15, 2000).[8] This episode elaborates the goings on when Krusty decides to drop his traditional slapstick in favour of emulating American alternative comedians like Bobcat Goldthwait and Janeane Garofalo. His new jokes are quite different, in fact anti-commercial: "And all I keep seeing is dead celebrities hawking products! You've got poor old Vincent Price floating around in a toilet keg telling me about the horrors of an unfresh bowl!" He even burns a dollar bill on stage so that "those fatcats won't get their grave robbing hands on it". The show clearly makes a comment of the social norms surrounding commercialism and 'authenticity'. The show also features the character of American talk-show host Jay Leno.[9] As he says to Krusty:

> I'm proud of you Krusty, oh sure, I've got material success, my own show, acres of cars, a nice microwave oven. But you're out on the edge, you're doing it for sheer thrill. If I wasn't afraid of clowns, I'd give you a big hug.

Given the success of his new humour, Krusty is eventually discovered by two advertising executives. When they offer him a deal to promote a new car, he replies: "Krusty's not for sale [...] take your corporate blood wagon and get the hell out!" Eventually, Krusty does sell out and he's back to his old self. The twin temptations of 'selling out' to consumerism and defining oneself against consumption are brought into stark relief. It seems that in Krusty's case, both possible identity positions are related to consumerism – its pervasiveness is apparent. To conclude with a comment by Krusty himself: "There's nothing those Madison Avenue grave robbers won't do to get us to buy their crap!"

South Park and cultural invasion

In addition to its critique of the nature and effects of contemporary forms of consumption, McDonaldization also addresses other cultural concerns. Ritzer proposes that, as a 'new American menace', McDonaldization is nothing less than a global invasion, a new form of cultural imperialism "spearheaded by such 'leaders' of American society as Mickey Mouse, Madonna and her most recent MTV video, the announcers on CNN and, most importantly from my point of view, clowns like Ronald McDonald" (Ritzer, 1998: 72). Ritzer sees the almost deterministic march of a monolithic process that threatens to envelop the globe in a uniform and debased cultural blanket. In contrast to such morbid fears, we ask therefore what might be a different cultural response to McDonaldization and the assumed cultural imperialism? To address this question, we turn to our third and final animated cartoon, *South Park*. This is a half-hour prime-time television show that has been on air since 1997 and tells the story of four children's experience of growing up in the fictitious Colorado town of South Park. This is not a story, however, of an idyllic childhood in American suburbia; it is a direct parody of such lifestyles as idealized in most American situation comedies.

A particular episode of *South Park* ('Gnomes', first aired on December 16, 1998) enables us to open up a space to explore an alternative critique of the global imperialism of mass consumerism (see Rhodes, 2002). The episode starts with the boys being asked to develop a presentation to their school board on a topic of their choice but related to local news. The study group for the assignment includes the usual gang of Stan, Kyle, Eric and Kenny, plus Tweek. Tweek is the son of the owner of South Park's coffee shop – a jittery kid, who is said to suffer from Attention Deficit Disorder, but whose behaviour is suspiciously like that of a child who has drunk far too much coffee. Tweek convinces the others to do their report on the underpants gnomes, who he describes as "the little guys that come into your room real late, late at night and steal your underpants". Earlier that day, Tweek's father meets John Poston from Harbuck's coffee corporation (a thin disguise for the coffee retailer Starbucks) who offers him $500,000 to buy out his store. When he refuses to sell, Poston tells him that he will open his Harbuck's store immediately next door to Tweek's coffee shop and ruin his business. Reflecting on how "the corporate machine is ruining America", Mr Tweek hatches a plan to get the boys to write their report about corporate takeovers. In the end, he writes the report himself and, having been unable to locate the underpants gnomes, the boys agree to present it.

The following day, they present the 'Tweek report' to the school board. It contains elements such as the following: "As the voluminous corporate automaton bulldozes its way through bantam America, what will become of the endeavoring American family? Perhaps there is no stopping the corporate machine". After hearing the report, the school board takes the Harbuck's case to the Mayor who decides that if more than half of the town's population vote in favour, she will not allow Harbuck's to open in South Park. A political campaign ensues. Mr Tweek and the school board use the kids in television commercials to sell their political beliefs. Poston, whose political arguments about free-enterprise fail, develops an advertising campaign targeting children to drink coffee – "It's yum diddly-icious. It makes you feel super", he says whilst dressed in a Joe Camel costume. "I have a surprise for you. The new kiddycinno from Harbuck's. More sugar and the other goodies kids like with all the caffeine of a normal Double Latte." This is a stand-off between cartoon advertising aimed at children and the use of children as mouthpieces for adult political interests.

As the day to vote for or against Harbuck's gets closer, the boys are asked to make another speech. As they futilely try to work out how to proceed, the underpants gnomes appear. Kyle asks them why they are stealing underpants, to which one of the gnomes replies – "stealing underpants ... big business". Kyle asks the gnomes to teach them about business. The gnomes tell the boys about their own business plan: phase one is to steal and collect underpants and phase three is 'profit'. The gnomes, who profess themselves to be 'geniuses about corporations', do not seem to have developed the details of phase two – in fact, the details of phase two seem inconsequential as long as it leads somehow to phase three. Already there is a subtext here that is a satirical critique of big business. It is possible that the 'gnomes' are an analogy for the 'gnomes of Switzerland', those iconic bastions of international capital and the glorification of money as a substance of desire in its own right.[10] Then, there is the simple association of corporate activity and underpants, an incongruous juxtaposition that undermines the pretensions of big business with the banality of underwear and the link with base human functions. The main satirical moment resides in the absurdist and partial business plan of the gnomes. First, it is based on theft – but more importantly, the plan is only concerned with ends, with profit. There is no consideration of means, which appear to be considered as irrelevant and unimportant. Milton Friedman would presumably be proud of such pure capitalist élan.

The following day, the boys, armed with the fresh knowledge garnered from the gnomes, address the town again. Inverting their previous speech provided by Mr Tweek, they now suggest that "Big corporations are good", because "without big corporations we wouldn't have things like cars and computers and canned soup". Moving on to talk specifically about Harbuck's, Stan suggests:

> Even Harbuck's coffee started off as a small, little business. But because it made such great coffee and because they ran their business so well, they

managed to grow and grow until it became the corporate powerhouse it is today. And that's why we should let Harbuck's stay.

The show ends as Poston and Mr Tweek start negotiating a deal for Mr Tweek to be the manager of the new Harbuck's.

Clearly, *South Park* offers an irreverent depiction of the business practices and cultural imperialism of large corporations. Like the mythical and allegorical gnomes, neither Tweek nor Harbuck's appear to be incorporating any genuine ethical considerations into their calculus. Initially, Poston attempts to mobilize the discourse of American free-enterprise to defend his corporation by saying "My argument is simple, this country is founded on free enterprise. Harbuck's is an organization that prides itself on great coffee!" His ensuing plan to seduce the youth of the town by marketing high-caffeine, high-sugar beverages (the 'kiddycinno'), however, suggests that it is a front for expansionist corporate agendas. Similarly, Mr Tweek's moral high ground is eroded by his willingness to exploit the children in pursuit of his crusade. Publicly, he positions himself as the innocent small business man whose honest livelihood it being put at risk by the evil forces of big business. He works to mobilize a discourse of honest work and family tradition – one that taps into that rich vein in the American psyche of the valiant individual up against a monolithic, corrupt and immoral system. When first offered $500,000 for his shop by Harbuck's, Mr Tweek replies:

> When my father opened this store thirty years ago, he cared only about one thing – making a great cup of coffee. Sure we may take a little longer to brew a cup, we may not give it fancy names. I guess we just care a little more. And that's why Tweek coffee is still home brewed with the finest beans we can muster. Yes, Tweek coffee is a simpler coffee for a simpler America.

Tweek's espoused high-minded American libertarian economic rhetoric and his anti-big business sentiments, however, are soon juxtaposed with his own tactics of using the boys as mouthpieces for his political convictions.

Unlike Poston and Mr Tweek, however, the underpants gnomes do not attempt to legitimate their behaviour with any high-minded politico-economic discourse. They have a message that is more direct and simple, one befitting the Gnomes of Zurich. This is a message of pure, 'libertarian' capitalism – one in which profit is the only animus and in which if that is the end, any means are justified. The means is so incidental that the underpant gnomes have not even troubled to elaborate them – phase two of their plan is left unspecified and indeterminate. The amorality of the ethos is cemented by the fact that phase one entails the stealing of underpants. It almost seems as if this is the only thing that the gnomes are able to do – in the parlance of business, it is their 'core competence'. For them, phase two needs no rhetorical support, no allusion to any meta-narratives of free enterprise or anything else, it merely needs serve the pure motive of profit. What is revealed is that the only difference between the gnomes, Tweek and Poston is that the gnomes are honest about their approach to business. Discourses of a quasi-socio-political and ethical nature are thus exposed as masks for darker and starker motives – motives which emerge in remarkable congruence to those articulated by Ritzer.

Critique from the inside

We concur with the view that "McDonaldization presents a concrete example of applied social analysis which clarifies important social developments in the present moment, calling attention to their costs and benefits, their positive and negative sides" (Kellner, 1999: 186). However, we also agree that this analysis "fails to adequately explicate its cultural dimensions" (187). In this chapter, we have provided one means for illustrating and addressing that deficiency. We have also tried to show how the ground and the space for a very effective critique of McDonaldization exist within popular culture itself. This demonstrates the more general thesis that popular culture can contain very subtle and nuanced critical analysis of the socio-cultural context of which it is a part and a product. In this case, such an analsyis offers an auto-critique that stands in contrast to Ritzer's invocation of a cultural process in which workers and consumers have little or no agency such that they are unable to respond to the structural forces of McDonaldization in any conscious, knowing or critical manner.

In having made a specific comparison between sociological and popular culture accounts of McDonalidization, we also take issue with critical positions where the critic purports to able to see and analyse that which the mere citizen cannot. The critic positions himself/herself as being able to determine what the citizen wants and needs since they are incapable of knowing that themselves – so enthralled are they by the magic of the modern consumer capitalism. Our argument directly opposes those critiques of popular culture that suggest that it is a degraded, banal and secondary form of culture to be studied only in so far as it provides an indication of the torpor of the masses, but not to be mined for insight, perspicacious parody or critical reflection. Such an analysis of the inevitable banalization of culture glosses the persistence of the diversity and differences that the analysis, ironically, laments the demise of. It is neglectful of the inherent productivity that the space of popular culture represents. It ignores the capacity of people to receive the significations of popular culture actively rather than passively and to play with, invert, subvert and rework them. We challenge the view of critics like Belk who promote this monolithic representation and point to the almost universal 'false consciousness' that infects the consumer:

> The illusions created by commercial interests have a religious character and promote a "fallacious paradise" ... [where] ... hyperreal consumer culture is a religion that is increasingly converting the world to a singular image of paradise as a standard package of branded consumer goods and services. The items in this package are promoted by media images such as Ronald

McDonald and his brethren and can be seen on global television programs, movies, sports stars, and tourists.

(Belk, 1996: 31, drawing on DeBord, 1970)

The phenomenon of McDonaldization has been typically met with much hostility and critique among intellectuals. This is often accompanied by a response that centres on a nostalgic call for community, authenticity and coherence in place of urban anomie, economic alienation and cultural rationalization (Turner, 1999). Whist such nostalgia might be comforting, we propose that the examples of popular culture that we have discussed here use parody and carnivalization as a significantly more successful and reflexive critical strategy.

What we have seen again in this chapter is that popular culture can be a site for a kind of inside-out, reflexive, auto-critique. We sympathize with the perspective that suggests that Ritzer and similar analysts pursue a somewhat elitist position that is outside-in and which elevates the perspective of the social critic enabling them to perceive and evaluate things that others cannot (Parker, 1998). In response, we hope that the critique that we have marshalled is as powerful, but avoids the elitist trap by deploying resources from within popular culture itself.

To conclude, we agree that phenomena such as McDonald's are important. What we argue against, however, are forms of critique that claim to step outside of culture and position their analysis above the object of their critique through an assumed privilege and inherent elitism. By drawing, in this case, on examples from television cartoons, we hope that we might contribute a perspective that recognizes the complex tensions that exist within culture. This is intended to show how a telling critique of great power, subtlety and nuance can be 'read', once again, within the constructions of popular culture itself.

8 Bruce Springsteen, management gurus and the trouble of the promised land

In this chapter, we turn our attention to a comparison between the representation of work and organizations in two quite particular examples of popular culture. The examples are a sample of contemporary popular management books and a sample of work-related themes in the popular music of Bruce Springsteen. Massive in popularity, our two examples are both commodified objects and texts emerging from Western culture and marketed and distributed around the world. Such texts contain the "ambiguities that necessarily attach themselves to objects produced in a society beset with contradictions" (Gunster, 2000: 67) and, as we try to illustrate in this chapter, important amongst these ambiguities are dys/utopian images of organized work.

Through our discussion, we illustrate that Springsteen's work engages with the ambiguities of Utopia to critically "articulate the problems facing workers coming to terms with [a] transformed industrial landscape" (Palmer, 1997: 106). We contrast this to those popular management books which provide an uncritical "hardheaded Utopia" (Gee *et al.*, 1996: 48) by marketing themselves "with the breathless hyperbole of global capitalism" (Parker, 2002b: 7) and the associated aesthetic spectacle (Clark and Greatbatch, 2004). Another key difference is that as manifested in such popular management books, popular culture speaks with a 'voice from above' that actively suppresses ambiguity and ignores power in order to reproduce a dominant ethos of contemporary capitalism. These books achieve this by professing a 'new work order' that promises more satisfying work, respect for diversity and the more democratic distribution of resources (Gee *et al.*, 1996).

While it is more than common for academic critiques of popular management to have the concomitant message that it should be replaced by 'superior' academic knowledge (Rhodes and Pitsis, 2007, see also Chapter 2), here we show how popular music can provide such an alternative. Indeed, we turn from popular management to popular music and in doing so find a more considered, nuanced, critical and sophisticated understanding of work relations in Springsteen – a performer widely heralded as "the chronicler and poet of ordinary Americans, a man whose music spoke to – and for – the people" (Cullen, 2005: 194). We argue that Springsteen uses a 'voice from within' to explore the ambiguities and paradoxes that emerge from the gap between real experience and utopian desire. While the popular management books provide uncritical support for its imaginary Utopia, Springsteen provides a critique of the promises of economic freedom through capitalism – promises which management writers are so often complicit in (re)producing. What this also shows is that the 'popularity' of a given work or genre is not necessarily a predictor of its content – as we shall see, both of our examples are massive in popularity but each constructs different representations of work and uses different (yet related) cultural discourses to do so.

This chapter starts by introducing Springsteen and the way the lyrics to his songs thematize working life in relation to a false promise of Utopia. These are themes that were repeated most prominently in his albums from the late 1970s to early 1980s – a time when, in the United States, "[t]he economic foundations of the industrial working class were disappearing, and the politics that once offered some protection had all but vanished" (Cowie and Boehm, 2006: 356). Following this introduction, and in contrast to Springsteen, we discuss the utopian tendencies that are represented in many popular management books – tendencies that seek to provide a justification for the legitimate rule of managers. Third, we bring Bruce Springsteen and his music back into the discussion as a possible antidote to such simplistically utopian perspectives. By reviewing the lyrics of a selection of his songs that speak of a representative experience of work, we suggest that Springsteen's corpus embodies a grounded understanding that speaks *through* work rather than just speaking *about* work and that critically portrays the complexities and ironies therein. This chapter concludes with a discussion of the implications of Springsteen's work to the critical appreciation and understanding of working life that forms the theme of the overall book.

Listening to Springsteen

> End of the day factory whistle cries
> Men walk through that gate with death in their eyes
> And you just better believe boy, somebody's gonna get hurt tonight
> It's the working, the working, just the working life
> 'Cos it's the working, the working, just the working life

The citation above is taken from Bruce Springsteen's song 'Factory' on his 1978 album *Darkness on the Edge of Town*. It is a song about hard and drudgerous labour governed by the factory whistle and locked in by iron factory gates. This is a work that destroys people while it gives them life. It is a bitterly iron-gated work whose irony is only ever worked out with pain and hurt. The people who work in Springsteen's factory are unable to escape the dull torment of their work and seem emasculated by their lack of power in the workplace (Palmer, 1997). Springsteen sings with a pain and resignation in his voice – "It's the working, the working, just the working life." Illustrative of many of Springsteen's songs, 'Factory's' subject is the difficulty and hardship of working life. He depicts the "hopes and fears of an ethnic working class from which he emerged with a clarity and empathy" (Cullen, 1997: 4) and chronicles the stories of "hard people living hard lives" (Sawyers, 2004: 1).

Although a short and simple song, 'Factory' is an example of a product of mass culture that can offer many possibilities for compelling critiques of organizations and work. Such popular music is the soundtrack to people's lives as it infiltrates and fills all manner of social spaces. The words that are sung ring through people's consciousnesses, providing lyrics that are a dominant way that knowledge is embodied and available in everyday life. The use of musical forms to embody knowledge is not new; lyric poetry and oral traditions have performed this function in many cultures, past and present. As a popular musician, Springsteen is also not alone in using lyrics to dramatize and discuss working conditions. His lineage as a musician can be traced back through the pre-war folk music of Woody Guthrie, the rock-and-roll rebellion of the 1950s and the protest music of the 1960s – each of which commonly discussed political aspects of work in their lyrics. In discussing his musical influence, Springsteen himself recognizes the class-based politics that he draws on lyrically:

> Up until the late seventies, when I started to write songs that had to do with class issues, I was influenced more by music like the Animals' "We Gotta Get Out of This Place" or "It's My Life (And I'll Do What I Want)" – sort of class-conscious pop records that I'd listen to-and I'd say to myself: "That's my life, that's my life!" They said something to me about my own experience of exclusion. I think that's been a theme that's run through much of my writing: the politics of exclusion [...] I'd been really involved with country music right prior to the album Darkness on the Edge of Town [1978], and that had a lot of affect on my writing because I think country is a very class-conscious music. And then that interest slowly led me into Woody Guthrie and folk music. Guthrie was one of the few songwriters at the time who was aware of the political implications of the music he was writing – a real part of his consciousness.
>
> (Springsteen cited in Percy, 1998)

In terms of contemporary artists, Springsteen is among many who have used the politics of work as a dominant thematic in their lyrics (see Rhodes, 2007). What makes his work particularly salient however is the way that he has engaged in a sustained examination of working life in specific relation to the utopianism of the American Dream. It is this aspect of his work that we focus on in this chapter. Thus, our main concern is on how Springsteen provides a unique "critique of the promise of political economy that spins out lies and engenders dreams that can never be fulfilled" (Pratt, 1990: 193).

If Springsteen himself dreamed of being a massively popular and respected rock star, however, his dreams have more than come true. Over his 30-year career, Springsteen has attained mass popular success as well as having gained critical acclaim. With 24 albums to his credit, he is one of the biggest selling rock artists of all time – his 1984 album *Born in the USA,* for example, sold 15 million copies, making it the Columbia record label's biggest selling album ever. Springsteen's success and influence on popular music places him alongside Chuck Berry, Elvis Presley and The Beatles. On March 15, 1999, he was inducted into the prestigious *Rock and Roll Hall of Fame,* where he is described as a pivotal figure in the evolution of rock and roll (Rock and Roll Hall of Fame, 2002). By the mid-1980s, Springsteen had become "the world's most successful white rock star since Elvis" (Shuker, 2001: 123).

In addition to his commercial success, artistically, Springsteen has been compared to American musical and literary giants, ranging from Woody Guthrie and Bob Dylan, to Walt Whitman and John Steinbeck. This has led him to be heralded as "the single most influential purveyor of literacy in what is often considered the non-literate culture of youth and rock music" (Branscomb, 1993: 29). It is through this literacy that Springsteen's allegorical lyrics use familiar characters and situations to tell big stories (Sanneh, 2002); a key theme in these stories being people's troubled experiences with work. This is a theme which lays out in uncompromising terms "the shattered lives and broken countenances that make up the dark side of American existence as it is experienced by working people for whom the American Dream is a taunting cruel, and ungraspable abstraction" (Smith, 2000: 303). Springsteen presents his stories through an implicit politic that tell about "people, their lives, and how they see and experience their place in the world" (Gencarelli, 1994: 282). As we will elaborate, it is this popular vision of working life, told with a voice from within, that is in critical and stark contrast to understandings of work that pervade much popular management literature.

In attesting to Springsteen's work as being of value to the understanding of organizations and working life, inevitably we present only one of many possible readings of his work, and many other readings are possible. Pratt (1990), for example, noted that during his 1984 presidential campaign, Ronald Reagan attempted to appropriate Spingsteen's song 'Born in the USA' as a patriotic anthem of faith in the American Dream – a move that clearly suggested a failure to see the song as "a cry from people who feel let down and put down by the country in which they live" (Gencarelli, 1994: 295). Reagan must have listened to the anthemic chorus where Springsteen loudly sings 'I was born in the USA', but seems to have not considered the other lyrics from the same song. For example, Reagan is unlikely to have found political value in reciting:

Got in a little home town jam
So they put a rifle in my hands
Sent me off to a foreign land to go and kill the yellow man

In response to Reagan's attention, Springsteen addressed a concert audience with the following comment: "the president was mentioning my name the other day, and I kinda got to wandering what his favorite album might be. I don't think it was *Nebraska.* I don't think he's been listening to this one" (cited in Sandford, 1999: 236). With that comment, he launched into the song 'Johnny

99' from *Nebraska* – a stark simple song, sung in a melancholy voice and accompanied only by guitar and harmonica that tells the story of a worker from an Auto plant who gets drunk after losing his job and kills someone (Cullen, 1997). Thus, as Springsteen himself seems to be suggesting, irrespective of the varied audience responses, it is both possible and useful to "analyze the political significance of identified themes, [and] the relation of that thematic content to political-economic context" (Pratt, 1990: 178). It is such an analysis that we pursue in this chapter. As with the other chapters, in providing this reading of Springsteen, we are not suggesting that ours is necessarily one shared by other listeners of his songs or that Springsteen's critical potential is one that is realized by his fans. More to the point, we try to take Springsteen on his own terms – as represented in his words and stories – and read him as a cultural critic.

In looking at the content of Springsteen's songs, one finds a sustained discussion of the relationship between the utopianism of the 'American Dream' and the hard realities of the lived experience of working life. As Gencarelli discussed, Springsteen's lyrical interest the 'American Dream' started to become evident in his third album *Born to Run* (1975). Prior to that, his lyrics centred more on "street life, wild youth, and about living on the verge of working class adulthood, but dreaming of a way out to something greater" (Gencarelli, 1994: 285). From the mid-1970s until the mid-1990s, the focus on the American Dream, as it related to the experience of work, was a dominant theme in his music; after which his interest turned to other political issues (e.g. the reflection on the 9/11 bombings in 2002's *The Rising*, or the anti-Iraq war sentiment in the title song to 2005's *Devils and Dust*).

When it comes to work, for Springsteen, the task is not to resolve this problematic relationship between utopian dreams and quotidian experience, but rather to deal with its actuality. As he sings in 'Tunnel of Love' (from the 1987 album of the same name), "you've got to learn to live with what you can't rise above". This sentiment is echoed in the earlier song 'The Promised Land' (from the 1978 album *Darkness on the Edge of Town*) where Springsteen's character sings "I've done the best to live the right way, I get up every morning and go to work each day." Work is seen as something that should be good and righteous, but in the face of working all day in a garage, the protagonist of the song sees his eyes going blind and his blood running cold. For him, the promise of work is broken, and it leaves the character feeling so weak that he wants to 'explode' and take a knife to cut the pain from his heart. This character realizes work's false promise as a dream that tears him apart and leaves him lost and broken-hearted but at the same time this is a dream that he does not know how to give up. The song chronicles a transition of "a relatively naïve white boy who is shocked to learn that the world is not his oyster" (Cullen, 1997: 64) yet it ends, ironically, with the dissonant realization that despite everything, he still believes in the promised land.

On close listening, one can be left with the feeling that the naïveté, which expects the promise to come true, is replaced by a knowledge that, despite the evidence to the contrary, the belief is so ingrained, so central, that one must still believe and live with the inability of the belief to be fulfilled. It might be that without the 'dream', however hollow, there would simply be nothing. As a result, one is left to manage the ambivalence of believing in the promised land whilst wishing for a storm that will:

Blow away the dreams that tear you apart
Blow away the dreams that break your heart
Blow away the lies that leave you nothing but lost and broken-hearted

Popular management

The second example of popular culture that we are concerned with is the popular management book. Our particular focus is on those (mainly American) management texts that emerged from the early 1980s as popular prescriptions for management practices in light of perceived requirements for organizational change in response to changing economic conditions. In recent years, many people involved in the formal and academic study of management have turned their attention to analysing this popular phenomenon of the management guru (see Chapter 2). This academic attention has seen management scholars take 'good sport' in critiquing, debunking and even ridiculing popular management theory and its pundits (Collins, 2001). The apparent seriousness of such critiques suggests that popular management is merely a form of entertainment (Crainer, 1998b) that is "philosophically impoverished, theoretically underdeveloped and empirically emaciated" (Jackson, 1996: 52). Indeed, "the dominating focus of research on management fashions centres on attempts to explain managers' enthusiasm for ideas that are *fundamentally flawed*" (Clark, 2004: 298, italics added). Purveyors of popular management are decried as 'witch-doctors' who peddle a modern-day snake oil that plays on the anxieties of managers (Micklethwait and Wooldridge, 1997) while delivering superstitious and 'technically inferior' forms of management (Abrahamson, 1996: 275). What this amounts to is a well-developed academic suspicion of popular management theory. This suspicion not only from those managerialist researchers who believe that popular management undermines 'our' corporations (Hilmer and Donaldson, 1996) but also from those of a more critical persuasion who see popular management as a town crier for the language of the new capitalism; a language presented in 'fast capitalist texts' that are silent on the dystopian realities of contemporary work (Gee *et al.*, 1996; see also Agger, 1989, 1992) despite fast capitalism's increasing speed (Agger, 2004).

The popularity of such books started with the rapid growth of interest in management, especially in the United States, that emerged as an attempt to come to terms with the rise of Japanese competition, advances in information technology and radical changes in working patterns (Micklethwait and Wooldridge, 1996) – a similar set of concerns to which Springsteen was reacting to very differently in his work from the late 1970s onwards. This spawned a new wave of management theory, management fashion and management guruism (Jackson, 2001b) that saw the number of business books published increase from 771 in 1975 to

3,000 in 1996 – an industry worth over one billion dollars in the United States alone (Kennedy, 1998). An important aspect of this growth in management books is the way they relate to the construction of what Gee *et al.* (1996) call a *new work order* – an ideal work culture that is reflexively created through the reading and writing of contemporary management fashion as manifested in 'fast capitalist texts' – those texts which glorify Agger's (1992, 2004) critical notion of fast capitalism. These texts, exemplified by popular management gurus such as Tom Peters, Peter Senge and Hammer and Champy are:

> A mix of history and description, prophesy, warning, prescriptions and rec-ommendations, parable (stories of success and failure) and large doses of utopianism. They announce a new "enchanted workplace", where hierarchy is dead and partners engage in meaningful but often fast past-paced and stressful work in a collaborative environment of mutual commitment and trust.
>
> (Gee *et al.*, 1996: 25)

As they are textually positioned, these new organizations exist to create new forms of identity – bosses become coaches, middle managers become team leaders and workers become associates, partners or knowledge workers. What Gee *et al.* (1996) observe is that although such textually constructed organi-zations tend to be celebratory and hortatory, they also display a lack of concern for morality and social justice. Further, fast capitalism is imperialistic – it seeks to take over the practice and social identities that were once the terrain of church, community, university and government discourse. This is created through organizational culture as manifested in 'visionary leadership' and 'core values'; it attempts to construct a more or less total and consuming life world for people which "seeks to gain a pervasive influence in every area of an employee's life" (Casey, 1995: 197). In such organizations, managerial control can be coupled with "vocabularies of team-work, quality consciousness, flexibil-ity, quality circles, learning organizations, which reconcile the normative and autonomous aspirations of the employees with the collective entrepreneurship of the 'culture' of organizations" (Chan, 2000: 28).

The management texts through which such cultures are proposed are fre-quently presented as "tales from management gurus and visionaries concerning the dramatic objectives of organizational turnaround and regeneration" (Jeffcut, 1994: 229). In such stories, managers are the heroes who have the 'right stuff' to lead their organizations to the utopian future. It is here that instrumental and authoritarian concerns appear to be thoroughly integrated and embodied in organizations through "extolling of the virtues and potentialities of heroic and romantic organizational transformation that are both total and unrealizable" (ibid.: 234). Further, such transformations, led by managerial elites who are the fittest and hence have risen to their positions of 'greatness' through a Darwinian process, need no justification – their market success and authority give them transformational license. The archetypes for the late modern organizations run by such managers are ones where loyalty, favouritism, informality and non-legality are emphasized over hierarchical compliance; technical training is replaced by loyalty, style and organizational fit; and fixed salaries are replaced by performance pay; and where rules are replaced by discretionary behaviour (Gephart, 1996). Such images of organizations – utopian dreamlands where heroic managers lead entrepreneurial and 'motivated' employees – become the 'other' against which managers and organizations are compelled to evaluate themselves and strive to become. As documented in popular management books, this is a textually fabricated organizational other imagined by those who seek to propose it as a possible organizational reality. Its status is that of a powerful and elitist imaginary – a reflexively constructed world grounded in the prescriptive practice of those who seek the power to define how the world 'should be'.

One feature of these texts is that they commonly take a neo-social Darwinist perspective on Utopia. Thus, like Herbert Spencer's nineteenth-century version of social Darwinism, popular management writing, either explicitly or implicitly, relies on a theory of social development justified and explained through calls to evolution and progress. For Spencer, this meant drawing on Darwin's work "concerning the evolutionary principle and natural selection, [and generalizing] the Darwinistic theory to provide understandings of individual and social life more generally" (Bowles, 1997). Needless to say, Spencer sold out public halls in late nineteenth-century New York when he visited, offering a theory that suggested that societies develop in accordance with the rule of the 'survival of the fittest' – where 'the best' aspects of culture and society triumph and endure. The gilded age could ask for no better ideology. In popular management today, a similar ethos is still evident in the approach to business strategy which suggests that organizations are in militaristic competition with each other and that the 'fittest' organizations are the ones that emerge victorious and successful in the battle (Byrne, 1999). It is ever a popular refrain.

In popular management, increased global competition has led to a revival in the sentiments of social Darwinism, which "enables its adherents to ignore the moral consequences of their behavior because the weeding out process supposedly happens through the operation of natural, impersonal forces" (Beyer and Nino, 1999: 289). This 'new social Darwinism' is one where the "survival of the fittest should be upheld by governments and societies as the determinant of market efficiency and the legitimacy of firms" (Brovetto *et al.*, 1999: 398). Collins and Porras' (1994) best-selling management book *Built to Last*[1] is a case in point. They state that in identifying the 'habits' of corporations with long-term success, they "found the concepts in Charles Darwin's *Origin of the Species* to be more helpful for replicating the success of certain visionary companies that any textbook on corporate strategic planning" (9). On this basis, they analysed organizations as species, which evolve so that the strongest organizational variations survive. Further, they argue that although this evolutionary metaphor is valuable, the difference between organizations and species is that evolution can be purposefully stimulated in organizations – "visionary companies more aggressively *harness* the power of evolution" (149, italics in original). They repeatedly quote Darwin's maxim: "Multiply, vary, let the strongest live, and the weakest die" (140, 146, 163). In invoking Darwinism, Collins and Porras' central argument is that there is a set of "distinguishing characteristics of the world's most enduring and successful corporations" related to "the *timeless* management principles that have consistently distinguished out- standing companies" (xxiii, italics in original). Of course, any organization that chooses to abide by these principles can count itself too amongst the 'fittest'.

Collins and Porras are a good example of a common trait in popular manage- ment writing – one where particular practices, habits, characteristics or attributes of successful companies are articulated as those which will lead to corporate prosperity and longevity. Much as the social Darwinism that preceded it, Collins and Porras appeal to a 'value neutral' social science to develop "a framework to describe social development and evolution" (Werhane, 2000: 191). Notably, one of the first major management books that both embodied and helped define this genre was Peters and Waterman's 1982 bestseller *In Search of Excellence*.[2] Peters and Waterman describe a particular organizational Utopia by defining attributes that designate companies that are 'excellent'. These excellent com- panies are those that achieve innovative performance that allows them to continually transform and adapt and are "brilliant at the basics" (13). Again, the message is a simple and clear combination of utopianism and Darwinism. *In Search of Excellence*, together with the publication of books like Deal and Kennedy's (1982) *Corporate Cultures* and Moss-Kanter's (1983) *The Change Masters* were part of a growing interest in management theory, organizational culture and the types of change required to create successful organizations. In prescribing particular models of organizational 'excellence', such popular man- agement theory most often relies on the promise of a utopian organization.[3] Such an ethos has, for example, led Hammer and Champy, in their 1994 best seller *Reengineering the Corporation*,[4] to claim that "America's largest corporations – even the most successful and promising among them – must embrace and apply the principles of business reengineering or they will be eclipsed by the greater success of those companies that do" (2). Again, the message is 'evolve or die' and the prescription is for a particular utopianist image of organizations and a putative means to achieve it. In such organizations, "leaders create a new tomor- row" (Belasco, 1990: 6) and "if America is to build on its past competitive strengths and to secure a better future for itself, innovation ... is a necessity not because it produces more profits but because it does ensure our *survival*" (Moss- Kanter, 1983, italics added).

As represented in such popular management books, the reality of actual organizations is contrasted against a utopian image. This is a simulacral reality that is textually created and against which organizations are positioned in infe- rior otherness – organizations and the people within them are told that in order to survive, they must evolve into the imaginary Utopias presented to them. These are 'designer cultures' that are deliberately defined by management and inhabited by 'designer employees' who will be "mediated through a rhetoric of self-actualisation, flexibility and hyper-adaptability" (Casey, 1995: 87). Such organizations are elitist, imaginary, utopian and simulacral. To sustain the notion of such a culture is to demand consensus – the hallmark of the 'strong' culture. It is here, however, that the unmanageability of the complexity of many organizational events is sidestepped in favour of a particular utopian point of view that suggests that managers have the power to define and dictate the cultures of their organizations – this amounts to an *"idyllic tyranny* in which any serious dissent is kept at bay or, even worse, rigorously suppressed" (ten Bos, 2000: 104).

Springsteen's troubled Utopia

Popular culture is a fragmentary kaleidoscope. While bosses were learning that elephants could dance (Belasco, 1990), it is not unlikely that, given the cohort, some of the dancing would have been to the music of Springsteen. Great rhythms, at least in the more upbeat material, but what about the words? In these words, dissent is neither kept at bay nor suppressed. Springsteen offers representations of work that are valuable because they speak from a place frequently muted in management discourse, a popular voice that provides a complex and broad ranging understanding of organization life. This is an example of mass culture that offers dramatic, intense and dynamic representation of organizations (Hassard and Holiday, 1998: 1) that, in the case of Springsteen, is spoken from the lyrical point of view of the worker in society; the kind of guy that Springsteen might have been had he not had musical talent.

Springsteen himself is well aware of the potential of music to provide productive insights into working life. In a 1981 concert, he told the audience of the importance of music to his own life:

> It wasn't until I started listening to the radio, and I heard something in those singer's voices that said there was more to life than what my old man was doing and the life I was living. And they held out a promise that every man has the right to live his life with some decency and some dignity. And it's a promise that gets broken every day in the most violent way. But it's a promise that never, ever dies, and it's always inside of you.
>
> (Cited in Cullen, 1997: 11)

What 'his old man was doing' was working – it is such a vision of working class work and life that is a motif that runs through Springsteen's work. In the song 'Out in the Street' (From the 1980 album *The River*), Springsteen juxtaposes the relationship people have with work to their lives outside of the workplace. He does this by singing from the perspective of the working everyman who is his common protagonist – this is a person who "works five days a week ... loading crates down at the dock". Such work is seen not as anything valuable in itself; it is a means to a non-work end. Here, it is *not-working* that is a form of freedom and a source of strength and self-worth (Cullen, 1997). With rock-and-roll verve, he sings: "Monday morning when the foreman calls time, I've already got

Friday on my mind." At work, he is dreaming about being 'out in the street' so that he can 'walk the way he wants to walk' and 'talk the way he wants to talk'. This is a simple song that contains the common view that work is oppressive, boring and means being at the beck and call of the foreman and the factory whistle. When at work, how a person walks and talks is regulated and controlled and the only hope is for the brief liberation available outside of the workplace – 'on the street'. Against the upbeat tempo of the song itself and Springsteen's lively pop-ish singing, this song seems to suggest that this hope might make it all worthwhile. His, however, is not the hope of a naïve child – it is a hope that fully recognizes its position against its alternatives.

This is further illustrated in the song 'Night' (from the 1975 album *Born to Run*) – one of Springsteen's first songs to explicitly deal with working life. Springsteen again juxtaposes working from non-working life in order to suggest the potential for escape. He starts "You get up every morning at the sound of the bell; You get to work late and the boss man's giving you hell." As the intensity of the song builds, Springsteen tells us how it is in the night – when work is done – that the irony of work reaches its boiling point.

> You're just a prisoner of your dreams
> Holding on for your life
> Cause you work all day
> To blow 'em away in the night

The point is that the utopian dream is something that can neither be destroyed nor easily fulfilled: despite its promise of liberation, its realization is that of potential imprisonment.

This sentiment of the oppressive nature of work is developed further in the 1980 song 'The River' (from the 1980 album of the same name). Again, the protagonist in this song is a working class man and it tells the story of his life in a small American town where "they bring you up to do, like your daddy done". At the beginning of the song, Springsteen suggests that the hardships of working life are ones that people are born into and compelled to participate in. He starts by telling us that when in High School, he and Mary used to drive out of the industrial valley of their home town to go where 'fields were green' to swim in the river. The water and swimming are a metaphor for escape – escape from the working life of the town into a transient state of utopian forgetfulness. For the hero of the song, however, the harsher vision of 'real life' takes over and the 'green fields' are only a passing fantasy. When Mary gets pregnant, they are forced to marry and for his nineteenth birthday, he sings that he got 'a union card and a wedding coat'. His wedding was not seen as an occasion for celebration – there were "no wedding day smiles, no walk down the aisles, no flowers, no wedding dress". On the night of the wedding, though, he and Mary still go down to the river, still hoping for an alternative to their lives.

As Springsteen's haunting singing tells the story, it becomes apparent that this alternative, this hope, is not forthcoming and he sings that "now I act like I don't remember, Mary acts like she don't care". What he is left with are the memories of his youth and of the river – memories that 'haunt him like a curse'. He asks "is a dream a lie that don't come true, or is it something worse". At the end of the song, he again goes down to the river, but this time the river is dry. Here, the relationship between life's utopian promise and the hard realities of lived experience are solemnly counterpoised in a dark image of hopelessness. For the character of the song, the dreams of his youth were cut off too early by the heart-breaking realities of adult responsibility. He acts like he doesn't remember but he remembers his dreams all too well.

Against the backdrop of such realities, in the song 'Reason to Believe' (from the 1982 album *Nebraska*), Springsteen sings that "at the end of every hard earned day people need some reason to believe". Through the sparse musical accompaniment and the howling vocals, he suggests that after the hardships and bitter ironies of life and work, people still feel that they must have an ideal to aspire to, a Utopia that although not realized is still required in order to make life meaningful – no matter how fragile that meaning might be. This Utopia, however, is not one to be taken as being either achievable or desirable. In the opening verse, he sings of a man who stopped his car on the highway and is looking at a dead dog:

> Seen a man standin' over a dead dog lyin' by the highway in a ditch
> He's lookin' down kinda puzzled pokin' that dog with a stick
> Got his car door flung open he's standin' out on Highway 31
> Like if he stood there long enough that dog'd get up and run
> Struck me kinda funny seem kinda funny sir to me
> At the end of every hard earned day people find some reason to believe

The dog is obviously dead but he seems to retain hope that it will come back to life. By articulating this hope, Springsteen appears to be offering "a cynical look at a species that despite all evidence to the contrary, absurdly insists on believing in something" (Branscomb, 1993: 38). It is this cynicism that Springsteen struggles with; as he himself has said: "the tricky thing about getting older is not giving into cynicism" (cited in Santaro, 1996: 36) and "the greatest challenge of adulthood is holding on to your idealism after losing your innocence" (cited in Anon., 1999: 52). It is this irrational faith of having 'something to believe' that appears to trouble Springsteen (Cullen, 1997) – a troubling that comes from the recognition of an inevitable and unresolvable tension.

This picture of the failed Utopia of work is given a more historical treatment in the song 'Youngstown' (from the 1995 album *The Ghost of Tom Joad*) where Springsteen tells the story of the industrialization of the north-east Ohio town of Youngstown. The song uses real events that happened in Youngstown in 1979 by which time three steel mills were closed down and where "no longer passive to their being systematically abandoned, local people protested, sought in vain to negotiate a buyout, and then took the matter to court. The judge ruled against them" (Byrne, 1999: 30). Springsteen tells us that it was in this town iron ore was discovered in 1803 and a blast furnace was built. It was there that the cannonballs used in the American Civil War were made and, for later wars, tanks and bombs were built. On returning from service in the war in Vietnam, just as his father had done on returning from World War II, the protagonist of the song takes a job in the plant – a job that allowed him to earn a living and raise a family. The work was required for subsistence, but it is portrayed as being destructive of meaningful experience, as, like his father used to say: "Them boys [the bosses] did what Hitler couldn't do." He ends by saying that when he dies, he does not want to go to heaven because "I would not do heaven's work well." Instead he wants to "stand in the fiery furnaces of hell."

Springsteen paints a harsh picture of American industrialism, one that makes soldiers wonder what they had been fighting for. This is tough, burning work that is both unavoidable and undesirable, one that makes a person so disenchanted with the false promise of modern Utopia that he resigns himself to a life, and death, in hell. Rather than celebrating organizational success, Springsteen instead gives voice to those rendered expendable by late twentieth-century American capitalism (Martin, 1996). This is not the stuff of the harmonious culture promised in the fast capitalist texts.

As these examples illustrate, a consistent motif and subject matter that runs through Springsteen's music is the experience of work. This thematization seeks to draw a contrast between the lived experience of work and the promise that it offers. This is a promise that is "lost but not forgotten, from the dark heart of a dream" (in 'Adam Raised a Cain' from the 1978 album *Darkness on the Edge of Town*). In contrast to the desire for organizational Utopia presented in managerial discourse, what Springsteen represents is a complex and unresolved relationship with Utopia. This is a Utopia whose promises have persistently been broken, yet can still not be forgotten. In the 1978 song 'Prove it all Night' (from the 1978 album *Darkness on the Edge of Town*), Springsteen sings:

> Everybody's got a hunger, a hunger they can't resist,
> There's so much that you want, you deserve much more than this,
> But if dreams came true, oh, wouldn't that be nice,
> But this ain't no dream we're living through tonight.

Perhaps it would be 'nice', but what happens then when the dreams go radically awry? The song 'Johnny 99' (from the 1982 album *Nebraska*) starts with Ralph losing his job at an Auto plant. Unemployed, the bank threatens to take away his house and, as he puts it, he had "debts no honest man could pay". Having lost his livelihood and feeling that he has lost his life, Ralph cracks and, drunk, he shoots a night clerk. He goes to the "part of town where when you hit a red light you don't stop" and starts waving a gun around, threatening to kill himself. Following his arrest, Ralph tells the judge that:

> Well your honor I do believe I'd be better off dead,
> So if you can take a man's life for the thoughts that's in his head,

Then sit back in that chair and think it over judge one more time,
And let 'em shave off my hair and put me on that killin' line.

It is not made clear what these thoughts might be, but one imagines that they have something to do with giving up on the utopian dream of the promised land that is so prevalent in Springsteen's work.

For Springsteen, the hopes of liberation and the realities of oppression exist both simultaneously and uncomfortably. He is aware of the potential harsh realities of work, but his characters are not fully resigned. There is still the possibility of an 'Independence Day' (from the 1980 album *The River*) where a young man can sing to his father "they ain't gonna do to me what I watched them do to you". Springsteen does not allow all of his characters to give up on their dreams, but he only allows the dreams to be retained against the lived experience of hardship and disappointment.

The broken promise of Utopia

Proposing Utopias suggests that "some form of imaginary is essential to human affairs" (Mazlish, 2003: 44). Thus, following Mannheim (1952), utopian thinking is seen by some as a requirement for a society because its absence would create a stasis that would relinquish people's ability to understand and shape history. In this sense, Utopia involves "a direct challenge to existing social order [and] potentially liberates thought and dramatically redirects action" (Ackroyd, 2002: 50). Although their Utopias are different to those that Mannheim might have imagined, the types of popular management books that we have reviewed in this chapter seem to attest to this principle. They present a new organizational Utopia with the aim of enabling managers to direct their organizational realities towards it. In doing so, they offer the evangelical promise of an organizational 'other' free from contradiction, irony and dysfunction. Such organizations are positioned similarly to the paternal colonialists or benevolent dictators of the past and seek to convert their existing (savage) cultures to new notions of culture (empowered, team based, harmonizing, learning, etc.) Further, it is suggested that such conversions are immanently possible. By making grand claims regarding the achievement of organizational change and harmony, popular management books stand above the organizations they talk about in order to proclaim what those organizations *should* do.

As ten Bos (2000) argues, the issue with popular management is not so much as popularity *per se*, but rather that its critical potential is "undermined because it is not able to get rid of utopian desires ... [and is] still imbued with rational-utopian tendencies such as the reduction of complexity and ambivalence" (11). As a popular artist, Springsteen presents a compelling counterpoint to such tendencies. Unlike much popular management, he is not enthralled by the simplicity of a work-based promised land; Springsteen's version of work is more ambiguous and complex. His critique is not one that stands above its subject but, rather, he speaks from the perspective of those people deeply embedded within working life. His songs are concerned with "the effects of poverty and uncertainty, the consequences of weakness and crime; they trawl through the murky reality of the American Dream; they contrast utopian impulses with people's lack of opportunity to do much more than get by" (Frith, 1988: 98). He does not (perhaps even cannot) discount Utopia, but he demonstrates an awareness of the potential effects of dreaming dreams that don't come true. This is not to say that he uses the notion of Utopia pejoratively to mean being out of touch with reality (Mazlish, 2003), impossible or misguided (Shklar, 1994).

For Springsteen, Utopia is very real in the sense that it frames the reality that his characters find so troubling. In exploring such troubles:

> the bulk of Springsteen's work uses class oppression as a vehicle for explor-
> ing themes of individual survival, [and] it works so well because the rocker
> absorbed his history lessons deeply. He readily sees both the distance
> between the promise of the United States and the often painful reality, as
> well as the power of music
>
> (Cowie, 2001: 115)

For Springsteen, the promises of the promised land, whilst still culturally compelling, have not been kept. The result is a tension between two realities – the utopian desire for redemption through work and the existential dissatisfaction with the experience of work. It is this Utopia, with its "promises of prosperity, equality and mobility for all, which haunts the working people who populate Springsteen's music" (Smith, 2000: 306). For Springsteen, there is an intense discrepancy between what work pretends to offer and what working people experience in 'reality' (ibid.).

The immediate similarity between Springsteen's music and the popular management books that have been discussed here is that they both reference and represent an image of Utopia as related to work. For popular management, this Utopia is one that is said to be achievable such that organizations can be transformed into better places where people work co-operatively in pursuit of visionary common goals. More specifically, contemporary managerial Utopias celebrate the heroic leaders, the entrepreneur, the excellent company and the portfolio worker such that the possibility of working poverty, inequality and other organizational ills is either "ignored or held to be temporary inconveniences" (Parker, 2002b: 5). Conversely, Springsteen attests to how the consequences of work are, for many people, relatively permanent inconveniences. For him, Utopia is not so achievable – instead, he invokes Utopia by retaining a belief in redemption through work whilst having to continually face evidence that suggests that this redemption cannot be easily realized. Springsteen's characters are able to portray a sense of anger and disillusionment whilst still being able to hold on to their dreams with the pride and will to survive them (Cullen, 1997). Hence, for Springsteen, the Utopia is complex and ironic, and for the management books, it is simple and putatively realizable.

It can be said that invoking Utopia immediately works to present a gap between existing and desirable states of affairs such that the basis of Utopia is a lack. Approaching Utopia thus requires some understanding of the nature of the relationship between the current reality and the imagined Utopia. Key to the difference in representations between Springsteen and the popular management books is the nature of this relationship. For popular management, the Utopia is seen as being immanently achievable without irony or contradiction. The gap only exists such that following the right advice can close it. Thus, current reality is merely a temporary state of affairs to be overcome in the search for progress. For Springsteen, however, it is an interrogation of this gap that is so critical. In doing this, the important insight that Springsteen offers emerges from his willingness to understand work and organizations from an ambivalent, ironic and contradictory perspective – one that speaks from the within in order to explore the complexity of understanding without seeking to 'get it right' with singular and final explanations or prescriptions. His is a poetics that emphasizes "egalitarianism; an instinctive compassion; a pragmatic skepticism toward utopian solutions; and ... a bracing humility about human endeavor" (Cullen, 1997: 198).

Unlike the management books, Springsteen does not attempt the utopian rhetoric which "promises to deliver a meaning which shatters social reality and replaces it with something better ... [where] people are empowered by their conviction in an, as yet, not existing circumstance" (Letiche, 1996: 207). This is problematic as management writing can employ a "politics of being conclusive" (Rhodes, 2001b) where, by both claiming and putatively enacting the ability to 'know', particular interests and ways of knowing become privileged over others. Here, popular managerial Utopias "take the dominant ideas from the most favoured part of the first world and then generalize them through airport bookstores across the globe" (Parker, 2002b: 5). Springsteen is more particular than general – he tells stories about people. The critical value of this lies in how, by looking for different voices and different understandings, it might be possible to reveal the ambiguities of social construction and the indeterminacy of organizational experience (Keenoy *et al.*, 1997). Such an attention to difference is not restricted to comparing the perspectives of different 'individuals' but, as seen in Springsteen's case, it is also about examining the internal conflicts that arise when multiple discourses are channelled through a single self. It is, for example, the conflict between the imagined Utopia and the experienced organization, rather than its resolution, that is a driving force.

With and without Utopia

Springsteen's characters do not necessarily offer any real (or imaginary) solutions to the problems of working life, but they do present a sensitive and critical portrait of the alienation and tension that so often results from work (Cowie, 2001). It is this acute sensitivity and empathy that we argue is of key value to the understanding of working life and of organizations – one without unreflexive false promises and one that acknowledges and represents some of the paradoxes and problems of work. Springsteen "compels a passionate understanding of people's lives – their emotions and imaginings, their jobs and their play" (De Curtis, 1992: 619) such that the experience of work can be understood in potentially new ways. It is here that:

> beneath the canvas [Springsteen] sees the interconnectedness of white and black, worker and boss, native and immigrant, and men and women, not in nostalgic terms that seek to deny conflict, but in gritty terms that can only be explored on the level of individual despair
>
> (Cowie, 2001: 117)

By relating to "people's lives, their work stresses, financial hassles, and emotional difficulties" (Shuker, 2001: 125), Springsteen's work provides a critical, literate and heartfelt study of the experience of work that oscillates between a faith in Utopia and the realization that its achievement is far from straightforward.

There is a profound irony of course: while the Tom Peters and Rosabeth Moss Kanters of the world have grown prosperous and wealthy through the promotion of their Utopias to the new class of managers and those who aspire to join them, so too has Bruce Springsteen reaped massive financial benefits from his work. However, it could be said that, in terms of the politics of mass culture, Springsteen's oral tradition remains far more powerful than the written, videoed or presentational culture of the management writers. It uses similar representational and promotional techniques – exemplary stories, personal appearances at which the author's authenticity can be judged and slick merchandizing, to sell a form of visceral release from the deadening reality of everyday life and work. In Springsteen, however, this produces a raw power that continues those traditions of rock-and-roll rebellion that every great artist from Little Richard, through Chuck Berry and Elvis Presley, through Bob Dylan, aspired to. In capturing the pain, he offers an antidote to the hot-gospelling style of the management preachers and draws instead on the great preachers of popular culture.

It seems ironic too that the artist who has brought a tradition of work critique in popular music to a peak should be known colloquially as 'The Boss'. While the readers of management books might aspire to being respected as bosses, Springsteen achieves his respect through anthems that undercut such respect at every turn of the screw on the working class lives of those he imagines from his remoteness. Of course, in popular culture, if the message is to succeed, how could it be otherwise?

9 Selling out

Authenticity, resistance and punk rock

Late 1970s punk rock band *The Sex Pistols* are a part of western cultural mythology. In the popular imagination, their "legacy still thrills" (Freeman-Greene, 2007). Nowhere is the contemporary salience of this myth more noticeable than in the reviews of Julien Temple's 2000 film *The Filth and the Fury: The Sex Pistols* – a documentary that chronicles the rise and fall of the band. As Scott (2000) recounted in the *New York Times:* "If you thought the passage of time had rendered *The Sex Pistols* quaint objects of pop-culture nostalgia, Julien Temple's electrifying new documentary will make you think again." As the review goes on to suggest, the cultural strength of *The Sex Pistols* myth is one that is deeply rooted in resistance and rebellion: "the filth and the fury of British punk rock at its moment of impact retains a surprising dignity. These guys hated everything, but at least they believed in something. Nihilism like this makes you glad to be alive." As former lead singer John Lydon (aka Johnny Rotten) recalls in the film itself, "we managed to offend all the people we were fucking fed up with". But they clearly did not offend everyone and still do not. In 2006, *The Sex Pistols* 1977 album *Never Mind the Bollocks* was ranked at 22 in *Q Magazine*'s list of 100 Greatest Albums of All Time.

More generally, the punk rock of the 1970s still holds cultural cache and its legacy is an inspiration to much popular music from grunge to hardcore (Bennett, 2001; Heylin, 2007). Even contemporary pop is not ignorant of the punk myth – in her massive 2006 hit, the Scottish popular musician Sandi Thom sang "I wish I was a punk rocker with flowers in my hair." Juxtaposing the rebellious spirit of 1960s flower power and 1970s anarchic punk, she justifies this wish with "In '77 and '69, revolution was in the air; I was born too late to a world that doesn't care." For Thom, these were times when "God saved the queen she turned a whiter shade of pale" – direct reference is being made here to the hits of *The Sex Pistols* in 1977 and Procol Harum more than a decade earlier. The ethos that Thom's lyrics, in part, suggest is one where late 1970s punk rock, as exemplified by the Pistols rebelliousness, is a symbol of meaningfulness that she does not find (but desires) in her own contemporary cultural context.

Punk meant something because it actively resisted the status quo. And this was a specific form of resistance that rejected what was seen as the overproduced narcissism and self-styled seriousness of 1970s art rock. It rejected too the 'peace and love' romanticism of the 1960s hippie culture – an empty dream that seemed an all too saccharine capitulation of the rebellious culture of 1950s rock and roll. Punk was a reaction not just to the ethos of such movements but also to their institutionalization such that "Punk musicians assumed the task of bringing back to rock the type of harsh rebellion, rough sound, musical simplicity and – mostly in Britain – direct reference in the lyrics to social issues (unemployment, inter-racial relations) which they thought were lost" (Regev, 1994: 94). As Grossberg (1990: 117) puts it:

> Punk attacked rock and roll for having grown old and fat, for having lost that which puts it in touch with its audience and outside of the hegemonic reality. It attacked rock and roll in the guise of megagroups and arena rock, hippies and baby boomers who had clearly become part of what was supposed to be outside of rock and roll.

Thom's contemporary lyrical mythologizing might place punk alongside 1960s mystical dreaming, but it severely underestimates their differences – while the hippies valourized dropping out of commercialized culture into a new Eden with flowers in their hair, the punks (especially the British ones[1]) fought and spat from within the hell on earth that they were thrown in to.

Another contemporary discussion of *The Sex Pistols* can be found on the website of the Canadian alternative radio station The Edge (2005) in a two-part article entitled 'The History of Selling Out'. This article does well to sum up the way that, within popular music, authenticity is an important marker of what people regard as musical integrity. In the first paragraph is the statement that "at its best, music is pure art, uncorrupted by any form of profit [...] it's an expression of [the performer's] inner most thoughts and feelings". As the article goes on to suggest, however, the connection of popular music and commerce make the desire for such purity unrealistic. The article points to how, in 1976, *The Sex Pistols* "were widely admired for how they managed to swindle hundreds and thousands of dollars out of two big record companies without so much as selling a single". The story concerns the situation where the band were caught in media controversy and record company bidding wars which ended up with them walking away with £120,000 in advances, for which they released no songs. As The Edge article describes it, "the prevailing sense amongst fans was that the Pistols had stuck it to the establishment and were laughing all the way to the bank".

The cultural logic was that *The Sex Pistols* had authenticity because they refused to sell out to big business, while still being able to reap the financial benefits that big business had to offer. This is not a "contemporary ideal of authenticity" based on the premise that "lying within each individual, there is a deep. 'true self' – the 'real me'" (Guignon, 2004: 6) but rather one that is "inextricably positioned within [or in relation to] structures maintained and manipulated by monolithic corporate power (well practiced of course, in the profitable exploitation of difference)" (Middleton, 2006: 204). By the advent of the 1970s, the desire to be a self that was not commercially determined or defined was as strong as ever, not the least because of the still growing incorporation of a corporatized consumption-driven culture into more and more aspects of daily life – a culture that offered a bitter and unavailable imagery to working-class kids who felt they had few attractive prospects. In place of utopian dreams, the sub-culture that *The Sex Pistols* were at the centre of offered the authenticity of a working-class 'street credibility' that was very much located on the street rather than in the pastoral hallucination of the meadow. Even their drugs of choice showed this distinction – no LSD or magic mushrooms to transport the mind elsewhere, but uppers and amphetamines to make the now all the more intense. This was not the bourgeois dream of heaven on earth, but a direct engagement with the world-weary practicalities of evening the score by screwing the system just like it had screwed you.

As prefaced above, what is interesting about *The Sex Pistols'* various dalliances with big business (in the form of record companies) is that it immediately brings together a prevalent cultural logic of capitalism, identity and resistance. In this chapter, we reflect on the example of *The Sex Pistols*, as an empirical case, in terms of what it suggests to theories of resistance – in particular resistance to capitalist organizations. In pursuing this, we note that the meaning of the music and its culture for fans and followers is not our particular focus. Instead, we concern ourselves with the relations between the musicians and the recording industry. We note here that while like any other form of music punk "isn't just about the politics of resistance", it can nevertheless be "one site where people 'make do' with what resources they have and resist the power structures that oppress them". This is particularly salient to punk given that it "is often highly political in so far as it is deeply bound to questions of resistance, social location and commodification" (Phillipov, 2006: 392) and that it was "the most focused political challenge rock had yet produced" (Simonelli, 2002: 127). In our discussion, we relate this resistance also to other more contemporary examples of popular music as it draws attention to a cultural tension between authentic identity and commerce.

The main issue that our discussion draws out is how punk rock, in its production, exemplifies a mode of resistance that is both relational in terms of capitalist culture and organizations, but also seeks to exceed it through a punk rock aesthetic where new forms of subjectivity can be fashioned in excess of that culture.[2] This is a case where resistance can be excessive of business organization in that it relies on a more autonomous cultural organization that is productive in its own right. The result is the possibility of a certain 'authenticity' that might enable formation of subjectivity that is not limited to (but does include) an expression of a negative opposition or relation to authority. Present too is the creation of a positive expression of style and self-formation (cf. Foucault, 1988).

In sum, we use the possibilities of authenticity in popular music to develop an understanding of resistance that is neither rooted in the notion of an authentically true, independent or self-contained primordial self, nor one that is limited to relational oppositionality. This attests to the idea that rock "is a place where oppositional ideas can be expressed and shared, and in this sense becomes a forum for subversion" (Irving, 1988: 167). In this chapter, we connect this subversion to a temporal notion of authenticity that is located in the ongoing production of the self towards an always futural ideal of authenticity. An authenticity 'to-come' (Derrida, 1995).

This chapter begins with a brief review of resistance theories within critical management studies (CMS) with particular reference to Foucault's (1979) notions of panoptic power and relational resistance. These resistance theories are considered in contrast to the discourse of authenticity that is found in rock music in general, with specific reference to punk rock and *The Sex Pistols*. From there, we continue with the story of *The Sex Pistols* and their record companies in relation to these notions of resistance and authenticity. The main point made is that *The Sex Pistols* illustrate a form of resistance that is able to engage subversively with corporate power and take advantage of it, while still maintaining an authenticity that enables identity to be formed, in part, outside of the resistance–compliance binary that posits the resistant subject as the other of commercial and corporate discourse. This chapter concludes by suggesting that authenticity as located in punk, rather than attesting to the primacy of a true self, or to the creation of a resistant subject, is best understood as a case of exercising a certain authentic power.

Resisting organized discipline

Resistance is clearly a key concept in the study of business and management, especially amongst those who exhibit a profound scepticism to the moral foundations of corporate and commercial practice. In particular, in those traditions associated with critical management studies (CMS) and Foucauldian-inspired theory, resistance has been understood specifically in terms of surveillance, power and subjectivity and generally in relation to the development of a (self)disciplining contemporary social forms (McKinlay and Starkey, 1998; Knights and McCabe, 1999; Fleming and Sewell, 2002; Fleming and Spicer, 2003). The key text informing such ideas is Michel Foucault's *Discipline and Punish* (1977). This line of thinking proposes that under the pervasive and perpetual gaze of the corporation, organizational surveillance renders subjectivity, self-disciplining (cf. Iedema *et al.*, 2006). This subjectivity is "the product of a plurality of disciplinary mechanisms, techniques of surveillance and power-knowledge strategies" (Knights and McCabe, 1999: 203) where people "ritually collude in the own exploitation [and] the space for recalcitrance is markedly reduced" (Fleming, 2005: 46).

The argument is that surveillance eventually makes people internalize power so they become self-disciplined rather than controlled by others (Townley, 1993). Following Foucault (1979), the corporation is considered as a kind of realization of Bentham's infamous imagined prison, the Panopticon. For employees, various electronic and managerial surveillance technologies are deployed such that people who work for organizations are thought to be constantly under the potential or actual gaze of the managerial or corporate eye.

Consciousness of this external gaze leads people to also gaze upon themselves, internalizing the corporate eye so that it envelops them in the disciplinary apparatus of the corporation. In the Panopticon-cum-organization, surveillance is power's mechanism. By account of this 'subjectification thesis' (Fleming and Spicer, 2003: 174), organizational practice creates self-disciplining subjects who always think that they may be being watched and hence comply as if they actually were (Foucault, 1977). As Foucault (1979: 201) puts it: "the surveillance is permanent in its effects, even if it is discontinuous in its action [...] the inmates should be caught up in a power situation of which they themselves are bearers".

In studies of work organizations, it has been claimed that the research and theory inspired by Foucault illustrates "how power and discipline actively construct conformist selves" and "how forms of power exert control over people, not least by shaping their identities and relationships" (Collinson, 2003: 536). In the contemporary organization, however, deploying this surveillance through the tradition of centralized control is insufficient and even unnecessary for the full force of self-discipline to be realized (Sewell and Wilkinson, 1992). Supplementing, complementing or substituting for central and formal surveillance, contemporary corporate power has become more diffuse, less obvious and more potent in lack of overt presence. Peer-observation, electronic surveillance, team-based organization, performance management, quality management, human resource management and a raft of other managerial practices are all seen to participate in the tangled web of surveillance practices and self-discipline. And it is these disciplinary practices which are thought to embody a mode of management that extends from the governance of labour and action into the manipulation and control of the identity and subjectivity of workers. Not limited to workers, this extends into organizational activities that seek to govern consumers through marketing activities that purport to falsely offer them freedom and autonomy (Hodgson, 2002). No longer satisfied with the overt exploitation of the productive value of workers or the consumptive value of consumers, the argument is that now it is the autonomous subjectivity of individuals that is regarded as an economic resource (Miller and Rose, 1990) – organizations feel that it is incumbent upon them to produce the 'appropriate individual' always willing and able to jump to the service of the organization of their own volition and without coercion (Alvesson and Willmott, 2002) whether it be at the work station or the shopping till. When everyone is a worker or a consumer, it seems corporations exercise a power that seeks to determine who people are.

At its most extreme surveillance and discipline in organizations might be thought of as exerting complete control over identity such that "employees are simply programmed automatons who diligently perform the logic of the dominant regime as it is engineered [...] so that there is no possibility for resistance" (Fleming and Sewell, 2002) just as it might render people as "particular kinds of consumer subjects" (Knights and Sturdy, 1997). But of course other possibilities are manifold and have been elaborated upon extensively in the management literature (e.g. Jermier *et al.*, 1994; Fleming and Spicer, 2003; Hodgson, 2003). Resistance is seen as important in that it provides people with the mechanisms through which to try and tilt the balance of power back in their own favour – even though that resistance is to be located in relation to the power which it counterbalances. In the case of workers, as Collinson (2003: 539) argues, "by engaging in resistance, employees often begin to construct an alternative, more positive sense of self to that provided, prescribed or circumscribed by the organization". Staying aligned with Foucauldian theory, resistance is considered to be implicit in the exercise of corporate power such that conformity, although demanded by disciplinary power, is not its inevitable outcome (Collinson, 2003). This reflects a reciprocal and relational theory of power where within every instance of power, the possibility of resistance is implied.

Of course, discipline does not create, and has not created, a new race of worker-robots or consumer-dopes pre-programmed with managerially sanctioned subjectivities. Following Foucault:

> Where there is power there will also be resistance and, just as power is a broad and agentless web, resistance forms through a myriad of points distributed across webs of power/knowledge in an irregular, localized fashion. There is no centrepoint for resistance but, at every point where power is constituted through discourse, there is also resistance.
>
> (Clegg *et al*., 2006: 300)

Resistance too can take many forms – whether it be, for example, through humour, irony, cynicism, scepticism, parody, bitching or fraud (Hardy and Clegg, 2006) as well as through acts of deliberate subversiveness or self-exclusion. The point is that while power in the form of the control of subjectivity is increasingly prevalent in commercial and organizational settings, they do not serve the goal of full and complete reconstitution of subjectivity (Knights and McCabe, 1999). Instead, "resistant selves constitute a primary means by which employees express their discontent about workplace processes. They may help subordinates in 'surviving' organizational regimes of tight control, surveillance and commodification" (Collinson, 2003: 539).

Authenticity in rock

The corporate and commercial power–knowledge regimes discussed above do not exist in a vacuum. They are related to, and are a part of, other aspects of culture that have their own historically formed discourses and practices. Nowhere is this more palpable than in rock music. The relationship between power and resistance in capitalist organizations has long been locatable in the cultural site of rock music – most particularly as it is articulated through a discourse of 'authenticity'. Authenticity is a key defining feature of rock, one that distinguishes it from its pop 'other'. As Middleton (2006: 203) puts it: "The discourse of authenticity within music culture still holds much of its critical primacy, as dismissive response to turn-of-the-century 'manufactured pop' and 'corporate hegemony' makes clear."

One of the central ideas is that that musicians should be true to their artistic integrity, rather that 'selling out' to the lure of the market and its populist sentiments – resistance to corporate discipline seems to be at the heart of rock sensibility. Here the commercial temptations to become the person who the market (as mediated by record companies) wants you to be must be resisted in order to be able to locate oneself in the subject position of the 'musician-as-artist'. Those who do conform to the expectations of the music business are often condemned as fakes – whether it be the manufactured pop of *The Monkees* in the 1960s, the lip-synching shenanigans of Milli Vanilli in the 1980s, the cultural pretensions of *Vanilla Ice* in the 1990s, or the reality television-produced idols of the 2000s, appearing to be who someone else wants you to be lacks what is considered as artistic credibility. Better by far, the story goes, to resist such disciplining pressures, and be yourself – an ethos that reflects deeply romanticized notions of art being the product of an asocial authentic creativity associated with a pre-modern humanity (Guignon, 2004).

In music, authenticity is related, as a prized value, to being real, honest, truthful, with integrity, actual, genuine, essential and/or sincere (Moore, 2002). This notion of authenticity is used to distinguish, for example, "the genuine from the counterfeit, the honest from the false, the original from the copy"; the dominant view being that "authentic music came from (perhaps even generated) authentic communities; the bogus stuff was produced by cynics and aimed at (perhaps even created) consumers mired in false consciousness – dope for dupers" (Middleton, 2006: 200). Such distinctions mark the stereotypified, romanticized and overstated bifurcation which contrasts "the social as 'other' to one's true self" (Guignon, 2004: 34). Key here is a crude cultural logic of authenticity that, in modern times, is constructed very much in relation also to a commercial 'other'. To be authentic as a musician means to write and perform from a position of cultural authority and creativity rather than adapting one's style to that which is most likely to be socially acceptable or commercially successful (Moore, 2002). The anti-commercial and resistant sentiment that informs the discourse of authenticity is obvious. The discourse of authenticity is also very much one of identity – the musician, to be authentic, must position his or her selfhood against that of the "commodified, fetishized icon" (Middleton, 2006: 200). Authenticity requires resistance to corporate discipline.

On face value, the idea of the authentic self in rock, as outlined above, is problematic because it fails to adequately account for the social character of identity. The modern authentic is often cast as that which is not an imitation or a counterfeit but is an originary and creative self. Authenticity is held to reside in a person's "uniquely personal, as opposed to culturally or socially shared, identity" (Ferrara, 1998: 5). As Goldstein and Rayner (1994: 368) describe, authenticity "announces that each individual is his or her own measure, and if I am not true to myself, I miss the significance of my life". The authentic self is capable of being corrupted by social or economic influences, so the story goes, but should try to stay true to its 'real' self. As Middleton (2006) traces it, authenticity as it is used in popular music goes back directly to the nineteenth-century romanticism and the enlightenment quest for genuine and true knowledge in the spirit of Kant and Rousseau; just as it can be traced to similar roots in management thinking (Fleming, 2005). It is through such a cultural legacy that authenticity is rendered in a discourse of the self – a free and true self seeking and awaiting self-knowledge and its expression. In this context, art qua music is of course important in that it is regarded as belonging to a moral sphere – great work created by great *men* of genius, each conceived of through concepts of "autonomy, self direction and the unitary self" (Middleton, 2006: 217).

Today authenticity is still wrapped up in terms of the relations between people and art, whereby art is seen as an expression of a romanticized notion of the authentic self. Moreover, as discussed earlier, commercialization is seen as an anathema to such artistic expression. This logic can be seen in how, for example, Alan Lomax's recording of Robert Johnson in the 1920s was authentic because Johnson played a hitherto unrecorded country blues that was not contaminated by big business. Conversely, Bob Dylan, who had earlier been lauded by the folk music cognoscenti for his adherence to their musical tradition, was booed at Newport in the 1960s for playing with a rock band because his 'fans' felt that he had betrayed the authenticity of his folk roots. "[H]e was decried as a 'sellout' by folknik purists" (Hentoff, 2006: 95).

It was in 1988 that Neil Young proudly anthemized This Note's For You in protest of the inauthenticity associated with musicians involved in product promotion and advertising. He yelled out: "Ain't singin' for Pepsi; Ain't singin' for Coke; I don't sing for nobody; Makes me look like a joke; This note's for you." More recently in 2000, Eminem famously announced himself as iconically authentic to his alter ego, rapping "I'm Slim Shady, yes I'm the real Shady; All you other Slim Shady's are just imitating." And in his call for authenticity, true to form, Eminem distances himself from commercial pop and locates himself close to rebellion and resistance:

> I'm sick of you little girl and boy groups, all you do is annoy me;
> So I have been sent here to destroy you;
> And there's a million of us just like me;
> Who cuss like me;
> Who just don't give a fuck like me.

The dominant role of authenticity in rock discourse is clearly illustrated by Chester's (1970: 78) comments on *The Band* in relation to their position in 1960s rock:

> Their intense professionalism and the rigor of their collective instrumental work have never been endangered by the demand of being cultural symbols as well as musicians (the ruin of such promising groups as Country Joe or the Doors), and these qualities are absolute requirements of the ultra-sensitive capacity to turn thought instantly into sound that intentional construction demands

As this snippet suggests, *The Band* are to be lauded because they are virtuoso musicians rather than cultural symbols whose own 'false' commercial personas might eclipse the requirements of the music.

Despite being labelled as a modernist notion (Brackett, 2002), the trace of authenticity discourse has not been erased from contemporary rock, even if that trace has been either commodified or parodied. Take for example Avril Lavigne, an entirely manufactured pop star whose skater-girl/rock chick persona launched on to the world stage in 2002. Lavigne's biographical details attest to her lack of rock authenticity (she was part of a manufactured band), yet still she could sing about authenticity; as she does, for example, in one of her biggest hits 'Complicated':

> Acting like you're somebody else gets me frustrated;
> Life's like this, you;
> And you fall and you crawl; and you break and you take;
> What you get and you turn it into; Honesty
> Promise me I'm never gonna find you fake it.

Faking it is the worst sin in rock. Resisting commercial capitulation is one of the greatest virtues.

In an odd juxtaposition, it seems that within popular music itself there is a logic at play quite similar to Adorno's (1941) trenchant critique of popular music as mindless repetition designed for mass appeal and cultural manipulation. So too is Adorno's prizing of the avant-garde as a bastion of non-commercial aesthetic values – tastes and preferences differ, but the belief in the Enlightenment logic appears to persist. For Adorno popular culture is inauthentic, but for today's music fan it is only some of this culture that is so. There are connections too in terms of anti-commercialism. Akin to Marx's base/superstructure distinction, the idea is that culture is linked to economy such that the things produced by the culture industry are in the service of that industry – at an economic and ideological level. The result, so the argument goes, is that people are hoodwinked into being unable to resist or critique capitalism because they lack an authentic culture through which to do so. The consciousness is falsified as commodified cultural products masquerade as originals. But, in the discourse of rock authenticity, while this masquerade is a constant threat, not all cultural products participate in it. Those judged as not doing so are the ones called authentic – and it is this judgment that goes by the name of 'selling out'.

Selling out

For both fans and rock musicians, the issue of 'selling out' has been an important part of rock music discourse, and one that is directly implicated with authenticity and resistance. The idea is that musicians should be true to their artistic integrity, rather that succumbing to the lure of the market and its populist sentiments. Importantly, this discourse does not condemn 'selling' per se, nor does it condemn popularity in its entirety. Rather, the main issue is that to be authentic the popularity and the large sales should be a by-product of the search for, and expression of, artistic integrity rather than a goal in and of itself. The artist should not be faking it but should somehow be conceived of as 'real'. Thus, key to the issue of authenticity in music is the relationship between the music itself and the commercial processes through which it is produced and distributed. In this sense, organizations – record companies, radio stations, etc. – are placed centrally in discussions of the aesthetics of rock. Most commonly, this placing is one that is critical, where it is assumed, for example, that A&R people of dubious artistic taste, greedy record company executives, manipulative producers and avaricious advertisers are a force against which the authentic musician must resist in order to retain his or her authenticity.

Despite a dominant logic that binarizes the distinction between commerce and authenticity, it remains the case that it is difficult "to maintain any absolute distinction between commercial exploitation on the one hand and creativity/ originality on the other, even though these categories are emphatically opposed in the value systems of most subcultures" (Hebidge, 1979: 95). Nevertheless, such distinctions provide ample material for song writing. As Davies, J (1996) explains, for example, The Clash's song 'Complete Control' provides a simple message of authenticity, that is: "The Clash's record company has reneged on a promise of artistic freedom made to the group." The lyric contrasts their wish to be 'artistically free' with CBS's desire to "make money" (8). As The Clash sang it: "They said we'd be artistically free; When we signed that bit of paper; They meant let's make a lotsa mon-ee; An' worry about it later" – but their message was not just a matter of autobiography: "This is Joe Public speaking; I'm controlled in the body, controlled in the mind; Total C-o-n control – that means you!" Foucault's idea of disciplinary power does not seem too far away.

Despite the cultural potency and persistence of the discourse of authenticity in popular music, the growth of mass culture and the culture industries in the twentieth century has for a long time been perceived as putting authenticity in jeopardy. Thus, as Connell and Gibson (2003: 19) suggest, a key way that authenticity in music is constructed "starts with assumptions about the moment of commodification, when indigenous or folk music traditions came into contact with wider musical economies". Such assumptions are based on the uneasy relationship between the values associated with music as a form of culture and music as a commodity to be sold. 'Selling out' is thus said to occur when the commodity values take precedence over cultural values. The situation contemporarily has become even more complicated as the notion of authenticity itself can be used as a marketing device designed to sell commodities – as with Avril Lavigne discussed earlier – and has in a sense become commodified. Nevertheless, authenticity remains as a residue of folk tradition and the romanticism of a mythical past unencumbered by the hegemony of capitalism, even when that hegemony is everywhere to be seen. The myth of authenticity and the hope for authenticity persevere despite its being headed off at every turn.

In relation to rock music, the discourse of 'selling out', in addition to being positioned in relation to commerce, is connected with a notion of authenticity that has been historically constructed in an odd combination of entertainment, social identity and "values such as resistance, refusal, alienation and marginality" (Connell and Gibson, 2003: 42). As Brackett (2002) points out, the development of a rock aesthetic based on a notion of authenticity and anti-commercialism emerged in the mid-1960s as an offshoot of the folk music revival of the late 1950s and early 1960s (Brackett, 2002; Frith, 1981) and subsequently as part of its transformation into folk rock. As part of that transformation, the rock musician, to be considered authentic, had not only to eschew himself or herself from commercial objectives, but also to be considered as a 'real' person unencumbered by the star quality of the teen idol even though it was such idolatry that characterized many of the original 1950s rock and rollers – Elvis Presley being the case in point.

Selling *The Sex Pistols*

To examine in more detail the relationship between music, authenticity, resistance and commerce, we now turn to the example of *The Sex Pistols*. In 1976, punk was emerging as a major force in British music – not the least as a result of manager Malcolm McLaren's efforts, for example, of organizing of the 'Punk Rock Festival' in London in September 1976 (Simonelli, 2002). Central to this were *The Sex Pistols*, the band who headlined that festival and who are now perhaps most strongly associated with punk iconography – while punk was very much alive in London in the mid-1970s, "it wasn't until the appearance of The Sex Pistols that punk began to emerge as a recognizable style" (Hebidge, 1979: 142). Under the direction of McLaren, they were an un-signed band that seemed to promise much in relation to potential record sales. An early recognition of this resulted in stiff competition between major record labels eager to cash in on the punk explosion. As Savage (1991) recounts, there were initially two record companies in the running for the Pistols contract – Polydor and EMI. Pushed along by McLaren's sales panache, EMI got the deal. McLaren reports that he said to EMI:

> If you can't help these kids then God help the industry [...] if you can't sign something that's new and young and in front of your eyes you're living in the past and you might as well shut up shop.
>
> (Savage, 1991: 224)

Spurred on by such an argument, EMI gave the band a £40,000 non-returnable advance for a two-year contract. As Savage (1991: 225) describes, this was a coup for EMI who lacked an adequately contemporary and future-oriented catalogue and a boon for the Pistols who could now both have a money to progress their careers and vindicating "their image as the Punk elite". It was 8 October 1976. Two months later on 1 December, the band were scheduled, at the last minute, to appear on the London evening television programme *Today*, hosted by Bill Grundy. What happened in this interview, and its aftermath, is a central story in the history and mythology of punk.

As well as the members of *The Sex Pistols*, numerous other punks were present at the interview. Notably, this entourage included the punk icon,

Siouxsie Sioux, of the band Siouxsie and the Banshees. At one point, Grundy turned his attention from the Pistols to the women who were present – especially Siouxsie. The script is like this:

GRUNDY: What about you girls behind?
GLEN: He's like yer Dad in' he, this geezer, or your Grandad?
GRUNDY: Are you worried or just enjoying yourself?
SIOUXSIE: Enjoying myself.
GRUNDY: Are you?
SIOUXSIE: Yeah.
GRUNDY: Ah, that's what I thought you were doing.
SIOUXSIE: I've always wanted to meet you.
GRUNDY: Did you really?
SIOUXSIE: Yeah.
GRUNDY: We'll meet afterwards, shall we?
[Siouxsie makes a moué.]
STEVE [JONES, THE SEX PISTOLS GUITARIST]: You dirty sod. You dirty old man.
GRUNDY: Well keep going chief, keep going. Go on you've got another ten
    seconds. Say something outrageous.
STEVE: You dirty bastard.
GRUNDY: Go on, again.
STEVE: You dirty fucker!
GRUNDY: What a clever boy!
STEVE: You fucking rotter!
[More laughter from the band and fans; Grundy closes]
GRUNDY: Well that's it for tonight. The other rocker, Eamonn, I'm saying
    nothing else about him, will be back tomorrow. I'll be seeing you soon. I
    hope I'll not be seeing you [to the band] again. From me though, goodnight.

(Savage, 1991: 259)

This exchange of sexual innuendo and coarse language caused a media uproar – an uproar that ironically ignored the rough edged but traditional chivalry of the Pistol's guitarist Steve Jones' defence of Siouxsie. As Jones puts it: "From that day on it was different. Before then, it was just music: the next day it was the media" (Savage, 1991: 260).[3] While punk was an established underground movement, it "first surfaced in the nation's consciousness with the aftermath of the Grundy interview" (Cobley, 1999: 174) through its coverage in both the London and national press and the association of punk with swearing, filth, degradation and a general downfall of society.

From the beginning, the issue of *The Sex Pistols* authenticity was very much a matter of public interest. Earlier in the interview, Grundy asked: "I'm told that the group has received £40,000 from a record company. Doesn't that seem ... er ... to be slightly opposed to their [*deep breath*] anti-materialistic view of life?" The answers from the band were "No. The more the merrier" and "we've fucking spent it ain't we" (Vermorel and Vermorel, 1978: 30).

By the next day, this short exchange had become headline news. As the right-wing tabloid the *Daily Mirror* puts it: "A pop group shocked millions of viewers last night with the filthiest language ever heard on British television" (Savage, 1991: 264). With another day gone by, there was a statement in the *Daily Mail* that started to pull at the heart strings of capitalism and authenticity:

> The ultimate peddlers of the pop industry – slick, agile of brain, fast of mouth – know that the same three chord product can be sold over and over again, as long as the package changes. Every financial year, the men who manipulate for money try to impose a fresh style. Increasingly they capitalize on a basic tide of behaviour: young people's instincts to outrage the older generation.
>
> (Savage, 1991: 266)

Amidst the chaos of the media coverage, followed by concert cancellations and radio play blacklisting of the single 'Anarchy in the UK', the band's (and McLaren's) relationship with EMI was at breaking point. By Christmas, the deal with EMI was dead. This was confirmed by an EMI press release on 5 January 1977 – both parties "mutually agreed to terminate their record contract. EMI feels it is unable to promote this group's records internationally in view of the adverse publicity that has been generated in the last two months" (Vermorel and Vermorel, 1978: 49).

In a song released later that year, on the album *Never Mind the Bollocks Here's The Sex Pistols*, they sang

> Don't judge a book just by the cover
> Unless you cover just another
> And blind acceptance is a sign
> Of stupid fools who stand in line
> Like
> E.M.I. E.M.I. E.M.I.

Finding another record company was not difficult, with CBS and Virgin Records in the early running. By 9 March, however, the band signed with A&M for an advance of £75,000. For the press, there was a public signing the following day outside of Buckingham palace, as a promotion for their first planned A&M single – the notorious 'God Save the Queen'. A&M said that "*The Sex Pistols* becoming available presented us with a unique business opportunity" (Vermorel and Vermorel, 1978: 66). A week later, after more press scandal mongering and political furore, A&M terminated the contract and the band and their handlers kept the cash. "A&M washed their hands of the group by destroying almost all of the 25,000 newly pressed singles. They also destroyed the metal masters. *The Sex Pistols* were now music industry pariahs" (Savage, 1991: 320).

As the Pistols notoriety continued to grow, on 12 May they were signed to

Virgin Records and their single 'God Save the Queen' was released on 27 May – timed to try and ensure that it would be in the top ten of the pop charts during Jubilee week. The single hit the charts at number 11, eventually rising to number 2 despite being banned by major retailers.

By that time, the nation's youth were singing along to the lyrics originally written down quickly by Lydon in a Hamstead squat (Savage, 1991):

> Don't be told what you want
> Don't be told what you need
> No future
> No future
> No future
> For you

It is unclear whether the Grundy incident was a premeditated media stunt or a spontaneous outburst, but either way it kicked off a form of public notoriety for *The Sex Pistols* that paved the way for their commercial success and cultural popularity – meanwhile Grundy himself was suspended from his job at Thames television for the incident (Simonelli, 2002). And all the time the Pistols were active in their resistance: in their "deliberate opposition to commercial rock music [… they …] flaunted their ineptitude as musicians, making noises that were louder, faster and noisier than anything most audiences had heard previously" (Moore, 2004: 312). The band created a perception of resistance and notoriety that was seen by sections of the fan base as a sign of authenticity – sticking it up with the big corporations, the established media, defacing images of the British monarchy and so forth were all readable as authentic rebellion and resistance, in particular to commercial institutions. As McLaren announced at the time: "We constitute a basic challenge to the whole way the record business is organized" (Simonelli, 2002: 131).

Resistance and authenticity

Having provided an account of *The Sex Pistols* relationship with the music industry and the public, the question we now turn to is whether Foucauldian inspired resistance theory or discussions of authenticity are adequate to explain what went on. *The Sex Pistols*, today widely regarded as the archetypal punk band, where at the helm of this then new music which promised not only a new social critique, but also a new type of free speech:

> it inaugurated a moment – a long moment, which still persists – when suddenly countless odd voices, voices no reasonable person could have expected to hear in public, were being heard all over the place […] there was an absolute denial of self-censorship in *The Sex Pistols'* songs that gave people who heard them permission to speak as freely.
>
> (Marcus, 1993: 3)

If power/knowledge "structures the sayable" (Townley, 2005: 646), *The Sex Pistols* appear not to have been listening, instead engaging in a radical agency enabled by counter-discourse (Moussa and Scapp, 1996). As a form of resistance, punk spat in the face of authority with abandon and without regard for the future. As Shuker (2001: 162) notes, the persistent theme of anarchy in punk culture "indicates a congruence between punk as music and the social location and values of the associated punk subculture [...] Music here exists very much within a broader set of social relations". It is within this set of social relations that the activities of *The Sex Pistols*, described above, appear to conform to a model of rock resistance "founded on the overturning of authority and a celebration of rebellion" (Rhodes, 2007: 32). This was a resistance positioned directly in opposition to the establishment, to commercial culture and to business – and to the forms of subjectivity that were projected on and through the youth of the day.

In their unique position in 1976/1977, *The Sex Pistols* were quite clearly acting in a way that rebelled against the dominant position that they may have been placed in by the music business – as dutiful contract holders expected to fulfil their end of the bargain as negotiated and legally inscribed. If this were read in terms of resistance theory in organization studies, it could be suggested that what was being resisted was big business' normalizing discourse that sought to contain and capitalize on rebellion as a marketing tool, while retaining the right to normalize musicians into particular forms of subject positions designed to render them productive, in both musical and economic terms. But, for the Pistols, the wild abandon of the particular variety of their resistance appeared both culturally and commercially unacceptable for their early record labels. Their resistance manifested in the way that it transgressed the boundaries of assumed marketability. The band could not be contained in terms of the marketing of resistance because it was too radical for the cultural sensibilities of the record companies (or at least in that the companies believed that their association with the Pistols would damage sales elsewhere in their catalogue).

As introduced earlier in this chapter, within the study of management and organizations, resistance to the disciplinary power of organizations can manifest in a number of ways, for example; the non-internalization of organizational values (Willmott, 1993), cynicism (Fleming and Spicer, 2003), humour (Taylor and Bain, 2003), partial subjectivization (Knights and McCabe, 1999) or active discontent (Collinson, 2003). Such approaches suggest that agency can be located in terms of the presumed power of organizations to normalize employees (Gabriel, 1999). Both Gabriel (1999) and Fleming and Sewell (2002) argue that in the face of disciplinary power, resistance might be locatable is various 'unmanaged' or 'invisible' sites. Here resistance "may well stop short of overt rebellion, although its impact may be just as disruptive (perhaps even more so)" – this is a resistance "conducted below the veneer of legitimacy; covert and seditious acts carried out in the silent spaces of everyday life" (Fleming and Sewell, 2002: 859–60). In terms of punk rock, this is a resistance that starts in the silent space of the gutter, only later to be heard loud and clear by all.

Punk emerged from a disenfranchised underclass of disaffected youth who were not really plugged into the establishment circuits of power and control and who while resisting that power did not have a full knowledge of it. It is this lack of knowledge that suggests that the punk resistance does not conform to the idea that resistance is necessarily located both within and against the disciplinary regimes of organizational control. Clegg *et al.* (2006) suggest "resistance to power, because it calls forth the appropriate sanctions, actually strengthens the organizational order, rather than weakening it". This last statement seems to hold true for those forms of resistance which are locatable entirely within the discursive bounds from which organizational authority and power emerge ... but this is not the only location, and certainly not the one we have been discussing here.

If resistance is only the other to power, then power is merely confirmed by its resistance. In such cases faced with the rules that seek to rationalize organizational authority, those who work in and for organizations might choose between resistance and obedience – while directly opposed to such rules, resistance is still defined in relation to those rules. Such a systemic notion of power/resistance fails to account for the potential for resistance to be exercised in a way that is not only constituted in relation to the rules from which relational resistance is marked. This is where punk and *The Sex Pistols* come in.

The point we are getting at is that modes of resistance can deploy cultural narratives that exist beyond or outside of the commercial or organizational system of discourse – this was the character of much of *The Sex Pistols* resistance. Such narratives flow through significations that are not contained wholly within commercial or organizational discourse; they exceed its bounds. On that basis, such narratives are able to enact a power that seems, ostensibly, to exist in its own right as well as being relative to power. When resistance is multi-focused, and dispersed across various sites and discursive moments, its connections to commercial culture or organizations cannot be so neatly delineated. *The Sex Pistols* were not alone in their cultural location but neither were they tightly connected the broader punk rock movement of the time. In punk, there was no centre or location to which establishment power regimes could target its disciplinary forces. There was of course the negative media coverage and the well-publicized banning of songs from radio airplay, but if anything, this bolstered punk's notoriety, familiarity and popularity. The dispersal of the mechanisms of consumer capitalism in the music industry over a broad range of economic, social and cultural institutions meant that the spontaneity and speed of punk's development rendered it beyond the panoptic gaze of any disciplinary power.

Rather than being just a power that is produced against (and hence defined by) that which is resisted, punk rock seemed to exceed the limits of what the system would allow or even be able to acknowledge. In other words, while on the one hand resistance has been conceived of as the resistance by deviance to organized authority, it is also possible that the cultural organization of that very resistance might itself be powerful in a non-secondary and non-derivative way. In other words, punk was part of the system that it rebelled against, but it was also more than that system.

What the example of *The Sex Pistols* shows is the possibility of a resistance that exceeds the discipline against which it is positioned. As Davies (1996: 5) describes it, this is not so much a "resistance to a dominant culture outside or against which it is conceived as existing" but rather a "subversiveness within that culture". More specifically:

> The strategy for subversion employed by McLaren and The Sex Pistols involved trying to steer the institutions of the mass media and icons of consumer culture against themselves, using their own signs and spectacles to expose the artificial and arbitrary nature of an apparently immutable social system.
>
> (Moore, 2004: 311)

This shift in focus from resistance to subversiveness is important. While conventional notions of resistance rest on the idea of acting out of an opposing force to power, the notion of subversiveness hones in more specifically on *undermining* that power or even *exceeding* its limits – and moreover this subversiveness is seen, in rock discourse, as authenticity par excellence (Regev, 1994). Part of this undermining was the way that punk, for both its musicians and its fans, appealed to a disaffected youth by saying to society: yes look how filthy, ugly, unpalatable, unruly, disturbing and disgusting we are, but we are created in your image; it is your social systems that have constituted us; it is your social and political systems that have created the conditions of no future and nihilism; it is your institutions that have left us 'pretty vacant'; it is your aesthetic institutions that have pushed us over into anti-style. But it also said: we are more than you.

In terms of *The Sex Pistols*, they were (with the political skills of Malcolm McLaren) able to undermine the various record companies for whom they were employed. The reason that this happened was precisely because they did not engage in (or possibly fully understand) the nature of the discourse against which they were rebelling. Even though McLaren was knowingly involved in a 'Rock 'n' Roll Swindle', his approach was more opportunistic than planned (Moore, 2004) – "it is difficult to know whether McLaren was operating on a chaotic series of intuitions or according to an orchestrated plan, but it was clear that he was the first rock manager to use the *subversive* possibilities of hype" (Harron cited in Bennet, 2001: 61, italics added). McLaren's espoused approach was based on the belief that "a rock and roll band could swindle the established order into bringing them into the system, then violently overthrow it" (Simonelli, 2002: 124). The result was a practice of abandon which saw the band spin out of control in their own activities with little concern for the consequences. Despite this, however, the band also conducted itself in a way that was not entirely opposed to the business – they were quite successful in using this business against itself in order to secure their own success, financially and otherwise, and McLaren was well known for boasting about the money he was making from record companies and film contracts (Huxley, 1999).

The notion of 'selling out' is complicated by punk, which retained an authenticity while at the same time having "no real problem with the idea of making large amounts of money" (Huxley, 1999: 96). In a sense, this might be described as a form of rock and roll resistance that, while enacted a discernable form of struggle, was doing so without any particular destination in mind (Grossberg, 1990). This is then a form of self-empowerment locatable within the unstable vectors of attitude, corporeal pleasure and youthfulness that might "energize new possibilities within everyday life" (Grossberg, 1990: 117). This attests to the idea that "popular culture can be a form of resistance" (Street, 1997: 12) but also that the cultural logics – in this case the rock and roll logics – provide cultural narratives for such resistance. This is not a resistance that is just oppositional, but one that is also creative and open-ended.

The form of resistance that *The Sex Pistols* encapsulate is, importantly, one that is not opposed, either practically or ideologically to business per se. In a sense what emerges out of their dealings with the record companies is a sense of renewed authenticity that is creatively crafted in the space between music and commerce. In other words, they sold without selling (themselves) out.

What's left of authenticity?

The example of *The Sex Pistols* various interactions with EMI, A&M and Virgin Records is now almost 30 years old. Despite this, a cultural interest in *The Sex Pistols* remains vibrant both for their now middle-aged contemporaries and for the punk legacy that still thrives today in rock music culture. If anything, this rock and punk rock ethos is deeply embedded in Western culture – an ethos of rebellion, abandon, recklessness and disregard for authority whose limits and trajectory are not entirely knowable. What this demonstrates is the possibility for a form of resistance that brashly offends authority and, in so doing, enables a particular form of authenticity that might enable one to 'become oneself'.

Peterson (2005: 1086) suggests that rather than being an intrinsic characteristic to an object, person or group, authenticity "is a claim that is made by or for someone, thing, or performance and either accepted or rejected by relevant others". By this account, authenticity is, following Goffman (1959), a form of impression management such that, for example, a person who wishes to be regarded as authentic must do so by managing his or her own performance in relation to how others will interpret it in the hope that the relevant attributions will be forthcoming – in other words, authenticity is "ascribed, not inscribed" (Moore, 2002: 210). For Peterson (2005: 1086), this 'authenticity work' is carried out in terms of relations to ethnic and cultural identity, group membership, artistic status and 'authentic' experience as well as the ways one's actions are regarded as being consistent with a single and valued sense of identity. It is in such ways that authenticity is "tied to identity and articulates the desire of consumers to differentiate themselves from the masses" (Gardner, 2005: 136) by first ascribing authenticity to particular forms of music and then by identifying with it in order to garner some of that authenticity for themselves. While this speaks as an example of the potential potency of subcultural identification in general, it was particularly pronounced in punk at the time: "No subculture has sought with more grim determination than the punks to detach itself from the taken-for-granted landscape of normalized forms, nor to bring down upon itself such vehement disapproval" (Hebidge, 1979: 19). There is an old joke where a perplexed middle-class parent asks the punk rocker teenager, "Why do you dress like that?" The teenager, who looks quite similar to all of the other punks, replies "because, I want to be different!" The weak humour of this is, of course, the idea that the teenager achieves no difference at all because he or she is exactly the same as all of those other people trying to be different. This, however, is a poor reading in that it assumes the desire to be different is a desire to be different from everyone else – that is the desire to be absolutely unique. Quite clearly, though the rebellious authenticity of punk is not necessarily about the absolute difference of the individual but rather about being different to that which they think is expected of them. This means being different to the bourgeois values being inscribed and represented by the parent: "I don't want to be different to them, I want to be different to you!" What this illustrates is that authenticity is located in the relation between self and other – the authentic punk is so because she/he is not who she/he is 'supposed' to be – and that difference is something that is ascribed to him or her as culturally meaningful by others.

For others, however, it may well have been the case that some notion of absolute individuality was, at least, an aspiration and part of the aesthetic – one importantly as far distanced as possible from the mass consumptive signifiers of identity available in the type of mass produced look available commercially (even though it was this ideal that Malcolm McLaren's sex clothing store in London came to pander to). We are careful here to neither totalize nor idealize punk. For some, the weekend punk for example, the Friday night insertion on the safety pin was a sellout, and punk chic as a fashion commodity was an appropriation. For some knowing punks, this was inevitable and punk was bound and intended to self-implode. It was always going to be a short, dark moment of challenge.

But punk was still a moment of challenge whose myth lives on today. Moreover, it was a challenge and a response to a "crisis of meanings caused by the commodification of everyday life" (Moore, 2004: 305) in postmodern culture. This response, Moore argues, appears in two contradictory ways. The first is a response to postmodernity characterized by a turning away from mass-mediated, consumer-driven society. The second is "quest for authenticity and independence from the culture industry" (307) through the formation of local institutions and alternative media (O'Connor, 2002). Concordantly, Moore argues that punk engages both with a 'culture of deconstruction' (informed by defiance, resistance and the parody of power) and with a 'culture of authenticity' (informed by autonomy from the culture industry and various forms of political criticism and activism). It is using these distinctions that we can regard calls to punk rock authenticity not just as a form of resistance that reinforces power through opposition but also one creative of the possibility of some degree of autonomous subjectivity.

What this suggests is the possibility of an authenticity that is not merely a ruse for resistance, nor does it necessarily rest on the assumption of a natural self to which one might return. As Butler (2003) argues, following Foucault, the concern here is not just with the formation of a subject rendered through surveillance and discipline (as outlined earlier in the chapter) but with self-formation. As Butler (2003: 19–20) writes:

> That the range of its possible forms is delimited in advance by such modes of subjectivation does not mean that the self fails to form itself, that the self is fully formed. On the contrary, it is compelled to form itself, but to form itself within forms that are already more or less in operation and underway. Or, one might say, it is compelled to form itself within practices that are more or less in place. But if that self forming is done in disobedience to the principles by which one is formed, then virtue becomes the practice by which the self forms itself in desubjugation, which is to say that it risks its deformation as a subject, occupying that ontologically insecure position which poses the question anew: who will be a subject here.

If we take Butler's statement in relation to authenticity – the notion of being a subject who is not entirely wrapped up in power and its resistance means not actually being a subject at all – at least not one that is present in existent practices. Authenticity is thus rendered as an anti-identity or an anti-subjectivity – it is the "deformation of the subject" (Butler, 2003: 20) understood in terms of both lack of form and aberration of form. The authentic self here is a flight from subjectivity. While such a flight, in an pure sense, seems untenable, what might still be salvaged is the way that subjectivity might still slip as it is in part located within power relations and in part is a departure from them – "rock and roll is a set of strategies for struggle, the nature and effects of which are never predetermined" (Grossberg, 1990: 122). Punk is then not entirely outside of power relations and their effects, but neither is it entirely within them. Anything that engages with the social in the way that punk does will inevitably be in the circuits of power, but focusing also on the potential for an exteriority, there is a need to point to a temporalization of the authentic subject as being en route to subjectivity (rather than trapped by it). The question asked is, "Who is the subject here?" (Butler, 2003: 20), but the answer is not locatable entirely in the here and now.

For Middleton (2006: 238), authenticity is best regarded (following Derrida) as spectral such that "even if its untruth is acknowledged, we still want it, and we want it all the more because this phantasmic version is all we have" where the spectre of authenticity is matched up to the "fetish power in consumption, each a verso of the other" (240). Here authenticity is guaranteed through the exchange of representations between self and other as mediated through culture and the culture industries. The 'real thing' (the authentic subject) is an object of desire for the uncommodified and the unfetishized. What Middleton gets at with this is a temporalization of authenticity – authenticity's futurization, rather than subjectivity's stranglehold in the determined possibilities of the present. The point that we can take from this is that authenticity does not need to be understood in terms of the return to an authentic self, but rather that authenticity is in Derrida's (1995) terms part of the 'to come'. Not a utopia to be imminently realized, but a spectral fantasy which exists outside of the day of judgment where the authentic will be divided from the inauthentic. In the present, this renders authenticity as 'undecidable' (Derrida, 1988) such that authenticity can never be determined once and for all but is instead a project characterized by anxiety and choice in the face of multiple positions of how one is to be and who one wants to be. This is an authenticity that relates to a moral self not in terms of the truth of self-sameness, but in terms of the responsibility for the madness of living without the knowledge of who one might be or how one's decisions might play out for both self and other.

The oppositional force of subculture is not limited to ritualistic or symbolic forms of resistance (cf. Hebidge, 1979) but might also be considered subversively productive of new forms of subjectivity. More generally, it might be the case that subcultures, and particularly youth subcultures, not only work and are powerful because they offer subjectivities and subject positions that are alternative to those that the mainstream offers, but also because they provide a platform against which to embark on uncharted trajectories. Rock, in particular punk rock, is thus rendered political at the level of the subject and its creative possibilities. This is no model to follow but rather an example of the possible. What this shows is that in a commodified culture dominated by commerce, there are possibilities for resistance and subversion that that do not always locate the self within the gaze commercially motivated institutions – even when that gaze seems insurmountably potent.

10 Sampling, tinkering and the glitch

Bricolage in popular music and in organization practice

Performers and producers of rap and hip-hop music might be forgiven for think-ing that they invented musical sampling. That is certainly not the case; it has, in fact, a long history (Rose, 1994), as we shall see. There has, however, clearly been an intensification of the use of sampling over the last couple of decades in contemporary popular music, in rap but also other musical sub-genres such as dance and acid jazz ... and even in contemporary 'classical' music. This intensi-fication has been enabled by certain technologies and driven by certain aesthetic tastes and artistic preferences. It has generated a good deal of discussion about the nature of music, particularly around the role of technology in music produc-tion, but also intense debates around notions of originality and authenticity in music and in artistic production more broadly. In that regard, this chapter occu-pies some of the same discursive space as other chapters in this book, particu-larly the previous one in that it raises important questions about the contemporary meaning of authenticity. Since popular music is big business, the commercial aspects of originality and authenticity have often been foregrounded in considerations of sampling. Most particularly, the use of samples has reener-gized discussions about originality, authorship and ownership, and the legalities of copyright have been invoked. We argue, then, that "sampling is a distinctly postmodern practice – indeed, exemplary. It engages in the aesthetics of pastiche and nostalgia. It constructs an assemblage of fragments – a bricolage" (West-wood, 1999: 196).

These are important matters that have wider import than simply the role and status of rap music and will be touched upon in this chapter. However, our main aim here is to use sampling as an example within popular culture of some of the particularities of the intersection of work practice and technology. We are particularly interested in exploring the ways in which that intersection is con-ducted in unplanned, unintended or accidental ways. Sampling is an exemplary form of the manipulation of technology to produce outcomes that go beyond the formal, official and/or intended uses of the technology. It is a form of 'tinker-ing', and this chapter explores some other examples from musical and other domains. We then relate this treatment of sampling explicitly to the notion of bricolage as first articulated by Lévi-Strauss (1966). Precise translations of the French term bricolage are not straightforward, but one clear connotation *is* 'tinkering' and so the relationship with sampling is quite clear. This chapter will discuss instances of tinkering in music practice but also the use and/or appropriation of technological malfunctions or unintended outcomes for functional or aesthetic purposes. Thus, some forms of music practice have identified glitches in certain technologies and worked to incorporate them for aesthetic effect into their music practice.

This chapter then argues that bricolage, tinkering and the constructive deployment of glitches are not merely restricted to practices within popular music production but are in fact more pervasive in work and organizational practice than is commonly acknowledged. The concept of bricolage has received only limited direct attention in management and organization studies (Baker *et al.*, 2003), in part, we surmise, because it poses a challenge to the rationalist assumptions embedded in the field's orthodoxy. There are instances of bricolage being applied in the areas of policy making (Freeman, 2005), organizational founding and entrepreneurial activity (Baker *et al.*, 2003; Baker and Nelson, 2005), information technology adoption (Ferneley and Bell, 2006), constructing organizational culture (Linstead and Grafton-Small, 1992), design (Louridas, 1999) and formulating strategy (Cunha and Cunha, 2006), and Cunha (2007) has attempted a summary.

Considerations of tinkering and bricolage open up a new space for exploration in organization studies, one that offers enhanced understanding of the nature of work practice and the intersection of work practice and the intersection of work and technology. The presence of bricolage, tinkering and glitches in organizational settings is a challenge to the formal, ordered, expected and rational aspects of organization and management practice. As such, they serve to undermine such features and offer a platform for a critique of them. Indeed, in more general terms, according to Derrida (1978), bricolage has a subversive quality since it is part of the threat to the centre, to logocentrism and to notions of an ordering origin that fixes and guarantees meaning.

Sampling/bricolage

The use of sampling and samples in contemporary music production and performance has become widespread and is present in a variety of musical forms and genres. Its greater visibility in recent times is perhaps through its extensive use in hip hop, rap, techno and related forms of popular music. There are somewhat varied views on precisely what constitutes sampling. Davies (1996: 3) suggest that originally it referred how the "waveform of any sound could be analyzed and/or synthesized in PCM [pulse-code modulation ...] by measuring its amplitude [...] at each of a sequence of vertical 'slices' taken many thousands of times per second". He acknowledges, however, that the meaning has altered and that since the 1970s it tends to refer to "the method by which special musical instruments or apparatus digitally 'record' external sounds for subsequent resynthesis" (Davies, 1996: 3). It is clear that digital technology has greatly facilitated the recording, archiving, retrieval and dispersal of sound and music and that this has greatly enabled the more extensive use of musical samples. It needs to be recognized that there are different ways of recording and storing sounds, musical sounds particularly, and reproducing them in different (musical) contexts and that this has a much longer history than digital sampling (Davies, 1996). It also needs to be recognized that the aesthetic accompanying such practice has appeared in other cultural forms and at other times – resonating for example with Dadaist use of readymades in altered contexts and to produce collages, both aural and visual. It resonates too with various experimental forms of writing such as William Burroughs' 'cut-up' technique, something also used by David Bowie in some of his earlier pop compositions, as well as more recently by *Nirvana's* Kurt Cobain.

Most typically today, we think of sampling as the insertion of one piece of recorded music, usually in a fragmented form, into a different musical composition or context. In this sense, sampling can be seen as the process of "putting heterogeneous elements into a new context" (Herzogenrath, 2000: 3). This manipulation of heterogeneous materials that are already to hand, and their deployment into new forms for different purposes, is at the heart of sampling and, we argue, fully resonant with bricolage. It is also part of a wider practice of tinkering with technology, using technology in unplanned, unanticipated ways to construct something new and of value to the producer/user/consumer.

The concept of bricolage came to prominence with its use by Levi-Strauss (1966) who considers it in complex ways, including its mythopoetic function; that is, its role in mythological thought in contrast to the formalisms of scientific thought. He refers also to bricolage 'on the technical level'. Derrida (1978: 85), commenting on this level, maintains that Levi-Strauss sees the bricoleur as:

> someone who uses "the means at hand", that is, the instruments he finds at his disposition around him, those which are already there, which had not been especially conceived with an eye to the operation for which they are to be used and to which one tries by trial and error to adapt them, not hesitating to change them whenever it appears necessary, or to try several of them at once, even if their form and their origin are heterogeneous – and so forth.

It is this sense of bricolage that is at issue in our deliberations in this chapter. We contend that sampling can be read as a form of bricolage in this sense – perhaps an exemplary form. More mundanely, we can note that the term comes from the French *bricoleur* and a simple English translation is problematical, but it is said to be in a similar connotational space to 'tinkering', and 'to fiddle', although some see it as best captured by the English compound 'do-it-yourself'.

Bricolage has been taken up and deployed in relation to a range of disciplines and fields. It has been widely used in art theory and practice, linked, for example, to Dadist and Surrealist practices involving 'found objects', collage and other techniques. Postmodern art is often described in ways associated with bricolage in terms of the assemblage and juxtaposition of heterogeneous materials and styles, often possessing different or even contrasting cultural and artistic references. Cultural studies theorists have used bricolage to refer to the transfer across cultural domains of objects and artefacts as part of identity formation processes. An example of relevance to us is the appropriation by punks of objects from the mundane, often domestic, domain to produce an ironic or paradic fashion statement. The use of wastebin liners as a mode of attire is a classic example. In information systems theory, Ciborra (1992, 1994, 1997) has applied the term to refer to the practice realities of work in developing information systems and related strategies in organizations – of which more later. As intimated, the term has been used in philosophy wherein Derrida suggests that all discourse is bricolage since every text draws upon the intertext and is an assembly of previous traces and heterogeneous materials. The contrast that Levi-Strauss makes between the bricoleur and the engineer or scientists is, for Derrida, spurious and indeed itself mythical. As he says:

> The notion of the engineer who had supposedly broken with all forms of bricolage is therefore a theological idea; and since Levi-Strauss tells us elsewhere that bricolage is mythopoetic, the odds are that the engineer is a myth produced by the bricoleur
>
> (Derrida, 1978: 285–6)

All discourse is bricolage, and both the scientist and the engineer cannot pretend to get outside or beyond that, both are *bricoleurs* too.

Common to these various conceptions is the notion of the *bricoleur* as someone who produces something through a practice that makes use of materials at hand and in ways contingent upon the particular context. It refers to an unplanned, underdetermined, non-systematized practice of solving problems in situ using materials to hand and a repertoire of techniques that are called up and combined for practical purposes in a contingently contextual manner. In his work on bricolage in information systems, Ciborra (1996) sees it as having three dimensions. The first sees bricolage in terms of tinkering or fiddling: the requirement in complex dynamic systems to tinker with the formal, organized and intended materials heuristically to ensure practical outcomes are actually attained. The second dimension refers to the trial-and-error nature of practice and of strategy formulation. There is affinity here with the practice turn in strategy and the perspective that strategy is emergent through bottom-up practices. The third dimension is the use of materials and processes in ways that they were not originally planned or designed for. These dimensions all reflect the practice of sampling. In a summary manner, Ciborra (1992: 49) defines bricolage as:

> tinkering through the combination of resources at hand. These resources become the tools and they define in situ the heuristic to solve the problem [...] bricolage is about leveraging the world as defined by the situation. With bricolage, the practices and the situations disclose new uses and applications of the technology and the things.

For the bricoleur resources are marshaled from an available set and in a sense 'invented' in relation to a situated task. Indeed, the repertoire of materials and procedures is developed through use, but each remains relatively undetermined and subject to future manipulations as the situation demands. Furthermore, "Not only are tools selected according to the bricoleur's purpose, but that purpose itself is shaped in part by the tools and material available. The properties of each, tools, materials and project, are uncovered in process" (Freeman, 2005: 7). This contrasts with a programmatic approach in which a problem is confronted with a predetermined set of tools designed for precisely that purpose – a caricature of what an engineer is presumed to do for instance. Whereas the engineer and the scientist are driven by a programmatic project and work through abstractions and structures to create events, the bricoleur is driven by his/her tools and materials and works concretely to produce structure out of events. The bricoleur works by a 'retrospective' assessment of his/her repertoire of materials tools and procedures for possibilities; he/she "interrogates all the heterogeneous objects that constitute his (sic) treasury" (Lévi-Strauss, 1966: 33) and constructs a situated response. It might be noted that some see scientific investigation that is qualitative, multimethodological and multitheoretical as a form of bricolage (Kincheloe, 2005).

Weick's notion of sense-making has been likened to bricolage and indeed he makes specific reference to the concept – describing it as "a process of sense-making that makes do with whatever materials are at hand [...] to use whatever resources and repertoire one has to perform whatever task one faces" (Weick, 1993a: 351–2). It is a form of 'practical intelligence' (Wagner, 2000) in which the bricoleur builds up a tacit knowledge and understanding of materials and processes through hands-on, trial-and-error manipulation. In this sense, it is different to the professed analytical, abstract approach said to characterize the scientist and, one might add, the supposedly rational organizational planner and strategist.

Sampling/bricolage and the postmodern aesthetic

The pop-rap song 'I'll Be Missing You' (1997) by Sean 'Puffy' Combs (aka Puff Daddy, aka P. Diddy) represents an interesting case of sampling in contemporary popular music. Produced as a tribute to his friend and fellow hip-hop artist Biggy Smalls (aka Notorious B.I.G.), who had been shot dead, it samples Samuel Barber's 'Adagio for Strings', the American Spiritual 'I'll Fly Away' and the hit song 'Every Breath You Take' by the rock/pop band *The Police*. The incorporation of these samples from very disparate musical genres reflects the kind of postmodern aesthetic that current musical sampling practice represents. Alper (2000), for example, points to "genre mixing, irony, humor, and self-parody, and the exploration of the surface characteristics of an artwork" as aspects of a postmodern aesthetic in modern music and other cultural forms.

The capacity to record, store and retrieve a vast and eclectic array of musical sounds, styles and genres means that there is a mammoth library of material with which to play. This is a repository that feeds the postmodern inclination to mix styles and genre, including historically disparate styles. The kind of mixing, for example, in which "eighteenth-century fugal techniques are conjoined with rock while cello quartets perform heavy metal" (Alper, 2000: 2). Alper (2000) provides other examples: hip-hop DJs sampling the work the composer Steve Reich to make remixes; the artist Cornelius combining Bach fugues with techno beats; the setting of heavy metal band *Metallica*'s music in a rearrangement for cellos by the group *Apocalyptica*. Here the musician is very much acting like a bricoleur and reflecting a postmodern concern with the surface qualities of music and sound; its sonic qualities, rather than musical structures. Rodgers (2003: 315) also argues that sampling represents a "postmodern contestation of the 'real'" and points to the practices of appropriation and pastiche, and the questioning of notions of authorship and authenticity sampling gives rise to. Music sampling then is, at one level, part of a wider cultural development in which a postmodern aesthetic has emerged and become significant in cultural practice and in our everyday cultural experiences.

The form of sampling in which portions of an existing piece of recorded music are digitally inserted into a different composition, often as a loop in rap and hip hop, has become entrenched as a routine practice in a number of musical genres. Although the practice per se might be considered postmodern, not all instances exhibit the genre mixing, pastiche or parodying that Alper and Rodgers refer to, while many do. From the beginning, the records used for 'scratching' and later for samples in rap and hip hop were often taken from what were considered classic, 'old-school' soul, funk and R and B music (Demers, 2003). Indeed, Rodgers also notes that musically, sampling has roots in "'Afro-diasporic' music practices including Caribbean 'versioning', bop 'quoting', and dub and reggae production techniques" (Rodgers, 2003: 313, see also Rose, 1994: 83–4). It is also suggested that in the early days of jazz, few songs/tunes that became standards were written compositions, rather they were "pieced together out of musical material that was floating loose around bandstands – fragments of hymns, blues, work songs, operatic arias, or traditional themes with ancient histories" (Collier, 1983: 140, cited in Frith, 1988). There is more than a hint of the bricoleur in this description.

There was a sense in early sampling that in accessing the 'old school' music, contemporary rap and hip hop was reproducing and keeping alive some of the authentic history of black experience in the USA, referencing, as it were, aspects of black cultural history thereby giving a political edge to the music. The Roots ?uestlove (aka Ahmir Thompson) maintains that the first use of a sample as a breakbeat (as opposed to merely a sound effect) was by the stadium rock band *Yes* when they incorporated five seconds of *Funk Inc*'s 'Owner of a Lonely Heart' (1972), itself a cover of *Kool and the Gang*'s 'Kool is Back' (cited in Marshall, 2006). This refers to the use of a digital sampler rather than a turntable or a live band to reproduce the sample, but clearly the reproduction by a live band, or the use of turntables, represents other modes of sampling.[1] However, Davies (1996: 10) notes that James Tenney produced 'Collage No. 1 (Blue

Suede)' in 1961 which features entirely of manipulations of the recording of Elvis Presley's 'Blue Suede Shoes'.

This practice of quoting or referencing from the past is another aspect of the postmodern aesthetic, one that includes repetition and excess, and excess through repetition. Sampling participates in what Plasketes (2005: 137) refers to as the 'Re-Age', the period from the 1980s till now in which US culture at least has been "operating on 'Re' mode control [...] an endless lifestyle loop of repeating, retrieving, reinventing, reincarnating, rewinding, recycling, reciting, redesigning and reprocessing". It is an age of covers and repeats or revisits and of a gleeful mixing of historical sources and references. It is an historical mingling matched by the playful mixing of genres and cultural forms. Boundaries – temporal, spatial and cultural – are dissolved, and hierarchies, for example of high art over low art, dismantled. It appeared as if "originality's merit had become outmoded" (Plasketes, 2005: 146). Certainly, the Re-Age raised issues of authenticity, originality, repetition, excess, appropriation, authorship, imitation and "an emphasis on commodity rather than concept" (ibid.). As an illustration of the excess of the cover version, he references Rhino Records release of an album consisting entirely of cover versions of the pop song 'Louie Louie'. The artist John Oswald produced a CD called 'Grayfolded' which consisted of the reproduction of 51 live performances of one Grateful Dead song (Davies, 1996). This repetition and excess is part of what Rodgers (2003) refers to as the "recombinant aesthetic of digital culture in general" (314) and is something that sampling is most clearly a part.

Herzogenrath (2000) argues that 'Techno' not only makes use of samples but also partakes of the postmodern aesthetic of excess and repetition. He references Deleuze's argument that 'proliferation is always a threat to order' and suggest that there is a subversive quality to 'techno'. He further suggests that in this excess and in the use of (and here he cites Szepanski, 1995: 137, 142) "a multitude of noises, shrieks, chirps, creaks and whizzes [...] all sounds traditionally associated with madness [...] Techno in this sense is schizoid music: it deconstructs certain rules and forms that that pop-music has inflicted on sounds". Herzogenrath argues, then, that Techno's deployment of 'unreasonable sounds *beyond* meaning' is subversive in the postmodern sense of releasing unrelenting and proliferating signifiers that 'forces signification against itself' and privileges the signifier over the signified. He also argues, incidentally, that the Techno 'raver', in the dissolutions of identity and ego that accompany the rave scene, participates in a kind of Lacanian *joissance* beyond the 'phallus', a state and experience beyond the expressible and beyond fatherly, rational control.

The workings of sampling/bricolage

Sampling involves the manipulation of technology and music to produce new effects; manipulations in which musical elements are taken out of their intended context and mixed with other elements taken from different contexts. In addition, sampling entails the deployment of technologies in ways for which they were not intended. These modes of manipulation are all also features of bricolage as noted above. In this section, we explore these workings of sampling and bricolage further. First, we briefly discuss the technology associated with the emergence and development of sampling.

Technological history and technology of sampling

The recent examples of digital musical sampling notwithstanding, sampling can be defined more broadly as the storing and replaying of sound from an original source on another, different piece of technology such that this secondary piece of technology reproduces the sound of the original. On this basis, sampling has a long history going back at least to the *hydraulis*, a pneumatic pipe organ developed in Roman times (Davies, 1996). In the 1980s *orchestrions* were developed which reproduced a range of different sounds. Another noteworthy development is *musique concrete*, initially introduced by Pierre Schaeffer in 1948 at the Paris radio station. This included the idea of an organ based on gramophone records with Schaeffer, like some form of proto-DJ, surrounded by dozens of turntables. Schaeffer was a clear precursor of the 'mixing' now so prevalent in hip hop and rap since he developed techniques for 'playing' several turntables and manipulating playback and level controls to construct sound collages. However, it was the *Mellotron*,[2] developed in 1964 and making use of magnetic tape that was labelled the first 'sampler'. Rick Wakeman, along with Dave Biro, developed and marketed the *Birotron* and the *Bandmaster Powerhouse Rhythm Machine* in the 1970s.

There represent the technological provenance of sampling which today, as noted, most typically refers to digital technology. This too though, according to Davies (1996), has a relatively long history going back as far as the 1930s when Reeves developed *pulse-code modulation* enabling 'slices' of sound to be taken thousands of times per second. The method more commonly associated with sampling today of digitally recording sound for its subsequent incorporation in another context was developed in the 1970s. Early synthesizers, such as the *Synclavier*, were effectively sampling devices that stored a range of sounds that could be reproduced. By the mid-1980s, samples were included as more or less standard in most manufacturers' electronic keyboards. The modern sampler is a hardware or software device (or an interface of the two) that records a sound signal as digital information and enables complex manipulations of that sound (Rodgers, 2003: 313). Rodgers (2003) reports that such machines became available at affordable prices when the *Ensoniq Mirage* was released in 1984 for US$2,000. Today, there are a range of machines available with varying degrees of sophistication and at different price points produced by major companies such as Yamaha and Akai. With these sounds can be stored and extensively manipulated, sliced, combined, sequenced, stretched, varied in pitch, amplitude and velocity, they can be filtered, looped and distorted in an endless array of possibilities.

From the 1990s onwards, sampled sounds have also become available on a commercial basis on CDs containing not only a vast array of recorded instruments and sounds but also rhythmic patterns that can be incorporated into other compositions. Such material is now also available online for download as well as integrated into the range of affordable computer based 'home studio' programmes such as Steinberg's Cubase or the range of products from TASCAM. This development adds to the dynamic through which musicians working with digital material become both consumers and producers. The digital musical sample is widely used in music composition and production across the spectrum of musical genres from rap to jazz to classical.

Manipulation and tinkering

Sampling exhibits something of the complexities of the interaction of technology and human action. It is clear that there is a material semiotic in sampling; it is constituted through a dynamic intersection of human agents, concepts/ideas and non-human technologies. What is apparent is that it not only exhibits qualities of bricolage in the sense of the marshalling of heterogeneous materials to produce new sonic outcomes, but that the performers are often also tinkering with technology. They are also marshalling technological elements into combinations, deploying technology for purposes for which it was not intended and intensely interacting with the technology in ways that exhibit qualities of performance and physicality. Both Science and Technology Studies (STS) and Actor-Network Theory (ANT) have, in different ways, explored such dynamics and revealed the subtleties of human-technology engagements. More specifically, Pinch and Bijsterveld (2004: 636) note that STS provides the intellectual platform for the emerging area of 'Sound Studies' which they position as the study of "the material production and consumption of music, sound, noise, and silence, and how these have changed throughout history and within different societies", doing so from within a broad, interdisciplinary framework. They note that STS has been dominated by the visual paradigm with the relative neglect of the sonic realm.

STS brings the conceptual and methodological tools for the inclusion, not only of the historical, cultural and social location of sound, but also its relation to "science and technology and its machines and ways of knowing and interacting". It is important to recognize, as noted earlier, that musical instruments are technologies – from the simple drum to the digital sampler. Indeed, "Musical instrument design is one of the most sophisticated and specialized technologies that we humans have developed" (Moog, cited in Pinch and Trocco, 2002: v). STS has shown the co-construction of technology and society and indeed the co-construction of technology, culture and identity (Oudshoorn and Pinch, 2003; Woolgar, 1991). Indeed, pursuing a Foucauldian analytic and going beyond the technology interface, Denora (1999) argues that music can be part of the *technology of the self*, part of how we construct and sustain our identities. Sampling is clearly a manipulation of technology and includes these human–technology interfaces and STS has started to investigate this sonic zone as a number of papers cited in this chapter bear witness.

A fundamental aspect of technological and musical manipulation in sampling is the method of 'scratching' developed by DJs in the Bronx and Harlem districts of New York in the late 1970s (Demers, 2003). This involves both the manual manipulation of technology and the putting to use of technology in unintended ways. The use of vinyl for scratching and sampling obviously provides for different sonic possibilities, and musicians using this technology seek different qualities from different vinyl recordings, sensing a different 'grain' or timbre form different sources. For some hip-hop artists, the 'dirty' grain of old vinyl is connected to notions of authenticity. It is also apparent that scratching requires a physical engagement with the technology; there is an embodiment in the production of music in this mode as there is, say, in blowing a trumpet, or keying a piano, an embodiment that works with the technology to release distinctive sounds. There is, then, a level of interaction and performance associated with the use of digital sampling as there is in music production via more traditional instruments too (Rodgers, 2003). Thus, in working with samplers, musicians seek to locate a feel and to work with physicality to engender an embodied, personalized element to the production of sound. Pinch and Trocco (2002) have argued for the need to understand the technologies of music through their use, 'reading' the 'scripts' that users embed in them (see Akrich, 1992).

This mode of sampling also involves old style DJs/MCs tinkering in the sense of 'digging' for old vinyl records in an "ongoing and circuitous archaeological process in which the producer hunts and gathers sounds" (Rodgers, 2003: 318). The invocation of 'archaeological' is not incidental since there is often an historical component involved wherein the samples found, selected and incorporated provide some historico-cultural reference of significance. The process involves constructing a 'collage' of sonic elements that constitute a polysemous composition, not just of sonic elements with their particular qualities, but also of these historico-cultural references.

Tinkering with gramophone records is not a recent phenomenon associated with DJs; it in fact has a long history, going back almost to their launch (Davies, 1996). Several artists had experimented with using gramophone records by altering speeds and direction and in combination to produce 'performances' in the 1920s and 1930s. The composer Hindemith recorded three studies using gramophone records that were tinkered with such a manner. The avant-garde composer John Cage composed a number of pieces, such as his 'Landscape No. 5' (1952), which used recorded layers of sound taken from large numbers of gramophone records. This is a pre-digital form of sampling, one involving a more direct manipulation of instruments and apparatus to produce new sounds. It is also a clear example of tinkering with technology and using it in ways other than that for which it was designed. In this regard, it is similar to 'scratching' which, as noted, is widely held to have been developed by DJs and MCs from the 1970s onwards, but is also used by composers such as Milan Knizak (1960s) and Christian Marclay (1970s) (Cutler, 1994) quite independently from that realm. A more recent composition by Shea *et al.* called 'Vinyl Reqiuem' (1993) uses over 200 vintage record plays controlled by three people (Davies, 1996). A different mode of tinkering is Laurie Anderson's replacement of a violin's bow strings with fine bits of recorded tape which are then repeatedly drawn across a replay head mounted on the violin to produce novel sounds (e.g. Tape Bow Violin, 1977, and Neo Violin, 1983). Anderson (1969) has consistently engaged in all manner of musical technology manipulations, including a symphony played on automobile horns.

Many of the ideas and methods from early vinyl sampling were reconfigured into digital sampling once that technology became available, especially at affordable prices. Even in digital sampling, there is a desire to reproduce the particular grain and timbre of such qualities (Marshall, 2006; Rodgers, 2003). Rodgers makes clear that samplers and other digital technologies are not 'fixed', immutable technologies that simply produce music automatically after 'programming' or at the press of a button. They have to be 'played' in the sense of manually manipulated, and there is an interaction between machine and musician. The language of sampling attests to this physicality with the techniques of 'chop-and-stab', 'crunching' 'mangling' 'cutting' or 'splicing' (Marshall, 2006). Indeed, musicians chose particular machines because of different and preferred interactive qualities and because of a capacity to intervene and customize the technology. There is a touch and a 'feel' to certain machines (Rose, 1994). There is then a considerable amount of interaction, not to say tinkering, with the technology, and this is not even considering the options for combining and utilizing different bits of technology, apparatus and software in different ways.

Sampling and other digital music tools also "have their own accompanying sets of gestures and skills that musicians are continually exploring to maximize sonic creativity and efficiency in performance" (Rodgers, 2003: 315). One example discussed by Rodgers is the attempt by electronic musicians to get 'grain' into their sound – to attend to and produce a certain timbre. 'Grain' is achieved through the processes of production, through the actions and decisions of the musician with respect to 'sound design'. This involves techniques such as 'spatialisation, panning, and effects processing' that are the musical gestures that reveal the "tactility and pleasurability of the recording process" (Rodgers, 2003: 317). The performance aspects of DJs and MCs who use 'scratching' is more obvious, but only obvious because of the visibility of the manual manipulations.

An interesting example of sampling and the manipulations involved comes from the duo known as Matmos.[3] They are habitual users of all manner of 'found sounds', including "contact microphones brushing human hair, the pages of a Bible turning, rock salt being crunched underfoot, aspirin tablets being thrown at a drum kit from the other side of a room", "amplified crayfish nerve tissue" and "– oh yes – the very real sound of human fat being sucked through tubes during liposuction surgery" (Doyle, 2004). One of their most notable albums is 'A Chance to Cut is a Chance to Cure' (2001) for which they recorded plastic surgeries performed on patients. As Drew, one of the duo, recalls, "I recorded three nose jobs, a chin implant, two laser eye surgeries and two liposuctions" (Doyle, 2004). The plastic surgery provided a wealth of sounds – some interesting, others less so:

> When they do the osteotomy in nose jobs, they slide a chisel inside the nose and they break the bones of the face with a hammer. But it kind of sounds like a pencil hitting a desk or something, it's really boring. Whereas other things that are pretty humble are actually really great – some of the brushes that they use to clean wound areas are cool, and the inflatable life support blanket is really great. They lay it over the patient and there's air streaming into it and sometimes it sounded really nice. It's not dramatic, y'know, it's a blanket. But as audio, it had this constant whirring rush that was really soft and beautiful and if you moved the microphone across it, you could actually play it.
>
> (Quoted in Doyle, 2004)

The sounds are manipulated extensively by Matmos, but the album primarily consists of the sounds of plastic surgery. There is a point, as Rodgers (2003: 319) points out, about the manipulations and endless revisions of the body available through plastic surgery and the sonic manipulations and endless revisions of sonic elements the musicians can produce. There is an endless tinkering with recorded sound by Matmos, and they often seek to mirror or parallel a recorded sound through a different mechanism back in the studio. For example, they sought to mirror the recorded sound of liposuction in the studio by having one of them sucking through a pen placed into a bowl of water. In another instance, they recorded someone playing a steel guitar in a sewer pipe and sought to parallel that through recording and amplifying the sound off blood rushing though the veins of one of the duo. This is embodied digital sound in a most direct manner. They also engage in an extensive tinkering with technology. They have an eclectic array of machines and software that they combine and work with and which they often employ or mix in unintended ways.

Some musicians are even attuned to and seek to deploy the particular sonic qualities of different sound studies within which the original sounds were produced. There is recognition among musicians, producers and sound engineers that different studios provide an environment that gives rise to different sound qualities and that these are embedded in recordings made in those studios. These differences are in part a result of the acoustic qualities of particular buildings and rooms, but also a function of differences in other technologies such as the type of microphones and amplifiers used, but also of 'miking' and 'amping' techniques (Marshall, 2006). This extends to the imperfections that might be present in particular contexts or inherent to particular types of technology. In pre-digital times, sound engineers would manipulate the space looking to create an artificial reverberation. This had become such a feature of popular music that digital technology has sought to reproduce it. As Théberge (1997) has noted this has resulted in a kind of second-order simulation, wherein digital reverb is a simulation of studio produced reverb, which was itself an artifice.

The role of sound engineers and producers is significant in the modern production of music since they are integral to the production of the final sound and are valued for their musical contribution (Hennion, 1989). Since so much music is recorded and mediated by complex recording technologies such as multitracking, the sound engineer role has risen progressively in significance to where they can legitimately be considered as co-producers of the music. As Horning (2004) argues, in the early days, sound engineers learnt by trial and error and developed, through effective listening and experimentation, tacit skills such as 'miking', 'reverb' and 'mixing', which would give distinctive sounds to recordings. Again, a significant amount of tinkering was involved, and they can clearly be conceived of as bricoleurs. Even with the increased sophistication of technology and a reduction in the necessity of tacit listening skills, there remain significant opportunities for manipulating the technology and a rich language to accompany it (Porcello, 2004).

As we have noted, tinkering with music-related technology is not confined to sampling, there have been many other instances throughout music history. Indeed, musical instrumentation history has its roots in the appropriation and manipulation of found objects, the horn, the animal skin, the hollowed piece of wood. Other examples from recent times include manipulations of the piano. A significant, recent example is the prepared piano made famous by John Cage. He experimented with a prepared piano first in 1938. Seeking to allow a single pianist to also provide a wider range of percussive and other sounds, Cage would attach nuts, bolts and pieces of rubber to the strings of the piano. Other composers such as Margaret Leng Tan, Philip Corner and Stephen Scott have also used this technique. In popular music, the Velvet Underground, the Grateful Dead, Elton John, David Bowie/Brian Eno and Muse have made use of prepared piano. There is also a history of using a 'prepared guitar' in a similar manner. Keith Rowe and Fred Frith were pioneers in the 1960s and 1970s – although the slide guitar, which can also be seen as a manipulation, dates back much further.

The guitar has been manipulated in other ways too as Waksman (2004) says "Tinkering has long been a part of the history of the electric guitar." The early development of the electric guitar took place in the garages and backyards of amateurs in suburban America. Indeed, Waksman (citing Gelber, 1997) attributes a significant impetus to technological tinkering to the growth of 'do-it-yourself' as a cultural phenomenon in the emergent suburbs of the USA in the early twentieth century.[4] Gerber sees this as driven by a masculine desire to resurrect manual labour to carve out a masculine space. Waksman (2004) notes too that a 'do-it-yourself' ethos penetrated parts of popular music, perhaps most notably in the punk movement of the 1970s–1980s, but also in hardcore and techno. This DIY aesthetic accompanied a general rise in the availability of technology in everyday life and the development of tinkering as an interest or hobby. One significant area of amateur technological tinkering was with radio. As Douglas (1987: 197) points out "In the hands of amateurs, all sorts of technological recycling and adaptive reuse took place." And as Waksman (2004: 679) adds, "radio tinkering became a model for popular uses of technology that were geared towards an active engagement with the technological artifact rather than idle consumption". Indeed, Les Paul and Leo Fender, the two central tinkerers with the electric guitar that Waksman focuses upon, were themselves amateur radio enthusiasts. Whilst Paul and Fender were producers of guitars, Waksman also focuses on the guitar tinkering of two players – Eddie Van Halen and Greg Ginn. Both were to become virtuosi players, and both were perpetual tinkerers with their instruments. As Waksman (2004: 676–7) argues, tinkering in these, as in other domains, serves a number of functions:

> exploring the ways in which technology can be put in the service of creating a certain kind of sound; [...] a way for musicians and instrument makers [...] to redesign the electric guitar to more individualized specifications; and [...] a mode of self-directed activity in which musicians have sought to carve out a sphere of "independence" from the broader structures that govern the music and guitar-manufacturing industries.

Individualization and independence are an important part of the alternative and sometimes resistive and subversive nature of technological tinkering in a way analogous to the challenge bricolage presents to the planned, intended, schematic, engineered processes within the formal arrangements of organizational practice. Paul and Fender challenged the assumptions of conventional, industrial guitar production and introduced manipulations that altered the instruments sonic possibilities. In some cases, tinkering is driven by a sheer fascination with the technology itself and challenges the normal instrumentalism of technology work (Turkle, 1984). The extent of technological manipulation and modification varies considerably – from minor adjustments to the complete assembly of a new device. Modifications of existing technology are most frequent with combinations of existing elements into new forms and uses being common.

Van Halen, for example, constructed hybrid guitars out of components from existing models. He did so in order to produce the sounds he wanted and to have a guitar match his own unique technique. It is, again, a way to locate an individualized sound and to challenge the standardizations and uniformities inherent to mass-produced products; he saw "his tinkering as a form of resistance to the pre-set options of existing electric guitar design" (Waksman, 2004: 693). This is the same ethos again driving the punk DIY aesthetic and the sampling within Techno; the same ethos driving sound engineers to produce their own distinctive sound by tinkering with studio technology and using tacit knowledge (Horning, 2004). These individualizing and resistive impulses sometimes result in outcomes that are able to penetrate the commercial zone and become incorporated into mainstream production. Thus, Van Halen's tinkerings became incorporated into standard models. There are numerous other examples; for instance, Takahashi (2000) shows how amateur tinkering in technology led to the development of a number of commercially viable electronic consumer goods in post-Second World War Japan. Whether this can be seen as re-appropriation by the mainstream is a moot point. Perhaps that does not matter, the challenging, resistive and individualizing actions of the tinkerer are sufficient to cause a change in the dominant systems.

Glitches

In talking about sound engineers tinkering above, we noted that this extended to the incorporation of imperfections in the technology and sound into the process. On occasion, technological imperfections become appropriated, valued and made part of the sonic construction. For the guitarist Ginn, the technique involved racking up the sound and distortion so that the resultant feedback became part of the desired sound. The use of distortion and feedback has been central in rock guitar, exemplified most dramatically by Jimi Hendrix in the 1960s. Van Halen also pushed the instrument to its limits looking for sounds the instrument was not designed to deliver. There is a wider point here though about tinkering and the location and use of the glitches and flaws in technology by the tinkerer. Part of the challenge to the formal, ordered and intended realm of organization and technology is engendered by tinkering locating, deploying and bringing value to the flaws and failings of technology. As Pinch and Trocco (2002: 223) suggest "All the best instruments in some sense do not 'work' as they are supposed to. It is the departures from theoretical models of instruments – the unexpected resonances and the like – that make an instrument particularly valued." In Techno and hip hop, the 'techniques of ab-use' (Herzogenrath, 2000), such as sampling and scratching, deploy the technology of records, turntables, computers, etc. in unintended ways; the same goes for the prepared piano or guitar. Each points to a deficiency, flaw or limitation in the technology as designed.

For some, this use of the flaws in musical technology is part of a reaction against what is seen as over precision, technological sophistication, sanitation and dehumanization of some forms of music. As Rodgers (2003: 316) puts it, "many musicians are contesting technological sophistication by incorporating audible 'glitches' into musical output, even making these the centerpiece of recordings". Sampling, in looking for the 'dirt' and 'grain' in vinyl, goes in this direction, but in some cases goes further in actively seek-out technological glitches so as to incorporate them into the composition or sound. Some musicians, in Techno for example, make use of the cheaper technology available and revel in and valourize the imperfections it includes. Such low-budget sound technology – referred to as 'lo-fi' – is seen by some as "a politicized expression of limited economic resources or as a critique of the pristine production values associated" with the mainstream music industry (Rodgers, 2003: 317). Cascone (2000) sees this as part of a post-digital reaction that some hard core, techno and sampling musicians invoke as a kind of 'aesthetics of failure'.

In music as bricolage, the music is emergent in practice and is constituted by what is possible at the time and what emerges in process. As Sherburne (2001: 66) suggests, in such a context, accidents have "equal rights within the composition as deliberate, conscious, or premeditated compositional actions or decisions". The DIY aesthetic of punk also revelled in the rawness and lack of sophistication in making music and positioned this against the sophistications of commercialized music and the arid musicianship of 'dinosaur rock'. The value of glitches and technological failure is also apparent in philately where the flawed stamp has more value than the properly reproduced one. There are probably many other areas where the glitch comes to have value, including in organizational contexts and remain to be explored. In a more general sense, we suggest that sampling, technological manipulations and the use of glitches that we have shown to be so prevalent and so integral to contemporary popular music are likely to be more pervasive features of organization and organizational practice than is currently acknowledged. We would argue that the discourse and rhetoric of rationality, order and control within both management and organization studies and in the language of practitioners has resulted in the elision of such practices. It is to those issues that we now turn.

Bricolage in/as organizational practice

It is interesting to note that Ciborra (1996, 1997, 1999, Ciborra, *et al* 2003) invokes the notion of bricolage in organizational contexts in relation to the unintended and the accidental and as a counterpoint to the planned, intended and programmatic. He uses the Mann Gulch disaster and the response to it as an example of organizational bricolage. The only person to act effectively in the disaster, Dodge, was able to construct sense where the routine organizational assumptions and practices of others had failed to find any. He acted as bricoleur using "his local context and the materials at hand to create a solution which should not have been open to him" (Stahl, 2005: 490). Similarly, the Apollo 13 disaster has also been examined as an example of bricolage in which heterogeneous materials – plastic bags and duct tape – were marshalled into an improvized, situated solution (Rerup, 2001 – cited in Cunha, 2007). Ciborra's analysis of the Mann Gulch disaster offers a reinterpretation that builds on Weick's (1993b) earlier analysis. We have already noted Weick's (1993a, 1996, 1998, Weick *et al* 2005) invocation of bricolage in organizations and his extensive exploration of the related notions of organizational improvization and sense making. In his work generally, Ciborra makes extensive use of bricolage in a direct manner to describe the actual practices of organizing and managing associated with information technology, including strategy formation processes. As Stahl (2005: 489) maintains, Ciborra sees strategy as more an account of attempts to 'muddle through', "to make sense of the situation and to use the local context as bricolage". In other words, strategy is a practical, situated activity in which the context determines what can be brought to bear, what resources are available, and so shape strategy formulation. Ciborra challenges notions of strategy as a rationally predetermined, planned activity.

As noted in the introduction, bricolage has received scant attention in organization and management studies (Baker *et al.*, 2003), in part, we suggested, because of the challenge it poses to the formal, intended, ordered and rational aspects of organizing and organization. Whilst the concept has been deployed by a small number of writers to explore various facets of practice, we maintain that the types of bricolage we witness in sampling are more pervasive in organizations than commonly acknowledged. Indeed, following Weick's line of reasoning, organizing itself, as a process, has great resonance with bricolage. Cunha (2007) argues too that bricolage is not to be viewed as some deviant organizational practice but as necessary to the practice of organization and management. A number of writers, including Weick, have pursued the notion of improvization with respect to management and organizing (e.g. Cunha *et al.*, 1999; Kamoche and Cunha, 2001, Kamoche *et al.* 2002; Vera and Crossan, 2004) and there is clearly a relationship between bricolage and improvization.

Existing work on bricolage and improvization mostly talks broadly about marshalling heterogeneous resources to deal with situations in context. What is absent is the kind of detailed attention to practice that we have seen in the popular music literature. What is also absent is the discussion of tinkering with technology so fulsomely discussed in relation to popular music production. One notable exception is the work of Orr (1996) in analysing the work of photocopier technicians. That detailed analysis reveals that in actual practice such workers are not working to an operating manual on determined and fixed technology as might be imagined. Like the sound engineer, they rely upon significant tacit knowledge to manipulate and tinker with the machines to keep them operational. Orr also points out, again paralleling sound engineers, that this role as bricoleur and improvizer is important in the construction of a professional identity. These workers are able to conceptualize themselves as creative and skilled trouble shooters possessing scarce and expert knowledge, not as low-level repair personnel working on routine technical problems.

Louridas' (1999) discussion of design as bricolage approaches a similar level of detail but in a more abstract form and following a close reading of Levi-Strauss. He notes that the designer works with materials that are available, "The means for the construction of his artifacts are taken from his surroundings" (Louridas, 1999: 8). The responses made are situationally determined and immediate, and the 'game' is to make do with what is available – this is contrasted to the engineer. Unlike the engineers, the designer must:

> determine which of his tools and materials are suitable for his purpose; he searches his inventory and chooses among the possible answers. He does not decompose the problem: his purpose is not to examine it analytically; he reorganizes his materials to create the structure of the envisaged artifact.
>
> (Louridas, 1999: 9)

We anticipate that such types of detailed study and analysis would reveal many other instances of technological manipulation and organizational bricolage in a range of domains. One barrier to this happening is the potentially challenging and subversive character of sampling/bricolage with respect to certain orthodoxies and assumptions.

The challenge and subversion of sampling/bricolage

If we return to musical sampling for the moment; the practice has created controversy, and indeed consternation, in two ways principally. One concerns arguments about the nature of music and perceptions of its quality. The other concerns sampling's challenge to notions of originality and authenticity. The latter has taken sampling into a legal imbroglio that continues to be played out in complex and dynamic ways. Rodgers (2003) summarizes these two points of critique as positioning sampling as either 'theft' or 'automation' but contests that neither is accurate. In both modes of criticism, there are shades of the old bifurcation between high and low culture, a bifurcation that has been under dissolution within a postmodern aesthetic.

The sample police: challenge to notions of originality, authenticity and quality

Some people find sampling an affront to their musical sensibilities. For them, sampling contributes to the broader malaise in which music is perceived to be increasingly de-humanized and de-skilled, and the machinic production of music that de-emphasizes the human component is lamented. Indeed, as Rodgers (2003: 313) suggests, many writers comment critically on an apparent "dissolution of boundaries between human-generated and automated musical expression". Perhaps forgetting that most non-vocal music is machine mediated, critics have attacked music produced via synthesizers, samplers or other electronic forms as somehow inferior to music produced on older technologies such as the piano or violin. For Rodgers (2003), although sampling uses a different technology, it exhibits all the creativity of other musical forms, requires equivalent musical skill and adheres to worthy aesthetic standards. She maintains that being able to use sampling requires as much learning, practice and playing skill as any other instrument and notions that it is simple and automatic are false. As noted earlier, she makes clear that sampling is not a merely automated process; samplers have to be 'played' and there is learning and skill associated with that. The sampler strives for a certain 'touch,' and aficionados recognize that different sampling technologies have different qualities and can be manipulated in different ways for different sonic effects.

At another level, sampling can clearly be considered as a creative process when the selection, modification, incorporation and synthesizing involved in composing music from samples is considered. It is a process akin to collage in the visual arts; a method afforded clear artistic merit and legitimacy. Sampling, as noted, requires another component that involves knowledgeable activity – the hunting and gathering of old vinyl and the marshalling of various musical samples and styles for not only sonic effect, but also their cultural and political references.

The second, and perhaps more important critiques, relate to sampling's violation of the values and norms of originality and authenticity that some hold as sacred within music specifically and the arts generally. Critics such as Goodwin (1990), for example, have dismissed this form of modern music as amounting to plagiarism, lacking in originality, being an affront to authenticity, and wallowing in a shallow pastiche rather than being music of substance.

The notion of authenticity in music, including, or perhaps particularly – as we have seen in Chapter 9 – in rock music, has in part been fed by notions of originality, but also of resistance to mere commercial motives. With respect to the former, Plasketes (2005: 152) argues, however, that by the late 1970s the postmodern condition had already "ruptured rock culture's aesthetic, shifting emphasis away from authenticity". Sampling expressly challenges notions of authenticity and originality while simultaneously resurrecting these same notions by different means. Sampling reflects the notion that all cultural products participate in a complex intertextuality and that any claim to originality is forgetful of this and the fact that cultural constructions are built upon and reflexively justified and legitimated by that which precedes them. For example, even at the level of genre if one considers the ineluctable dependence and embeddedness of rock and roll in the blues, what claims for originality can be made?

Originality is permanently problematized by such intertextuality, dependence and indebtedness – the question is one of degree and explicitness. Plasketes (2005) also reminds us that an aesthetic of excess, repetition and appropriation impels not only sampling, but the proliferation of the 'cover' version and the endless recycling of songs. Like sampling, covering sometimes instills a response through the recontextualization of the original or by an unusual juxtaposition. Who, for example, can forget *The Sex Pistols* appropriation of the crooner standard, 'My Way' and Sid Vicious' snarling, defiant and violent rendition?

The questions of originality, authority and authenticity amounts to a twofold challenge to the music industry. First, notions of authenticity for some equate to non-commercialization. That is, authentic music and authentic musicians produce music for motives other than commercial ones, and the incorporation of music into the machinations of a monolithic music industry is perceived as 'selling' out and an erosion of authenticity (see Chapter 9). Second, there is a challenge to authority as ownership and hence to commercial, proprietary claims to music.

Commercialization has increasingly been accompanied by claims on intellectual property, and so the challenge to originality and authenticity posed by sampling has increasingly been embroiled in legalistic contestations over intellectual property. However, it ought to be noted that appropriating, referencing and quoting other, earlier music has been a feature of almost every form of music in the second half of the twentieth century. Using the actual recordings of other artists, however, has been interpreted as raising different issues, especially when such recordings are owned not by the musicians who produced them but by music companies. Interestingly, the 1911 Act in the USA stated that the purchaser of a gramophone record secured the rights to all public performances; it was only with the advent of extensive radio play of recorded music that music companies become worried and lobbied for changes in the law (Frith, 1988). Initial copyright laws were designed to protect and encourage the creative process by giving protection to the composer of music, it was not until later that protection shifted to those (music companies increasingly) who had acquired ownership and rights of the material musical artefact – published and recorded music.

As Frith (1988: 71) argues:

> Quiet as it's kept, the rationale of copyright law isn't that private property is the highest philosophical good. It's to provide economic incentive for the spread of ideas and information, incentive that would presumably be vitiated were works open to unlimited reproduction and resale.

Copyright laws have increasingly been used to protect copyright owners' monopoly rights. With changes in the technologies of reproduction, and especially latterly with digital technologies and open mechanisms of distribution through the Internet, the issue becomes less about recorded or published music itself, but rather one of *access*. As Christgau (1986: 40) maintains: "In an age when all products of the mind have been commoditized, the freedom to sell equals the freedom to disseminate." Such a mindset brings music companies into direct conflict with samplers and mixers.

Music companies employ 'sample police' (Marshall, 2006: 869) to detect unauthorized sampling. The distribution of music on the Internet and the operations of companies like Kazaa and Napster in establishing free sharing through P-to-P networks heightened the alarm among music companies who launched legal, lobbying and technical campaigns to reassert their control of the production and distribution of music.[5] BMI, for example, developed the Musicbot, a device that searches the Web and monitors the use of music files so as to expose those instances where a fee ought to have been paid (Jones, 2000). Music companies are also strategically reassessing their business models to properly incorporate the new digital, Internet-enabled distribution systems. Even back in the 1980s, Frith (1988) went so far as to suggest that for the music industry, the business was no longer production or distribution, but the creation of rights (of ownership). For some, the Internet and its (relatively) open architecture and access provides for a means to re-democratize music. Some musicians are uploading their material and making it available on the Internet to be downloaded by their fans thus cutting out any industry mediation. Some are even doing this for free, thus removing the commercialization of music altogether, taking music back to a pre-commercial time.

The invocation of copyright in relation to sampling remains contested however, with many musicians rejecting this interpretation and continuing to use samples in their work. As Marshall (2006) notes, for some established musicians with contracts with bigger companies, there are sufficient resources to buy the rights to use samples.[6] But there are plenty of other musicians who continue to use samples and get away with it because they are not visible enough and so pass under the 'radar' of the 'sampling police'. There is an active resistance in some quarters with sampling used to make a cultural and political statement. As Rodgers (2003: 313) points out "Most scholars writing on the use of samplers express anxiety over the dissolution of boundaries between human-generated and automated musical expression, and focus on the copyright infringement issues surrounding sampling practices without adequately exploring samplists' musical and political goals."

It is important to note that issues of originality, ownership and copyright are not confined to the music industry. Intellectual property (IP) has become something of a mantra latterly, particularly in an era of the so-called knowledge economy. Companies have been impelled to take all manner of measures to protect their IP and fight for copyright and patent rights. Equally, operators in many domains have sought to appropriate the technologies of reproduction and to make copies of all manner of goods – from clothes to electronic hardware. At the time of writing, the governments of more than one country are legitimizing the reproduction of generic drugs by local companies in defiance of the patent rights of some of the larger pharmaceutical companies. There is not the space to explore these densely political challenges to originality and 'copyright' here, but they need to be noted as a further manifestation of the challenge of samplingesque practices.

There are also areas of technological tinkering and modification that are apparent in a wide range of areas, but which do not appear to be much attended to in the academic literature. The point here is that sampling, tinkering, DIY and bricolage are all challenges to the intended order of things. They threaten to usurp the structures, systems, processes, technologies and objects that have been formally, officially and rationally constituted; they are, further, a challenge to the proprietary and exclusive claim on such things. Tinkering with cars, to take another example, has significantly bypassed the automobile companies, especially in terms of after-sales service and the surrounding support industries. We have seen how they have taken steps to limit the options for amateur tinkering through, for example, increasingly sophisticated technology and the sealing of components. The original, be it original song, original manufactured automobile component or original designer shirt, is all subject to unplanned manipulation and copying in a vast panoply of subversive acts of repetition and excess such that the divisions between copy and original are thoroughly blurred and the claims to ownership thoroughly muddled.

The politics of sampling/bricolage

There is, as is by now apparent, a political dimension to sampling/bricolage. The politics of sampling include the resistances both to notions of originality and authenticity and to the appropriations and legalisms of the music industry and its business cohorts discussed above. Additionally, the appropriations and pastiche some sampling revels in is actually "musically and politically constructive, capable of encompassing a complex web of historical references and contesting dominant systems of intellectual property and musical ownership" (Rodgers, 2003: 314). That is, in the hands of some composers and musicians sampling is a deliberate subversion, or at least interrogation, of the orthodoxies of musical and cultural production, accomplished by posing questions about authorship, originality and ownership. Bourgeois, modernist cultural and aesthetic sentiment had individualized creativity, artistic output, and cultural production, and elevated notions of originality. The forces of capitalist consumerism and commercialization have additionally introduced commoditization, proprietary ownership and commercial value for all cultural products. For some musicians, sampling provides a vehicle for contesting such interpolations. Rose (1994) holds that this is the case for some hip-hop and rap artists who see themselves as confronting a dominant and dominating (white) music industry. There is clearly a politics to sampling – both in the sense of its challenge to both bourgeois and modernist notions of originality and commercial conceptions of value and intellectual property, but also through constructing or reconstructing a statement by the invocation of particular cultural and historical references.

The latter references processes, in some sampling, of direct politicization through the quoting or referencing of political activism from the old blues and soul repertoire. Thus, 'old school' hip hop includes references from 1970s soul and blues that sometimes have activist or other political connotations. In a more general sense, the juxtaposition of disparate forms and styles as well as being an expression of a postmodern aesthetic can also be read as a political statement. Such referencing can be used to parody, subvert or critique that which is referenced as well as valuorizing it or invoking it for positive purposes. For example, the quoting by Puff Daddy of music of elements from the white classical tradition provides an ironic inversion of the long history of white appropriations of black music in rock, pop and jazz. There is something of an intersection or resonance of this reference to Afro-American musical forms with the disputations over copyright.

As Frith (1986: 63) notes "Copyright laws defines music in terms of 19th century Western conventions and is not well suited to the protection of Afro-American musicians' improvisational art or rhythmic skills." This would be true of the traditions of such forms as the blues and jazz in which tunes are assembled from disparate elements, passed on by modelling, observing or word of mouth and constructed in performance in an improvized manner. One might say that these are forms of musical bricolage and that contemporary notions of copyright do not sit well with such traditions. Furthermore, the possibilities of recording technology and multitracking mean that a particular music production might take place in several stages, over time and involving different sets of people in a further process that approximates a bricolage. The act of creation becomes diffuse and dispersed and the attribution of ownership and copyright further problematized. Frith (1986: 66) provides an interesting example, one that also features music in an Afrodiasporic context:

A group of Jamaican session musicians put down a rhythm on a multichannel recording tape. It becomes the property of a producer. Sometime later a pianist adds some "fill-ins" and a basic melodic structure. Over the next year a number of artists record songs with melodic differences over the top of this tape. This happens all the time in Jamaica. Who are the composers? How should copyright fees be divided?

Today, there are network music recording studios that exist in a virtual space (Théberge, 2004). Musicians from anywhere can upload music files, add elements to a mix and work on a composition.

The political statements in sampling are not always associated with social activism or social protest and equality. In the context of a global music business, samples are available from musical forms from all around the world. There are opportunities to appropriate sounds from all manner of contexts and sometimes this can take the form of a kind of musical colonialism or even orientalism in which the music of third world cultures can be appropriated and incorporated into Western music in ways that extract additional value and/or which seeks to provide exotic referencing (Rose, 1994; Taylor, 2001). For example, the album 'Duck Rock' compiled/produced by Malcolm McLaren[7] features an eclectic mix of music and sampled elements from world music, hip hop as well as sonic elements taken from old records, recorded on African streets, or sourced from American radio – the originators and composers of which are not acknowledged on the album. Frith (1988: 66) makes the point that the obvious appropriations never drew the attention of the copyright 'police' largely because "its quotes came from third world or folk artists and record companies who lacked clout".

The challenge and subversion of rational over-determination in organizations

As is now clear, sampling is a challenge to the formal, planned and intended regimes of music production particularly those governed by the aesthetics of the orthodox and the imperatives of the music industry. Similarly, technological manipulation and the appropriation of the glitch challenges the intended uses of technology and the ordered regimes of organizationally sanctioned technological deployment. It can also be argued that the operation of bricolage in organizations is a challenge to and potential subversion of the ordered, intended, rational structures and processes that are often presumed to be essential for effective organizational functioning.

We have seen how with Ciborra bricolage is a meaningful description of what is required as practice in complex, turbulent organizations. Ciborra maintains that to function in such environments organizations must become adept at tinkering. That is, tinkering and bricolage are required for the effective emergence of organizational strategies and responses that enable organizations to compete and survive. He contrasts this to the formulaic, blueprint, pre-figured approach to strategy and to the attempts by management practitioners and management academics alike to produce neat, simple and enclosing models of organizational function, strategy and change. His research shows organization members to often be desirous of predictability and stability and to find change threatening and destabilizing. Neat and simple models have appeal, of course, because they pretend to help cope with such threats and uncertainties. As Verjans (2005: 505) argues, commenting on Ciborra, such people will, in all probability:

> relate to such "necessary fictions" as plans, project timelines, deadlines and milestones, in order to retain a certain form of "mental" control over the situation. A concept such as "bricolage" or improvisation is meaningless and even threatening to them, because it does not allow for planning, control or predictability

Indeed, we can shift that argument and say that bricolage is a managerial and organizational inevitability and as such is a threat to the rationalist assumptions of order that sustains the discourse that perpetuates these 'necessary fictions'.

In the broadest sense, the entry of bricolage as organizational practice exposes "the weaknesses of some of the assumptions about rationality that we find in business studies" (Stahl, 2005: 487). For Ciborra, this extends to a critique of the scientism of management and organization studies and the adherence to models of investigation derived from the natural sciences. He joins with poststructuralists in casting doubt on the presumed objectivity, logical rationalism and value-neutral assumptions embedded in orthodox, neo-positivist management and organization studies, including his own domain of information systems. He is sharply critical of the detached rationality and the falsely 'heroic' management that he sees in information systems – perspectives that distort not only the realities confronted by organizations but also the realities of how practitioners actually go about their work and problem solving. For him, the reality is that they are bricoleurs. This is true at the micro-level of operational activity, at the level of tinkering with machines, as well as at the level of strategy, which Ciborra sees as fundamentally a process of 'muddling through' of attempts at sense making in the particularities of situated contexts, deploying whatever is at hand at the time to do so. It is true of the programmer as bricoleur (Turkle, 1995) as it is of policy makers (Freeman, 2005). The analysis of the Mann Gulch disaster is an example of the failures of rational systems and the attempt to pin down complex realities in prefigured systems. It suggests that in insisting on purely rational, programmatic approaches to things managers are mislead – and in this case dangerously so.

The tinkering and manipulation of technology represents another area of challenge to ordered and ordering orthodoxies. The examples of technological tinkering we have examined are instances of the appropriation of a given technology by a user and its modification in terms of form and function to suit some individualized purpose the person has. Technology is put to uses for which it was not intended, combined in unusual ways, tampered with to produce unintended effects and customized to suite the user. These activities are a challenge to any notion of technological determinism. Technology is not fixed and static, it is often, perhaps more often than is commonly acknowledged, worked upon and interacted with in a dynamic fashion. There are attempts to individualize the technology, and as we have seen, the technological manipulations people make can be a significant element in their identity formation. This would be true of sampling artists, of guitarists like Van Halen and Ginn, but also of custom car enthusiasts and, importantly, Orr's photocopier technicians. There is a challenge here to the standardization imperatives of technology and production and the rational ordering that implies. There is also a challenge to and subversion of the standardizations and uniformities of the market as users and consumers individualize things through their manipulations. This can be seen as part of the resistance to mass consumerism and people's attempts to individuate and differentiate, even if that is through the reproductions and repetitions of sampling.

Bricolage is not a negative and destructive challenge; it offers a realistic way of understanding organizational practice. It has, as noted, been relatively neglected in management and organization studies. The neglect stems in part from the challenges to rational ordered practices that both practitioners and academics seem keen to hang on to. Bricolage rattles those presumed certainties and those prospects of order. It appears messy to any neo-positivist overly rationalist purview. The tendency to view management and organization as rationally ordered is still pervasive. As Cunha (2007) suggests, management is still most often portrayed as an abstract rather than a practical activity and organizational thinking still informed by a Newtonian logic (Tsoukas and Knudsen, 2003). Organization and management studies, in consequence, primarily attempt to provide managers with simplified, rational, often linear models and associated tools.

Managers themselves are often impelled to concur with such representations and to position and define themselves as purely rational actors in a universe which can be made sense of and ordered by here have, of course, been plenty of detractors of this view – from Lindblom to Mintzberg, to Weick, to Chia – but this has not been the dominant orthodoxy nor has much of that critique focused on the mundane practices of the manager. There is a relative neglect of the manager as bricoleur and of processes of organizational bricolage. We have suggested that, in part, this is because bricolage looks 'messy' in the context of the dominant structural-functionalist paradigm with its emphasis on order, linearity and rationality. In the discourse of contemporary management and the rationalist assumptions that embody it, the manager is more likely to be represented as a resource planner rather than bricoleur, and the organization characterized as rationally ordered, with rational planning, and rational resource allocation rather than as bricolage. This representational preference is as salient in the academic literature as it is in among practitioners. Orthodox organization studies emphasize rational processes and focus on the abstractions of management and organization to the relative neglect of practice, practical intelligence, improvization, accident and serendipity. This leads to a distorted and partial representation and understanding of organization and organizing. The processes of sampling and tinkering, isomorphic with the process of bricolage, are, we submit not only more pervasive in organizations than is recognized in the orthodoxy; they are inherent to and necessary for the practices of organizing and management.

Notes

1 Introduction: organizations and popular culture

1 *The Simpsons* in 7(2001a) and Rhodes and Pullen (2007), *Dilbert* in Czarniawska and Rhodes (2006) and Kessler (2001), *Looney Toons* on Rehn (2004), the rock music examples in Rhodes (2004, 2007), *Rising Sun* in Foreman and Thatchenkery (1996), *Peter Pan* in Aaltio-Marjosola and Lehtin (1998), *Star Wars* in Grice and Humphries (1997) and *Judge Dredd* in Parker (1998a).

2 Management as popular culture

1 You can download their study guides, watch the set films, take a test online costing US$10, and if you pass (and you can keep taking the test till you do), you receive a Hollywood MBA certificate (framed for an additional fee). Presumably to avoid any legal wranglings, they put in parentheses after Hollywood MBA – (Master of Bijou Advice)!

2 This status was superseded by Moore's *Bowling for Columbine* (2002) and *Fahrenheit 9/11* (2004).

3 We have put 'knowledge' within quotes here to signify its problematic status, particular given the concerns of the chapter. We were tempted to put it under erasure (~~knowledge~~) after Derrida (1976), but, like Warhol's soup cans, having been done once, it becomes tiresome and uncreatively imitative to repeat the point.

4 The *Wharton School* was established in 1881 by Joseph Wharton within the University of Pennsylvania as the first business school within a university system. It might be noted that Andrew Ure began teaching management at Anderson's College in Glasgow around the same time. Also it could be argued that the Ecole Supérieure de Commerce of Paris founded in 1819 was the first school of administration, but it had some national specificities and certainly did not spawn the expansion that the US model did. And just as an indication of scale today, over 100,000 people graduate with MBAs in the USA alone every year.

5 Perhaps a statement more true of the United Kingdom and Europe than the USA, but the general point is still valid.

6 Clark and Greatbatch (2004) report that Tom Peters confessed in an interview with *Fast Company* that he faked the data for *In Search of Excellence*, declaring that he thought that to be 'pretty small beer'.

7 The HBR can itself be seen as a prime exemplar of the blurring of the lines between academic, practitioner and popularist modes of representation.

8 Sturdy notes that presenting this in tabular form necessarily leads to some generalizations. The article explicates the nuances and complexities.

9 See www.evidence-basedmanagement.com/. (site visited 1 February 2007)

3 Articulating organization studies and popular culture

1 Although organization theorists have found value in studying and theorizing organization in terms of aesthetics knowledge and discourse (Gagliardi, 1996; Strati, 1999; Linstead and Hopfl, 2000), this has not been extended to the aesthetic and epistemic value of music that uses work as its theme. [Note, however, that songs written by people in organizations have been discussed in relation to organizational aesthetics (see Nissley, 2002).]

4 Men, non-men and masculinity in *Glengarry Glen Ross:* the retardations of the masculine in contemporary capitalistic organizations

1 It should perhaps be noted that the focus is very much on the US variant of the capitalist ethos ... it is a moot point what extension this has internationally or universally.
2 The play premiered in London in 1983 and appeared in print in 1984 (Mamet, 1984). The film version of *Glengarry Glen Ross* was released in 1992, directed by James Foley.
3 The first in 1951, then as a CBS television adaptation in 1966, and finally the Volker Schlondorff version produced in 1985.
4 The main characters are as follows: the four salesmen – Ricky Roma (played by Al Pacino), George Aaronow (played by Alan Arkin); Dave Moss (played by Ed Harris) and Shelley Levene (played by Jack Lemon); John Williamson, the office manager (played by Kevin Spacey); Blake, the 'young gun' manager from head office (played by Alec Baldwin); James Lingk, the duped customer (played by Jonathon Price); Baylen, the detective (played by Jude Ciccolella).
5 The Cadillac Eldorado is an iconic American luxury car.
6 The 'business trilogy' are the three plays *GGR, American Buffalo* and *Speed-the-Plow* that each deal with business-related themes.
7 The use of the phrase 'corrosion of character' of course provides an echo of Sennett (1998); it is partly an incidental and partly an intended echo, we are aware of Sennett's assessment of the damaging effects of contemporary capitalism and business on character. It is an assessment that resonates with that Mamet, but there are differences in argument and focus and, of course, the time frame and the state of the business system is different.
8 We recognize that there has been a growing body of work that provides such an articulation since, and the work of Sennett (1998) is one example.
9 There is resonance here with the notions of restricted linguistic codes as articulated originally by Bernstein (1966, 1971).
10 Loman is the lead character in *DoS.*

5 Commerce is our goal: corporate power and the novum in *Blade Runner*

1 'Science fiction' is commonly abbreviated as either SF or sf. In this chapter, we use the full term 'science fiction' – where the abbreviation is used it is done so only in order to reproduce direct quotations from others.
2 Comments made in this chapter are based only on the 1992 version. There were three main differences between the two versions. First, the earlier one had a 'voice over' from Deckard, the main character, running through the film and thus providing some (over) direction for the audience. Second, the 1992 version introduced more fully the possibility that Deckard is a replicant. Third, the ending of the 1982 version is more romanticized – rather than, as in the more ambiguous 1992 version where Rachael and Deckard enter an elevator with no specific direction implied, the film ends more 'happily' with the pair driving away with the new knowledge that Rachael has no expiration date. For a discussion of some of the implications of these differences, see Begley (2004).

6 From the '*The Rag Trade*' to '*Ab Fab*': representations of work, gender and the politics of difference in British sitcoms

1 These analytic objectives are pursued via an analysis of a sample of British sitcoms. The sample is drawn from comprehensive lists (British Sitcom Guide, 2006; Guide to Comedy, 2006) and particular cases chosen on the basis of ensuring a selection across the time frame, the presence of the focused-upon themes and the relative popularity/impact of the sitcom (determined by number of episodes and series and listing on a poll of viewers – the British Sitcom Guide).

2 The lower case is intentional and is the standard representation for the show.

3 ITMA is an acronym for 'It's That Man Again' which was a catchphrase used by the British newspapers whenever Hitler laid claim to some new territory.

4 Other female characters were Mrs. Mopp, Poppy Poopah and Mona Lot.

5 Wolfe and Cheney are men and in terms of the gendered organization of sitcom and other media it might be noted that until the 1980s the vast majority of writers and producers in the United Kingdom were male. For some, this accounts for the type of programmes made and the characters developed for women to play (Gray, 1994). The existence of an exclusive 'boys club' of produces and writers has been blamed in part for the lack of female representation in the industry, with Gray (1994) noting that male producers in the United Kingdom have often been reluctant to use women writers and that unless you are part of the (male) 'light entertainment club', it can be very hard to 'break into'. Since the 1980s, there has been a gradual expansion of women involved in writing and production in British television, including comedy. The work of Carla Lane, Victoria Wood, Dawn French and Jennifer Saunders has been significant.

6 Sitcoms with leading female characters whilst not as common as those with a male focus were developed at this time. For example, there was *Gert and Daisy* produced in 1959 and *Winning Widows* appeared in 1961 with its two female lead characters.

7 *The Liver Birds* (1969–1979, 1996); *Butterflies* (1978–1983); *Solo* (1981–1982); *Bread* (1986–1991).

8 These were the main characters in the first two series.

9 Which carries the tag line "For men who should know better"!

10 One of the main writers, Jimmy Perry, had worked as a Butlin's 'Redcoat', and the other, David Croft, had also worked as an actor and then producer of holiday camp shows.

11 The mini-skirt did not appear until the mid-1960s.

12 This provides an interesting contrast with the male-dominated and more recent *Absolute Power* where the PR firm is enormously influential and totally without ethics.

13 Exemplified to some extent by Tom Peters – see Chapter 2.

7 The reception of McDonald's in sociology and television animation

1 It is not clear whether or not, in the course of researching his books, Ritzer actually spoke to or interviewed any actual McDonald's employees.

2 At the same time mounting a critique of that other icon of global consumer capitalism – Coca-Cola. Incidentally, Coca-Cola is the exclusive supplier of soft drinks to McDonald's, and Ritzer (1998) refers to coca-colonization as a process similar to McDanaldization.

3 Ritzer himself uses – *ization* neologisms widely – in his 1998 book *The McDonaldization Thesis* as well as McDonaldization, he also proposes that we have coca-colonization, Disneyization, Las Vegasization, McDisneyization, sneakerization, Snickerization and Toyotaization as well as the more standard fare of Americanization, westernization, globalization, glocalization etc.

4 This is a small sample of Krusty products. Under the title 'Merchandizing, thy name is Krusty …', Richmond and Coffman (1997: 208–9) list more than 60 such products as they have appeared in various episodes.

5 This citation is taken from Richmond and Coffman (1997: 102) and Cherry (1996).

6 The citations we use from this episode are taken from Chen (1992).

7 From the episode 'Kamp Krusty' (Production code 8F18, original air date 1 October 1992).

8 The citations we use for this episode are taken from Wierney (2000).

9 As is common in *The Simpsons*, this episode features 'real-life' entertainers doing their own voice overs for their animated images.

10 "Swiss bankers are often called 'gnomes', after the trolls of Swiss mythology. They are said to have great power, but are seldom seen-and are discreet to the point of being elusive and enigmatic." See summary of, 'Swiss gnomes and global investing', audio-cassette produced by Knowledge Products available at: http://know-products. store.yahoo.net/swissgnomes.html (site visited 1 November 2007).

8 Bruce Springsteen, management gurus and the trouble of the promised land

1 As reported on Jim Collins (2003) website, *Built to Last* spent almost five years on *Business Week*'s bestseller list, has had over 70 printings and has been translated into 16 languages.

2 The cover of the current edition of the book reports that it has sold over three million copies and was on the *New York Times*' bestseller list for over three years.

3 This growing interest in utopian images of organizations in the early 1980s is bleakly contrasted by Springsteen's album *Nebraska* – a chilling depiction of the underside of American industrialism that was released in the same year as the publication of *In Search of Excellence*.

4 As reported on Michael Hammer's company website (Hammer and Company, 2003), *Reengineering the Corporation* has not only sold more than two million copies and been translated into 30 languages, but it also "introduced the business world to the power of radical change … put the word 'reengineering' into the English language … [and is] the most successful business book of the last decade".

9 Selling out: authenticity, resistance and punk rock

1 Punk rock originated in the United States with bands like The New York Dolls and The Patti Smith Group, it is Malcolm McLaren who is largely credited for bringing to it Britain. As Irving (1988) explains, transported to British context, however, its meaning changed significantly. In the USA, early 1970s punk never really became popular – it was intimately associated with the New York art scene and was largely based on stylistic protests. In Britain, however, punk latched on to working class sub-culture and dropped its artistic pretensions. Not only did British punk adopt a political (rather than stylistic) protest, but it also had "a huge impact on all levels of British society, making people feel rage, fear, guilt, and compassion simultaneously" (168).

2 Our discussion in this chapter focuses on rock music, and punk rock in particular. That is not to say that other forms of cultural activity and expression cannot be understood as a mode of excessive resistance. In music hip-hop and various underground movements are also examples. What we do argue, however, is that in punk rock this resistance takes a particular subcultural form that for some is elevated to a cultural archetype.

3 Perhaps so for Jones, but it must be noted that McLaren has always argued hat he was media savvy from the outset and was well aware of the commercial benefits of controversy. In late 1977, McLaren launched *The Sex Pistols* first (and only) US tour he

booked the first concerts in the Southern cities of Atlanta, Memphis and San Antonio in anticipation of more sensationalized media coverage (Moore, 2004). It was McLaren, too, who placed the communist hammer and sickle emblem on the back drop of the set of the band *The New York Dolls* when he managed them in the early 1970s in New York.

10 Sampling, tinkering and the glitch: bricolage in popular music and in organization practice

1 The first commercial album using the turntable in this way *?uestlove* identifies as *Grandmaster Flash and the Furious Five's* 'The Adventures of Grandmaster Flash on the Wheels of Steel' in 1981. That song sampled, among other things *Queen's* 'Another One Bites the Dust' and *Blondie's* 'Rapture'. Grandmaster Flash is widely credited with pioneering MCing, and the use of turntables in performance and even with coining the term 'hip hop'.
2 Later marketed as the *Novatron*.
3 *Matmos* are Martin Schmidt and Drew Daniel who, as well as producing their own work, programme a lot of material for the artist Bjork.
4 Note that 'do-it-yourself' is considered by some to be the most appropriate English translation of bricolage.
5 For example, the Secure Digital Music Initiative (SDMI), developed by a coalition of music industry stakeholders (in music publishing and distribution, telecommunications firms, Internet businesses, consumer electronics and computer companies), is working to find a standardized protection scheme.
6 This can be very restrictive since the licensing fees for a single song can be as much as US$78,000 (Marshall, 2006).
7 McLaren is former manager of *The Sex Pistols* (See Chapter 9). Given the album's nature, the producer Trevor Horn and the arranger Anne Dudley ought to be acknowledged.

References

Aaltio-Marjosola, I. and Lehtinen, J. (1998) Male Managers as Fathers? Contrasting Managers, Fatherhood and Masculinity, *Human Relations*, 51(2): 121–36.

Abrahamson, E. (1991) Management Fads and Fashions: The Diffusion and Rejection of Innovations, *Academy of Management Review*, 16(3): 586–612.

Abrahamson, E. (1996) Management Fashion, *Academy of Management Review*, 21(1): 254–85.

Abrahamson, E. and Fairchild, G. (1999) Management Fashion: Lifecycles, Triggers, and Collective Learning Processes, *Administrative Science Quarterly*, 44: 708–40.

Ackerman, D. (2002) The 20 Most Influential Business Books, *Forbes Magazine*, available at: www.forbes.com/2002/09/30/0930booksintro.html (visited 1 March 2005).

Ackroyd, S. (2002) Utopia or Ideology: Karl Mannheim and the Place of Theory, in M. Parker (ed.) *Utopia and Organization*, pp. 40–58, Oxford: Blackwell.

Adams, S. (1996) *The Dilbert Principle: A Cubicle's-Eye View of Bosses, Meetings, Management Fads, and Other Workplace Afflictions*, New York: Harper Business.

Adams, S. (2002) *Dilbert and the Way of the Weasel*, HarperCollins.

Adorno, T. (1941) On Popular Music, in S. Frith and A. Goodwin (eds) (1990) *On Record*, pp. 301–14, London: Routledge.

Adorno, T. and Horkheimer, M. (1944) *Dialectic of Enlightenment*, London: Verso.

Agger, B. (1989) *Fast Capitalism: A Critical Theory of Surveillance*, Urbana: University of Illinois Press.

Agger, B. (1992) *Cultural Studies as Critical Theory*, London: The Falmer Press.

Agger, B. (2004) *Speeding Up Fast Capitalism: Cultures, Jobs, Families, Schools, Bodies*, Boulder, CO: Paradigm.

Akrich, M. (1992) The De-Scription of Technical Objects, in W.E. Bijker and J. Law (eds) *Shaping Technology/Building Society*, pp. 206–24, Cambridge, MA: MIT Press.

Albran, K. (1974) *The Profit*, Los Angeles, CA: Price/Stern/Sloan Publishers.

Alper, G. (2000) Making Sense Out of Postmodern Music? *Popular Music And Society*, 24(4): 1–14.

Alvesson, M. (1993) Organisations as Rhetoric: Knowledge Intensive Firms and the Struggle with Ambiguity, *Journal of Management Studies*, 30(6): 997–1019.

Alvesson, M. (1998) Gender Relations and Identity at Work: A Case Study of Masculinities and Femininities in an Advertising Agency, *Human Relations*, 51(8): 969–1005.

Alvesson, M. and Billing, Y.D. (1992) Gender and Organisation: Towards a Differentiated Understanding, *Organisation Studies*, 13: 73–103.

Alvesson, M. and Skoldberg, K. (2000) *Reflexive Methodology, New Vistas for Qualitative Research*. London: Sage.

Alvesson, M. and Willmott, H. (2002) Identity Regulation as Organizational Control: Producing the Appropriate Individual, *Journal of Management Studies*, 39(5): 619–44.

Angus, I. and Langsdorf, L. (eds) (1993) *The Critical Turn: Rhetoric and Philosophy in Postmodem Discourse*, Carbondale and Edwardsville: Southern Illinois University Press.

Anon. (1999) The Old 'New Dylan', *The Nation*, 13 December: 52.

Apter, M.J. (1982) 'Fawlty Towers' – A Reversal Theory Analysis of a Popular Television Comedy Series, *Journal of Popular Culture*, 16(3): 128–38.

Badaracco Jr, J.L. (2006a) Leadership in Literature, *Harvard Business Review*, March: 47–55.

Badaracco Jr, J.L. (2006b) *Questions of Character: Illuminating the Heart of Leadership Through Literature*. Harvard, MA: Harvard Business School Press.

Badenhausen, R. (1998) The Modern Academy Raging in the Dark: Misreading Mamet's Political Incorrectness in Oleanna, *College Literature*, 25(3): 1–19.

Baker, E. and Nelson, R.E. (2005) Creating Something from Nothing: Resource Construction Through Entrepreneurial Bricolage, *Administrative Science Quarterly*, 50: 329–66.

Baker, T., Miner, A.S. and Eesley, D.T. (2003) Improvising Firms: Bricolage, Account Giving and Improvisational Competencies in the Founding Process, *Research Policy*, 32: 255–76.

Bakhtin, M.M. (1984a) *Rabelais and His World*, Trans. Hélène Iswolsky, Bloomington: Indiana University Press.

Bakhtin, M.M. (1984b) *Problems of Dostoyevsky's Poetics*, Ed. and trans. Caryl Emerson, Minneapolis: University of Minnesota Press.

Baritz, L. (1960) *The Servants of Power: A History of the Uses of Social Science in American Industry*, Westport, CT: Greeenwood.

Barley, S.R., Meyer, G.W. and Gash, D.C. (1988) Culture of Cultures: Academics, Practitioners and the Pragmatics of Normative Control, *Administrative Science Quarterly*, 33: 24–60.

Barrett, F. (1996) The Organisational Construction of Hegemonic Masculinity: The Case of the US Navy, *Gender, Work and Organisation*, 3(3): 129–41.

Barthes, R. (1977) *Image, Music, Text*. Ed. and trans. Stephen Heath, New York: Hill.

Bartunek, J.M. and Spreitzer, G.M. (2006) The Interdisciplinary Career of a Popular Construct Used in Management: Empowerment in the Late 20th Century, *Journal of Management Inquiry*, 15(3): 255–73.

Battaglia, D. (2001) Multiplicities: An Anthropologists Thoughts on Replicants and Clones in Popular Film, *Critical Inquiry*, 27(3): 493–514.

Bauman, Z. (1993) *Postmodern Ethics*, Cambridge, MA: Basil Blackwell.

Bauman, Z. (1995) *Life in Fragments. Essays in Postmodern Morality*, Cambridge, MA: Basil Blackwell.

Begley, V. (2004) Blade Runner and the Postmodern: A Reconsideration, *Literature/Film Quarterly*, 32(3): 186–92.

Belasco, J.A. (1990) *Teaching the Elephant to Dance: Empowering Change in Your Organization*, New York: Crown.

Belk, R.W. (1996) Hyperreality and Globalization: Culture in the Age of Ronald McDonald, *Journal of International Consumer Marketing*, 8(3/4): 23–76.

Benders, J. and van Veen, K. (2001) What's in a Fashion? Interpretative Viability and Management Fashions, *Organization*, 8(1): 33–53.

Bennet, O. (2001) *Cultural Pessimism: Narratives of Decline in the Postmodern World*, Edinburgh: Edinburgh University Press.

Bennett, A. (2001) *Cultures of Popular Music*, Buckingham: Open University Press.

Bennis, W.G. and O'Toole, J. (2005) How Business Schools Lost Their Way, *Harvard Business Review*, 83(5): 96–105.

Bernstein, B. (1966) Elaborated and Restricted Codes: An Outline, *Sociological Inquiry*, 36(2): 254–61.

Bernstein, B. (1971) *Class, Codes and Control*, vol. 1, London: Paladin.

Beyer, J.M. and Nino, D. (1999) Ethics and Cultures in International Business, *Journal Of Management Inquiry*, 8(3): 287–97.

Beynon, J. (2002) *Masculinities and Culture*, Buckingham; Philadelphia, PA: Open University.

Bhabha, H.K. (1994) *The Location of Culture*, London; New York: Routledge.

Bigsby, C.W.E. (1985a) *A Critical Introduction to Twentieth-Century American Drama, Volume Three: Beyond Broadway*, Cambridge: Cambridge University Press.

Bigsby, C.W.E. (1985b) *David Mamet*, London/New York: Methuen.

Black, E. (2001) *IBM and the Holocaust: The Strategic Alliance Between Nazi Germany and America's Most Powerful Corporation*, New York: Crown.

Bloomfield, B.P. and Vurdubakis, T. (1994) Re-Presenting Technology: It Consultancy Reports as Textual Reality Constructions, *Sociology*, 28(2): 455–77.

Boje, D.M. (2001) *Narrative Methods for Organizational and Communication Research*, London: Sage.

Boje, D.M. and Rhodes, C. (2005) The Virtual Leader Construct: The Mass Mediatization and Simulation of Transformational Leadership, *Leadership*, 1(4): 407–28.

Boje, D.M. and Rhodes, C. (2006) The Leadership Style of Ronald McDonald: Double Narration and Stylistic Lines of Transformation, *The Leadership Quarterly*, 17(1): 94–103.

Booker, M.K. (2006) *Alternate Americas: Science Fiction Film and American Culture*, Westport, CT: Praeger.

Bowes, M. (1990) Only When I Laugh, in A. Goodwin and G. Whannel (eds) *Understanding Television*, pp. 128–40, London: Routledge.

Bowles, M. (1997) The Myth of Management: Direction and Failure in Contemporary Organizations, *Human Relations*, 50(7): 779–803.

Bowman, J. (1993) Leave It to Beavis, *New Criterion*, 12(4): 5–62.

Boyce, Mary E. (1996) Organisational Story and Storytelling: A Critical Review, *Journal of Organisational Change Management*, 9(5): 5–26.

Brabazon, T. (2005) What Have You Ever Done on the Telly?: The Office, (Post) Reality Television and (Post) Work, *International Journal of Cultural Studies*, 8(1): 101–17.

Brackett, D. (2002) 'Where's It at?': Postmodern Theory and the Contemporary Musical Field, in J. Lochhead and J. Auner (eds) *Postmodern Music/Postmodern Thought*, pp. 207–31, New York: Routledge.

Branscomb, H.E. (1993) Literacy and a Popular Medium: The Lyrics of Bruce Springsteen, *Journal of Popular Culture*, 27(1): 29–42.

Brawer, R.A. (1998/2000) *Fictions of Business: Insights on Management from Great Literature*, New York: Wiley.

Brereton, P. (2001) Utopianism and Fascist Aesthetics: An Appreciation of 'Nature' in Documentary Film/Fiction, *Capitalism, Nature, Socialism*, 12(4): 33–50.

Brewis, J. (1998) What Is Wrong with this Picture? Sex and Gender Relations in Disclosure, in J. Hassard and R. Holliday (eds) *Organization Representation: Work and Organization in Popular Culture*, pp. 83–100, London: Sage.

Brewis, J. and Linstead, S. (2000) *Sex, Work, and Sex Work: Eroticizing Organization*, London: Routledge

Brewis, J., Hapton, M.P. and Linstead, S. (1997) Unpacking Priscilla: Subjectivity and Identity in the Organization of Gendered Appearance, *Human Relations*, 50(10): 1275–305.

British Sitcom Guide (2006) Available at: www.british-sitcom.co.uk/list.shtml (visited 9 December 2006).

Brittan, A. (1989) *Masculinity and Power*, Oxford: Basil Blackwell.

Brovetto, P.R., Carruth, R. and Pasquero, J. (1999) Guest Editors' Introduction to the Special Issue, *Business and Society*, 38(4): 396–401.

Brown, R.H. (1992) *Writing the Social Text*, New York: Walter De Gruyter.

Brown, T. (1996) The Deeper Side of Dilbert, *Management Review*, 85(2): 48–52.

Brown, T. (1997) What Does Dilbert Mean to HR? *HR Focus*, 74(2), 12–13.

Bruno, G. (1987) Ramble City: Postmodernism and 'Blade Runner', *October*, 41: 61–74.

Buchanan, A. and Huczynski, D. (2003) *Organizational Behavior: An Introductory Text Fifth Edition*, Harlow: Prentice Hall.

Buchanan, D. and Huczynski, A. (2004) 'Images of Influence: Twelve Angry Men and Thirteen Days', *Journal of Management Inquiry*, 13: 312–23.

Burke, P. (1978) *Popular Culture in Early Modern Europe*, London: Temple Smith.

Burrell, G. (1993) Eco and the Bunnymen, in J. Hassard and M. Parker (eds) *Postmodernism and Organisations*, pp. 71–82, London: Sage.

Burrough, B. and Helyar, J. (1992) *Barbarians at the Gate: The Fall of Rjr Nabisco*, New York: Harpercollins.

Butler, J. (2003) What Is Critique? An Essay on Foucault's Virtue, available at: www.law.berkeley.edu/cenpro/kadish/what%20is%20critique%20J%20Butler.pdf (visited 19 July 2004).

Butsch, R. (1992) Class and Gender in Four Decades of Television Situation Comedy: Plus Ça Change, *Critical Studies in Mass Communication*, 9: 387–99.

Byers, T.B. (1987) Commodity Futures: Corporate State and Personal Style in Three Recent Science-Fiction Movies, *Science Fiction Studies*, 14(3): 326–39.

Byrne, E.F. (1999) Give Peace a Chance: A Mantra for Business Strategy, *Journal of Business Ethics*, 20: 27–37.

Cannadine, D. (1990) *The Decline and Fall of the British Aristocracy*, Yale University Press.

Cannadine, D. (1999) *The Rise and Fall of Class in Britain*, New York: Columbia University Press.

Carilli, J. and Campbell, T. (eds) (2005) *Women and the Media: Diverse Perspectives*, University Press of America.

Carroll, D.C. (1987) *David Mamet*, Basingstoke: Macmillan.

Carter, V.K. (2000) *Learning from Work: Thinking Aversively About Dilbert*, D.Ed., Pennsylvania State University, DAI.

Cascone, K. (2000) The Aesthetics of Failure: 'Post-Digital' Tendencies in Contemporary Computer Music, *Computer Music Journal*, 24(4): 12–18.

Casey, C. (1995) *Work, Self and Society: After Industrialism*, London: Sage.

Catano, James V. (2001) *Ragged Dicks: Masculinity, Steel, and the Rhetoric of the Self-Made Man*, Carbondale: Southern Illinois University Press.

Chalmers, L.V. (2001) *Marketing Masculinities: Gender and Management Politics in Marketing Work*, Westport, CT: Greenwood Press.

Chambers, I. (1985) *Urban Rhythms, Pop Music and Popular Culture*, London: Macmillan.

Champoux, J.E. (1999) Film as a Teaching Resource, *Journal of Management Inquiry*, 8(2): 206–17.

Champoux, J.E. (2001) *Using Film to Visualize Principles and Practices: Organizational Behavior*, Cincinnati, OH: South-Western College Publishing.

Chan, A. (2000) *Critically Constituting Organization*, Amsterdam: John Benjamins.

Chen, R. (compiler) (1992) Episode Capsule: Krusty Gets Busted, *The Simpsons Archive*, available at: www.snpp.com/episodes/7G12.html (visited 27 May 2003) (original episode written by J. Kogen and W. Wolodarsky).

Cheng, C. (ed.) (1996) *Masculinities in Organisations*, Thousand Oaks, CA: Sage.

Cherry, J.A. (compiler) (1996) Episode Capsule: Lisa's First Word, *The Simpsons Archive*, available at: www.snpp.com/episodes/9F09.html (visited 27 May 2003) (original episode written by G. Apple and M. Carrington).

Chester, A. (1970) Second Thoughts on a Rock Aesthetic: The Band, *New Left Review*, 62: 75–82.

Chia, R. (1996) *Organizational Analysis as Deconstructive Practice*, Berlin: de Gruyter.

Chia, R. (2003) Ontology: Organizations as 'World-Making', in R.I. Westwood and S.R. Clegg (eds) *Debating Organisation: Point/Counterpoint in Organisation Studies*, pp. 98–113, Oxford: Blackwell.

Christgau, R. (1986) Down by Law, *Village Voice*, 25 March.

Ciborra, C. (1992) From Thinking to Tinkering: The Grassroots of Strategic Information Systems, *The Information Society*, 8: 297–309.

Ciborra, C. (1994) From Thinking to Tinkering, in C. Ciborra and T. Jelassi (eds) *Strategic Information Systems*, Chichester: John Wiley and Sons.

Ciborra, C. (1996) The Platform Organization: Recombining Strategies, Structures, and Surprises, *Organization Science*, 7(2): 103–18.

Ciborra, C. (1997) Improvising in the Shapeless Organization of the Future, in C. Sauer and P.W. Yetton (eds) *Steps to the Future; Fresh Thinking on the Management of IT-Based Organizational Transformation*, pp. 257–77, San Francisco, CA: Jossey-Bass.

Ciborra, C. (1999) Notes on Time and Improvisation, *Accounting, Management and Information Technologies*, 9(1): 77–94.

Ciborra, C., Braa, K., Cordella, A., Dahlbom, B., Failla, A., Hanseth, O., Hepsø, V., Ljungberg, J., Monteiro, E. and Simon, K. (eds) (2003) *From Control to Drift: The Dynamics of Corporate Information Infrastructures*, Oxford: Oxford University Press.

Cicourel, A.V. (1964) *Method and Measurement in Sociology*, London: Collier-Macmillan.

Clark, D. (1990) Cagney and Lacey: Feminist Strategies of Detection, in M.E. Brown (ed.) *Television and Women's Culture: The Politics of the Popular*, pp. 117–33, London: Sage.

Clark, T. (2004) The Fashion of Management Fashion: A Surge Too Far? *Organization*, 11(2): 297–306.

Clark, T. and Greatbatch, D. (2004) Management Fashion as Image-Spectacle: The Production of Best-Selling Management Books, *Management Communication Quarterly*, 17(3): 396–424.

Clark, T. and Salaman, G. (1998) Telling Tales: Management Gurus' Narratives and the Construction of Managerial Identity, *Journal of Management Studies*, 35(2): 137–61.

Clegg, S.R. (1992) Postmodern Management? *Journal of Organization Change Management*, 5(2): 31–49.

Clegg, S.R. (2005) Puritans, Visionaries and Survivors, *Organization Studies*, 26(4): 527–45.

Clegg, S.R. and Hardy, C. (1996) Representations, in S. Clegg, C. Hardy and W.R. Nord (eds) *Handbook of Organization Studies*, pp. 676–708, London: Sage.

Clegg, S.R. and Hardy, C. (1999) *Studying Organization: Theory and Method*, London: Sage.

Clegg, S.R., Courpasson, N. and Phillips, N. (2006) *Power in Organizations*, Thousand Oaks, CA: Sage.

Clemens, J.K. and Mayer, D.F. (1999) *The Classic Touch: Lessons in Leadership from Homer to Hemingway*, New York: Contemporary Books.

Clemens, J.K. and Wolff, M. (1999) *Movies to Manage By: Lessons in Leadership from Great Films*, New York: Contemporary Books.

Cleveland, J.N., Stockdale, M. and Murphy, K.R. (2000) *Women and Men in Organisations: Sex and Gender Issues at Work*, Mahwah, NJ: Lawrence Erlbaum.

Cobley, P. (1999) Leave the Capitol, in R. Sabin (ed.) *Punk Rock: So What?* pp. 170–86, London: Routledge.

Cohen, K.F. (1998) *Forbidden Animation: Censored Cartoons and Blacklisted Animators in America*, Jefferson, NC: McFarland.

Cohen, S. (1991) *Rock Culture in Liverpool: Popular Music in the Making*, Oxford: Clarendon Press.

Collier, J.L. (1983) *Louis Armstrong*, New York: Oxford University Press.

Collins, D. (2000) *Management Fads and Buzzwords: Critical–Practical Perspectives*, London: Routledge.

Collins, D. (2001) The Fad Motif in Management Scholarship, *Employee Relations*, 23(1): 26–37.

Collins, D. (2003) The Branding of Management Knowledge: Rethinking Management 'Fads', *Journal of Organizational Change Management*, 16(2): 186–204.

Collins, D. (2004) Who Put the Con in Consultancy? Fads, Recipes, and 'Vodka Margarine', *Human Relations*, 57(5): 553–72.

Collins, J. (1989), *Uncommon Cultures: Popular Culture and Postmodernism*, London: Routledge.

Collins, J. (1995) *Architectures of Excess: Cultural Life in the Information Age*, London: Routledge.

Collins, J.C. (2003) JimCollins.Com: Library, available at: www.jimcollins.com/lib/books.html (visited 4 April 2003).

Collins, J.C. and Porras, J.I. (1994) *Built to Last: Successful Habits of Visionary Companies*, New York: Harper Collins.

Collinson, D.L. (1992) *Managing the Shopfloor: Subjectivity, Masculinity and Workplace Culture*, Berlin: De Gruyter.

Collinson, D.L. (2003) Identities and Insecurities: Selves at Work, *Organisation*, 10(3): 527–41.

Collinson, D.L. and Hearn, J. (1994) Naming Men as Men: Implications for Work, Organisation and Management, *Gender, Work and Organisation*, 1(1): 2–20.

Collinson, D.L. and Hearn, J. (eds) (1996) *Men as Managers, Managers as Men: Critical Perspectives on Men, Masculinities and Managements*, London: Sage Publications.

Collinson, D.L. and Hearn, J. (2005) Men and Masculinities in Work, Organizations, and Management, in M. Kimmel, J. Hearn and R.W. Connell (eds) *The Handbook of Studies on Men and Masculinities*, Thousand Oaks, CA: Sage.

Comer, Debra R. and Cooper, Elizabeth A. (1998) Gender Relations and Sexual Harassment in the Workplace: Michael Crichton's Disclosure as a teaching tool, *Journal of Management Education*, 22(2): 227–41.

Connell, J. and Gibson, C. (2003) *Sound Tracks: Popular Music, Identity and Place*, London: Routledge.

Connell, R.W. (1995) *Masculinities*, Oxford: Polity Press.

Connell, R.W. (2005) *Masculinities*, 2nd ed., Crows Nest, New South Wales: Allen and Unwin.

Corbett, M. (1995) Reconstructing Human-Centred Technology: Lessons from the Holly-wood Dream Factory, *AI and Society*, 12: 214–30.

Corbett, M. (1998) Sublime Technologies and Future Organization in Science Fiction Film, in J. Hassard and R. Holliday (eds) *Organization Representation: Work and Organization in Popular Culture*, pp. 247–58, London: Sage.

Coupland, D. (1996) *Microserfs*, New York: Regan Books.

Coupland, D. (2006) *JPod: A Novel*, London: Bloomsbury.

Cowie, J. (2001) Fandom, Faith and Bruce Springsteen, *Dissent*, Winter: 112–17.

Cowie, J. and Boehm, L. (2006) Dead Man's Town: 'Born in the USA' Social History, and Working Class Identity, *American Quarterly*, 58(2): 253–378.

Craib, I. (1988) *Experiencing Identity*, London: Sage.

Crainer, S. (1998a) In Search of the Real Author, *Management Today*, May: 50–4.

Crainer, S. (1998b) *The Ultimate Guide to Business Gurus*, Capstone: Oxford.

Crawford, M. (1989) Humor in Conversational Context: Beyond Biases in the Study of Gender and Humor, in R.K. Unger (ed.) *Representations: Social Constructions of Gender*, pp. 155–66, New York: Baywood.

Cullen, J. (1997) *Born in the USA: Bruce Springsteen and the American Tradition*, London: Helter Skelter.

Cullen, J. (2005) *Born in the USA: Bruce Springsteen and the American Tradition*, 2nd edn, Middletown: Wesleyan University Press.

Cunha, M.P. (2007) Bricolage in Organizations, Working Paper, Lisbon: Faculdade De Economia, Universidade Nova De Lisboa.

Cunha, M.P. and Cunha, J.V. (2006) Towards a Complexity Theory of Strategy, *Management Decision*, 44: 839–50.

Cunha, M.P., Cunha, J.V. and Kamoche, K. (1999) Organizational Improvisation: What, When, How and Why, *International Journal of Management Reviews*, 1: 299–341.

Cusack, M., Jack, G. and Kavanagh, D. (2003) Dancing with Discrimination: Managing Stigma and Identity, *Culture and Organization*, 9(4): 295–310.

Czarniawska, B. (1995) Rhetoric and Modern Organizations, *Studies in Cultures, Organizations and Societies*, 1(2): 147–52.

Czarniawska, B. (1996) *Management She Wrote: Organization Studies and Detective Stories*, Göteborg: Gothenburg Research Institute.

Czarniawska, B. (1997) *Narrating the Organization: Dramas of Institutional Identity*, Chicago, IL: University of Chicago Press.

Czarniawska, B. (1999) *Writing Management: Organization Theory as a Literary Genre*, Oxford: Oxford University Press.

Czarniawska, B. and de Monthoux, P.G. (eds) (1994) *Good Novels, Better Management: Reading Organizational Realities in Fiction*, London: Routlege.

Czarniawska, B. and Rhodes, C. (2006) Strong Plots: The Relationship Between Popular Culture and Management Theory and Practice, in P. Gagliardi and B. Czarniawska (eds) *Management and Humanities*, pp. 195–220 Edward Elgar.

D'Acci, J. (1994) *Defining Women: Television and the Case of Cagney and Lacey*, Chapel Hill: University of North Carolina Press.

Dalton, M.M. and Linder, L.R. (eds) (2005) *The Sitcom Reader: America Viewed and Skewed*, New York: State University of New York Press.

210   *References*

Danaher, K. (ed.) (1997) *Corporations Are Gonna Get Your Mama: Globalization and the Downsizing of the American Dream*, Monroe, ME: Common Courage Press.

Dasgupta, R. (2000) Performing Masculinities? The 'Salaryman' at Work and Play, *Japanese Studies*, 20(2): 189–200.

Davies, H. (1996) A History of Sampling, *Organised Sound*, 1(1): 3–11.

Davies, J. (1996) The Future of 'No Future': Punk Rock and Postmodern Theory, *Journal of Popular Music*, 29(4): 3–25.

Davis, J.A. (2000) Dilbert as Organizational Analyst, *Dissertation Abstracts International, Section A: The Humanities and Social Sciences*, 2001 June, 61(12): 4755, University of Kansas.

de Curtis, A. (1992) Bruce Springsteen, in A. De Curtis and K. Henke (eds) *The Rolling Stone Illustrated History of Rock And Roll*, 3rd edn, pp. 619–25, New York: Random House.

de Marco, T. (1997) *The Deadline: A Novel About Project Management*, New York: Dorset House.

Deal, T.E. and Kennedy, A.A. (1982) *Corporate Cultures: The Rites and Rituals of Corporate Life*, Harmondsworth: Penguin Books.

DeBord, G. (1970) *Society of the Spectacle*, Detroit: Black and Red.

Dellinger, K. (2004) Masculinities in 'Safe' and 'Embattled' Organisations: Accounting for Pornographic and Feminist Magazines, *Gender and Society*, 18(5): 545–66.

Demastes, W. (1988) *Beyond Naturalism: A New Realism in America Theatre*, Westport, CT: Greenwood Press.

Demers, J. (2003) Sampling the 1970s in Hip-Hop, *Popular Music*, 22(1): 41–56.

Denora, T. (1999) Music as a Technology of the Self, *Poetics*, 17(1): 31–56.

Derrida, J. (1976) *Of Grammatology*, Baltimore: Johns Hopkins University Press.

Derrida, J. (1978) Structure, Sign, and Play in the Discourse of the Human Sciences, in J. Derrida (ed.) and Alan Bass (trans.) *Writing and Difference*, pp. 278–94, London: Routledge.

Derrida, J. (1988) Afterword: Toward and Ethic of Discussion, in G. Graf (ed.) *Limited Inc.*, pp. 111–54, Evaston, IL: Northwestern University Press.

Derrida, J. (1995) *The Gift of Death*, Chicago: Chicago University Press.

DeVault, M.L. (1990) Novel Readings: The Social Organization of Interpretation, *The American Journal of Sociology*, 95(4): 887–921.

Dick, P. (1968) *Do Aliens Dream of Electric Sheep?* Garden City, NY: Doubleday.

Dickens, P. (2000) *Social Darwinism: Linking Evolutionary Thought to Social Theory*, Buckingham: Open University Press.

Docker, J. (1994) *Postmodernism and Popular Culture: A Cultural History*, Cambridge: Cambridge University Press.

Donaldson, L. (1996) *For Positivist Organization Theory: Proving the Hard Core*, London: Sage.

Donaldson, L. (2001) *The Contingency Theory of Organizations*, Thousand Oaks, CA: Sage.

Donaldson, L. (2003) Position Statement for Positivism, in R.I. Westwood and S.R. Clegg (eds) *Debating Organisation: Point/Counterpoint in Organisation Studies*, pp. 116–27, Oxford: Blackwell Publishing.

Douglas, S.J. (1987) *Inventing American Broadcasting, 1899–1922*, Baltimore, MD: Johns Hopkins University Press.

Douglas, W. and Olson, B.M. (1995) Beyond Family Structure: The Family in Domestic Comedy, *Journal of Broadcasting and Electronic Media*, 39: 236–61.

Dow, B.J. (1996) *Primetime Feminism: Television, Media, Culture and the Women's Movement Since 1970*, Philadelphia: University of Pennsylvania Press.

Downs, A. and Stogner, C. (1995) *Corporate Executions: The Ugly Truth About Layoffs – How Corporate Greed Is Shattering Lives, Companies, and Communities*, New York: Amacom.

Doyle, T. (2004) Matmos: The Art of Cut and Paste, *Sound On Sound*, May, available at: www.Soundonsound.Com/Sos/May04/Articles/Matmos.Htm (visited 1 February 2007).

du Gay, P. (1996) Making Up Managers: Enterprise and the Ethos of Bureaucracy, in S.R. Clegg and G. Palmer (eds) *The Politics of Management Knowledge*, pp. 19–35, London: Sage.

Dubnick, M. (2000) Movies and Morals: Energizing Ethical Thinking Among Professionals, *Journal of Public Affairs Education*, 6(3): 147–59.

Durkin, K. (1985) Television and Sex Role Acquisition 2: Effects, *British Journal of Social Psychology*, 24: 191–222.

Dyrud, M.A. (1998) Ethics a la Dilbert, *Business Communication Quarterly*, 61(4): 113–18.

Elasmer, M., Hasegawa, K. and Brain, M. (1999) The Portrayal of Women in U.S. Prime Time Television, *Journal of Broadcasting and Electronic Media*, 44: 20–34.

Feldman, D.C. (2000) The Dilbert Syndrome: How Employee Cynicism About Ineffective Management Is Changing the Nature of Careers in Organizations, *American Behavioral Scientist*, 43(8): 1286–300.

Ferneley, E. and Bell, F. (2006) Using Bricolage to Integrate Business and Information Technology Innovation in SMEs, *Technovation*, 26: 232–41.

Ferrara, A. (1998) *Reflective Authenticity: Rethinking the Project of Modernity*, London: Routeldge.

Feuer, J. (2001) The Unruly Woman Sitcom ('I Love Lucy, Roseanne, Absolutely Fabulous'), in G. Creeber (ed.) *The Television Genre Book*, pp. 60–71, London: British Film Institute.

Finnegan, R. (1989) *The Hidden Musicians: Music Making in an English Town*, Cambridge: Cambridge University Press.

Finney, G. (1994) *Look Who's Laughing: Gender and Comedy*, Langhorne: Gordon and Breach.

Fisher, R. (1997) Teachers and Hegemony Sucks: Examining Beavis and Butt-Head for Signs of Life, *Educational Studies*, 23(3): 417–29.

Fiske, J. (1987) *Television Culture*, London: Routledge.

Fiske, J. (1989) *Understanding Popular Culture*, London: Unwin Hyman.

Fitting, P. (1987) Futurecop: The Neutralization of Revolt in Blade Runner, *Science Fiction Studies*, 14(3): 340–53.

Fleming, P. (2005) Metaphors of Resistance, *Management Communication Quarterly*, 19(1): 45–66.

Fleming, P. and Sewell, G. (2002) Looking for the Good Soldier, Svejk Alternative Modalities of Resistance in the Contemporary Workplace, *Sociology*, 36(4): 857–73.

Fleming, P. and Spicer, A. (2003) Working at a Cynical Distance: Implications for Power, Subjectivity and Resistance, *Organization*, 10: 157–79.

Foreman, J. and Thatchenkery, T. (1996) Filmic Representations for Organizational Analysis: The Characterization of a Transplant Organization in the Film Rising Sun, *Journal of Organizational Change Management*, 9(3): 44–62.

Foucault, M. (1977) *Discipline and Punish: The Birth of the Prison*, Harmondsworth: Penguin.

Foucault, M. (1988) *The Care of the Self: History of Sexuality 3*, New York: Vintage.

Fournier, V. and Grey, C. (2000) At the Critical Moment: Conditions and Prospects for Critical Management Studies, *Human Relations*, 53(1): 7–32.

Fouts, G. and Burggraf, K. (1999) Television Situation Comedies: Female Body Images and Verbal Reinforcements, *Sex Roles*, 40(5/6): 473–81.

Freedman, C. (2000) *Critical Theory and Science Fiction*, Wesleyan University Press.

Freeman, F. (2005) *Policy Making as Bricolage: Uncertainty, Rationality and Learning in Public Health*, Working Paper, Edinburgh: University of Edinburgh.

Freeman-Greene, S. (2007) Never Mind the Bollocks, Here's to Punk Music, *The Age*, 5 May, available at: www.theage.com.au/articles/2007/05/03/1177788304477.html (visited 7 May 2007).

Friedman, S.G. (1985) The Gritty Eloquence of David Mamet, *New York Times*, 21 April: 40.

Frith, S. (1981) *Sound Effects: Youth, Leasure and the Politics of Rock and Roll*, New York: Pantheon Books.

Frith, S. (1988) Copyright and the Music Business, *Popular Music*, 7(1): 57–75.

Frith, S. (1996) *Performing Rites: Evaluating Popular Music*, Oxford: Oxford University Press.

Frith, S. (1998) *Music for Pleasure: Essays in the Sociology of Pop*, New York: Routledge.

Frith, S. (2004) Towards and Aesthetic of Popular Music, in S. Frith (ed.) *Popular Music Vol. IV: Music and Identity*, pp. 32–47, London: Routledge.

Frost, P.J., Moore, L., Louis, M., Lundberg, C. and Martin, J. (1991) *Reframing Organizational Culture*, Newbury Park, CA: Sage.

Frost, P.J. (1993) *Toxic Emotions at Work*, Boston, MA: Harvard Business School Press.

Frost, P.J., Mitchell, V.F. and Nord, W.R. (eds) (1997) *Organizational Reality: Reports from the Firing Line*, 5th edn, Reading, MA: Addison Wesley.

Frost, P.J., Nord, W.R. and Krefting, L. (eds) (2004) *Managerial and Organizational Reality*, Pearson.

Furusten, S. (1999) *Popular Management Books: How They Are Made and What They Mean for Organisations*, London: Routledge.

Gabriel, Y. (1999) Beyond Happy Families: A Critical Reevaluation of the Control–Resistance–Identity Triangle, *Human Relations*, 52(2): 179–203.

Gabriel, Y. (2000) *Storytelling in Organisations: Fact, Fictions and Fantasies*, Oxford: Oxford University Press.

Gagliardi, P. (1996) Exploring the Aesthetic Side of Organizational Life, in S.R. Clegg, C. Hardy and W. Nord (eds) *Handbook of Organization Studies*, London: Sage.

Galbraith, J.R. (1980) Applying Theory to the Management of Organizations, in W.M. Evan (ed.) *Frontiers in Organization and Management*, pp. 151–67, New York: Praeger.

Gallivan, J. (1999) Gender and Humor: What Makes a difference? *North American Journal of Psychology*, 1: 307–18.

Game, A. and Pringle, R. (1983) *Gender at Work*, Sydney: George Allen and Unwin.

Gardner, J. (1994) Leave It to Beavis, *National Review*, 48(6): 60–3.

Gardner, R.O. (2005) Tradition and Authenticity in Popular Music, *Symbolic Interaction*, 28(1): 135–44.

Garsten, C. and Grey, C. (1997) How to Become Oneself: Discourses of Subjectivity in Post-Bureaucratic Organisations, *Organization*, 4: 211–28.

Gee, J.P., Hull, G. and Lankshear, C. (1996) *The New Work Order: Behind the Language of the New Capitalism*, St. Leondards: Allen And Unwin.

Geis, D.R. (1992) David Mamet and the Metadramatic Tradition: Seeing 'the Trick from the Back', in L. Kane (ed.) *David Mamet: A Casebook*, New York: Garland.

Gelber, S. (1997) Do-It-Yourself: Constructing, Repairing and Maintaining Domestic Masculinity, *American Quarterly*, 49(March): 66–112.

Gencarelli, T. (1994) Trying to Learn How to Walk Like the Heroes: Bruce Springsteen, Popular Music, and the Hero/Celebrity, in S.J. Drucker and R.S. Cathcart (eds) *American Heroes in a Media Age*, pp. 281–300, Creskill, NJ: Hampden Press.

Gephart Jr, R.P. (1996) Management, Social Issues, and the Postmodern Era, in D.M. Boje, R.P. Gephart Jr and T.J. Thatchenkery (eds) *Postmodern Management and Organization Theory*, pp. 21–44, Thousand Oaks, CA: Sage.

Gerlach, N. (1996) The Business Restructuring Genre: Some Questions for Critical Organization Analysis, *Organization*, 3: 425–53.

Gherardi, S. and Poggio, B. (2001) Creating and Recreating Gender Order in Organisations, *Journal of World Business*, 36(3): 245–59.

Godelier, M. (1980) Work and Its Representations: A Research Proposal, *History Workshop Journal*, 10(1): 164–74.

Goffman, E. (1959) *The Presentation of Self in Everyday Life*, New York: Doubleday.

Golding, P. and Murdock, G. (1991) Culture, Communication and Political Economy, in J. Curran and M. Gurevitch (eds) *Mass Media and Society*, pp. 15–32, London: Edward Arnold.

Goldratt, E. (1997) *The Critical Chain*, Aldershot: Gower Publishing.

Goldratt, E. and Cox, J. (1984) *The Goal: Beating the Opposition*, Aldershot: Gower Publishing.

Goldstein, J. and Rayner, J. (1994) The Politics of Identity in Later Modern Society, *Theory and Society*, 23(3): 367–84.

Good, G., Porter, M. and Dillon, M.G. (2002) When Men Divulge: Portrayals of Men's Self-Disclosure in Prime Time Situation Comedies, *Sex Roles*, 46(11/12): 419–28.

Goodwin, A. (1990) Sample and Hold: Pop Music in the Digital Age of Reproduction, in S. Frith and A. Goodwin (eds) *On Record: Rock, Pop, and the Written Word*, pp. 258–74, New York: Pantheon Books.

Gosling, J. and Mintzberg, H. (2003) The Education of Practicing Managers, *MIT Sloan Management Review*, 45(4): 19–25.

Gosling, J. and Mintzberg, H. (2006) Management Education as If Both Matter, *Management Learning*, 37(4): 419–29.

Gottlieb, R. (1978) The 'Engine' that Drives Playwright David Mamet, *New York Times*, 15 January, Sec. 2: 4.

Gowler, D. and Legge, K. (1983) The Meaning of Management and the Management of Meaning: A View from Social Anthropology, in M.J. Earl (ed.) *Perspectives on Management*, pp. 197–233, Oxford: Oxford University Press.

Gramsci, A. (2001) *Selections from Cultural Writings*, D. Forgacs and G. Nowell-Smith (eds) and W. Boelhower (trans.), London: Electric Book Company.

Gray, F. (1994) *Women and Laughter*, Houndmills: Macmillan.

Greenbaum, A. (1999) Brass Balls: Masculine Communication and the Discourse of Capitalism in David Mamet's Glengarry Glen Ross, *The Journal of Men's Studies*, 8(1): 33–44.

Greenwood, M. (2000) The Study of Business Ethics: A Case for Dr Seuss, *Business Ethics: A European Review*, 9(3): 155–62.

Grewell, G. (2001) Colonizing the Universe: Science Fictions Then, Now, and in the (Imagined) Future, *Rocky Mountain Review*, 55(2): 25–47.

Grey, C. (1994) Career as a Project of the Self and Labour Process Discipline, *Sociology*, 28(2): 479–97.

Grey, C. (1999) We Are All Managers Now; We Always Were: On the Development and Demise of Management. *Journal of Management Studies*, 36(5): 561-585.

Grice, S. and Humphries, M. (1997) Critical Management Studies in Postmodernity: Oxymorons in Outer Space? *Journal of Organization Change Management*, 10(5): 112–25.

Grint, K. (1994) Reengineering History: Social Resonances and Business Process Reengineering, *Organization*, 1(1): 179–201.

Grint, K. (1997) *Fuzzy Management*, Oxford: Oxford University Press.

Grint, K. and Case, P. (1998) The Violent Rhetoric of Reengineering – Management Consultancy on the Offensive, *Journal of Management Studies*, 35(5): 557–77.

Grossberg, L. (1990) Is Their Rock After Punk? in S. Frith and A. Goodwin (eds) *On Record*, pp. 111–24, London: Routledge.

Grossberg, L. (1992) *We Gotta Get Out of This Place: Popular Conservatism and Post-modern Culture*, New York: Routledge.

Guest, D. (1990) Human Resource Management and the American Dream, *Journal of Management Studies*, 27: 377–97.

Guide to Comedy (2006) Available at: www.bbc.co.uk/comedy/guide/ (visited 1 December 2006).

Guignon, C. (2004) *On Being Authentic*, London: Routledge.

Gunster, S. (2000) Revisiting the Culture Industry Thesis: Mass Culture and the Commodity Form, *Cultural Critique*, 45: 40–70.

Gunter, B. (1995) *Television and Gender Representation*, London: John Libbey.

Gussow, M. (1984) Real Estate World a Model for Mamet: His New Play Draws on Life, *New York Times*, 28 March: C19.

Haley, C. (2001) Science Fiction and the Making of the Laser, in W. Smith, M. Higgins, M. Parker and G. Lightfoot (eds) *Science Fiction and Organization*, pp. 31–40, London: Routeldge.

Hall, S. (1994) Reflections upon the Encoding/Decoding Model: An Interview with Stuart Hall, in J. Cruz and J. Lewis (eds) *Viewing, Reading, Listening*, Boulder, CO: Westview.

Hall, S. (1996) On Postmodernism and Articulation: An Interview with Stuart Hall, in D. Morley and K.-H. Chen (eds) *Stuart Hall: Critical Dialogues in Cultural Studies*, pp. 131–50, London: Routledge.

Hall, S. and Whannell, P. (1964) *The Popular Arts*, London: Hutchinson.

Hamamoto, D.Y. (1989) *Nervous Laughter: Television Situation Comedy and Liberal Democratic Ideology*, New York: Praeger.

Hammer and Company (2003) Publications, available at: www.hammerandco.com/publications-corporation.asp (visited 4 April 2003).

Hammer, M. and Champy, J. (1994) *Reengineering the Corporation: A Manifesto for Business Revolution*, New York: Harpercollins.

Hancock, P. and Tyler, M. (2004) 'MOT Your Life': Critical Management Studies and the Management of Everyday Life, *Human Relations*, 57(5): 619–45.

Handy, C. (1983) *Understanding Organisations*, London: Penguin.

Handy, C. (1985) *Gods of Managemen: The Changign Work of Orgaizations*, Oxford: Oxford University Press.

Harbison, F. and Myers, C.A. (1959) *Management and the Industrial World: An International Analysis*, New York: McGraw-Hill.

Hardy, C. and Clegg, S.R. (2006) Some Dare Call It Power, in S.R. Clegg, C. Hardy, T. Lawrence and W. Nord (eds) *The Sage Handbook of Organization Studies Second Edition*, pp. 774-6, London: Sage.

Harrington, C.L. and Beilby, D.D. (2005) Constructing the Popular: Cultural Production and Consumption, in C.L. Herrington and D.D. Beilby (eds) *Popular Culture: Production and Consumption*, pp. 1–16, London: Blackwell.

Harris-Fain, D. (2005) *Understanding Contemporary American Science Fiction, 1970–2000*, University of South Carolina Press.

Hartley, J. (2001) Situation Comedy – Part 1, in G. Creeber (ed.) *The Television Genre Book*, London: British Film Institute.

Harvard Business School (2006) *Our History*, Boston, MA: Harvard Business School, available at: www.hbs.edu/about/history.html (visited 12 November 2006).

Hassard, J. and Holliday, R. (eds) (1998) *Organization Representation: Work and Organization in Popular Culture*, London: Sage.

Hassard, J. and Parker, M. (eds) (1993) *Postmodernism and Organizations*, London: Sage.

Haywood, C. and Mac an Ghaill, M. (2003) *Men and Masculinities: Theory, Research, and Social Practice*, Philadelphia, PA: Open University.

Hearn, J. (1992) *Men in the Public Eye: The Construction and Deconstruction of Public Men and Public Patriarchies*, London: Routledge.

Hearn, J. (1994) The Organisation(s) of Violence: Men, Gender Relations, Organisations, and Violences, *Human Relations*, 47(6): 731–55.

Hearn, J. and Morgan, D. (eds) (1990) *Men, Masculinities and Social Theory*, London: Unwin Hyman.

Hebidge, D. (1979) *Subculture: The Meaning of Style*, London: Methuen.

Hegele, C. and Kieser, A. (2001) Control the Construction of Your Legend or Someone Else Will: An Analysis of texts on Jack Welch. *Journal of Management Inquiry*, 10(4): 298-302.

Heinecken, D. (2003) *The Warrior Women of Television: A Feminist Cultural Analysis of the New Female Body in Popular Media*, New York: P. Lang.

Helford, E.R. (ed.) (2000) *Fantasy Girls: Gender in the New Universe of Science Fiction and Fantasy Television*, Lanham, MD: Rowman and Littlefield.

Hengen, S. (ed.) (1998) *Performing Gender and Comedy: Theories, Texts and Contexts*, Amsterdam: Gordon and Breach.

Henkin, B. and Fish, J.M. (1986) Gender and Personality Differences in the Appreciation of Cartoon Humor, *Journal of Psychology*, 120(2): 157–75.

Hennion, A. (1989) An Intermediary Between Production and Consumption: The Producer of Popular Music, *Science, Technology and Human Values*, 14: 400–24.

Hentoff, N. (2006) Interview with Nat Hentoff, Playboy Match 1966, in J. Cott (ed.) *Dylan on Dylan*, pp. 93–112, London: Hodder and Stoughtopn.

Henriques, J., Hollway, W., Urwin, C., Venn, C. and Walkerdine, V. (1984) *Changing the Subject*, London: Metheun.

Henson, K.D. and Rogers, J.K. (2001) Why Marcia You've Changed! Male Clerical Temporary Workers Doing Masculinity in a Feminized Occupation, *Gender and Society*, 15(2): 218–38.

Herzog, T.R. (1999) Gender Differences in Humor Appreciation Revisited, *Humor – International Journal of Humor Research*, 12(4): 411–23.

Herzogenrath, B. (2000) Stop Making Sense: Fuck 'Em and Their Law (… It's Only I and O but I Like It …), *PMC*, 10(2).

Heylin, C. (2007) *Babylon's Burning: From Punk to Grunge*, London: Penguin/Viking.

Higgins, M. (2001) Introduction: More Amazing Tales, in W. Smith, M. Higgins, M. Parker and G. Lightfoot (eds) *Science Fiction and Organization*, pp. 1–12, London: Routeldge.

Higgins, S. (1999) *Movies for Leaders: Management Lessons from Four All-Time Great Films (Management Goes to the Movies)*, Cowles Pub. Co.

Hilmer, F. and Donaldson, L. (1996) *Management Redeemed: Debunking the Fads that Undermine Our Corporations*, New York: Free Press.

Hobbs, R. (1998) Teaching with and About Film and Television Integrating Media Literacy Concepts into Management Education, *Journal of Management Development*, 17(4): 259–72.

Hodgson, D. (2002) 'Know Your Customer': Marketing, Governmentality and the 'New Consumer' of Financial Services, *Management Decision*, 40(4): 318–28.

Hodgson, D. (2003) Taking it Like a Man: Masculinity, Subjection and Resistance in the Selling of Life Assurance, *Gender, Work and Organisation*, 10(1): 1–21.

Holbert, R.L., Shah, D.V. and Kwak, N. (2003) Political Implications of Primetime Drama and Sitcom Use: Genres of Representation and Opinions Concerning Women's Rights, *Journal of Communication*, 53(1): 45–60.

Höpfl, H. (2002) Hitchcock's Vertigo and the Tragic Sublime, *Journal of Organizational Change Management*, 15(1): 21–34.

Hopton, J. (1999) Militarism, Masculinism and Managerialisation in the British Public Sector, *Journal of Gender Studies*, 8(1): 71–83.

Horning, S.S. (2004) Engineering the Performance: Recording Engineers, Tacit Knowledge and the Art of Controlling Sound, *Social Studies of Science*, 34(5): 703–31.

Huczynski, A.A. (1993) *Management Gurus: What Makes Them and How to Become One*, London: Routledge.

Huffington, A. (2003) *Pigs at the Trough: How Corporate Greed and Political Corruption Are Undermining America*, New York: Crown.

Huxley, D. (1999) 'Ever Get the Feeling that You've Been Cheated?' Anarchy and Control in the Great Rock 'n' Roll Swindle, in R. Sabin (ed.) *Punk Rock: So What?* pp. 81–99, London: Routledge.

Iedema, R., Rhodes, C. and Scheeres, H. (2006) Surveillance, Resistance, Observance: Exploring the Teleo-Affective Intensity of Identity (at) Work, *Organization Studies*, 27(8): 1111–30.

Irving, K. (1988) Rock Music and the State: Dissonance or Counterpoint? *Cultural Critique*, 10: 151–70.

Jackson, B. (1996) Reengineering the Sense of Self: The Manager and the Management Guru, *Journal of Management Studies*, 33(5): 571–90.

Jackson, B. (2001a) Art for Management's Sake? *Management Communication Quarterly*, 14(3): 484–90.

Jackson, B. (2001b) *Management Gurus and Management Fashions: A Dramatistic Inquiry*, London: Routledge.

James, B. (1998) The Political Consequences of the Commercialization of Culture, *Journal of Communication*, Autumn: 155–61.

Jameson, F. (2005) *Archeologies of the Future: The Desire Called Utopia and Other Science Fiction*, London: Verso.

Jeffcut, P. (1994) From Interpretation to Representation in Organizational Analysis: Postmodernism, Ethnography and Organizational Symbolism, *Organization Studies*, 15(2): 241–74.

Jenkins, M. (1997) The Dystopian World of Blade Runner: An Ecofemist perspective, *Trumpeter*, 14: 4, available at: www.icaap.org/iuicode?6.14.4.2 (visted 12 January 2007).

Jennings, D. (1967) *We Only Kill Each Other: The Life and Bad Times of Bugsy Siegel*, Prentice-Hall.

Jermier, J., Knights, D. and Nord, W. (1994) *Resistance and Power in Organizations*, London: Routledge.

Jevons, M. (1998) *Deadly Indifference: A Henry Spearman Mystery*, Princeton, NJ: Princeton University Press.

Johnson, P.R. and Indvik, J. (1999) Organizational Benefits of Having Emotionally Intelligent Managers and Employees, *Journal of Workplace Learning*, 11(3): 84–8.

Johnson, S. and Blanchard, K. (1981) *One Minute Manager*, Berkley, CA: Berkley Trade.

Jones, C., Anand, N. and Alvarez, J.L. (2005) Manufactured Authenticity and Creative Voice in Cultural Industries, *Journal of Management Studies*, 42(5): 893–9.

Jones, M.T. (1998) Blade Runner Capitalism, the Transnational Corporation, and Commodification, *Cultural Dynamics*, 10(3): 287–306.

Jones, S. (2000) Music and the Internet, *Popular Music*, 19(2): 217–30.

Jurkiewicz, C.L. and Giacalone, R.A. (2000) Through the Lens Clearly: Using Films to Demonstrate Ethical Decision-Making in the Public Service, *Journal of Public Affairs Education*, 6(4): 257–65.

Kafner, S. (1997) *Serious Business: The Art and Commerce of Animation in America from Betty Boop to Toy Story*, New York: Scribner.

Kahn, J.S. (1995) *Culture, Multicultural, Postculture*, London: Sage.

Kamoche, K.N. and Cunha, M.P. (2001) Minimal Structures: From Jazz Improvisation to Product Innovation, *Organization Studies*, 22: 733–64.

Kamoche, K.N., Cunha, M.P. and Cunha, J.V. (eds) (2002) *Organizational Improvisation*, London: Routledge.

Kavanagh, D., Kuhling, C. and Keohane, K. (2005) The Odyssey of Instrumental Rationality: Confronting the Enlightenment's Interior Other, in S. Linstead and A. Linstead (eds) *Thinking Organization*, pp. 157–79, London: Routledge.

Keenoy, T., Oswick, C. and Grant, D. (1997) Organizational Discourses: The Postmodern Condition Revisited, *Organization*, 4(1): 114–29.

Kellner, D. (1999) Theorizing/Resisting McDonaldization, in B. Smart (ed.) *Resisting McDonaldization*, pp. 186–206, London: Sage.

Kemske, F. (1993) *The Virtual Boss*, North Haven, CT: Catbird.

Kemske, F. (1996) *Human Resources: A Business Novel*, London: Nicholas Brealey.

Kennedy, C. (1998) *Guide to the Management Gurus*, London: Random House.

Kenny, M. and Stevenson, N. (2000) Masculinity: A Risky Path to Take? in J. Rutherford (ed.) *The Art of Life: On Living, Love and Death*, pp. 135–51, London: Lawrence and Wishart.

Kerfoot, D. and Knights, D. (1993) Management, Masculinity and Manipulation: From Paternalism to Corporate Strategy in Financial Services in Britain, *Journal of Management Studies*, 30(4): 659–78.

Kerfoot, D. and Knights, D. (1996) The Best Is Yet to Come? The Quest for Embodiment in Managerial Work, in D.L. Collinson and J. Hearn (eds), *Men as Managers, Managers as Men*, pp. 78–98, London: Sage.

Kerfoot, D. and Knights, D. (1998) Managing Masculinity in Contemporary Organisational Life: A Managerial Project, *Organisation*, 5(1): 7–26.

Kerman, J.B. (1991) Introduction, in J.B. Kerman (ed.) *Retrofitting Blade Runner*, pp. 1–3, Bowling Green, OH: Bowling Green State University Popular Press.

Kessler, E.H. (2001) The Idols of Organizational Theory: From Francis Bacon to the Dilbert Principle, *Journal of Management Inquiry*, 10(4): 285–97.

Khurana, R. (2002) *Searching for a Corporate Savior: The Irrational Quest for Charismatic CEOs*, Princeton, NJ: Princeton University Press.

Kieser, A. (1997) Rhetoric and Myth in Management Fashion, *Organization*, 4(1): 49–74.

Kilduff, M. (2001) Hegemonic Masculinity and Organisational Behavior, in R.T. Golembiewski (ed.) *Handbook of Organizational Behavour*, 2nd edn, New York: Marcel Decker.

Kincheloe, J.L. (2005) On to the Next Level: Continuing the Conceptualization of the Bricolage, *Qualitative Inquiry*, 11(3): 323–50.

Kirkham, P. and Skeggs, B. (1998) Absolutely Fabulous: Absolutely Feminist? in C. Geraghty and D. Lusted (eds) *The Television Studies Book*, pp. 287–300, London: Arnold.

Knights, D. and Kerfoot, D. (2004) Between Representations and Subjectivity: Gender Binaries and the Politics of Organisational Transformation, *Gender, Work and Organisation*, 11(4): 430–54.

Knights, D. and McCabe, D. (1999) 'Are there no limits to authority?' TQM and organizational power, *Organization Studies*, 20: 197–224.

Knights, D. and Sturdy, A. (1997) Marketing the Soul: From the Ideology of Consumption to Consumer Subjectivity, in D. Knights and T. Tinker (eds) *Financial Institutions and Social Transformations: International Studies of a Sector*, pp. 158–88, London: Macmillan.

Kondo, D.K. (1990) *Grafting Selves: Power, Gender and Discourses of Identity in a Japanese Workplace*, Chicago, IL: University of Chicago Press.

Korte, D. (1997) The Simpsons as Quality Television, *The Simpsons Archive*, available at: www.snpp.com/other/papers/dk.paper.html (visited 21 May 2003).

Kostera, M. (1997) Personal Performatives: Collecting Poetical Definitions of Management, *Organization*, 4(3): 345-353.

Kotthoff, H. (2000) Gender and Joking: On the Complexities of Women's Image Politics in Humorous Narratives, *Journal of Pragmatics*, 32(1): 55–80.

Kotthoff, H. (2006) Gender and Humour: The State of the Art, *Journal of Pragmatics*, 38: 4–25.

Krukowski, Lucian (1992) *Aesthetic Legacies*, Philadelphia, PA: Temple University Press.

Kuhn, A. (ed.) (1990) *Alien Zone: Cultural Theory and Contemporary Science Fiction Cinema*, New York: Verso.

Kumar, K. (1984) The Social Culture of Work: Work, Employment and Unemployment as Ways of Life, in K. Thompson (ed.) *Work, Employment and Unemployment*, Milton Keynes: Open University Press.

Laclau, E. (1977) *Politics and Ideology in Marxist Theory*, London: New Left Books.

Laclau, E. and Mouffe, C. (1985) *Hegemony and Socialist Strategy*, London: Verso.

Laclau, E. and Mouffe, C. (2001) *Hegemony and Socialist Strategy*, 2nd ed., London: Verso.

Lafaurie Jr, R.A. (compiler) (1996) Episode Capsule: 22 Short Films About Springfield, *The Simpsons Archive*, www.snpp.com/episodes/3F18.html (visited 27 May 2003) (original episode written by R. Appel, D.S. Cohen, J. Collier, J. Crittenden, G. Daniels, B. Forrester, R. Pulido, S. Tomkins, J. Weinstein and M. Groening).

Lahr, J. (1983) *Programme Notes for Glengarry Glen Ross*, London: National Theatre (cited in Anne Dean, *David Mamet: Language as Dramatic Action*, Rutherford, NJ: Fairleigh Dickinson University Press).

Lampert, M.D. and Ervin-Tripp, S.M. (1998) Exploring Paradigms: The Study of Gender and Sense of Humor Near the End of the 20th Century, in W. Ruch (ed.) *The Sense of Humor: Explorations of Personality Characteristic*, pp. 231–70, Berlin: Mouton de Gruyter.

Leahey, M. (1982) The American Dream Gone Bad, *Otherstages*, 4 November: 3.

Lee, J. (1995) Subversive Sitcoms: Roseanne as Inspiration for Feminist Resistance, in D. Dines and J.M. Humez (eds) *Gender, Race and Class in Media: A Text Reader*, pp. 469–75, Thousand Oaks, CA: Sage.

Lee, M. (2002), Management History as Told by Popular Culture: The Screen Image of the Efficiency Expert, *Management Decision*, 40(9): 881–94.

Lefanu, S. (1988) *In the Chinks of the World Machine: Feminism and Science Fiction*, London: The Women's Press.

Letiche, H. (1996) Postmodernism Goes Practical, in S. Linstead, R. Grafton Small and P. Jeffcut (eds) *Understanding Management*, pp. 192–211, London: Sage.

Lev, P. (1998) Whose Future? Star Wars, Alien and Blade Runner, *Literature/Film Quarterly*, 26(1): 30–7.

Lévi-Strauss, C. (1966) *The Savage Mind*, London: Weidenfeld and Nicholson.

Lewis, K.L., Schmisseur, A.M., Stephens, K.K. and Weir, K.E. (2006) Advice on Communicating During Organizational Change: The Content of Popular Press Books, *Journal of Business Communication*, 43(2): 113–37.

Lewis, L. (1992) *The Adoring Audience: Fan Culture and Popular Media*, London: Routledge.

Lindvall, T.R. and Melton, J.M. (1997) Towards a Post-modern Animated Discourse, in J. Pilling (ed.) *A Reader in Animation Studies*, pp. 203–20, London: John Libbey.

Linstead, S. (2000) Ashes and Madness: The Play of Negativity and the Poetics of Organization, in S. Linstead and H. Hopfl (eds) *The Aesthetics of Organization*, pp. 61–92, London: Sage.

Linstead, S. (2001) Rhetoric and Organizational Control: A Framework for Analysis, in R.I. Westwood and S. Linstead (eds) *The Language of Organisation*, pp. 217–40, London: Sage.

Linstead, S. (2003) Question Time: Notes on Altercation, in R. Westwood and S.R. Clegg (eds) *Debating Organization*, pp. 368–79, Oxford: Blackwell.

Linstead, S. and Grafton-Small, R. (1992) On Reading Organizational Culture, *Organization Studies*, 13(3): 331–55.

Linstead, S. and Hopfl, H. (eds) (2000) *The Aesthetics of Organization*, London: Sage.

Loebbecke, J.K. (1999) *The Auditor: An Instructional Novella*, Upper Saddle River, NJ: Prentice Hall.

Lorber, J. and Farrell, S.A. (eds) (1991) *The Social Construction of Gender*, Newbury Park, CA: Sage.

Lotz, A.D. (2006) *Redesigning Women: Television After the Network Era*, University of Illinois Press.

Louridas, P. (1999) Design as Bricolage: Anthropology Meets Design Thinking, *Design Studies*, 20(6): 517–35.

Lupton B. (2000) Maintaining Masculinity: Men Who Do 'Women's Work', *British Journal of Management*, 11(Special Issue): S33–48.

Lyotard, J.F. (1993) *The Postmodern Explained: Correspondence, 1982–1985*, D. Barry, B. Maher, J. Pefanis, V. Spate and M. Thomas (trans.), Minneapolis: University of Minnesota Press.

Malking, J.R. (1992) *Verbal Violence in Contemporary Drama*, Cambridge: Cambridge University Press.

Mamet, D. (1977) *American Buffalo*, New York: Grove.

Mamet, D. (1984) *Glengarry Glen Ross: A Play*, 1st edn, New York: Grove Press.

Mamet, D. (1986) *Writing in Restaurants*, New York: Penguin Books.

Mamet, D. (1988), *Speed-the-Plow*, New York: Grove.

Mamet, D. (1989a) In the Company of Men, in *Some Freaks*, New York: Viking Press.

Mamet, D. (1989b) Women, in *Some Freaks*, pp. 21–26, New York: Viking Press.

Mamet, D. (1992) *Oleanna*, New York: Vintage.

Management Goes to the Movies (MGTM) (2006) Available at: www.moviesforbusiness.com/ (visited 16 November 2006).

Mannheim, K. (1952) *Ideology and Utopia*, New York: Harcourt, Brace and Co.

Manzoni, J.-F. and Barsoux, J.-L. (2002) *The Set-Up-To-Fail Syndrome: How Good Managers Cause Great People to Fail*, Boston, MA: Harvard Business School Press.

Marc, D. (1997) *Comic Visions: Television Comedy and American Culture*, Malden, MA: Blackwell.

Marc, D. (1998) *Comic Visions: Television Comedy and American Culture*, 2nd edn, Malden MA: Blackwell.

Marcus, G. (1993) *In the Fascist Bathroom: Punk in Pop Music, 1977–1992*, London: Penguin.

Marcus, G. and Fischer, M.J. (1986) *Anthropology as Cultural Critique: An Experimental Moment in the Human Sciences*, Chicago, IL: University of Chicago Press.

Marshall, W. (2006) Giving Up Hip-Hop's Firstborn: A Quest for the Real After the Death of Sampling, *Callaloo*, 29(3): 868–92.

Martin, G. (1996) Hey Joad, Don't Make It Sad … (Oh, Go On Then), *New Musical Express*, 9 March.

Martin, P.Y. (2001) Mobilizing Masculinities: Women's Experience of Men at Work, *Organization*, 8(4): 587–618.

Mayerle, J. (1991) Roseanne, How Did You Get Inside My House – A Case Study of a Hit Blue-Collar Situation Comedy, *Journal of Popular Culture*, 24(4): 71–88.

Mazlish, B. (2003) A Tale of Two Enclosures: Self and Society as a Setting for Utopias, *Theory, Culture and Society*, 20(1): 43–60.

Mazza, C. (1998) The Popularization of Business Knowledge Diffusion: From Academic Knowledge to Popular Culture? in J.L. Alvarez (ed.) *The Production, Diffusion and Consumption of Business Knowledge*, pp. 164–81, London: Macmillan.

McCance, D. (2002) Crossings: An Interview with Aritha van Herk, *Mosaic*, 36(1): 1–19.

McConnell, F. (1994) Art Is Dangerous: Beavis and Butthead, for Example, *Commonweal*, 14 January: 28–30.

McCracken, S. (1998) *Pulp: Reading Popular Fiction*, Manchester: Manchester University Press.

McDonagh, C. (1992) Every Fear Hides a Wish: Unstable Masculinity in Mamet's Drama, *Theatre Journal*, 44(2): 195–205.

McEachern, C. (1999) Comic Interventions: Passion and the Men's Movement in the Situation Comedy, Home Improvement, *Journal of Gender Studies*, 8(1): 5–19.

McGuigan, J. (1992) *Cultural Populism*, London: Routledge.

McKinlay, A. and Starkey, S. (1998) *Foucault, Management and Organization Theory*, London: Sage.

McKinley, W. (2003) Methodology, in R.I. Westwood and S.R. Clegg (eds) *Debating*

Organisation: Point/Counterpoint in Organisation Studies, pp. 140–56, Oxford: Blackwell Publishing.

McKinley, W. and Mone, M.A. (1998) The Re-Construction of Organization Studies: Wrestling with Incommensurability, *Organization*, 5(2): 169–89.

McKinley, W., Mone, M.A. and Moon, G. (1999) Determinants and Development of Schools in Organization Theory, *Academy of Management Review*, 24: 634–48.

McNamara, K.R. (1997) Blade Runner's Post-Individual Worldspace, *Contemporary Literature*, 38(3): 422–46.

Meyers, M. (ed.) (1999) *Mediated Women: Representations in Popular Culture*, Cresskill, NJ: Hampton Press.

Micklethwait, J. and Wooldridge, A. (1996) *The Witch Doctors: Making Sense of the Management Gurus*, New York: Random House.

Micklethwait, J. and Wooldridge, A. (1997) *The Witch Doctors: Making Sense of the Management Gurus*, London: Mandarin.

Middleton, R. (1990) *Studying Popular Music*, Milton Keynes: Open University Press.

Middleton, R. (2006) *Voicing the Popular: On the Subjects of Popular Music*, New York: Routledge.

Miller, A. (1958) *Death of a Salesman: Certain Private Conversations in Two Acts and a Requiem*, New York: Viking Press.

Miller, A. (1961) *Death of a Salesman*, Harmondsworth, Middlesex: Penguin Books.

Miller, P. and Rose, N. (1990) Governing Economic Life, *Economy and Society*, 19: 1–32.

Mills, A. (1998) Cockpits, Hangars, Boys and Galleys: Corporate Masculinities and the Development of British Airways, *Gender, Work and Organisation*, 5(3): 173–88.

Mills, A.J. and Tancred, P. (eds) (1992) *Gendering Organisational Analysis*, Newbury Park, CA: Sage.

Milner, A. (2004) Darker Cities: Urban Dystopia and Science Fiction Cinema, *International Journal of Cultural Studies*, 7(3): 259–79.

Mintz, L.E. (1985a) Situation Comedy, in B. Rose (ed.) *TV Genres*, pp. 105–29, Westport, CT: Greenwood Press.

Mintz, L.E. (1985b) Ideology in the American Situation Comedy, *Studies in Popular Culture*, 8(2): 42–51.

Moore, A. (2002) Authenticity and Authentication, *Popular Music*, 21(2): 209–23.

Moore, R. (2004) Postmodernism and Punk Subculture: Cultures of Authenticity and Deconstruction, *The Communication Review*, 7: 305–27.

Morgan, M. (1987) Television, Sex-Role Attitudes, and Sex-Role Behavior, *Journal of Early Adolescence*, 7: 269–82.

Morreale, J. (ed.) (2002) *Critiquing the Sitcom: A Reader*, Syracuse: Syracuse University Press.

Morrow, M. (1999) 'But Beavis, Everything Does Suck': Watching Beavis and Butt-Head Watch Videos, *Popular Music and Society*, 23(3): 31–41.

Moss-Kanter, R. (1983) *The Change Masters: Corporate Entrepreneurship at Work*, London: Unwinhyman.

Moussa, M. and Scapp, R. (1996) The Practical Theorizing of Michel Foucault: Politics and Counter-Discourse, *Cultural Critique*, 33: 87–112.

Moylan, T. (2001) *Scraps of the Untainted Sky*, Westport, CT.

Mumby, D. (1998) Organizing Men: Power, Discourse, and the Social Construction of Masculinity(s) in the Workplace, *Communication Theory*, 8: 164–83.

Mundorf, N., Bhatia, A., Zillmann, D., Lester, P. and Robertson, S. (1988) Gender

Differences in Humor Appreciation, *Humor – International Journal of Humor Research*, 1(3): 231–43.

Myrdal, G. (1958) *Value in Social Theory*, London: Routledge.

Negus, K. (1996) *Popular Music in Theory*, Cambridge: Polity.

Nissley, N. (2002) Tuning-In to Organizational Song as Aesthetic Discourse, *Culture and Organization*, 8(1): 51–68.

Nkomo, S.M. and Cox Jr, T. (1996) Diverse Identities in Organisations, in S.R. Clegg, C. Hardy and W. Nord (eds) *Handbook of Organisation Studies*, pp. 338–56, London: Sage.

Novick. J. (1984) Mamet, *Village Voice*, 3 April: 89.

Novitz, D. (1992) *The Boundaries of Art*, Philadelphia, PA: Temple University Press.

O'Connor, A. (2002) Local Scenes and Dangerous Crossroads: Punk and Theories of Cultural Hybridity, *Popular Music*, 21(2): 225–36.

O'Sullivan, J. and Sheridan, J. (2005) The King Is Dead, Long Live the King: Tall Tales of New Men and New Management in the Bill, *Gender, Work and Organization*, 12(4): 299–318.

Olson, B. and Douglas, W. (1997) The Family on Television: Evaluation of Gender Roles in Situation Comedy, *Sex Roles*, 36(5–6): 409–27.

Orr, J. (1996) *Talking About Machines: An Ethnography of a Modern Job*, Ithaca, NY: Cornell University Press.

Ouchi, W. (1981) *Theory Z: How American Management Can Meet the Japanese Challenge*, Reading, MA: Addison-Wesley.

Oudshoorn, N. and Pinch, T. (eds) (2003) *How Users Matter: The Co-Construction of Users and Technologies*, Cambridge, MA: MIT Press.

Pagel, S. and Westerfelhaus, R. (2005) Charting Managerial Reading Preferences in Relation to Popular Management Theory Books, *Journal of Business Communication*, 42(4): 420–48.

Palmer, G. (1997) Bruce Springsteen and Masculinity, in S. Whiteley (ed.) *Sexing the Groove: Popular Music and Gender*, pp. 100–17, London: Routledge.

Parker, M. (1998a) Judgement Day: Cyborganization, Humanism and Postmodern Ethics, *Organization*, 5(4): 503–18.

Parker, M. (1998b) Manufacturing Bodies: Flesh, Organization, Cyborgs, in J. Hassard, R. Holliday and H. Willmott (eds) *Organization Representation: Work and Organization in Popular Culture*, pp. 71–86, London: Sage.

Parker, M. (1998c) Nostalgia and Mass Culture: McDonaldization and Cultural Elitism, in M. Alfine, J.S. Caputo and R. Wynard (eds) *McDonaldization Revisited: Critical Essays in Consumer Culture*, Westport, CT: Praeger.

Parker, M. (2002a) *Against Management*, Cambridge: Polity.

Parker, M. (2002b) Utopia and the Organizational Imagination: Outopia, in M. Parker (ed.) *Utopia and Organization*, pp. 1–8, Oxford, Blackwell.

Parker, M., Higgins, M., Lightfoot, G. and Smith, W. (1999) Amazing Tales: Organization Studies as Science Fiction, *Organization*, 5(4): 579–90.

Parkin, D. and Maddock, S. (1995) A Gender Typology of Organisational Culture, in C. Itzin and J. Newman (eds) *Gender, Culture and Organisational Change: Putting Theory into Practice*, pp. 68–80, London: Routledge.

Patient, D., Lawrence, T.B. and Maitlis, S. (2003) Understanding Workplace Envy Through Narrative Fiction, *Organization Studies*, 24(7): 1015–44.

Percy, W. (1998) Rock and Read: Will Percy Interviews Bruce Springsteen, *Doubletake*, 12, available at: www.doubletakemagazine.org/mag/html/backissues/12/index.html (visited 20 June 2003).

Peters, T. (1999) *The Brand You 50: Or: Fifty Ways to Transform Yourself from an 'Employee' into a Brand that Shouts Distinction, Commitment, and Passion!* New York: Knopf.

Peters, T. and Austin, N. (1985) *A Passion for Excellence*, New York: Random House.

Peters, T.J. and Waterman Jr, R.H. (1982) *In Search of Excellence: Lessons from America's Best Run Companies*, New York: Harper and Row.

Peterson, M. (2006) *Consumption and Everyday Life*, London: Routledge.

Peterson, R.A. (2005) In Search of Authenticity, *Journal of Management Studies*, 42(5): 1083–98.

Pfeffer, J. (1982) *Organizations and Organization Theory*, Boston, MA: Pitman.

Pfeffer, J. (1993) Barriers to the Advance of Organizational Science: Paradigm Development as a Dependent Variable, *Academy of Management Review*, 18: 599–620.

Pfeffer, J. (1997) *New Directions for Organization Theory: Problems and Prospects*, New York: Oxford University Press.

Pfeffer, J. and Fong, C. (2002) The End of Business Schools? Less Success Than Meets the Eye, *Academy of Management Learning and Education*, 1(1): 78–95.

Pfeffer, J. and Sutton, R.I. (2006a) *Hard Facts. Dangerous Half-Truths and Total Nonsense: Profiting from Evidence-Based Management*, Harvard, MA: Harvard Business School Press.

Pfeffer, J. and Sutton, R.I. (2006b) Evidence-Based Management, *Harvard Business Review*, 84(1): 62–75.

Pfeffer, J. and Sutton, R.I. (2006c) Profiting from Evidence-Based Management, *Strategy and Leadership*, 34(2): 35–43.

Pfeffer, J. and Sutton, R.I. (2006d) A Matter of Fact, *People Management*, 28 September, 25-30.

Phillipov, M. (2006) Haunted by the Spirit of '77: Punk Studies and the Persistence of Politics, *Continuum: Journal of Cultural Studies*, 20(3): 383–93.

Phillips, N. (1995) Telling Organizational Tales: On the Role of Narrative Fiction in the Study of Organizations, *Organization Studies*, 16(4): 625–49.

Phillips, N. and Zyglidopoulos, S. (1999) Learning from Foundation: Asimov's Psychohistory and the Limits of Organization Theory, *Organization*, 6(4): 591–608.

Pinch, T. and Bijsterveld, K. (2004) Sound Studies: New Technologies and Music, *Social Studies of Science*, 34(5): 635–48.

Pinch, T. and Trocco, F. (2002) *Analog Days. The Invention and Impact of the Moog Synthesizer*, Harvard, MA: Harvard University Press.

Plasketes, G. (2005) Re-Flections on the Cover Age: A Collage of Continuous Coverage in Popular Music, *Popular Music and Society*, 28(2): 137–61.

Plato (1955) *The Republic*, Harmondsworth: Penguin.

Pondy, L.R., Frost, P.J., Morgan, G. and Dandridge, T.C. (eds) (1983) *Organizational Symbolism*, Greenwich, CT: JAI Press.

Porcello, T. (2004) Speaking of Sound: Language and the Professionalization of Sound-Recording Engineers, *Social Studies of Science*, 34(5): 733–58.

Porter, M.J. (1998) The Structure of Television Narratives, in L.R. Vande Berg, L.A. Wenner and B.E. Gronbeck (eds) *Television Criticism*, pp. 140-57, Boston: Houghton-Mifflin.

Postman, N. (1987) *Amusing Ourselves to Death*, London: Methuen.

Powell, G.N. and Veiga, J.E. (1986) Using Popular Music to Examine Management and OB Concepts: A Rejoinder to Springsteen's Thesis, *Organizational Behavior Teaching Journal*, 10: 79–81.

Prasad, P. (1997) The Protestant Ethic and the Myth of the Frontier: Cultural Imprints, Organisational Structuring and Workplace Diversity, in P. Prasad, A.J. Mills, M. Elmes and A. Prasad (eds) *Managing the Organisational Melting Pot: Dilemmas of Workplace Diversity*, pp. 129–47, Thousand Oaks, CA: Sage.

Pratt, R. (1990) *Rhythm and Resistance: The Political Uses of American Popular Music*, Washington, DC: Smithsonian Institute Press.

Prokos, A. and Padavic, I. (2002) 'There Oughtta Be a Law Against Bitches': Masculinity Lessons in Police Academy Training, *Gender, Work and Organization*, 9(4): 439–59.

Puffer, S. (1991) *Managerial Insights from Literature*, Boston, MA: PWS-Kent Publishing.

Puffer, S. (ed.) (2004) *International Management: Insights from Fiction and Practice*, London: M.E. Sharpe.

Pullen, A. and Rhodes, C. (2008) Dirty Writing, *Culture and Organization*.

Regev, M. (1994) Producing Artistic Value: The Case of Rock Music, *The Sociological Quarterly*, 35(1): 85–102.

Rehn, A. (2004) *The Serious Unreal*, Dvalin Books.

Rehn, A. and Skold, D. (2005) 'I Love the Dough': Rap lyrics as a minor economic literature, *Culture and Organization*, 11(1): 17–31.

Rerup, C. (2001) 'Houston, We Have a Problem': Anticipation and Improvisation as Sources of Organizational Resilience, *Comportamento Organizacional E Gestao*, 7: 27–44.

Rhodes, C. (2000) Reading and Writing Organizational Lives, *Organization*, 7(1): 7–29.

Rhodes, C. (2001a) D'oh: The Simpsons, Popular Culture and the Organizational Carnival, *Journal of Management Inquiry*, 10(4): 374–83.

Rhodes, C. (2001b) *Writing Organization: (Re)Presentation and Control in Narratives at Work*, Amsterdam: John Benjamins.

Rhodes, C. (2002) Coffee and the Business of Pleasure: The Case of Harbucks vs. Mr. Tweek, *Culture and Organization*, 8(4): 293–306.

Rhodes, C. (2004) Utopia in Popular Management Writing and the Music of Bruce Springsteen: Do You Believe in the Promised Land? *Consumption, Markets and Culture*, 7(1).

Rhodes, C. (2007) Outside the Gates of Eden: Utopia and Work in Rock Music, *Group and Organization Management*, 32(1): 22–49.

Rhodes, C. and Brown, A. (2005) Writing Responsibly: Narrative Fiction and Organization Studies, *Organization*, 12(4).

Rhodes, C. and Pitsis, A. (2008) Organization and Mimetic Excess: Magic, Critique and Style, *Group and Organization Management*.

Rhodes, C. and Pullen, A. (2007) Humour, Work and the Grotesque Body: Mr. Burns and The Simpsons Cartoon Carnival, in R. Westwood and C. Rhodes (eds) *Humour, Organizations and Work*, pp. 161–79, London: RouteldgeFalmer.

Rhodes, C., Rhodes, J. and Rhodes, D. (2005) Jackass, in C. Jones and D. O'Doherty (eds) *Organize! Manifestos for the Business School of Tomorrow*, Stockholm: Dvalin Press.

Richardson, L. (1994) Writing: A Method of Inquiry, in N.K. Denzin and Y.S. Lincoln (eds) *Handbook of Qualitative Research*, pp. 516–29, Thousand Oaks, CA: Sage.

Richmond, R. and Coffman, A. (eds) (1997) *The Simpsons: A Complete Guide to Our Favorite Family*, New York: Harper Collins.

Ritzer, G. (1996) *The McDonaldization of Society: An Investigation into the Changing Character of Contemporary Social Life*, revised edn, Thousand Oaks, CA: Sage.

Ritzer, G. (1998) *The McDonaldization Thesis*, London: Sage.

Ritzer, G. (1999) Assessing the Resistance, in B. Smart (ed.) *Resisting McDonaldization*, pp. 234–55, London: Sage.

Ritzer, G. (2004) *The McDonaldization of Society, Revised New Century Edition*, Thousand Oaks, CA: Sage.

Roberts, A. (2006) *The History of Science Fiction*, Houndmills: Palgrave.

Roberts, J. (2005) The Ritzerization of Knowledge, *Critical Perspectives on International Business*, 1(1): 56–63.

Roberts, R. (2001) *The Invisible Heart: An Economic Romance*, Cambridge, MA: MIT Press.

Robyns, C. (1991) Beyond the First Dimension: Recent Tendencies in Popular Culture Studies, in Joris Vlasselaers (ed.) *The Prince and the Frog*, Leuven: ALW.

Rock and Roll Hall of Fame (2002) Bruce Springsteen: Performer, available at: www.rockhall.com/hof/inductee.asp?id=194 (visited 15 July 2002).

Rodgers, T. (2003) On the Process and Aesthetics of Sampling in Electronic Music Production, *Organised Sound* 8(3): 313–20.

Roper, M. (1994) *Masculinity and the British Organisation Man Since 1945*, Oxford: Oxford University Press.

Rose, T. (1994) *Black Noise: Rap Music and Black Culture in Contemporary America*, Hanover and London: Wesleyan University Press.

Ross, A. (1989) *No Respect: Intellectuals and Popular Culture*, London: Routeldge.

Roudané, M.C. (1986) An Interview with David Mamet, *Studies in American Drama, 1945–Present, 1*

Rowe, D. (1995) *Popular Cultures*, London: Sage.

Rowe, K. (1995) *Unruly Woman: Gender and the Genres of Laughter*, Austin: University of Texas Press.

Sandford, C. (1999) *Springsteen: Point Blank*, London: Warner Books.

Sanneh, K. (2002) Springsteen Issues a Call to 'Rise Up' After 9/11, *New York Times*, 9 August: 3.

Santaro, G. (1996) Bruce Springsteen; Down the River, *The Nation*, 11 November: 34–6.

Savage, J. (1991) *England's Dreaming: The Sex Pistols and Punk Rock*, London: Faber.

Savran, D. (1988) *In Their Own Words: Contemporary American Playwrights*, New York: Theatre Communications Group.

Savran, D. (1992) *Communists, Cowboys, and Queers: The Politics of Masculinity in the Work of Arthur Miller and Tennessee Williams*, Minneapolis: University of Minnesota Press.

Sawyers, J.S. (2004) *Introduction*, in J.S. Sawyer (ed.) *Racing in the Street: The Bruce Springsteen Reader*, pp. 1–28, New York: Penguin.

Schlosser, E. (2001) *Fast Food Nation: The Dark Side of the American Meal*, London: Penguin.

Science Fiction Studies (1999a) Chronological Bibliography of Science Fiction History, Theory, and Criticism, *Science Fiction Studies*, available at: www.depauw.edu/sfs/biblio.htm (visited 21 January 2006).

Science Fiction Studies (1999b) Special Issue on Science Fiction and Queer Theory, *Science Fiction Studies*, 26(1): 1–52.

Scott, A.O. (2000) The Filth and the Fury, *New York Times*, available at: http://movies2.nytimes.com/gst/movies/movie.html?v_id=184581 (visited 20 June 2005).

Senge, P. (1990) *The Fifth Discipline*, London: Random House.

Sennett, R. (1998) *The Corrosion of Character*, New York: W.W. Norton Press.

Sewell, G. and Wilkinson, B. (1992) 'Someone to Watch over Me': Surveillance, Discipline and the Just-in-time Labour Process, *Sociology*, 26: 271–89.

Sherburne, P. (2001) Mistaken Identity, *XLR8R*, 48: 65–7.

Shklar, J.N. (1994) What Is the Use of Utopia? in T. Siebers (ed.) *Heterotopia: Postmodern Utopia and the Body Politic*, pp. 40–57, Ann Arbor: University of Michigan Press.

Showalter, E. (1992) Acts of Violence: David Mamet and the Language of Men, *Times Literary Supplement*, 6 November.

Shuker, R (2001) *Understanding Popular Music*, 2nd edn, London: Routledge.

Signorielli, N. (1989) Television and Conceptions About Sex Roles: Maintaining Conventionality and the Status Quo, *Sex Roles*, 21: 341–60.

Silverstein, M. (1995) 'We're Just Human': 'Oleanna' and Cultural Crisis, *South Atlantic Review*, 60(2): 103–20.

Simonelli, D. (2002) Anarchy, Pop and Violence: Punk Rock Subculture and the Rhetoric of Class, 1976–1978, *Contemporary British History*, 16(2): 121–44.

Simpson, R. (2004) Masculinity at Work: The Experiences of Men in Female Dominated Occupations, *Work, Employment and Society*, 18(2): 349–68.

Sinclair, A. (2000) Teaching Managers About Masculinities: Are You Kidding? *Management Learning*, 31(1): 83–102.

Slack, J.D. (1996) The Theory and Method of Articulation in Cultural Studies, in D. Morley and K.-H. Chen (eds) *Stuart Hall: Critical Dialogues in Cultural Studies*, pp. 112–30, London: Routledge.

Smart, B. (ed.) (1999) *Resisting McDonaldization*, London: Sage.

Smith, G. (2000) Whitman, Springsteen, and the American Working Class, *The Midwest Quarterly*, 41(3): 302–20.

Smith, G.D. and Winchester, H.P.M. (1998) Negotiating Space: Alternative Masculinities at the Work/Home Boundary, *Australian Geographer*, 29(3): 327–39.

Smith, W., Higgins, M., Lightfoot, G. and Parker, M. (eds) (2001) *Science Fiction and Organization*, London: Routledge.

Sochen, J. (ed.) (1991) *Women's Comic Visions*, Detroit: Wayne State University Press.

Solomon, N. (1997) *The Trouble with Dilbert: How Corporate Culture Gets the Last Laugh*, Monroe, ME: Common Courage Press.

Spangler, L.C. (2003) *Television Women from Lucy to Friends: Fifty Years of Sitcoms and Feminism*, New York: Praeger.

Spell, C.S. (2001) Management Fashions: Where Do They Come from, and Are They Old Wine m New Bottles? *Journal of Management Inquiry*, 10(4): 358–73.

Srinivas, N. (1999) Managers as Androids: Reading Moral Agency in Phillip Dick, *Organization*, 6(4): 609–24.

Stableford, B. (1987) *The Sociology of Science Fiction*, San Bernardino, CA: Borgo.

Stahl, B.S. (2005) The Obituary as Bricolage: The Mann Gulch Disaster and the Problem of Heroic Rationality, *European Journal of Information Systems*, 14: 487–91.

Storey, J. (1998) *An Introduction to Cultural Theory and Popular Culture*, Atlanta: University of Georgia Press.

Strati, A. (1999) *Aesthetics and Organizations*, London: Sage.

Street, J. (1997) *Politics and Popular Culture*, Cambridge: Polity Press.

Strinati, D. (2005) *An Introduction to Theories of Popular Culture*, 2nd edn, London: Routledge.

Sturdy, A. (2004) The Adoption of Management Ideas and Practices: Theoretical Perspectives and Possibilities, *Management Learning*, 35(2): 155–79.

Suvin, D. (1979) *Metamorphoses of Science Fiction: On the Poetics and History of a Literary Genre*, New Haven, CT: Yale University Press.

Suvin, D. (1988) *Positions and Presuppositions in Science Fiction*, Kent, OH: Kent State University Press.

Suvin, D. (1990a) Counter Projects: William Morris and Science Fiction of the 1880s, in R. Garnett and R.J. Ellis (eds) *Science Fiction Roots and Branches*, London: Macmillan.

Suvin, D. (1990b) Novum Is as Novum Does, in K. Sayer and J. Moore (eds) *Science Fiction, Critical Frontiers*, Basingstoke: Macmillan.

Swartz, M. and Watkins, S. (2003) *Power Failure: The Inside Story of the Collapse Of Enron*, New York: Doubleday.

Swingewood, Alan (1998) *Cultural Theory and the Problem of Modernity*, London: Macmillan.

Szepanski, A. (1995) Den Klangstrom Zum Beben Bringen, in Hrsg. Philipp Anz/Patrick Walder, *Techno*, Zürich: Ricco Bilger.

Takahashi, Y. (2000) A Network of Tinkerers: The Advent of the Radio and Television Receiver Industry in Japan, *Technology and Culture*, 41(3): 460–84.

Taussig, M. (1993) *Mimesis and Alterity: A Particular History of the Senses*, New York: Routledge.

Taylor, P. and Bain, P. (2003) 'Subterranean Worksick Blues': Humour as Subversion in Two Call Centres, *Organization Studies*, 24(9): 1487–509.

Taylor, T.D. (2001) *Strange Sounds: Music, Technology and Culture*, New York and London: Routledge.

Telotte, J.P. (ed.) (1995) *Replications: A Robotic History of Science Fiction Film*, New York: Verso.

ten Bos, R. (2000) *Fashion and Utopia in Management Thinking*, Amsterdam; Philadelphia, PA: John Benjamins.

ten Bos, R. and Rhodes, C. (2003) The Game of Exemplarity: Subjectivity, Work and the Impossible Politics of Purity, *Scandinavian Journal of Management*, 19(4): 403–23.

The Edge (2005) *102.1 The Edge*, available at: www.edge.ca/ongoinghistory/sp_selling_out2.cfm (visited 21 July 2005).

Théberge, P. (1997) *Any Sound You Can Imagine. Making Music/Consuming Technology*, Hanover, NH: Wesleyan University Press.

Théberge, P. (2004) The Network Studio: Historical and Technological Paths to a New Ideal in Music Making, *Social Studies of Science*, 34(5): 759–81.

Thomas, A.B. (1993) Sacred Cows and Other Animals, *Times Higher Education Supplement*, 26 November.

Tolson, A. (1977) *The Limits of Masculinity*, London: Tavistock.

Townley, B. (1993) Foucoult, Power/Knowledge and its Relevance for Human Resource Management, *The Academy of Management Review*, 18 (3): 518–54.

Townley, B. (2005) Controlling Foucault, *Organization*, 12(5): 643–48.

Tronnes, M. (ed.) (1999) *Closers: Great American Writers on the Art of Sellin*, New York: St. Martin's Griffin.

Tsoukas, H. and Knudsen, C. (2003) Introduction: The Need for Meta-Theoretical Reflection in Organization Theory, in H. Tsoukas and C. Knudsen (eds) *The Oxford Handbook of Organization Theory*, pp. 1–36, Oxford: Oxford University Press.

Tuchman, G. (1978) The Symbolic Annihilation of Women by the Mass Media, in

G. Tuchman, A.K. Daniels and J. Benet (eds) *Hearth and Home: Images of Women in Mass Media*, pp. 3–38, New York: Oxford University Press.

Turkle, S. (1984) *The Second Self: Computers and the Human Spirit*, New York: Simon and Schuster.

Turkle, S. (1995) *Life on the Screen: Identity in the Age of the Internet*, New York: Simon and Shuster.

Turner, B.S. (1999) McCitizens: Risk, Coolness and Irony in Contemporary politics, in B. Smart (ed.) *Resisting McDonaldization*, pp. 83–100, London: Sage.

UC Berkley (2006) Blade Runner (motion picture): A Selective Bibliography of Materials in the University of California Berkeley Library, available at http://lib.berkeley.edu/MRC/bladerunner.html (visited 5 January, 2007).

Vaill, P.B. (1981) Thoughts on Using Poetry in the Teaching of OB, *Organizational Behavior Teaching Journal*, 6: 50–1.

Van Maanen, J. (1995) Style as Theory, *Organization Science*, 6: 133–43.

Vera, D. and Crossan, M. (2004) Theatrical Improvisation: Lessons for Organizations, *Organization Studies*, 25: 727–49.

Verjans, S. (2005) Bricolage as a Way of Life – Improvisation and Irony in Information Systems, *European Journal of Information Systems*, 14: 504–6.

Vermorel, F. and Vermorel, J. (1978) *Sex Pistols: The Inside Story*, London: Star Books.

Vorlicky, R. (1995) *Act Like a Man: Challenging Masculinities in American Drama*, Ann Arbor: The University of Michigan Press.

Wagg, S. (1998) *Because I Tell a Joke or Two: Comedy, Politics and Social Difference*, London: Routledge.

Wagner, R.K. (2000) Practical Intelligence, in R.J. Sternberg (ed.) *Handbook of Intelligence*, pp. 380–95, New York: Cambridge University Press.

Waksman, S. (2004) California Noise: Tinkering with Hardcore and Heavy Metal in Southern California, *Social Studies of Science*, 34(5): 675–702.

Ward, C. (1986) *Goodnight Campers! The History of the British Holiday Camp*, London: Mansell.

Watson, T.J. (1994) Management 'Flavours of the Month': Their Role in Managers' Lives, *International Journal of Human Resource Management*, 5: 893–909.

Watson, T.J. (1996) Rhetoric, Discourse and Argument in Organizational Sense-Making: A Reflexive Tale, *Organization Studies*, 16 (5): 805–21.

Watson, T.J. (2000) Ethnographic Fiction Science: Making Sense of Managerial Work and Organizational Research Processes with Caroline and Terry, *Organization*, 7(3): 489–510.

Webber, R.A. (1969) Convergence or Divergence? *Columbia Journal of World Business*, 4(3): 75–83.

Weick, K.E. (1993a) Organizational Redesign as Improvisation, in G.P. Huber and W.H. Glick (eds) *Organizational Change and Redesign*, pp. 346–79, New York: Oxford University Press.

Weick, K.E. (1993b) The Collapse of Sensemaking in Organizations: The Mann Gulch Disaster, *Administrative Science Quarterly*, 38(4): 628–52.

Weick, K.E. (1996) *Sensemaking in Organizations*, Newbury Park, CA: Sage.

Weick, K.E. (1998) Improvisation as a Mindset for Organizational Analysis, *Organization Science*, 9: 543–55.

Weick, K.E., Sutcliffe, K.M. and Obstfeld, D. (2005) Organizing and the Process of Sensemaking, *Organization Science*, 16(4): 409–22.

Weiss, A. (1995) *Our Emperors Have No Clothes: Incredibly Stupid Things Corporate*

Executives Have Done While Reengineering, Restructuring, Downsizing, Taming, Team-Building, Frankin Lakes, NJ: Career Press.

Werhane, P.H. (2000) Business Ethics and the Origins of Contemporary Capitalism: Economics and Ethics in the Work of Adam Smith and Herbert Spencer, *Journal Of Business Ethics*, 24: 185–98.

Westwood, R.I. (1999) A 'Sampled' Account of Organization: Being a De-Authored, Reflexive Parody of Organization/Writing, *Studies in Cultures, Organisations and Societies*, 5: 195–233.

Westwood, R.I. (2004) Comic Relief: Subversion and Catharsis in Organizational Comedic Theatre, *Organization Studies*, 25(5): 775–95.

Westwood, R.I. and Kirkbride, P.S. (2000) International Strategies of Corporate Culture Change: Emulation, Consumption and Hybridity, in U. Haley (ed.) *Strategic Management in the Asia Pacific: Harnessing Regional and Organisational Change for Competitive Advantage*, Oxford: Butterworth-Heinemann.

Westwood, R.I. and Clegg, S. (eds) (2003) *Debating Organisation: Point/Counterpoint in Organisation Studies*, Oxford: Blackwell Publishing.

Westwood, R.I. and Rhodes, C. (eds) (2007) *Humour, Work and Organisation*, London: Routledge.

Whitney, J. and Packer, T. (2000) *Power Plays: Shakespeare's Lessons in Leadership and Management*, New York: Simon and Schuster.

Whyte, W. (1957) *The Organization Man*, London: Penguin.

Wierney, H.M. (compiler) (2000) Episode Capsule: The Last Temptation of Krust, *The Simpsons Archive*, www.snpp.com/episodes/5F10 (visited 27 May 2003) (original episode written by D. Cary).

Williams, C.L. (1995) *Still a Man's World: Men Who Do Women's Work*, Berkeley: University of California Press.

Williams, R. (1976) *Keywords*, London: Fontana.

Willis, P. (1990) *Learning to Labor: How Working Class Kids Get Working Class Jobs*, New York: Columbia University Press.

Willmott, H. (1993) Strength Is Ignorance; Slavery Is Freedom: Managing Culture in Modern Organizations, *Journal of Management Studies*, 30: 515–52.

Woolgar, S. (1991) Configuring the User: The Case of Usability Trials, in J. Law (ed.) *A Sociology of Monsters*, pp. 58–97, London: Routledge.

Worster, D. (1994) How to Do Things with Salesmen: David Mamet's Speech-Act Play, *Modern Drama*, 37: 375–90.

Young, C.M. (1993) Huh-huh, Huh-huh, *Rolling Stone*, 633: 42–6.

Zayani, M. (1997) Review of Criticism, 39(4): 628–33.

Zeifman, H. (1992) Phallus in Wonderland: Machismo and Business in David Mamet's American Buffalo and Glengarry Glen Ross, in Leslie Kane, *David Mamet: A Casebook*, pp. 123–36, New York and London: Garland Publishing, Inc.

Zorn, T.E., Page, D.J. and Cheney, G. (2000) Nuts About Change: Multiple Perspectives on Change-Oriented Communication in a Public Sector Organization, *Management Communication Quarterly*, 13(4), 515–66.

Index

234   *Index*